MONUMENTS AND MEMORY

Cultural Heritage Studies

UNIVERSITY PRESS OF FLORIDA

Florida A&M University, Tallahassee
Florida Atlantic University, Boca Raton
Florida Gulf Coast University, Ft. Myers
Florida International University, Miami
Florida State University, Tallahassee
New College of Florida, Sarasota
University of Central Florida, Orlando
University of Florida, Gainesville
University of North Florida, Jacksonville
University of South Florida, Tampa
University of West Florida, Pensacola

MONUMENTS AND MEMORY

Archaeological Perspectives on Commemoration

EDITED BY
John H. Jameson, Sherene Baugher,
and Richard Veit

Foreword by Katherine Hayes

UNIVERSITY PRESS OF FLORIDA

Gainesville/Tallahassee/Tampa/Boca Raton
Pensacola/Orlando/Miami/Jacksonville/Ft. Myers/Sarasota

Cover: *Pulling Down the Statue of George III at Bowling Green, July 9, 1776*, by William Walcutt (Courtesy: Lafayette College Art Collection, Easton, Pennsylvania).

References to internet websites (URLs) were accurate at the time of writing. Neither the author nor University Press of Florida is responsible for URLs that may have expired or changed since the manuscript was prepared.

Copyright 2025 by John H. Jameson, Sherene Baugher, and Richard Veit
All rights reserved
Published in the United States of America

30 29 28 27 26 25   6 5 4 3 2 1

Library of Congress Cataloging-in-Publication Data
Names: Jameson, John H., editor. | Baugher, Sherene, 1947– editor. | Veit, Richard F., 1968– editor. | Hayes, Katherine Howlett, author of foreword.
Title: Monuments and memory : archaeological perspectives on commemoration / edited by John H. Jameson, Sherene Baugher, Richard Veit ; foreword by Katherine Hayes.
Other titles: Cultural heritage studies.
Description: Gainesville : University Press of Florida, 2025. | Series: Cultural heritage studies | Includes bibliographical references and index. | Summary: "This volume examines many different public monuments, exploring the cultural factors behind their creation, their messages and evolving meanings, and the role of such markers in conveying the memory of history to future generations"— Provided by publisher.
Identifiers: LCCN 2024016814 | ISBN 9780813079233 (hardback) | ISBN 9780813070902 (pdf) | ISBN 9780813073576 (ebook)
Subjects: LCSH: Monuments—United States. | Memorialization—United States. | Monuments—United States—Public opinion. | Collective memory—United States. | BISAC: SOCIAL SCIENCE / Archaeology | HISTORY / Social History
Classification: LCC E159 .M656 2024 | DDC 363.6/90973—dc23/eng/20240429
LC record available at https://lccn.loc.gov/2024016814

The University Press of Florida is the scholarly publishing agency for the State University System of Florida, comprising Florida A&M University, Florida Atlantic University, Florida Gulf Coast University, Florida International University, Florida State University, New College of Florida, University of Central Florida, University of Florida, University of North Florida, University of South Florida, and University of West Florida.

University Press of Florida
2046 NE Waldo Road
Suite 2100
Gainesville, FL 32609
http://upress.ufl.edu

CONTENTS

List of Figures vii

List of Tables ix

Foreword xi

1. Introduction 1

   Sherene Baugher, Richard Veit, and John H. Jameson

2. Monuments and Memories: Irish, Polish, and Haudenosaunee Engagements with the Heritage Narratives of the American Revolutionary War 21

   Brant Venables

3. The Fredericksburg Slave Auction Block: A Monumental Reminder of Race Relations in Virginia 40

   Kerri Barile Tambs

4. "Each Soldier's Grave a Shrine": Confederate Cemetery Monuments 56

   Jeffrey Smith

5. Remembering, Reconciliation, and Forgetting: Monuments of Northern Cemeteries for Confederate Prisoners of War, Especially Elmira 74

   Sherene Baugher

6. Race, Gettysburg Memory, and the Jenkins Monument in Pennsylvania, 1990s–2020 92

   Hilary N. Green

7. Confronting Confederate Narratives: Archaeology at the Judah P. Benjamin Confederate Memorial at Gamble Plantation Historic State Park 107

   S. Matthew Litteral and Diane Wallman

8. Hidden in Public: The Power of the Memorial Landscape and the Archaeology of a Cornerstone Deposit from Louisville's Confederate Monument   126

    M. Jay Stottman

9. Pullman: A Model Town Becomes a National Monument   144

    Mark Cassello

10. A Feminist Intersectional Perspective Addressing the Dearth of Statues of Women and Minorities Resulting from the Great Predominance of Racist Patriarchal Public Statues in the United States   163

    Suzanne Spencer-Wood

11. Three Ways of Remembering World War I: The Sledmere Memorials, Yorkshire, England   186

    Harold Mytum

12. Memorializing Defeat: Remembering Civil Wars in Finland and USA   202

    Timo Ylimaunu and Paul R. Mullins

13. The Forgotten War Memory Boom: State and Local Korean War Memorials, 1987–2003   219

    Levi Fox

14. "Be Assured That . . . All . . . Memorials Will Be Kept Sacred and Beautiful": The Life Cycle of Memorials at Fort Monmouth, New Jersey   237

    Melissa Ziobro

15. Cannons by the Courthouse: War Memorials, Memory, and Commemoration in Modern Suburbia   255

    Richard Veit, Mark Cianciosi, and Joshua Butchko

16. Contested Monuments, Contested Spaces, and Contested Narratives   275

    Lu Ann De Cunzo

List of Contributors   293

Index   297

FIGURES

1.1. Bronze statue of Harriet Tubman in Auburn, New York 7
1.2. Memorial to Tomochichi in Wright Square, Savannah 9
1.3. Statue of George III 10
1.4. Statue of Garibaldi 11
2.1. Map of New York, USA, and Ontario, Canada 22
2.2. The Joseph Brant Monument in Brantford, Ontario, Canada 28
2.3. Statues on the Joseph Brant Monument 29
2.4. The Kościuszko Monument and the Timothy Murphy Monument 32
3.1. December 26, 1853, advertisement in the *Fredericksburg News* 44
3.2. Photo of auction block in 1898 45
3.3. A trio of photos of the auction block 47
4.1. Mount Olivet Confederate Monument 57
4.2. Plan for Confederate Circle 62
4.3. Confederate Pyramid, Hollywood Cemetery, Richmond 65
4.4. Confederate Monument, Fairview Cemetery 69
5.1. Granite monument at Finn's Point Cemetery, New Jersey 80
5.2. Monument to the victims of the Shohola train wreck 85
5.3. Confederate Monument in the Elmira Prisoner of War Camp Cemetery 86
5.4. Memorial to John W. Jones in the Elmira Prisoner of War Camp Cemetery 87
6.1. Jenkins Monument 93
6.2. Before and after photographs of the Jenkins Monument 99
6.3. *A Gathering at the Crossroads* monument 100
7.1. Location of Gamble Plantation 108
7.2. Digital Terrain Model of Ellenton 114
7.3. Gamble's map of the plantation and the Gamble mansion before restoration 119

7.4. Gamble plantation sugar mill ruins 121
8.1. The monument just after dedication in 1895 130
8.2. Daniel Boone commemorative silver spoon and a sealed brass tube 135
8.3. Ribbon from a badge printed with "CONFEDERATE ASSOCIATION OF KY May 11, 1891" 136
8.4. The monument's new landscape in Brandenburg, Kentucky 140
9.1. Historic Pullman rowhouses 146
9.2. Visitors attend the annual Pullman House tour 150
9.3. National A. Philip Randolph Pullman Porter Museum 153
9.4. Pullman National Monument Visitors Center under construction 158
10.1. The 1921 *Woman's Movement* in the Capitol Rotunda 171
10.2. The 1998 First Wave Statue Exhibit 172
10.3. The Boston Women's Memorial and the Harriet Tubman Memorial 174
10.4. Boblo Boat company dock building and the Zakrzewska building 179
11.1. Eleanor Cross and Wagoners' Memorial 189
11.2. The Boer War Memorial 191
11.3. Panel scenes A, B, C, and D on the Wagoners' Memorial 196
12.1. Red's memorials 206
12.2. Memorials in Ulvila and at Kitula mass grave in Akaa 209
12.3. Monument dedicated to Jefferson Davis 211
13.1. Korean War Memorials in Baltimore and Albany 223
13.2. Korean War Memorials in New York City and St. Joseph 224
13.3. Korean War Memorials in Wisconsin and Pennsylvania 228
13.4. Korean War Memorials in New Jersey and Pennsylvania 231
14.1. The Avenue of Memories and its first memorial plaque 242
14.2. The World War II memorial viewing stand 245
14.3. The Spanish–American War memorial 249
15.1. "Billy Yank" Hackettstown's Civil War Memorial 257
15.2. Hill of Heroes at Paterson and the All-Veterans Memorial at Mount Olive 261
15.3. Old One Horn, a Revolutionary War cannon 264
15.4. World War I German cannon and M 17 Light Tank 267
15.5. Graph showing number of markers erected per conflict 268

TABLES

7.1. Gamble Plantation Enslaved Laborer Demographics 117
8.1. Objects Found in the Box by Category 134

FOREWORD

Katherine Hayes

There has been a lot of ink spilled on monuments in the past few years. As the editors and authors of this volume observe, the sense of timelessness that surrounds monuments has been widely and perhaps irrevocably disrupted by the events and activism of the past decade in particular. I write this foreword from the city of Minneapolis, where Native activists and their allies have long been vocal in asserting the impacts of monumental memory in the form of public art (the *Scaffold* sculpture at the Walker Art Museum), statuary (the figure of Columbus which stood at the state capitol in St. Paul until it was pulled down), and environments (like the former Lake Calhoun with the reclaimed name of Bde Maka Ska). This is also a place where communities have grappled with new forms of remembrance, of the case cited by so many of the authors within this volume—the murder of George Floyd by former Minneapolis police officer Derek Chauvin. Unlike so many of the Confederate monuments, which were placed, most often, by White southerners in an effort to reshape the narrative of the Civil War to the Lost Cause, the planning for monuments and other kinds of memorials (through public art, place names, etc.) in Minneapolis is considering the needs and sentiments of many stakeholders. It is also happening in a context in which the "battle"—how to rethink policing and public safety in light of racial oppression—is not over. It offers, therefore, an intriguing comparison to the archaeological interpretations in this volume, in which monuments placed in the past are thickly contextualized to reveal whose actions and intentions created them, and what impact they have had in their lifetimes. And like many artifacts stashed away in dusty corners or infrequently visited repositories, heritage professionals and some members of the public struggle with the implications of choosing to no longer preserve them. For each, remembering that context is crucial.

    This volume reflects the fact that Confederate monuments and Civil War memory still loom large in the tensions around how we should or could think about monuments generally. The persistence of the Lost Cause narrative, and its dissemination across a wide variety of media, are reminders of the perceptive work of Haitian anthropologist Michel-Rolph Trouillot when he cautioned historians of the "ivory tower" that history is wrought and transmitted and often has greater impacts from *outside* of the academy than from within. The authors of this volume take up their charge to examine how sources, archives, and narratives are made instead of fixating solely on whether they meet academic standards. The Lost Cause narrative certainly does not, yet it persists and continues to do damage—in part because of its monumentality. Those ongoing damaging effects, as eloquently described in Hilary Green's chapter, lie at the heart of efforts to remove monuments.

But as with the comparison to contemporary commemoration efforts, the focus on Confederate and Civil War memory benefits from a comparison from other historical conflicts, whether they are wars or class conflict or the struggle for gender, racial, and ethnic representation. The case studies of these commemorations—on the Korean War, on an historic district celebrating labor history, on immigrant and Indigenous service in the military, on Finnish Civil War memory as a contrast to the American—highlight both the complexities of monumental memory, and also an absence of attention. These comparisons prompt the questions of who has the means and the authority to install monuments, and for what purpose? Are the decision-makers in community with the person or circumstances which are memorialized, or is there a paternalistic appropriation at work? Historians Lisa Blee and Jean O'Brien have provided a powerful example of the latter in their book *Monumental Mobility,* detailing the placement of statues of Massasoit—a Pokanoket leader in the seventeenth century—far to the west in the twentieth century by descendant settlers in an ongoing effort to control historical narratives about Native peoples. When we shift our attention away from the lightning-rod Confederate monuments to cases like these, we more clearly see the double-edged nature of monumental memory: a monument indeed materializes memory, but it does so by sacrificing nuance and context. That may suit the purposes of some, but it is at odds with the kind of community-based memory which relies on personal and intergenerational transmission with or without a material placement. This volume provides clear examples of memory's conflicted relations with monuments, for if it were otherwise we would not need an archaeological perspective on them.

References

Blee, Lisa, and Jean M. O'Brien
   2019   *Monumental Mobility: The Memory Work of Massasoit.* Chapel Hill: The University of North Carolina Press.

Trouillot, Michel-Rolph
   1995   *Silencing the Past: Power and the Production of History.* Boston: Beacon Press.

1

Introduction

SHERENE BAUGHER, RICHARD VEIT, AND JOHN H. JAMESON

Monuments, statues, memorials, and other sites of commemoration are artifacts with temporal and cultural contexts and close associations with history and memory. A common definition of artifacts in the archaeological sense is anything produced within a cultural system or by humans. As archaeologists, we like to say that every artifact has an associated story or stories. In reference to our volume theme, every monument or statue is an artifact with its own story, or stories, about how, why, and where it was produced and used. But, as a practical matter, not every artifact can or should be preserved. We make choices based on time and space limitations, but we must acknowledge that other factors, notably political, economic, and social circumstances, also affect what is preserved and why. Like memories, monuments can be soothing, inspirational, and sometimes traumatic. In this volume, we examine monuments, famous and forgotten, great and small, to understand the cultural and historical factors that shaped their creation, maintenance, and removal. We aim to bring archaeological and cultural heritage perspectives to bear on a category of highly visible artifacts imbued with meaning and meant to convey information to future generations. The monuments we have chosen to examine represent conflict and silenced histories. The conflict can be a result of wars and their aftermath or the many ways people in power attempt to control those with less power, such as the maintenance of white supremacy, power over formerly enslaved African Americans, dispossessed Native Americans, and the second-class status of women and minorities, especially Asian Americans, preventing them from voting, owning property, or even controlling where they could live and work. Why are some events and individuals commemorated and others forgotten or erased? What factors drive the erection of monuments and other forms of commemoration? Should we preserve, remove, replace, or destroy them? How does the public interact with monuments? How do monuments reflect and shape our national mythology? Our topics encompass highly and emotionally charged topics and accompanying publicity that has emerged from the struggle to preserve or remove monuments of conflict. Our discussions are interwoven with legacies associated with Native Americans, African Americans, immigrants, and women. We include reflections on how these topics and controversies impact current events and movements, such as the January 6 insurrection, the Black Lives Matter movement, immigration challenges, and gender discrimination. Today, some Americans are challenging the monuments that try to freeze American history at one point in time and reflect a narrow view of our heritage.

Power of Place

Dolores Hayden (1997) discussed how sites have what she calls "the power of place." She focuses on places of memory and history for African Americans in Los Angeles. There are numerous examples of the power of place for Native Americans. Indigenous people had most of their lands forcefully taken from them, sometimes even to create National Parks, but these sacred sites have "the power of place" (Burnham 2000; Keller and Turek 1998). Pueblo Indians still leave offerings at Mesa Verde in Colorado and Chaco Canyon in New Mexico. Monuments such as Medicine Wheel in Wyoming and Petroglyph National Monument in New Mexico had been threatened by commercial development despite being sacred sites (Baugher 2005).

For European Americans, the power of place and the sacred essence of a site can be seen in historic battlefields, from Revolutionary War battlefields to Pearl Harbor. Battlefields are places of conflict where numerous monuments are erected often to commemorate the soldiers whose lives were lost. The power of place is recognized in countries with the renaming of streets. In Barcelona, Spain, for example, commemoration narratives have transformed square names in the city into sites of memory, where both integration processes and a sense of belonging operate among all communities involved: exiles, migrants, and locals (Colomer 2021).

While Hayden thought of a location's positive power, monuments can also convey a terribly negative power. People are now challenging past and present power relations in the heritage narratives reflected in specific monuments. These power relations involve nationalism, imperialism, colonialism, cultural elitism, Western triumphalism, and social exclusion based on class, ethnicity, gender, and white supremacy. They have all strongly influenced how monuments are created, maintained, and preserved.

Silenced History

People in power have the economic, political, and social power to erect monuments, pay for commemoration ceremonies, and establish national, state, and local heritage sites (Kammen 1993, Shackel 2003). Heritage scholar David Lowenthal (1985), in his book, *The Past is a Forgotten Country,* has written extensively about the theme of exclusionary memory and how some people and subordinate groups are written out of history and out of a community, a state or province, or even a nation's collective memory. Paul Shackel (2003) describes how people in power seek to control how history is remembered. Minorities are silenced, and their participation in the building and growth of a city, county, or nation's history is purposefully ignored and forgotten.

Haitian anthropologist Michel-Rolph Trouillot's 1995 book, *Silencing the Past: Power and the Production of History,* examined the Haitian revolution, perhaps the most successful slave revolt in the Americas, and revealed the inequality of power in who is remembered and even how leaders like Sans Souci are written out of history. Trouillot goes beyond the Haitian example and takes a global perspective on silences and commemorative ceremonies, especially on the remaking of Columbus as a religious and ethnic icon. His analysis of identity politics in America is especially relevant to our study of monuments and silenced history.

Columbus has served as a positive symbol of exploration and Western expansion, with little attention paid to the resultant stealing of native land and the enslavement of indigenous people as part of the doctrine of discovery. By 1892, the United States had 28 monuments to Columbus, and in 2021, there were 121 Columbus monuments (Schiffman 2022). The monuments to Columbus have been a source of pride for Italian Americans, who faced discrimination as immigrants. However, Indigenous Americans have protested Columbus statues for decades, and scholars have written about the negative legacy of Columbus. By 2021, Columbus statues represented more than half of the 69 controversial non-Confederate statues that were removed (Thompson 2022:169).

Columbus monuments are not the only ones to represent silenced indigenous history. In the American Southwest, they include the monuments to Juan De Oñate y Salazar and Diego De Vargas. De Oñate led an entrada in 1598 that explored the Great Plains and the lower Colorado River basin, resulting in the colonization of what today is New Mexico. When a group of his men attempted to seize supplies from the indigenous inhabitants of Acoma Pueblo, they were driven off with a loss of life. De Oñate dispatched a punitive expedition that seized the community, resulting in the deaths of between 500 and 800 Acomans, with between 70 and 80 warriors and 500 noncombatants captured. Male captives over twenty-five years of age were to have their right foot cut off and were to endure twenty-five years of slavery; female captives over the age of twelve and younger men were to endure twenty years of slavery, while younger children were placed as servants in Spanish households (Roberts 2004:89–90).

The colony De Oñate established struggled to survive. Settlers found the arid land challenging, and the local Pueblo inhabitants were beset by Franciscan missionaries who forced conversions and demanded food, supplies, and labor to build missions (Gutiérrez 1991:77). In 1680, following years of abuse, the Pueblo people revolted, driving the colonists out of New Mexico. In 1692, the Spanish returned to New Mexico (Liebmann 2012:183). Although sometimes described as a bloodless reconquest by the new Governor, Diego de Vargas, it was not. For instance, at Jemez Pueblo, 84 men were killed, and 361 were captured (Roberts 2004:206).

Controversial statues of Oñate and Vargas were erected and have been a source of pride to Catholic Hispanic communities in New Mexico, people who have also been treated as second-class citizens by White Protestant European Americans, while being a source of the silenced history of murder and enslavement for Pueblo people. In 1994, a statue of the conquistador was erected near Alcalde, New Mexico. The statue was vandalized in 1998, and its right foot was cut off (Roberts 2004:97). It was subsequently repaired, but the Oñate visitor's center was closed. A statue of Vargas erected in 2007 in San Antonio's Cathedral Park was moved in 2020 to private property (Thomas 2021).

Perhaps the most controversial monuments in the United States are the Confederate monuments in public squares, prominent locations on public land, and in front of government buildings. These represent the silenced history of slavery and the mythology of the Lost Cause. It is essential to examine the intentions of the people who erected these statues, which some of our authors do in their chapters. Briefly, the South lost the war but won the battle for the narrative. Following the war and continuing today, the Lost Cause of the Confederacy, or simply the Lost Cause, defines the war as a struggle primarily waged to save the Southern way of life and to protect states' rights, including the right to secede from the Union. It does not mention the "right" to continue slavery, even though it was a key point in the Confederate Constitution (Commager 1973). It promotes the belief that slavery was just and moral because the enslaved were happy, even grateful. It overlooks that slavery made economic prosperity possible but at a horrible cost. Thus, the Lost

Cause denies the central roles of slavery and white supremacy in the build-up to and outbreak of the war.

After the war, organizations on both sides erected monuments, usually in cemeteries or battlefields, to remember the soldiers who died. Indeed, the Gettysburg battlefield is so replete with monuments that it appears to be a military sculpture garden. But these are battlefield commemorations.

In the South, many of the monuments went beyond cemetery memorials. Ninety-three percent of Confederate monuments were erected after 1895 (Cox 2003:50). As historian Karen Cox (2003:1) writes that the United Daughters of the Confederacy in raising monuments were on a campaign of vindication in which they "aspired to transform military defeat into a political and cultural victory, where states' rights and white supremacy remained intact." The main two waves of Confederate memorialization, during the Jim Crow era and again in the mid-twentieth-century Civil Rights Movement, coincided with the fiftieth and one-hundredth anniversaries of the war. Notions of white supremacy were used to perpetuate racism and racist power structures during the "Jim Crow era" in the American South that emphasized the supposed chivalric virtues of the antebellum South. Cox (2021:21) writes that Confederate monuments were "intentional statements about who made the laws and who enforced them." Through the erection of prominent Confederate monuments and selective writing of Southern history textbooks (which still continues), advocates of the "Lost Cause" sought to ensure that future generations of Southern Whites would learn about the South's "true" reasons for fighting the war, "using the language of states' rights justify slavery and de jure segregation," reinforce the belief in the inferiority of Blacks, and continue to support white supremacist policies (Cox 2003:162). The horrors of slavery, especially the rape of Black enslaved women by White men, are ignored.

The American Civil War 54th Massachusetts Memorial in Boston is the only nineteenth-century war monument portraying a positive depiction of African Americans. It was once viewed as a memorial to Robert Gould Shaw, the abolitionist leader of a famous African American regiment, the 54th Massachusetts; today, the monument is recognized for its depiction of the bravery of the Black soldiers (Shackel 2003:128–143). The monument has Shaw on his horse and is surrounded by his Black soldiers as they march into battle.

Another way to silence history is not to recognize the accomplishments of minorities. Where are the monuments to prominent nineteenth-century Black leaders like Harriet Tubman, Sojourner Truth, and Frederick Douglass? Harriet Tubman was recognized in the nineteenth and twentieth centuries for her heroic work on the Underground Railroad, as a nurse and spy during the

Civil War, and her leadership in carrying out the 1863 successful Combahee River Raid in which Union soldiers freed over 700 enslaved Black Americans. In 1915, a bronze plaque to Harriet Tubman was placed on the county courthouse wall in Auburn, New York, where Tubman lived after the Civil War until her death in 1913. However, it was not until the 1990s and primarily in the twenty-first century that fifteen Tubman statues were erected (Harriet Tubman Monuments 2023). In 2022, at the CIA headquarters in Virginia, the agency erected a monument to Harriet Tubman as a successful Civil War spy, and the statue is a copy of the original in Auburn, NY (Figure 1.1) (De Luce 2022). In evaluating who should be remembered, the Newark, New Jersey government removed a statue of Columbus and, in 2023, replaced it with a monument to Harriet Tubman (Barron 2023).

Authorized Heritage Discourse

Laurajane Smith (2006:29) has written about "Authorized Heritage Discourse," how the meaning of a monument is presented and serves to continue the status quo of people in power, and how minorities are silenced. In 2010, scholars from the UK, Sweden, and Australia (including Smith) created the Association of Critical Heritage Studies (ACHS) "to promote a new way of thinking about and doing heritage" (ACHS 2012). These scholars promote robust analysis and criticism of monuments and heritage sites and ask uncomfortable questions to bring the interests of the marginalized and excluded to the forefront (ACHS 2012).

The public worldwide has begun to challenge the power relations of monuments since the murder of George Floyd in 2020, together with other egregious contemporary events in the United States, like the Charleston murders in 2015 and the violent Unite the Right Rally in Charlotteville in 2017. In 2020, in London, people toppled the statue of Edward Colston, who made a seventeenth-century fortune from trading in enslaved West Africans (Elks 2020). We now see the active participation of people and communities who have been marginalized, demanding a say in what monuments are on display in town squares, in front of governmental buildings, and other publicly owned places. But movements to remove monuments go back to antiquity. This is often associated with the Latin phrase, *Damnatio memoriae*, or condemning of memory. For instance, later Egyptian pharaohs went to great lengths to erase the names and images of Akhenaten and his immediate successors from Egypt's monumental landscape (Silverman et al. 2006:183).

Figure 1.1. A bronze statue of Harriet Tubman in Auburn, New York. The statue by Brian P. Hanlon was dedicated in November 2018. Photo by Sherene Baugher, 2023.

The Illusion of the "Permanent" Monument

The archaeologist's stock in trade is the study of monuments; the Rosetta Stone, Trajan's column, Angkor Wat, and Mayan stelae were all intended to convey information to future generations. They are unusual in their longevity and "afterlife" (Cherry 2013). Other monuments had much shorter lives. Indeed, we have witnessed the recurring historical impulse to break or destroy images for religious or political reasons. Like the Egyptian example cited above, images of kings were defaced during the French Revolution. These events provide historical contexts for the modern movement to remove or destroy controversial monuments.

The commemoration of Tomochichi, a Native American leader significant to the history of Georgia, illustrates the impact of changing social and political values on preserving monuments. Erected in the center of Percival (later Wright) Square in Savannah in 1739, the Tomochichi Monument may well have been the first public monument in America and was unique in the colonial era in honoring a Native American. The disappearance of the monument from the documentary record within a few decades and the ensuing century-long period of neglect of the Indian chief's memory speak to the precarious nature of memorials. The construction of a garden mound on the site of his grave in 1871 and its removal in 1882 to make room for a large monument to leading Savannah industrialist William Washington Gordon initially provoked no public opposition. The gradual rekindling of interest in Tomochichi's memory and specifically in his burial site, however, led to the erection of a new monument in 1899 by the Georgia Colonial Dames, which some have erroneously concluded and frequently repeated in the twentieth century that the Gordon Monument destroyed the Tomochichi Monument (Williams 2012; NSCDA 2020). The Georgia Historical Commission later placed a large marker in Savannah's Wright Square, which details the achievements of the Yamacraw chieftain (Figure 1.2). Further commemorations of Tomochichi in the twentieth century redefined his significance, placing him on par with James Oglethorpe as a co-founder of Georgia. In 2005, Savannah's Tomochichi Federal Building and U.S. Courthouse were renamed in his honor.

Our focus is mainly on American monuments, and America is replete with monuments in public squares throughout the country. Monuments reflect the interests, artisanship, and politics of different periods. Political activism can profoundly shape the monumental landscape. The Stamp Act of 1765 rocked the colonies and seemed to symbolize the erosion of British liberties. That Act's repeal in 1766 led to widespread celebrations and calls for monuments to highlight the king's beneficence and the role of Prime Minister William Pitt in securing the Act's repeal.

In New York City, not one but three monuments were proposed to commemorate this auspicious event: a liberty pole, a statue of Pitt in bronze, and a gilded lead statue of King George III. The liberty pole would prove a lightning rod for political protests and became "the rallying point of New York City's Radical Whigs" (Olsen 2020:3). Indeed, it was so offensive that British troops took it down only to see it re-erected by the Whigs. This would happen not once but several times, with the pole increasingly armored against attack.

Other "liberty poles," albeit less armored, were repeatedly erected and taken down in other colonies, reflecting the ebb and flow of political and military changes during the revolutionary years. Ironically, the remains of

Figure 1.2. Memorial to Tomochichi. Wright Square, Savannah, Georgia. Photo by John H. Jameson, 2022.

a liberty pole and presumably related memorial plaque reading "A.D. 1827" (probably placed during the later monument installation) in Savannah, Georgia, were discovered during the installation of a monument obelisk honoring Revolutionary War heroes (Stewart 1993).

Certainly, the monumental equestrian statue of George III, erected on a marble base, was more formal and less vernacular than the liberty poles. Commissioned in 1766, it took some time for sculptor Joseph Wilton to produce and was erected in 1770 at Bowling Green in Lower Manhattan. Funded by the New York State Assembly, it was meant "to perpetuate to the latest posterity, the deep Sense This Colony has, of the eminent and singular Blessings derived from him, during His Most auspicious Reign" (Olsen 2020:2). The statue was loosely based on a monumental equestrian statue of Marcus Aurelius on the Capitoline Hill in Rome. Interestingly, the long-lived statue of the philosopher-emperor Aurelius has survived to the present day, while George III's has not. A patriot mob tore it down on 9 July 1776 (Figure 1.3). This was motivated both by politics, coming only days after the Declaration of Independence, and by pragmatism—the tons of lead that comprised the statue was of great value to the ill-equipped military forces of the young United States. Today, fragments of the statue, which were not cast into musket balls, survive

Figure 1.3. *Pulling Down the Statue of George III at Bowling Green, July 9, 1776*. Oil on canvas, 51-⁵/₈ × 77-⁵/₈ inches, by William Walcutt in 1857. (Courtesy: Lafayette College Art Collection, Easton, Pennsylvania).

in museums, including Philadelphia's Museum of the American Revolution. Indeed, scientific research by archaeologist Dan Sivilich has confirmed that the statue was melted down and its raw material recast as musket balls (Sivilich 2016:121–127).

The years after the American Revolution saw monuments erected to commemorate that conflict, its battles, and key participants (Chambers 2012). However, some of these never fully got off the ground. For instance, in Newark, New Jersey's Military Park, a brown sandstone slab, inscribed with the dates 1826 and 1906, sits under some shrubbery next to Gutzon Borglum's looming bronze statue, *Wars of America*. Its inscription reveals that it was associated with a planned monument celebrating America's independence that never fully materialized.

Other monuments have had lives and stories much different than their creators expected (Antonello and Cushing 2021). To wit, the statue of the unifier of Italy, Giuseppe Garibaldi, in New York City's Washington Square. Erected in 1888, the statue shows a standing Garibaldi who appears painfully twisted as he is about to draw his sword (Figure 1.4). This awkward pose results from a major alteration in the plans for the monument. As initially proposed, the figure was meant to be part of a grouping of three statues: Garibaldi, a bugler, and an infantry soldier standing on a rocky crag. Funding came from the siz-

Figure 1.4. *Garibaldi Being Cleaned*. Painting by Elizabeth Nottingham, 1935, Virginia Museum of Art. This painting shows workers cleaning the statue of Garibaldi. Note the figure's awkward pose.

able Italian immigrant community in New York. There were cost overruns; the single statue of Garibaldi cost more than the estimate for all three figures, leading to a radical revision of the monument (Miller 2010). The result was that the completed statue of Garibaldi had its legs bent to fit on a flat granite base. The statue's sculptor, Giovanni Turini, called the foundry workers who did this "cruel amputators" (Miller 2010). Calls to replace the awkward sculpture appeared regularly, but it has stood the test of time. However, it was recently tagged with graffiti, perhaps by individuals who mistook Garibaldi for some other historical figure, possibly Columbus.

Often, in the contemporary moment, we think of monument defacement and removal as political actions by marginalized communities, but some occur as a backlash to Black Lives Matter in the toppling of statues of abolitionists. For example, in 2020, a statue of Frederick Douglass was detached from its base in Rochester, New York (Gold 2020). In Madison, Wisconsin, protesters toppled a statue of Hans Christian Heg, a White abolitionist who fought against the Confederacy (Andrea 2020). Our authors discuss the messages and challenges of the monuments.

Chapters in This Book

Our chapters address diverse monuments and are in chronological order based on the historical event and the heritage narrative. The common theme is that the monuments represent an archaeology of conflict. The conflict could be a war, enslavement, or disenfranchisement regarding the right to vote. A thematic thread that runs through many chapters is silenced history. The chapters examine archaeologically revealed histories that have been obscured or poorly understood. All the chapters explore the social and cultural factors that influence the erection of monuments, such as economics, class, race, and immigration.

In chapter 2, Brant Venables analyzes the Saratoga monuments to Polish engineer Thaddeus Kościuszko and Irish American Timothy Murphy and the Joseph Brant Mohawk Indian monument in Brantford, Ontario. Venables demonstrates how ethnic groups in the nineteenth and early twentieth centuries were aware of the importance of challenging the authorized heritage discourse. These three groups raised money to create their own monuments when their role in history was being silenced. Venables examines how ethnic groups have engaged with nationalistic heritage narratives by emphasizing their own sacrifice, martial valor, and patriotism.

Kerri Barile and Brad Hatch, in chapter 3, discuss how archaeologists examined an object known as the "slave auction block" in Fredericksburg, Virginia. The block has an oral legacy of selling enslaved individuals. There is no archival evidence of this block, but the slave auctions took place in front of or on the hotel's porch by the block. This chapter explores the place of archaeology in ongoing debates regarding this significant object, one in denial (claiming it was a carriage step) and the other affirming the infamous slave history of Fredericksburg.

In chapter 4, Jeffrey Smith examines military monuments in Southern cemeteries immediately after the war and their impact on collective memory in commemorating Civil War dead. Smith examines how the role of the Ladies Memorial Associations and, later, the United Daughters of the Confederacy in funding these monuments in cemeteries sought to wrap the Lost Cause narrative into the sacred ground where the remains of the Confederate soldiers are buried. He analyzes how the living used the rhetoric of mourning to sanctify the Lost Cause.

Sherene Baugher focuses on the Northern prisoner of war camp cemeteries in chapter 5. Most of these camps buried the Confederate dead in mass burials. Confederate monuments in these cemeteries are analyzed. The Elmira prisoner of war (POW) camp cemetery in Elmira, New York, differs from the other camps because it has markers on individual graves due to the work of a formerly enslaved person involved in the Underground Railroad who was the sexton of the POW cemetery. With his monument, the narrative that this was a war to end slavery is not forgotten.

In chapter 6, Hilary Green discusses Brigadier General Albert Gallatin Jenkins's monument commemorating his Confederate advance into Pennsylvania during the Gettysburg campaign. However, Jenkins is infamous for brutally rounding up and kidnapping free Black men, women, and children in Pennsylvania and sending them south to be sold into slavery. Green discusses how descendants, including Green, protested this monument. She provides an insider understanding of the decades of trauma suffered by the survivors, this silenced history, and why this Confederate monument should be removed. The Jenkins Monument was removed in 2020, and a Black Civil War monument was erected.

In the following chapter, S. Matthew Litteral and Diane Wallman discuss the Gamble Plantation along the Manatee River in Florida, where presentations designed by the United Daughters of the Confederacy have emphasized the White power structure at the plantation, especially in providing a haven for Judah P. Benjamin, the Confederate Secretary of State who sought to escape to England at the end of the war. The plantation mansion houses a Confederate Museum, keeping the story of the enslaved mostly hidden. Archaeological research at the site is helping to raise awareness of the silenced history of the enslaved.

Jay Stottman, in chapter 8, analyzes Louisville's Confederate Monument on the University of Louisville's main campus. During the disassembly of the monument, a cornerstone box containing commemorative objects was found. Stottman discusses these objects, their relationship to the "Lost Cause," and how they reflected women's roles in perpetuating this narrative. He demonstrates that public monuments are invariably tied to a community's value systems and how this monument was simply moved to another city that supported a pro-Confederate monument.

In chapter 9, Mark Cassello focuses on the Pullman National Monument in Illinois, a large historic site, as a monument. He describes the Town of Pullman (1880–1907), built by George Pullman for workers who produced his luxurious railroad cars. However, the Pullman Strike of 1894 severely damaged Pullman's reputation and that of his town. This site is placed within the context of labor history and the role of the Black porters. Cassello examines how changes to the landscape, competing official and vernacular interests, and racism contribute to why some events, individuals, and structures are commemorated and others are not.

In the following chapter, Suzanne Spencer-Wood focuses on the silenced history of American women. She provides a feminist perspective that the androcentrism of patriarchy has resulted in the great predominance of statues memorializing men and very few statues commemorating women, especially minority women, who are primarily silenced in the historical narrative, reflecting their marginalization in life. Spencer-Wood investigates categories of women's statues that embody a variety of intersecting ideologies of gender, race, and class and convey messages about the place of women of different races and ethnicities in American society.

In chapter 11, Harold Mytum describes the Sledmere Memorials in Yorkshire, England, designed and paid for by Sir Mark Sykes. These monuments were exceptional in their scale, quality, and messages. Chivalry, paternalism, xenophobia, and romanticism are all evoked in the context of loss, sacrifice, and memory. These memorials are expressions of a larger culture and are tied to Sykes with his idiosyncratic intentions, experiences, and understandings.

Timo Ylimaunu and Paul Mullins, in chapter 12, compare the civil wars in Finland and USA and their divergent outcomes regarding commemoration. In twentieth-century Finland, the winning side, the Whites, organized violent revenge against the Reds, with many dying in POW camps. The Whites erected memorials representing their victory. In the United States, the narrative of the defeated Confederacy is dramatically different. The authors examine how memorials to these two civil wars, and the sides that lost the wars, expressed a vastly different range of sentiments, including reconciliation, mourning the dead, contemporary activism, ideological distortions, silenced histories, and false narratives.

In chapter 13, Levi Fox examines dozens of state and local Korean War monuments from 1987 to 2003 that were constructed both before and after the national dedication of the Korean War Veterans Memorial in 1995. He examines how early monuments call the war a "forgotten war." He discusses who funded the monuments, the time, the material and size of the memorial, and their location. He analyzes the narrative and symbolism to reveal how the Korean War has become "un-forgotten" over the last several decades.

Historian Melissa Ziobro, in chapter 14, examines the Fort Monmouth, New Jersey, Memorialization Committee records from the 1940s through the early twenty-first century. She highlights the logistics behind memorialization: who/what gets memorialized, when, where, why, and how. Her chapter considers what happens when memorials are abandoned. While she examined memorials on military property, she suggested questions we should ask about monuments on any property, including locating descendant communities and how we might proceed with removing and possibly relocating monuments.

Richard Veit, Mark Cianciosi, and Josh Butchko continue the examination of New Jersey's war memorials in chapter 15. They focus on how and why some conflicts are commemorated and others are overlooked. Monuments commemorating battles from the Revolutionary War to the Gulf Wars are examined. Particular attention is paid to two factors that drive commemoration: periodicity, the celebration of 50-, 100-, and 200-year anniversaries after the conflict, and participant life-course, with many memorials constructed as veterans become elderly. Other factors, such as economics, class, race, and immigration, are explored. Monuments reflecting silenced history are discussed.

In the final chapter, Lu Ann De Cunzo provides a detailed commentary on the chapters. She also adds her global perspectives on monuments and silenced history, especially regarding the brutal treatment of women.

Conclusions

America's monuments tell the story of the nation. They reflect a narrative emphasizing select events and individuals, often conflicts and White men. Government agencies erected some monuments, but many are the work of private initiatives and organizations. In the late twentieth century, the authorized heritage narrative has come under attack, and a broader, more inclusive narrative is taking place. This transition has caused some historic monuments to be removed. Some have found this shocking, assuming monuments were permanent landscape fixtures. They are not, as the chapters in this volume indicate. Monuments are erected, removed, modified, and preserved as their interpretation and meanings evolve. Nevertheless, they are powerful cultural landscape elements and create historical narratives and memories.

Black Lives Matter and systemic racism are front and center in discussions of monuments. Nations are re-examining the treatment of indigenous people, racial and ethnic minorities, and women. Our discussion of heritage is timely. A common thread in these chapters is the focus on historical and contemporary conflict over the role of monuments. In a post–George Floyd era, monuments can make previously silenced voices heard; they can be empowering by affirming the identity and restoring the dignity of marginalized groups.

Our chapters examine cultural heritage as background to the erection of monuments and memorials. There are six chapters on the controversial monuments of the American Civil War, examining who designed and paid for the monuments and what messages they were trying to convey. Authors explore how these monuments reflected the South's myth of the Lost Cause and the silenced history of slavery. Why and how these myths were allowed to perpetuate, whether connected to the American Civil War or civil wars in other countries, is analyzed. However, this book is not just about commemoration associated with the American Civil War. We include conflict memorials associated with other wars, including the Revolutionary War, World War I, and the often-overlooked Korean War. Our authors examine the changing goals in raising these military monuments and the transformations in how these monuments are viewed over time. Finally, what happens to military monuments when the sites are decommissioned will continue to challenge people in the twenty-first century.

While some authors in this volume discussed monuments associated with overt white supremacy, others focus on largely heretofore suppressed narratives. A challenge many colleagues face is developing a narrative for complicated heritage landscapes representing diverse stakeholders. Another is when archaeological facts and community-remembered history are not the same. With silenced history, erecting their own monuments was not an option open to Blacks, even if they had the funds, given their second-class status. Seeing a monument erected to a man who caused great harm to a community and decades of trauma to the survivors still presents challenges to having the monument removed. Finally, the lack of monuments to women of all races and classes raises the issue of control of the heritage narrative by White powerful males.

America, and much of the world, is changing, and we are becoming multicultural societies. We can learn from the past but not live in the past. What is encouraging is that within recent decades, statues have been erected for people of diverse races, religions, and ethnicities, and the contributions of women of all races and classes are being recognized. For example, in the twenty-first century in the United States, thirteen monuments depicting the silenced history of slavery were erected, plus ten statues to Frederick Douglass and four to Sojourner Truth (Contemporary Monuments to the Slave Past 2023). While many of these monuments are located on university campuses or in northern states, the trend away from commemorating White powerful males also exists in Southern states. For example, Calhoun Square in Savannah, Georgia, named for the pro-slavery leader John C. Calhoun, who served as vice president of the United States from 1825 to 1832, has been renamed. The new name chosen for the square is Susie King Taylor, known for her work in Savannah and elsewhere as the first Black nurse during the American Civil War.

Will the trend continue with future monuments and memorials that are inclusive, revealing silenced histories, or will they continue what has been called "an authorized heritage narrative" that reflects the status quo of the established people in power? We urge readers to explore the monumental landscapes they inhabit and examine the messages those monuments seek to convey to future generations.

References

ACHS (Association of Critical Heritage Studies)
- 2012 2012 Manifesto. https://www.criticalheritagestudies.org/history, accessed 9 May 2021.

Andrea, Lawrence
- 2020 Hans Christian Heg was an Abolitionist Who Died Trying to End Slavery. What to Know About the Man Whose Statue Was Toppled in Madison. *Milwaukee Journal Sentinel*, 24 June. https://www.jsonline.com/story/news/local/wisconsin/2020/06/24/hans-christian-hegs-abolitionist-statue-toppled-madison-what-know/3248692001/, accessed 1 May 2023.

Antonello, Alesandro, and Nancy Cushing
- 2021 Re-storying Monuments: Forum Introduction. *History Australia* 18(4):747–752.

Barron, James
- 2023 A Monument to Harriet Tubman Replaces a Columbus Statue in Newark. *New York Times*, 9 March. https://www.nytimes.com/2023/03/09/nyregion/harriet-tubman-monument-newark.html, accessed 4 May 2023.

Baugher, Sherene
- 2005 Sacredness, Sensitivity, and Significance: The Controversy Over Native American Sacred Sites. In *Heritage of Value, Archaeology of Renown: Reshaping Archaeological Assessment and Significance*. Clay Mathers, Tim Darvill, and Barbara Little, eds. Pp. 248–275. Gainesville, FL: University Press of Florida.

Burnham, Philip
- 2000 *Indian County, God's Country: Native Americans and National Parks*. Washington, D.C.: Island Press.

Chambers, Thomas A.
- 2012 *Memories of War: Visiting Battlegrounds and Bonefields in the Early American Republic*. Ithaca, NY: Cornell University Press.

Cherry, Deborah
- 2013 The Afterlives of Monuments. *South Asian Studies* 29(1):1–14.

Colomer, Laia
- 2021 Memorializing Forced Migration and Beyond. Commemorating Salvador Allende in Barcelona as Memory-work in the Context of Civic Memory and

the Politics of Belonging. *International Journal of Cultural Heritage Studies* 28(1):92–108.

Commager, Henry Steele, ed.
  1973 The Constitution of the Confederate States of America, March 11, 1861. *Documents of American History, Ninth Edition*. Englewood Cliffs, NJ: Prentice-Hall.

Contemporary Monuments to the Slave Past
  2023 Collections. https://www.slaverymonuments.org/collections/browse, accessed 8 May 2023.

Cox, Karen L.
  2003 *Dixie's Daughters: The United Daughters of the Confederacy and the Preservation of Confederate Culture*. Gainesville, FL: University Press of Florida.
  2021 *No Common Ground: Confederate Monuments and the Ongoing Fight for Racial Justice*. Chapel Hill, NC: The University of North Carolina Press.

De Luce, Dan
  2022 CIA Honors Underground Railroad and Civil War Hero Harriet Tubman as a Model Spy with a New Statue. NBC News 1 October 2022. https://www.nbcnews.com/politics/national-security/cia-honors-underground-railroad-hero-harriet-tubman-model-spy-new-stat-rcna50159, accessed 17 April 2023.

Elks, Sonia
  2020 Toppling of UK Statue Fuels Debate on Monuments to Slave Traders. Reuters 8 June, https://www.reuters.com/article/us-minneapolis-police-protests-britain-s/toppling-of-uk-statue-fuels-debate-on-monuments-to-slave-traders-idUSKBN23F2FD, accessed 20 April 2023.

Gold, Michael
  2020 Who Tore Down This Frederick Douglass Statue? *New York Times*, 7 July. https://www.nytimes.com/2020/07/07/nyregion/frederick-douglass-statue-rochester.html, accessed 1 May 2023.

Gutiérrez, Ramón A.
  1991 *When Jesus Came, the Corn Mothers Went Away: Marriage, Sexuality, and Power in New Mexico, 1500–1846*. Redwood City, CA: Stanford University Press.

Harriet Tubman Monuments
  2023 Harriet Tubman Auburn, New York. https://www.harriettubmanmonuments.slaverymonuments.org/items/show/1205, accessed 18 April 2023.

Hayden, Dolores
  1997 *The Power of Place: Urban Landscapes as Public History*. Cambridge, MA: MIT Press.

Kammen, Michael
  1993 *Mystic Chords of Memory: The Transformation of Tradition in American Culture*. New York, NY: Vintage Books.

Keller, Robert H., and Michael F. Turek
  1998 *American Indians & National Parks*. Tucson, AZ: The University of Arizona Press.

Liebmann, Matthew
   2012   *Revolt: An Archaeological History of Pueblo Resistance and Revitalization in 17th Century New Mexico.* Tucson, AZ: University of Arizona Press.

Lowenthal, David
   1985   *The Past Is a Forgotten Country.* New York, NY: Cambridge University Press.

Miller, Tom
   2010   The "Atrocious" Garibaldi Statue in Washington Square. https://daytoninmanhattan.blogspot.com/2010/08/atrocious-garibaldi-statue-washington.html, accessed 21 August 2021.

NSCDA (National Society of Colonial Dames of America)
   2020   Great American Treasures. https://www.greatamericantreasures.org/destinations/tomochichi-monument/, accessed 15 July 2022.

Olsen, Eric P.
   2020   Tearing Down Monuments in Revolutionary New York City. Manuscript on file, Morristown National Historical Park, Morristown, NJ.

Roberts, David
   2004   *The Pueblo Revolt: The Secret Rebellion that Drove the Spaniards out of the Southwest.* New York, NY: Simon and Schuster.

Schiffman, Rebecca
   2022   What's the Deal with Christopher Columbus Monuments? Art & Object. https://www.artandobject.com/news/whats-deal-christopher-columbus-monuments, accessed 2 May 2023.

Shackel, Paul A.
   2003   *Memory in Black and White: Race, Commemoration, and the Post-Bellum Landscape.* Corr. 5th edition. Walnut Grove, CA: AltaMira Press.

Silverman, David P., Josef W. Wegner, and Jennifer Houser Wegner
   2006   *Akhenaten and Tutankhamun, Revolution and Restoration.* Philadelphia, PA: University of Pennsylvania Museum of Archaeology and Anthropology.

Sivilich, Daniel M.
   2016   *Musket Ball and Small Shot Identification: A Guide.* Norman, OK: University of Oklahoma Press.

Smith, Laurajane
   2006   *Uses of Heritage.* London, UK: Routledge.

Stewart, Dorothy H.
   1993   The Monuments and Fountains of Savannah. A Report on an Internship for the Savannah Park and Tree Department. Copy on file at the Department of History, Armstrong State College, Savannah, GA.

Thomas, Sean P.
   2021   Don Diego de Vargas Statue Found in Backyard of Home/Business. *Sante Fe Mexican,* 15 February. https://www.santafenewmexican.com/news/local_news/don-diego-de-vargas-statue-found-in-backyard-of-home-business/article_ff8ca6d0-6fac-11eb-9e1c-530ed60bb115.html, accessed 1 May 2023.

Thompson, Erin L.
   2022   *Smashing Statues: The Rise and Fall of America's Public Monuments.* New York, NY: W. W. Norton.

Trouillot, Michel-Rolph
   1995   *Silencing the Past: Power and Production of History*. Boston, MA: Beacon Press.

Williams, Robin B.
   2012   The Challenge of Preserving Public Memory: Commemorating Tomochichi in Savannah. In *Preservation Education & Research,* 5: 1-16.

2

Monuments and Memories

Irish, Polish, and Haudenosaunee Engagements with the Heritage Narratives of the American Revolutionary War

Brant Venables

Memorializations at military heritage sites track the ways American society constructs and then reconstructs its understandings of important events. As archaeologists, we can analyze the layers of meaning and the transformations in the heritage narratives at military sites by studying the memorials as aboveground artifacts. This study examines a Saratoga monument dedicated to Polish American engineer Thaddeus Kościuszko, the Saratoga monument to Irish American Timothy Murphy, and the Joseph Brant monument in Brantford, Ontario (Figure 2.1). These three monuments serve as examples of how the Polish, Irish, and Haudenosaunee First Nations in Canada consciously utilized the themes of lauding heroes and martial courage through their commemoration of American Revolutionary War figures important to each community's heritage narrative.

Theoretical Positioning

An integral part of this examination is "discourses." As Greg Marston (2004:35) notes, "There are many conflicting and overlapping definitions of discourse formulated from various theoretical and disciplinary standpoints. The simplest understanding of discourse is 'language as social practice.'" Because language is not separated or external to any society, it is informed by "other non-linguistic features of society" (Marston 2004:35). As Ruth Wodak and Michael Meyer (2009:2–3) note, "discourse" is not limited strictly to language but can encompass "anything from a historical monument, a *lieu de mémoire* [place of memory], a policy, a political strategy, narratives in a restricted broad sense of the term, text, talk, a speech, topic-related conversations, to language per se." To provide a consistent understanding of what is

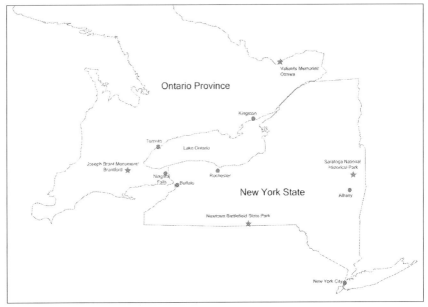

Figure 2.1. Map of New York, USA, and Ontario, Canada, showing the locations of the Newtown Battlefield State Park, Saratoga National Historical Park, Joseph Brant Monument, and Valiants Memorial. Map by Brant Venables, 2021.

meant by "discourse," in this chapter, it refers to the spoken and written words (both in documents and inscribed on physical artifacts like monuments) that bring about "material consequences" (Smith 2006:14).

As a part of heritage, discourse is not limited to the singular moment of a monument's dedication, speech given, or essay penned. Rather, it can often include one generation's reactions and engagement with texts or monuments conceived by a prior generation. When this engagement occurs with discourses crafted by a generation that has long since passed away, this may produce material consequences independent of the original actors (Smith 2006:14). A recent example of such discourses having material consequences are debates over the numerous monuments to Confederate figures that occupy public squares throughout the United States. Though the actors that erected these monuments are long dead, the discourses created by these monuments erected in public spaces shaped how the Civil War has been understood for decades by valorizing the Confederates who rebelled against the United States to preserve slavery and white supremacy.

As news coverage over recent years has shown, African Americans, who were historically marginalized and excluded from the heritage narrative of the United States, have heavily critiqued the racist symbolism of the monuments. Resistance to the calls to remove the monuments frequently invokes the ideas of heritage, particularly the belief that their existence creates a societal obligation to preserve and protect them as embodiments of the country's "heritage." This concept of obligatory stewardship and evocation of the heritage being a symbol of a shared common identity is what Laurajane Smith (2006:29) describes as the "Authorized Heritage Discourse." Briefly Authorized Heritage Discourse (abbreviated as AHD) is a dialogue that emphasizes aesthetically pleasing material objects, sites, places, or landscapes as a means of fostering an obligatory sense of stewardship for the current generation and crafting a common identity based on this past (Smith 2006:29). According to Smith, Authorized Heritage Discourse creates an imperative that the material object or place in question must be preserved for future generations (Smith 2006:29). This imperative further undermines attempts in the present to alter or change the meaning of a heritage site unless done under the supervision of heritage professionals (Smith 2006:29). By smoothing over conflicts and societal differences, Authorized Heritage Discourse serves to craft "conservative, if not reactionary, and distinctly Western, social messages" (Waterton et al. 2006:339).

Another function of Authorized Heritage Discourse is defining heritage as a passive experience: "visitors are led to, are instructed about, but are then not invited to engage with" (Smith 2006:31). The developments of heritage tourism influence this passive experience since the 1980s, which has led to the critique of heritage as simple entertainment (Smith 2006:32–33). However, this approach of treating heritage tourists as "passive consumers" serves the goals of Authorized Heritage Discourse through the quick rebuke many heritage professionals level against non-professionals such as reenactors that begin taking an active role in heritage (Smith 2006:34).

Site Backgrounds

The Saratoga National Military Park is located north of Albany and south of Lake George. The National Park Service runs this heritage site which includes numerous monuments placed on the battlefield during the late nineteenth and early twentieth centuries by private individuals or groups. During the fall of 1777, this heritage site was the location of one of the most decisive battles of the American Revolution.

In 1777, the British sought to follow up on the military successes of 1776 (Mackesy 1993:103). However, these successes did not deal a decisive blow, ending the rebellion in the colonies. General John Burgoyne proposed a three-pronged assault by three armies that would meet at Albany, New York

(Holmes and Smith-Holmes 2012:28). One prong of the assault would be conducted by an army striking southward from Canada and proceeding south along the Hudson River (Holmes and Smith-Holmes 2012:28). The second prong of the assault came from what is now western New York, with that army moving east along the waterways of the Mohawk River Valley (Holmes and Smith-Holmes 2012:28). The final prong was to be made up of troops garrisoned in British-occupied New York City who would strike northward along the Hudson River (Holmes and Smith-Holmes 2012:28). If successful, the British would end the war in a single decisive campaign by seizing control of the Hudson and Mohawk Rivers, key transportation highways in the eighteenth century, and cutting New England off from the rest of the colonies (Taylor 2016:179).

General John Burgoyne led the army tasked with seizing control of the Hudson River. On 13 June 1777, Burgoyne's army departed from St. Johns north of Lake Champlain (Ketchum 1997:130–133). After swiftly taking Fort Ticonderoga on 6 July by occupying the heights of Mount Independence, the British army rapidly traveled down the Hudson toward Albany (Luzader 2010:55–56).

It was not until the Battle of Bennington that Burgoyne's army met more than minor resistance. The battle began as a raid into Vermont, searching for horses for the German dragoons, cattle, and other supplies (Luzader 2010:94–95; Gabriel 2012:18). Up until this point, Burgoyne's army had relied on supply lines stretching from Canada, and as the army marched further down the Hudson, the logistics of supplying the army became progressively worse (Luzader 2010:94). Leading the raid was Lieutenant Colonel Friedrich Baum, who anticipated swiftly overwhelming the untested Continental forces guarding the depot (Luzader 2010:97). However, though the bulk of the forces had never seen combat, the Continental forces were double the size of Baum's and successfully enveloped Baum's troops on 16 August (Luzader 2010:105). This decisive defeat of Burgoyne's raiding party at Bennington set the stage for the Battles of Saratoga one month later.

Even though Continental General Horatio Gates had gathered a force of comparable size to Burgoyne's by early September, he recognized that the German and British infantry's superior training and experience weighted any battle in favor of Burgoyne (Luzader 2010:204). Seeking to offset that advantage, Gates moved his troops to Bemis Heights, which had a commanding view of the valley and the Hudson River below (Luzader 2010:204–205). The Polish engineer Thaddeus Kościuszko chose the locations and directed the construction of defensive works (Ketchum 1997:351).

The First Battle of Saratoga occurred on 19 September 1777, on the fields of a Loyalist farmer, John Freeman, who had gone north to join Burgoyne's army early in the campaign (Ketchum 1997:354). General Gates ordered Daniel Morgan, with his famous Morgan's Rifles light infantry, and Henry Dearborn, with additional infantry, to harass the British forces advancing on the Continental defenses' left flank (Ketchum 1997:360). When Morgan's Rifles spied the advancing British light infantry, they unleashed a devastating volley that sent the British into retreat (Ketchum 1997:360). A swift British counterattack forced Morgan's Rifles to retreat and regroup (Ketchum 1997:363). After both sides regrouped, the brunt of the fighting focused on the British line's center, which led to a pitched battle between the British regulars and Morgan's light infantry (Ketchum 1997:363–366). Though the British ultimately emerged victoriously, they failed to dislodge the Continental forces along Bemis Heights (Taylor 2016:181; Starbuck 1999:21).

On the morning of 21 September, as Burgoyne and his generals debated what to do next, a letter from General Henry Clinton arrived stating that Clinton would attempt to march 2,000 troops north from New York City to Burgoyne's aid (Ketchum 1997:375). Encouraged by this news, Burgoyne ordered his army to construct defensive redoubts of earth and timber and wait for relief (Ketchum 1997:375–376).

On 7 October, Burgoyne sent a reconnaissance in force under General Simon Fraser's command to probe the Continental left flank (Luzader 2016:26). As this reconnaissance force moved into the Berber Wheatfields, the Continentals attacked as British foragers were harvesting much-needed wheat (Luzader 2010:283–284).

Forced to retreat under a relentless Continental attack, General Fraser attempted to rally his outnumbered men in a spirited rear-guard action (Luzader 2016:28). Irish American Timothy Murphy fired the shot that mortally wounded Fraser (Ward 1952:529). This initial skirmish rapidly spread to a large battle. The massed Continental army, now numbering some 13,000 men to Burgoyne's 7,000, launched attacks against the main British defensive line (Luzader 2010:282). The Continentals successfully overwhelmed the 200 German *Jägers* manning the Breymann Redoubt on the British right flank. With the entire rear of the British army now threatened, they were forced to fall back to their final defensive position known as the Great Redoubt (Luzader 2010:297).

Slowly retreating northward, the beleaguered British army arrived at the town of Saratoga on 9 October (Luzader 2016:30). Exhausted and unable to retreat further, the British dug in and weighed their options while waiting in desperate hope a relief force would arrive (Luzader 2010:310–314). On 17 October, Burgoyne's army surrendered (Riedesel 1965:63; O'Shaughnessy 2013:146). As a result, Louis XVI and France's government, already aiding the Continentals with supplies and increasingly inclined in the Rebels' favor, formally allied France with the Continental Congress following the battle (O'Shaughnessy 2013:163–164; Ward 1952:540).

Following the Battle of Saratoga in October 1777, the British shifted their strategy from deploying Loyalist and First Nation forces as supplements to regular British military units to guerrilla forces. Butler's Rangers, Brant's Volunteers, and other Native American or Loyalist units patrolled the southern, eastern, and western boundaries between Native American and European American settlements, ranging from Ohio to the St. Lawrence River (Holmes 1977:2).

These forces engaged in raids against Continental agricultural settlements to disrupt supply lines and tie up troops sent to defend against these raids, thus preventing them from being used in the main theaters of war (Fischer 1997:20). The Continental forces deployed along the frontier matched their enemies' tactics by launching raids of their own against Loyalist and neutral or pro-British Native American settlements (Taylor 2006:8, 43–45). These devastating raids contrasted with the previous year's lengthy campaigns and continued until the end of the war in 1783 (Shy 1990:184–186; Fischer 1997:19–20; Taylor 2006:91; Mackesy 1993:130–136).

These changes in tactics saw civilian populations get swept up in a cycle of raids and counterraids that came to define the war along the frontiers of Pennsylvania and New York. However, the Continentals conveniently forgot their own raids' brutality and their contributions to this cycle of horror. In 1779, General George Washington issued orders to General John Sullivan to launch a campaign against the Haudenosaunee (Flick 1929:90). General Washington envisioned three goals for the campaign: first, conduct the expedition with a minimal drain on Continental resources; second, conduct the invasion during the season when it would do the most damage to the Native Americans; and third, if the Continentals had sufficient forces, to rout the Native Americans from what is now central and western New York (Williams 2005:192). The Continentals justified the Sullivan Campaign as a punishment for the Crown-allied Haudenosaunee for their 1778 raids against Continental settlements (Williams 2005:185–186, 227).

Acknowledging the Continental's numerical superiority, the Loyalists and Crown-allied Native Americans chose Newtown's small settlement for an ambush. Major John Butler commanded the Crown's roughly 200 non-Indian forces, chiefly drawn from the Loyalist unit Butler's Rangers. Joseph Brant

(Mohawk), Old Smoke (Seneca), and Hoch-ha-dunk (Delaware) led the four hundred Crown-allied Native Americans made up primarily of Seneca, Mohawk, and a few Delaware (Flick 1929:136–139).

Despite the efforts of Brant and Butler to conceal their forces, Continental scouts discovered the ambush. This allowed Sullivan to deploy the full might of 4,000 strong army against the roughly six hundred Loyalist and Crown-allied Native Americans (Fischer 1997:93; Graymont 1972:206–213). Despite the overwhelming odds and lack of artillery, the outnumbered Crown forces held the Continental forces at bay for two hours (Williams 2005:269). An attack by Continental infantry, supported by an artillery barrage, on the Crown forces' left flank necessitated their withdrawal or risk becoming surrounded (Public Archaeology Facility 2010:22–23).

The Battle of Newtown was the only major battle of the Sullivan Campaign (Graymont 1972:218). By the end of the campaign, the Continentals had destroyed 40 Native American towns, burned 160,000 bushels of corn and vegetables, ruined apple and peach orchards, and taken $30,000 worth of plunder (Williams 2005:293).

As a result of the devastation, the Haudenosaunee fled to Fort Niagara, seeking protection, food, and supplies from the British (Williams 2005:291–292). However, the British failed to provide sufficient supplies to adequately support the more than five thousand refugees (Williams 2005:292; Graymont 1972:220). A brutal winter, one of the worst recorded, added to the hardship (Fischer 1997:192). The Continentals offered provisions and supplies to any Native Americans who entered into a treaty with them, turned on the British at Fort Niagara, and delivered the fort over to Continental control (Williams 2005:293–294). Despite their desperate situation, the pro-Crown Haudenosaunee at Fort Niagara refused to betray their allies, and so Fort Niagara remained in British hands (Williams 2005:293–294). With this rejection of the offer of supplies, Sullivan was content to allow the Haudenosaunee refugees' humanitarian crisis to tax the British military's logistics and finances (Williams 2005:293–294).

Following the conclusion of the American Revolution, John Butler, Joseph Brant, the men they led in war, and their families fled to Canada and numerous other Loyalist and First Nation peoples who had sided with the Crown.

Memorials and Heritage Discourses

After the smoke of combat wafted away, the armies left, and the battlefields of Saratoga and Newtown returned to civilian use as farmland. Beginning with Civil War battlefields, especially Gettysburg in 1863, and then expanding

Figure 2.2. The Joseph Brant Monument in Brantford, Ontario, Canada. Photo by Brant Venables, 2016.

to Revolutionary War military sites, memorials served as platforms to craft national mythologies and laud military heroes. The Authorized Heritage Discourse adjusted to evoke national founding mythologies that resonated the most with contemporary audiences.

By the 1870s, with the approach of the Centennial of the American Revolution, the Authorized Heritage Discourse at Saratoga and Newtown championed the patriotism and heroic virtues of the Continental soldiers. Contrasting the Continentals' virtues were the Loyalists, First Nations peoples, British Regulars, and Hessian soldiers who, as enemies of the rebelling colonists, were portrayed as unpatriotic, prone to barbarism, tools of oppression, or unscrupulous mercenaries.

In contrast to the emerging Authorized Heritage Discourse in the 1870s on the United States side of the border, in 1874, the Hereditary Chiefs of the Six Nations Reserve at Grand River, Ontario, proposed a monument to Joseph Brant (Figure 2.2). They allocated $5,000 to the project in 1877 (Grand

Irish, Polish, and Haudenosaunee Engagements and the American Revolutionary War · 29

Figure 2.3. Statues on the Joseph Brant Monument: *A*, depicts Native Americans from the Mohawk, Tuscarora, and Oneida Nations; *B*, depicts Native Americans from the Seneca, Onondaga, and Cayuga Nations. Photos by Brant Venables, 2016.

River Branch—United Empire Loyalists' Association of Canada 2017). Over the next few years, donations to cover the $16,000 cost of the monument were gathered from the Six Nations Reserve, the Chippewas, the Canadian government, the Ontario government, the City of Brantford, Ontario, Brant and Bruce County, and private donations (United Empire Loyalists' Association of Canada 2017). The diverse contributions demonstrate the broad-based support for the Joseph Brant memorial in Canada.

Percy Wood from London, England, designed the monument, utilizing the likenesses of a chief from each of the Six Nations for the statues at the monument's base. These statues at the base represented the peoples that made up each of the Six Nations: Mohawk, Oneida, Tuscarora, Onondaga, Cayuga, and Seneca (Grand River Branch—United Empire Loyalists' Association of Canada 2017) (Figures 2.3a and 2.3b). The base of the monument forms a Union Jack with Joseph Brant's statue rising from the center (United Empire Loyalists' Association of Canada 2017). At the Six Nations' request, Percy Wood included the symbols of the Bear, Wolf, and Turtle Clans (United Empire Loyalists' Association of Canada 2017).

The British government donated 13 bronze cannons from Wellington's victory at Waterloo in 1815 and the Crimean War of 1853–1856 to be melted down to make the statues (Grand River Branch—United Empire Loyalists' Association of Canada 2017). The donation was an important symbolic act recognizing Joseph Brant as worthy of the military prestige embodied by artillery.

On 11 August 1886, Chief Ka-non-kwe-yo-the set the cornerstone of the monument (United Empire Loyalists' Association of Canada 2017). At the ceremony, William Cockshutt read a poem written by Pauline Johnson of the Six Nations Reserve specifically for the occasion (Grand River Branch—United Empire Loyalists' Association of Canada 2017).

The poem opens by speaking to Canadians of European descent and alluding to Canada's recent independence in 1867 and the role Native Americans played in the history leading up to this point:

> Young Canada with mighty force sweeps on/To gain in power and strength before the dawn/That brings another era, when the sun/Shall rise again, but sadly shine upon/Her Indian graves and Indian memories./For as the carmine in the twilight skies/Will fade as night comes on, as fades the race/That unto Might and doubtful Right gives place./And as white clouds float hurriedly and high/Across the crimson of a sunset sky/Altho' their depths are foamy as the snow/Their beauty lies in their vermillion glow./So, Canada, thy plumes were hardly won/Without allegiance from thy Indian son. (Grand River Branch—United Empire Loyalists' Association of Canada 2017)

Even as this opening acknowledges that the Six Nations people are not the power they once were, it establishes their equal claim to a place in the country.

Further reinforcing this point is the passage that Joseph Brant, along with the First Nation peoples who fought beside him, are heroes to both the Six Nations and Canada.

> Thy [Canada's] glories, like the cloud, enhance their charm/With red reflections from the Mohawk's arm./Then meet we as one common brotherhood/In peace and love, with purpose understood/To lift a lasting tribute to the name/Of Brant, who linked his own with Britain's fame./Who bade his people leave their Valley Home/Where nature her fairest aspects shone,/Where rolls the Mohawk River and the land/Is blest with every good from Heaven's hand,/To sweep the tide of home affections back/And love the land where waves the Union Jack. (Grand River Branch—United Empire Loyalists' Association of Canada 2017)

Pauline Johnson's poem further reinforces this challenge to the Continental-centric interpretation of patriotism in the United States by heralding Joseph Brant's patriotism. That Joseph Brant's alliances were not fickle is emphasized in her lines describing Joseph Brant's choice to move to Canada, "where waves the Union Jack" rather than remain in the land invaded by the Continentals.

The monument also subtly challenges anti–Native American sentiment in Canada by stating that both Joseph Brant and the Six Nations strictly observed treaties. This challenges any contemporary racist Canadian perceptions that Native Americans could not be trusted to uphold treaties or that

Native American treaty violations perpetrated contemporary conflicts. Like the United States, Canadians held similar racist ideas while also celebrating Canada's nineteenth-century development from colony to dominion in the British Commonwealth. Johnson's poem directly challenges racist heritage narratives that erased First Nation peoples from Canada's history. She asserts that Canada's Native American allies' sacrifices in war and the deaths of countless Native Americans won Canada's status as a dominion in the Commonwealth.

In contrast to the elaborate monument in Brantford, Ontario, and the dedication ceremony was the dramatically different portrayal of Joseph Brant and the Haudenosaunee occurring concurrently at the Newtown Battlefield in the 1870s. For the Centennial anniversary, this obligated reframing the Continentals' brutality leading up to, during, and after the Sullivan Campaign.

Exemplifying how this brutality was reframed as a virtue at the Centennial memorialization at Newtown was General William Tecumseh Sherman's keynote speech. Famous for his capture of the Confederate city of Atlanta, Georgia, and his subsequent "March to the Sea" during the Civil War, in 1879, Sherman was the four-star commanding general of the entire United States Army directly involved in the ongoing Indian Wars in the western United States (Utley 1973:15–16). In his speech, Sherman explicitly tied the Sullivan Campaign to current events:

> We are all at war. Ever since the first white man landed upon this continent, there has been a battle. We are at war to-day [sic]—a war between civilization and savages. Our forefathers . . . came to found an empire based upon new principles, and all opposition to it had to pass away. . . . [Washington] gave General Sullivan orders to come here and punish the Six Nations, for their cruel massacre in the valley of the Wyoming. . . . General Sullivan obeyed his orders like a man and like a soldier, and the result was from that time forward, your people settled up these beautiful valleys all around here. . . . This valley was opened to civilization; it came on the heels of General Sullivan's army, and has gone on, and gone on until to-day [sic]. The same battle is raging upon the Yellow Stone. (Cook 1887:439)

By tying the Sullivan Campaign to current events, he helped justify the campaign's brutality. He also established continuity that conveyed that patriotic heroes were fighting the battles out west because of patriotic heroes worthy of the present Centennial celebration of the Battle of Newtown.

In the nineteenth and early twentieth centuries, there was substantial nativist prejudice toward non-Anglo-Saxon immigrants. Of relevance to this study

Figure 2.4. A, The Kościuszko Monument in Saratoga, New York. B, The Timothy Murphy Monument in Saratoga, New York. Photos by Brant Venables, 2014.

was the prejudice toward Irish and Eastern European immigrants. Within the United States, nativist movements such as the Know-Nothing Party asserted that immigrants' true allegiance would always be to another country like Ireland or, in the case of Irish Catholics, to the foreign entity of the Pope (Orser 2007:110; Samito 2009:32). When the Civil War erupted, numerous immigrants served in defense of the United States. When the Civil War ended, veterans memorialized their service in cities, towns, and former battlefields throughout the country and slowly formed the monumental landscapes we are familiar with today. Immigrants who were veterans used memorializations of their military service to challenge nativist and bigoted discourses by asserting their loyalty to the United States. When the country began preparations to celebrate the Centennial of the Revolutionary War, this pattern transferred over.

While not the first monument at the Saratoga Battlefield dedicated to Kościuszko, the 1936 Kościuszko monument was the first placed on the battlefield definitively connected to commemorative efforts led by Polish Americans (Figure 2.4a). This is because the monument specifies Polish Americans erected it, including those from Albany, Amsterdam, Cohoes, Schenectady, Troy, and Watervliet, all located in New York. This coincided with New York Governor Herbert H. Lehman sending an urn filled with soil from one of the Continental earthworks laid out by Kościuszko to Poland around July 1936. Lehman did so at the request of F. Piskorski, chairperson of the Greater Poland, Silesian, and Pomeranian Alliance of America organization, with the soil to be made part of the Marshal Pilsudski Memorial Mound (Halpin 1936).

This demonstrates that Polish people saw Kościuszko as a national hero and a natural choice for Polish Americans to emphasize as a Revolutionary War hero to their community.

Beginning in 1950 and continuing for the remainder of the twentieth century, an organization known as the Polish American Congress held annual commemorations at the 1936 Kościuszko monument, celebrating the pride in their heritage and long tradition of loyalty displayed to the United States. The Polish American Congress was formed in May 1944 at Buffalo, New York, by individuals representing Polish communities from across the United States (Pienkos 2013). The organization expressed unwavering support for the defeat of the Axis and called for the restoration of Poland's independence after the war (Pienkos 2013). Although they failed to secure Poland's independence, it remained an active organization throughout the Cold War (Pienkos 2013).

Irish Americans also engaged with the heritage discourses of Saratoga. This engagement revolved around Timothy Murphy, an Irish American in Daniel Morgan's Rifle Corps, who is now recognized for firing the shot that mortally wounded British General Simon Fraser during the First Battle of Saratoga on 19 September 1777. In the late nineteenth century, when memorials were first being placed at Saratoga, who deserved credit for this fatal shot was more ambiguous.

In 1887, Daniel Morgan's great-granddaughter dedicated a monument to him which gave Daniel Morgan, not Timothy Murphy, credit for killing General Fraser:

Saratoga 1777
Here Morgan
Reluctant To Destroy
So Noble A Foe, Was
Forced By Patriotic
Necessity To Defeat And
Slay The Gentle And
Gallant FRASER

To Commemorate
The Magnanimity
Of MORGAN'S Heroic
Nature And His Stern
Sense Of Duty To His
Country, This Tablet
Is Here Inscribed
By

Virginia Neville Taylor
Great Grand Daughter
Of
Gen. DANIEL MORGAN

While the Morgan monument does not explicitly claim that he fired the fatal shot, the particular phrasing implies Morgan was more directly involved in shooting Fraser than was likely the case. Additionally, the wording that emphasizes Morgan's role as exemplary patriotic behavior is an example of how Authorized Heritage Discourse frames individuals and events to create narratives of heroes or villains.

It was not until 1913 that Timothy Murphy had a monument that acknowledged him by name and challenged the portrayal of events present on Daniel Morgan's monument (Figure 2.4b). The monument was dedicated by the Ancient Order of Hibernians, an Irish American organization founded in 1836 when Irish miners who made up the Hibernian Benevolent Society in Pennsylvania merged with the St. Patrick's Fraternal Society in New York City (Mike McCormack 2020). Due to the hostility toward Irish immigrants and Catholics in general during the nineteenth century, members of organizations like the Hibernians often acted to protect Irish communities and churches from violence by nativists, including members of the Know-Nothing Party (Mike McCormack 2020).

The Murphy monument did more than challenge the heritage narrative created by the Morgan monument. The monument also commemorates all Continental soldiers of Irish descent who gave their lives at Saratoga:

This Monument Is Erected by the Ancient Order of Hibernians of Saratoga County
   to the Memory Of Timothy Murphy
   Celebrated Marksman Of Colonel Morgan's Rifle Corps Whose Unerring Aim Turned The Tide Of Battle By The Death Of The British General Frazer On October 7, 1777. Thereby Adding To The World's History One Of Its Decisive Battles. In This Monument Is Commemorated Heroic Deeds Of Hundreds Of Other Soldiers Of Irish Blood Who Laid Down Their Lives On This Bloody Field That The Union Of States Might Be Triumphant.

Unlike the Morgan monument, which utilized broader, more abstract expressions of patriotism and heroism, the Murphy monument focused on the impact Murphy's slaying of Fraser had on the battle to establish Murphy's heroism and patriotism.

Beyond this, the Murphy monument's dedication to all Irish soldiers who fought for the rebel's cause is significant not just as a clear expression of loyalty to the country and pushback on nativist prejudice but the particular way this emphasis is made—the explicit mention that these Irish soldiers gave their lives for the Continental cause. This specific framework has its roots in the Irish monuments from the Civil War. Prime examples of this heritage framing are the monuments to the Irish Brigade at Gettysburg's Civil War battlefield in Pennsylvania. The 1888 Irish Brigade monument had the following inscription that, much like Murphy's monument decades later, focused on the theme of sacrifice: "The brigade entered the battle . . . 530 strong, of which this contingent, composing three battalions . . . [the] original strength [of these three] battalions was 3,000 men."

A second Irish Brigade monument erected, this one to the Brigade's chaplain, Father Corby, replicated this theme focusing on loss. The monument was constructed in 1910, three years before Timothy Murphy's at Saratoga, a sculpture of Father Corby, and was placed on the rock Corby stood on to administer general absolution to the Irish Brigade moments before they went into combat during the Battle of Gettysburg. The Catholic Church only permits general absolution, forgiving the sins of a large group of people without hearing individual confessions in extreme circumstances such as imminent death. By choosing to memorialize the moment when Corby gave general absolution to the Irish Brigade, it reminds viewers that many of the men he gave absolution to died in the next few hours of bloody conflict. Therefore, the Murphy monument at Saratoga is consistent with the themes expressed at other Irish American military monuments, chiefly a theme of loss and sacrifice as a demonstration of Irish American loyalty and patriotism in the United States' service.

Conclusion

The poem "The New Colossus" was written by New York poet Emma Lazarus in 1883 to help raise funds for a giant pedestal to support the Statue of Liberty. The poem's famous lines "Give me your tired, your poor,/Your huddled masses yearning to breathe free,/The wretched refuse of your teeming shore./Send these, the homeless, tempest-tost to me,/I lift my lamp beside the golden door!" evokes the compassion and haven immigrants hoped to find in the country when they arrived. The monuments to Thaddeus Kościuszko and Timothy Murphy expressed the dedication immigrants had to these ideals and called on viewers to reflect on how many immigrants gave their lives in pursuit of those ideals. Meanwhile, across the border in Canada, the Six Nations challenged the biased and racist heritage narratives in the United States by constructing a monument to Joseph Brant, asserting their heritage narrative that Joseph Brant was a Haudenosaunee and Canadian hero.

Together, these case studies demonstrate that non-dominant ethnic groups understood monuments and commemorations' power and exercised their agency to share their own heritage narratives with the broader populace. The impact of this agency can be seen at the Saratoga Battlefield where today there is interpretive signage that acknowledges Timothy Murphy's role. In Canada, the impact of the First Nations from Grand River, Ontario, can be seen in the Valiants Memorial located in Ottawa, Canada, which was installed in 2006 by the Canadian government. The Valiants Memorial pays "tribute to the people who have served [Canada] in times of war and the contribution they have made in building [Canada]" (Government of Canada 2006). Among the figures honored in the memorial is Joseph Brant.

The Joseph Brant Monument in Ontario demonstrates that awareness of heritage discourses' implications and their construction existed in the nineteenth century. Moreover, the Six Nations' hereditary chiefs in Ontario showed awareness of how to utilize heritage narratives to challenge discriminatory heritage discourses through both the physical symbolism used in the monument itself and the symbolism of the poem read at the dedication ceremony. The Kościuszko and Timothy Murphy monuments erected in the early twentieth century by Polish American and Irish American communities demonstrate similar awareness and engagement with heritage discourses. In the case of the Irish Americans, they explicitly transplant Civil War memorialization efforts aimed at challenging nativist bigotry over to a Revolutionary War site. They use monuments and commemorative speeches to reinforce further the Irish community's longstanding loyalty to the United States' causes. This study shows that monuments' utilization to promote specific discourses and heritage narratives was a well-understood rather than arcane concept.

References

Cook, Frederick, ed.
    1887   *Journals of the Military Expedition of Major General John Sullivan Against the Six Nations of Indians in 1779 with Records of Centennial Celebrations.* Auburn, NY: Knapp, Peck, & Thomson.

Fischer, Joseph R.
    1997   *A Well-Executed Failure: The Sullivan Campaign Against the Iroquois, July-September 1779.* 1st edition. Columbia, SC: University of South Carolina Press.

Flick, Alexander C.
    1929   *The Sullivan-Clinton Campaign In 1779: Chronology and Selected Documents.* Albany, NY: The University of the State of New York, Albany.

Gabriel, Michael P.
   2012   *The Battle of Bennington: Soldiers & Civilians*. Charleston, SC: History Press.

Government of Canada
   2006   Valiants Memorial Unveiled. News releases. Government of Canada: News. https://www.canada.ca/en/news/archive/2006/11/valiants-memorial-unveiled.html, accessed 21 January 2018.

Grand River Branch—United Empire Loyalists' Association of Canada
   2017   The Joseph Brant Monument. http://www.grandriveruel.ca/Grand_River_Brant_Monument.htm, accessed 12 September 2016.

Graymont, Barbara
   1972   *The Iroquois in the American Revolution*. 1st edition. Syracuse, NY: Syracuse University Press.

Halpin, John L.
   1936   Soil Was Taken from the Saratoga Battlefield to Become Part of the Marshal Pilsudski Memorial Mound in Poland. Box 9, Folder 1: Legal Size Box Jul-Sep 1936. Saratoga National Historical Park, State of New York Conservation Department.

Holmes, Donald C.
   1977   *Butler's Rangers*. Ottawa: Sir Guy Carleton Branch, United Empire Loyalists. http://www.uelac.org/PDF/Formation-of-Butlers-Rangers.pdf, accessed 13 February 2012.

Holmes, Timothy, and Libby Smith-Holmes
   2012   *Saratoga: America's Battlefield*. Charleston, SC: The History Press.

Ketchum, Richard M.
   1997   *Saratoga: Turning Point of America's Revolutionary War*. New York, NY: Henry Holt.

Luzader, John
   2016   The Coming Revolutionary War Battles at Saratoga. In *The Saratoga Campaign: Uncovering an Embattled Landscape*. William A. Griswold and Donald W. Linebaugh, eds. Pp. 1–38. Hanover, NH: University Press of New England.

Luzader, John F.
   2010   *Saratoga: A Military History of the Decisive Campaign of the American Revolution*. 1st paperback edition. New York, NY: Savas Beatie.

Mackesy, Piers
   1993   *The War for America: 1775–1783*. Lincoln, NE: University of Nebraska Press.

Marston, Greg
   2004   Social Policy and Discourse Analysis: Policy Change in Public Housing. Aldershot, Hants, UK: Ashgate.

McCormack, Mike
   2020   An Updated History of the Ancient Order of Hibernians in America. Ancient Order of Hibernians. http://www.aoh.com/aoh-history/, accessed 17 October 2016.

Orser, Charles E.
   2007   *The Archaeology of Race and Racialization in Historic America*. Gainesville, FL: University Press of Florida.

O'Shaughnessy, Andrew Jackson
   2013   *The Men Who Lost America: British Leadership, the American Revolution, and the Fate of the Empire*. New Haven, CT: Yale University Press.

Pienkos, Donald
   2013   Origins of the Polish American Congress. http://www.pac1944.0rg/pac-history/origins-of-the-polish-american-congress/, accessed 25 October 2016.

Public Archaeology Facility
   2010   *Documentary Research Report and Research Design Revolutionary War Newtown Battlefield Project (August 29th, 1779) Chemung County, New York, Grant # GA-2255-08-017*. Report to the American Battlefield Protection Program, National Park Service, Washington, D.C. by the Public Archaeology Facility of Binghamton University, Binghamton, NY.

Riedesel, Friederike Charlotte Luise
   1965   *Baroness von Riedesel and the American Revolution: Journal and Correspondence of a Tour of Duty, 1776–1783*. Marvin L. Brown, trans. Chapel Hill, NC: The University of North Carolina Press.

Samito, Christian G.
   2009   *Becoming American under Fire: Irish Americans, African Americans, and the Politics of Citizenship during the Civil War Era*. Ithaca, NY: Cornell University Press.

Shy, John
   1990   *A People Numerous & Armed: Reflections on the Military Struggle for Independence*. Ann Arbor, MI: The University of Michigan Press.

Smith, Laurajane
   2006   *Uses of Heritage*. London, UK: Routledge.

Starbuck, David R.
   1999   *The Great Warpath: British Military Sites from Albany to Crown Point*. Hanover, NH: University Press of New England.

Taylor, Alan
   2006   *The Divided Ground: Indians, Settlers, and the Northern Borderland of the American Revolution*. New York, NY: Vintage Books.
   2016   *American Revolutions: A Continental History, 1750–1804*. 1st edition. New York, NY: W. W. Norton & Company.

United Empire Loyalists' Association of Canada
   2017   Joseph Brant Memorial Statue. http://www.uelac.org/Loyalist-Monuments/Brant-Joseph.php, accessed 12 September 2016.

Utley, Robert M.
   1973   *Frontier Regulars: The United States Army and the Indian, 1866–1891*. New York, NY: Macmillan.

Ward, Christopher
   1952   *The War of the Revolution*. New York, NY: Macmillan.

Waterton, Emma, Laurajane Smith, and Gary Campbell
   2006   The Utility of Discourse Analysis to Heritage Studies: The Burra Charter and Social Inclusion. *International Journal of Heritage Studies* 12(4):339–355.

Williams, Glenn F.
   2005   *Year of the Hangman: George Washington's Campaign Against the Iroquois.* Yardley, PA: Westholme.

Wodak, Ruth, and Michael Meyer
   2009   Critical Discourse Analysis: History, Agenda, Theory and Methodology. In *Methods of Critical Discourse Analysis.* 2nd edition. Ruth Wodak and Michael Meyer, eds. Pp. 1–33. London, UK: SAGE.

3

The Fredericksburg Slave Auction Block

A Monumental Reminder of Race Relations in Virginia

Kerri Barile Tambs

It was dark; daylight was just starting to appear. Eight people gathered on a street corner for a small public works project. Brick pavers were pulled up, some dirt was shoveled out, stone and brick were removed, an archaeologist scraped the earth, and the area was covered back over. It took less than an hour. But this was no ordinary public works project, and it was not an ordinary morning. This was the removal of an incredibly significant stone object during a nationwide movement that rocked many American communities. It was 5 June 2020, on the northwest corner of the intersection of William and Charles Streets in Fredericksburg, Virginia. The historical era was the Black Lives Matter movement. The object was a 2.5 ft. tall, 20 in. wide column of sandstone colloquially known as the "auction block" or "slave auction block"—an object that enslaved individuals purportedly stood on to be sold as chattel. Small in size, the presence of this object had a long and deep impact on this historic community as a monument to pervading racism in this Southern city.

Prior to its removal, the object was marked only by a small bronze plaque that read: "AUCTION BLOCK. Fredericksburg's Principal Auction Site in Pre-Civil War Days for Slaves and Property." Information on the block was presented in numerous area tour guides and history books, but the data were equally as abbreviated, as the history of this block came not from records and research but primarily from over a century of oral tradition. While the block sat silently on the street corner, public discourse grew. Some said enslaved people stood on the stone to be auctioned off; others said it was merely a carriage step. Some sat in vigil near the stone to pray for those who were dehumanized on this corner; others stood on the block and posed to take tasteless photographs. On the extreme side, a few took a hammer to the stone to deface its surface. Regardless of opinion, the block was a symbol of tension and oppression, discord that reached its zenith in the summer of 2020.

This chapter focuses on the history and use of the block and the dialogue on race and memorialization, as well as the development of local narratives over time. Its colloquial story is based on oral history. Extensive scholarly research and archaeological studies on the object were not completed until 2017 and 2018. These inquiries provided an alternative version of the pervading story of its use that stood in conflict with the public narrative; however, this information was understandably sidelined as a city was forced to confront its tumultuous and uncomfortable past.

The Politics of Memory

Views of history and historical events have always been political. Individuals interpret past events through their knowledge, experiences, and locale (Kurtz 2018:9). This practice often results in fixed memories, wherein the historical narrative becomes "fact" once it is repeatedly processed through the lens of personal interpretation of historical data. At times, this process moves beyond the individual to a larger population, wherein the altered data becomes part of the collective memory. What needs to be considered, though, is that "history is different from memory. While history/historical narratives are 'representations of what is no longer,' detached and prone to reinterpretations, memory is always (subjectively) 'real'; lived, signified, and enacted by individuals of the community" (Chow 2015:193). This poses a challenge for those who are working with historical data to interpret the past in the public realm.

The ways in which history and historic places in America are interpreted and portrayed have changed over time. From the reverence of our "founding fathers" in the nineteenth century to the proliferation of historic house museums in the 1920s and 1930s, early commemoration revolved around sites related to notable individuals and events of our past (i.e., Sodaro 2018:13). Almost all of these places were associated with the lives and actions of White, wealthy males. This activity continued through the Bicentennial in the 1970s, when the reverence of our Colonial past pervaded our cultural fabric. It was not until the 1980s and 1990s that there was a notable shift in the study and commemoration of others. This shift included not only exploring the pasts of non-White and non-male groups but also acknowledging the more traumatic episodes of history. Moody (2020:181) and others refer to this time as a global "memory boom," a period when there was an international effort to acknowledge both alternative and darker aspects of history. This included the slave trade and slavery, as well as other episodes of human oppression and degradation. The paradox, though, was that although this was an international movement, the focus on history shifted to the local level—away from the great man theories to the individual actors and communal places with a significant local impact (Moody 2020:183).

Archaeology has been at the forefront of expanding our studies on subjugated groups, especially at the local level, since the 1980s (for example, Conkey and Spector 1984; Otto 1984; Singleton 1990). The historical presence of the "other" can often be found below ground in non-biased forms when compared to some written records. This has allowed archaeologists to be key players in the development of alternative narratives of our past wherein subjugated groups have a voice. This work has allowed specialists to examine the historical role of women (for example, Conkey and Gero 1991; Gibb and King 1991; Spencer-Wood 1987), those of color (for example, Babson 1988; Deagan 1983; Joyner 1984), people with lower social and economic status (for example, Mrozowski et al. 1986; Orser 1988), and individuals on the geographic margin of populated places (for example, Beaudry 1986; Hardesty 1988), among others. These studies have all provided an alternative story to the status quo. "Critically evaluating and challenging the dominant narrative can enable a very different view of the past and a new reality in the present" (Shackel 2013:3).

The archaeological voice, though, does not exist in a vacuum. Just as history is political, so are the findings of archaeologists exploring the past. This is particularly true in the exploration of race and identity, wherein multiple avenues of inquiry are intertwined (Labode and Levin 2016:10). Archaeologists must not only ensure that their voice is heard but, more importantly, filter their findings through additional data sets and the public narrative to fully understand the implications of alternative theories. As stated by archaeologist Barbara Little (2013:128):

> If we recognize and fully embrace the concept that our social science is embedded in our political and social context, then we need to recognize that our scholarship cannot stand alone or offer a disconnected authority. Archaeological expertise is unique and important, and it is a valid and valuable part of the collaboration necessary to make sense of our historical trajectories. Collaboration with other epistemologies and experiences is essential.

The Fredericksburg slave auction block site provided an opportunity to not only explore the history of this significant object but also to filter this data through the lens of oral tradition. How the public perceives an archaeological site and the data that is shared is just as informative as the data that comes from the dirt.

The Fredericksburg Slave Auction Block Study

Fredericksburg, Virginia, founded in 1728, is located approximately halfway between Washington, DC, and Richmond. In 2018, the Virginia Department of Transportation (VDOT) teamed with the City of Fredericksburg to commence a series of improvements to sidewalks, crosswalks, and other public roadside facilities in the historic core. Among the locations set for improvements was the intersection of Charles and William Streets, the location of the block. Recognizing the data potential of this resource and immense public interest, VDOT and the City engaged Dovetail Cultural Resource Group (Dovetail) to complete archival research and archaeological studies on the block prior to developing improvement plans (Hatch et al. 2019).

History and Public Recollections

Archival research confirmed that the block was installed around 1843 as part of the redevelopment of this corner. Recognizing the lack of first-class hostelries with large public spaces, Joseph Sanford built the United States Hotel at 401–405 William Street, a three-story, five-bay brick building (Hatch et al. 2019). Like many communities, the surrounding streets were composed of packed earth. Some streets had slightly elevated masonry sidewalks, while others did not. To increase the prominence of his new establishment, Sanford installed brick pavers to create a flat sidewalk in front of the new hotel as a pedestrian area. The stone auction block was installed just prior to laying the brick pavers; it was part of the original exterior design (Hatch et al. 2019). Insurance policy assessed the building alone at $13,850, suggesting that this new hotel was not modestly constructed (Fredericksburg Land Tax Records n.d.; Mutual Assurance Society n.d.). In fact, a few of the town's more notable citizens were lodgers, including Fredericksburg Mayor R.B. Semple, lawyer William H. Fitzhugh, merchant William F. Cheek, and barkeeper William P. Ellis, along with several clerks, painters, and other tradespeople (United States Federal Population Census 1850). Sanford owned and operated the United States Hotel from 1843 until 1851, when he sold the property to James Chartters, who renamed the business the Planter's Hotel (Hennessey 2017).

Taverns, inns, and hotels provided lodging for travelers in the eighteenth and nineteenth centuries but were also places for social gatherings, public auctions, and political events—thereby serving as communication hubs in

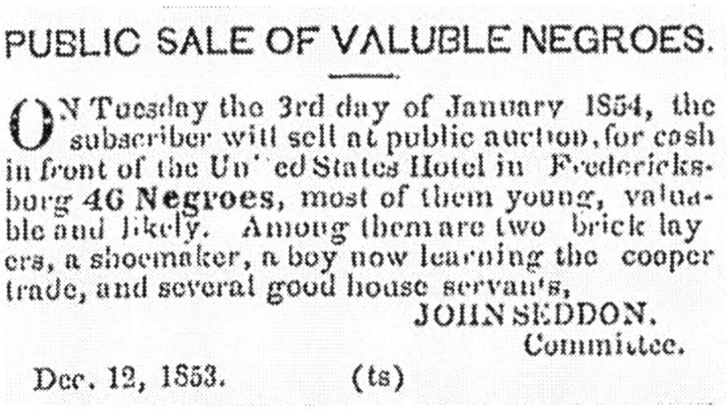

> **PUBLIC SALE OF VALUBLE NEGROES.**
>
> ON Tuesday the 3rd day of January 1854, the subscriber will sell at public auction, for cash in front of the Un'ed States Hotel in Fredericksburg 46 **Negroes**, most of them young, valuable and likely. Among them are two brick layers, a shoemaker, a boy now learning the cooper trade, and several good house servan's,
>
> JOHN SEDDON.
> Committee.
>
> Dec. 12, 1853. (ts)

Figure 3.1. December 26, 1853, advertisement in the *Fredericksburg News* (*Fredericksburg News* 1853:3). From the collections of Dayton History.

towns of all sizes for people of various socioeconomic backgrounds. Situated along one of Fredericksburg's major thoroughfares, the United States Hotel/Planter's Hotel is known to have been the site of many public auctions throughout the mid-nineteenth century. At these auctions, enslaved people appear to have been regularly sold along with personal property and real estate of area residents. The earliest known ad appeared in the 20 November 1846, edition of the *Richmond Enquirer* noting the sale of 40 enslaved people "near the United States Hotel" in Fredericksburg (Hennessy 2017). Newspaper ads show that sales were repeated each year until the Civil War. While it is probable that the stone was somehow used during some of these auctions, none of the advertisements reference the block specifically. Several ads, though, mention the sales "in front of the hotel," while some state that the sales would occur "before the front door" (for example, *Fredericksburg News* 1850, 1853).

The hotel continued in operation through the early twentieth century. In 1904 and again in the 1920s, the streets and sidewalks around the hotel were modified to raise the street level. The brick pavers were removed and then reinstalled in the late twentieth century.

The block has had an incredible amount of public interest over the past 150 years. The first known reference to the site specifically as "a slave auction block" is by a Civil War veteran returning to Fredericksburg in 1893 (Hennessy 2017). An image of the stone taken in 1898 by Albert Kearns shows the stone in context, straddling the edge of the road and sidewalk.

Kearns labeled the image as the "slave block" (The Albert Kern Collection at Dayton History 1898). A gas lantern had been installed adjacent to the stone sometime in the late nineteenth century. In the decades that followed, the "slave block" became a monument of historical interest, with several African Americans recounting their experiences visiting the site. Some even posed on or near the block for photographs. By 1913, the ideology of the stone as a "slave block" had risen in the ranks of Virginia lore, and the Association

Figure 3.2. Photo of auction block in 1898, looking south along Charles Street. Photo from The Albert Kern Collection at Dayton History, 1898.

for the Preservation of Virginia Antiquities sought to place a marker at the site to describe its historic use (Hennessy 2017). It is unknown if the marker was installed. Throughout the remainder of the twentieth century, the block remained a central object in downtown Fredericksburg, both physically and psychologically.

The block continued to be at the center of ongoing dialogues regarding the place of slavery in the historical narrative. Some residents and historians believed that the block, in its current location, provided an excellent in situ tool to discuss the horror of the practice of slavery and is a harsh reminder of our past to future generations. Others believed that the block was a derisive and particularly cruel object that should not be left sitting at a busy city intersection, especially without interpretation, and it should be removed.

Archaeology and Contextual Research

On-site studies at the corner of William and Charles Streets in 2018 included archaeological excavations and an in-depth examination of the physical components of the block. One 1.6 × 1.6 ft. test unit (TU 1) was placed against the object. Work commenced with the removal of a modern brick sidewalk. While not removed archaeologically, the sidewalk represented a culturally modified layer; thus, it was documented as Stratum I during the excavation.

Upon removal of the sidewalk materials, TU 1 unit was laid in adjacent to the block and excavation commenced. A total of three additional strata (labeled Stratum II–Stratum IV) were encountered in the unit below the brick sidewalk. Stratum II, which ranged from 0.2–0.5 ft., included fill brought in during the twentieth century to level and raise the sidewalk and street area. Only one artifact was found within the soil, a small fragment of undecorated creamware (1762–1820). At the base of Stratum II, archaeologists encountered several fragments of early twentieth-century, rough-tempered pavement near the eastern balk of the unit, along William Street.

Below the pavement fragments, Stratum III was approximately 0.5 ft.feet thick and covered the entire unit. It comprised nineteenth-century fill. Numerous small- and medium-sized brick paver fragments were also noted throughout the matrix. Eight artifacts, all very fragmented, were found in Stratum III—two undecorated creamware (1762–1820), two clear bottle glass, one green bottle glass, one slate, one aqua glass insulator fragment, and one oyster shell. The presence of the glass insulator gives the layer a *terminus post quem* of 1880.

At the base of Stratum III, the team uncovered the bottom of the block. The block sat on a pad made of unmortared brick that created a level platform for stone installation. Soil surrounding the pad, labeled as Stratum IV, was excavated to a depth of 0.2 to 0.4 ft., at which point the team hit a sterile sandy clay loam excavation of the unit ceased. Only one artifact was found in Stratum IV, a small fragment of dark green bottle glass. Based on the presence of the bottom of the stone and brick pad, as well as the general paucity of artifacts, this stratum was interpreted as the original nineteenth-century fill brought in to surround the block and its base. Based on analysis of the soils, the ground surface at the time of installation was about 1 ft. lower than it is today, thus the block would have appeared about a foot taller, 3.5 ft. in height above the ground surface.

Figure 3.3. *A*, Graffiti placed on the Auction Block in May 2020. Photograph Courtesy of the Fredericksburg Area Museum. *B*, Archaeological Profile of TU 1 at the Auction Block in November 2018. Photo by Dovetail Cultural Resource Group. *C*, The Block wrapped and secured for removal on June 5, 2020. Photo by Dovetail Cultural Resource Group.

Upon completion of the archaeology, the block itself was examined to understand its materials and size. The block is made of Aquia sandstone; however, it is not formed of the pure, soft sandstone used in numerous eighteenth-century buildings around Fredericksburg but a coarser variety that contains an abundance of large inclusions. This coarse sandstone was used in the area after around 1820, once veins of the refined sandstone had been depleted (i.e., Barile et al. 2008; Barile et al. 2014). The block was formed through rough cleaving using chisels and picks and later smoothed through fine chiseling and sanding. It is not circular but actually ovoid in shape.

To help identify the original use of the block, the team compared the archaeological and archival data against carriage blocks, slave auction blocks, road markers, and other streetside objects. The study showed that historic carriage blocks in Fredericksburg, or "upping stones" as they were also known, were much shorter. None were more than 1.5 ft. off the ground, and all were placed directly adjacent to the street. Most also tended to be as wide as the tread of a typical staircase or larger to facilitate use. At the time it was put in place, the top of the slave auction block was 3.5 ft. above the ground surface. It also was not at the edge of the street where a carriage could pull up but rather surrounded by the sidewalk; the sidewalk was not narrowed, thus bringing the block to the street/sidewalk interface until the late nineteenth century, as seen in the 1898 Kearns photograph. The preponderance of evidence suggested it did not function as a carriage block.

The object was also examined for use as a block on which enslaved individuals stood for sale as chattel. The stone is approximately 20 in. in diameter with a slight slope. This narrow width would have made balancing on top extremely difficult. The cleaved "step" that can be seen on the north side appears to be a natural break in the soft sandstone that occurred decades earlier. It is uneven and has a 45° angle. There are no chisel marks or other evidence that it was purposely cut as a step to get on top of the stone. The team also compared the block to sketches of slave auctions in progress as well as images captured of known Southern auction blocks in the twentieth century, most notably photographs collected by the Historic American Building Survey (HABS) in the early twentieth century. Historical depictions of auctions and auctioneers do often show individuals standing at an elevated height above the crowd, presumably to provide the audience with a clearer image of the items being sold. An 1861 image of a slave auction in Richmond, Virginia, was accompanied by a narrative describing the event:

> The auction rooms for the sale of Negroes are situated in the main streets, and are generally the ground floors of the building; the entrance-door opens straight into the street, and the sale room is similar to any other auction room . . . placards, advertisements, and notices as to the business carried on are dispensed with, the only indications of the trade being a small red flag hanging from the front door post, and a piece of paper upon which is written . . . this simple announcement—'Negroes for sale at auction.' . . . (The Atlantic Slave Trade and Life in the Americas 2015)

Places where slaves were auctioned in the South are diverse and include market buildings, specific rooms, stages, and blocks of varying sizes. A slave auction block in Campbell County, Virginia, recorded in HABS, noted that "according to tradition, these original stone features were used in the auction and sale of slaves. The smaller of the two elements was used by the auctioneer, while the stone table was used to display the best qualities of the slaves. The authenticity of this story has not been documented" (HABS 1960). Also recorded as a "slave auction block," a wide stage located inside the St. Louis Hotel in New Orleans, Louisiana, was recorded circa 1906 (Detroit Publishing Company 1906). All images depict a wide platform.

While the Fredericksburg block was likely not purposefully intended for use as a standing platform for auctioneers or enslaved people, it may have had a more tangential association with the auction industry and thus achieved its moniker through oral tradition. The square hole through the center of the block was purposefully cut and utilized. The hole measures about 2 in. in diameter with straight sides. Through a comparison with objects found in other communities, historians have suggested that a metal rod was inserted into the center of the stone, and a tablet or metal sheet was affixed to the rod for use as a signpost (Hatch et al. 2019:72). It is probable that a sign affixed to this object advertised many activities in the hotel, including the sale of enslaved individuals. If this is true, the block indeed has a notable association with the slave industry. There is no question that slave sales occurred at this corner and in the adjacent hotel; as noted above, numerous newspaper accounts testify to this fact. The probability of enslaved individuals standing on this particular object though, as repeatedly stated in the oral histories, is low.

The results of the 2018 archival research and archaeological study were summarized in a report and submitted to VDOT, the Virginia State Historic Preservation Office, Fredericksburg city staff and city council, the local paper, and local libraries. Although several articles appeared in the local newspaper, the Fredericksburg *Free Lance-Star,* the data was not embraced. The idea of enslaved people standing on the block for sale or as a carriage stone pervaded. While the work did not meet with active resistance from the community or scholars (for example, Shackel 2013:6), it was put aside in favor of the common stories. This highlights two elements: one, a reiteration of the importance of the public memory; and two, a focus on what the public memory says about current race relations in this Virginia city. The groups who referred to it as a slave auction block and a carriage step were quite different.

A Revised Public Dialogue

Between the November 2018 dig and June 2019, over half a dozen meetings and public talks were held to discuss the future of the block and its place in the community. Many of the meetings we led by the International Coalition of Sites of Conscience—hired by the City in 2019 to understand public opinion of this object. The meetings were well attended, tense, honest, and engaging. The primary outcome was that attendees fell into three camps: those who felt that the block should stay in situ with better interpretation; those who thought the block should be moved to the Fredericksburg Area Museum and interpreted there; and those who felt that the block should be destroyed. Public comments proliferated on social media, most notably on Facebook, each time the *Free Lance-Star* published an article on the ongoing study. Comments numbered in the thousands and were extraordinarily varied, representing the disparate opinions and intense emotions on this topic:

(1) From the philosophical reason to keep it: "Trying to remove it from public view, and not where it was historically, is wrong. It may be offensive to some, but it belongs out where people can see it 24 hours a day and remember what it stands for."

(2) To the emotional reasons to remove it: "Those of us descendants of slaves don't need a reminder of that disgusting, disgraceful history everytime we are in the area trying to enjoy our lives!"
(3) From the pragmatic view: "Part of the impetus for moving it was to preserve it physically and so that is not treated as playground equipment, with kids climbing on it having no idea of it's history."
(4) To very distinct comments on who's opinion should count "If you're not a black resident of Fredericksburg, your opinion doesn't matter here."

And many quoted the most famous archaeologist in the world, Indiana Jones: "That belongs in a museum!"

What was missing during the talks and public media blitzes, though, were the details that had been uncovered during the 2018 excavation. The goal of the meeting was to discuss the future of the block, not the past. A more nuanced understanding of its place in Fredericksburg's historic narrative, though, could have led to an intricate discussion on the development of the city's current racial tension. However, this approach was eschewed in favor of a future-focused outcome.

As the International Coalition of Sites of Conscience was performing its study, the City continued to be challenged regarding the appropriateness of retaining the block on the street corner. Due to this pressure, on 11 June 2019, the Fredericksburg city council voted to remove the auction block from its current site and place it in the Fredericksburg Area Museum prior to the completion of the study. The community was stunned. This vote was not on the formal meeting agenda, and citizens and scholars did not have the opportunity to comment on the motion or to pass along any data.

The next 12 months were filled with extensive meetings and dialogues on the removal of this object. Local business leaders sued the City to keep the block on the corner, as the object was an important element of the streetscape. More importantly, to the business owners, it was viewed as an important component of area heritage tourism, bringing potential customers to this part of town. Its removal, they stated, would have a negative impact on their revenue and visibility in the community. The lawsuit was eventually dismissed. City staff worked with the Fredericksburg Area Museum to discuss the creation of an exhibit on the block, with the stone itself as the central object. The City Public Works Department and Planning Department concurrently orchestrated the painstaking and careful physical movement of the 800-pound block of stone. Although the archaeological data acquired in 2018 was not absorbed in the public narrative, the City recognized the archaeological potential of this area and included an archaeologist from Dovetail in all of their meetings. The block was to be thoroughly explored archaeologically prior to its removal.

Removing a Monument of Hate

The carefully orchestrated archaeological study did not occur. On 25 May 2020, George Floyd was killed in Minneapolis, Minnesota. This action led to nationwide discord in cities large and small. Protests occurred in downtown Fredericksburg every night for over three weeks. Many of the marches ended at the auction block—the site of rallies, speeches, and prayers. While most of the protesters were peaceful, others expressed their dismay for this object through the application of extensive graffiti on all sides of the block in red, green, and yellow spray paint, which soaked into the porous sandstone. Chants of "remove the block" could be heard throughout the historic core.

The City decided to remove the block during an emergency public works project on the morning of 5 June 2020. An archaeologist from Dovetail was on site to document the entire process and perform limited excavation once the block had been removed. A temporary interpretive sign was placed on the site to explain the process.

After the removal, the archaeologists worked closely with the City and the Fredericksburg Area Museum to clean the block using archivally sound methods. After intensive dialogues among all parties, it was decided to leave the graffiti on the stone. Not only would removal likely cause physical damage to the friable material, but the graffiti was now part of the new history of this significant object. Like many artifacts found in memorial settings today, viewing the graffiti will allow future generations to "confront past violence as a way of moving forward" (Sodaro 2018:4). The block and associated interpretive data went on display in the Fredericksburg Area Museum in 2021.

Conclusions: A Community That May Never Heal

This small object continues to be at the center of a major controversy. Research suggests that the stone was a signpost outside of a hotel. The sign likely advertised the sale of enslaved human beings sold on this corner and inside the adjacent building in the decades prior to the Civil War. Unfortunately, no other signposts currently exist or have been located in historic photographs of Fredericksburg to verify this interpretation. To this extraordinarily racialized community, regardless of its historic use, the block is a monument to the discord that has existed for well over a century. The unrest came to a head in 2019 and 2020, and numerous formal and informal meetings were held to discuss the block and share opinions. The quantity of voices that became involved in the dialogue regarding the memorialization and study of this object were innumerable, and the opinions were vastly varied. During the tumultuous summer of 2020, the object was removed and prepared for interpretation in the local museum. As stated by historian Pok Yin S. Chow (2015:205): "Public acknowledgements and other forms of symbolic reparations may not be able to satisfy the deep wounds of victims and families of grave atrocities and their accompanying senses of injustice and hurt." The actions taken regarding the auction block, though, and the data acquired during the associated studies, can provide information on the development of toxic relations and the pervasiveness of public memory.

While archival research and archaeological study suggest that the block was not used as a physical platform for the sale of enslaved people but rather a signpost, its ties to the general action of selling people and its extraordinary significance cannot be denied, making this a monument of immense importance. Moreover, the development of oral traditions on this block and the dialogues held before its removal are of equal significance when evaluating this object and its place in Fredericksburg's history. According to the Fredericksburg Area Museum, the future interpretation of this monument will include all aspects of past and present to tell its tale in its new setting within the museum. In addition, the City is preparing on-site interpretive elements to share the story of the auction block in its former space. Proper interpretation has the potential to craft what Dell Upton (2015) calls the practice of "dual heritage," presenting an object purposefully created for one use to illustrate a counternarrative. This action is performed in memorial settings all around the world (Sodaro 2018:2), and it will be used in both interpretive settings for auction block data.

The dialogues on the Fredericksburg slave auction block directly reflect the ongoing national debates on the interpretation of slavery and slave-associated places/people on public monuments. Should they remain as an important reminder of the horror of our past? Or should they go to remove blatantly racist narratives from our public places? Regardless of the outcomes, the debates themselves offer important insight into political and racial tensions in our diverse society—debates that are themselves history making. Both in its new home at the Fredericksburg Area Museum and through on-site interpretation, the Fredericksburg auction block will continue to highlight both historic and current racial tensions and be a monument to this debate for many years to come.

Acknowledgments

First and foremost, thanks to the editors for organizing this volume. The studies presented here reflect the hard work of many historians, archaeologists, and planners from several groups, including Dovetail, the Historic Fredericksburg Foundation, Inc., the Fredericksburg Area Museum, and others. In particular, Danae Peckler performed the historical research, while D. Brad Hatch was the project manager of the undertaking. Archaeological studies were carried out by the author and Jonas Schnur, with the author present on the morning of the block's removal. Most importantly, thank you to VDOT and the City of Fredericksburg for their proactive sponsorship of studies on the block prior to and during its removal. The archaeological data is now gone, but the records will speak to the past well into the future.

References

Albert Kern Collection at Dayton History, The
   1898   *Glass-Plate Negative—Slave Block—Fredericksburg, VA, 1898*. Item K.4.3.064. Copyright, Dayton History. Electronic document, https://daytonhistory.pastperfectonline.com/photo/DAF7A375-DBD1-4207-B7AA-786718819720, accessed December 2018.

Atlantic Slave Trade and Life in the Americas, The
   2015   "Slave Auction, Richmond, Virginia, 1861." Slavery Images: A Visual Record of the African Slave Trade and Slave Life in the Early African Diaspora. Electronic database, http://www.slaveryimages.org/detailsKeyword.php?keyword=auction&recordCount=23&theRecord=0, accessed December 2018.

Babson, David W.
   1988   *The Tanner Road Settlement: The Archaeology of Racism on Limerick Plantation*. Volumes in Historical Archaeology IV. Columbia: South Carolina Institute of Archaeology and Anthropology, University of South Carolina.

Barile, Kerri, Earl Proper, Caitlin Oshida, and Kerry González
   2014   *Phase I Archaeological and Historical Investigations at the Riverfront Park Area (44SP0069) in Fredericksburg, Virginia*. Fredericksburg, VA: Dovetail Cultural Resource Group.

Barile, Kerri S., Kerry Schamel-González, and Sean P. Maroney
   2008a   *"Inferior to None in the State": The History, Archaeology, and Architecture of the Marriott Hotel Site in Fredericksburg, Virginia*. Fredericksburg, VA: Dovetail Cultural Resource Group.

Beaudry, Mary C.
   1986   The Archaeology of Historical Land Use in Massachusetts. *Historical Archaeology* 20(2):38–46.

Chow, Pok Yin S.
   2015   Memory Denied: A Commentary on the Reports of the UN Special Rapporteur in the Field of Cultural Rights on Historical and Memorial Narratives in Divided Societies. *The International Lawyer* 48(3):191–213.

Conkey, Margaret, and Joan Gero
  1991   *Engendering Archaeology: Woman and Prehistory*. Cambridge, UK: Blackwell Press.
Conkey, Margaret, and Janet Spector
  1984   Archaeology and the Study of Gender. *Advances in Archaeological Method and Theory* 7:1–38.
Deagan, Kathleen
  1983   *Spanish St. Augustine: The Archaeology of a Colonial Creole Community*. New York, NY: Academic Press.
Detroit Publishing Company
  1906   *Old Slave Block in St. Louis Hotel, New Orleans, La.* Louisiana. Detroit Publishing Company, Library of Congress Prints and Photographs Division, Washington, D.C. Electronic document, https://www.loc.gov/item/2016806002/, accessed December 2018.
Fredericksburg Land Tax Records
  n.d.   Fredericksburg Land Tax Records. Misc. years. Transcribed edition, Fredericksburg Research Resources, University of Mary Washington Department of Historic Preservation. Electronic documents, http://resources.umwhisp.org/fredburg.htm, accessed November 2018.
Fredericksburg News [Fredericksburg, Virginia]
  1850   Public Sale of Negros. 27 August:3.
  1853   Public Sale of Valuable Negros. 26 December:3.
Gibb, James G., and Julia A. King
  1991   Gender, Activity Areas, and Homelots in the 17th Century Chesapeake Region. *Historical Archaeology* 25(4):109–131.
Hardesty, Donald L.
  1988   *The Archaeology of Mining and Miners: A View from the Silver State*. Special Publication 6. Ann Arbor, MI: Society for Historical Archaeology.
Hatch, D. Brad, Kerri S. Barile, Danae Peckler, and Kerry S. González
  2019   *Archaeological Testing of the George Street Tunnel and Intersection of William and Charles Street, City of Fredericksburg, Virginia*. Fredericksburg, VA: Dovetail Cultural Resource Group.
Hennessey, John
  2017   The Slave Auction Block at William and Charles. *Mysteries and Conundrums: Exploring the Civil War-era Landscape in the Fredericksburg & Spotsylvania Region*. Electronic document, https://npsfrsp.wordpress.com/2017/09/14/the-slave-auction-block-at-william-and-charles/, accessed November 2018.
Historic American Building Survey (HABS)
  1960   Green Hill Slave Auction Block, HABS VA-605. Orville W. Carroll, National Park Service. Washington, D.C.: Library of Congress Prints and Photographs Division. Electronic document, https://www.loc.gov/item/va0279/, accessed November 2018.
Joyner, Charles
  1984   *Down by the Riverside: A South Carolina Slave Community*. Urbana, IL: University of Illinois Press.

Kurtz, Hilda E.
    2018   Introduction to the Special Forum: In the Aftermath of the Hate Rally in Charlottesville. *Southeastern Geographer* 58(1):6–9.

Labode, Modupe, and Kevin M. Levin
    2016   Reconsideration of Memorials and Monuments. *History News* 71(4):7–11.

Little, Barbara J.
    2013   Reversing the Narrative from Violence to Peace: Some Thoughts from an Archaeologist. *Historical Archaeology* 47(3):124–129.

Moody, Jessica
    2020   *The Persistence of Memory: Remembering Slavery in Liverpool, "Slaving Capital of the World."* Liverpool, UK: Liverpool University Press.

Mrozowski, Stephen A., Grace H. Ziesing, and Mary C. Beaudry
    1986   *Living on the Boot: Historical Archaeology at the Boot Mills Boarding Houses in Lowell, Massachusetts.* Amhurst, MA: University of Massachusetts Press.

Mutual Assurance Society of Virginia
    n.d.   *Mutual Assurance Society Policies. Misc. Years.* Electronic index, Fredericksburg Research Resources, University of Mary Washington Department of Historic Preservation. Microfilm edition, Central Rappahannock Regional Library, Fredericksburg, Virginia.

Orser, Charles
    1988   *The Material Basis of the Postbellum Tenant Plantation: Historical Archaeology in the South Carolina Piedmont.* Athens, GA: University of Georgia Press.

Otto, John S.
    1984   *Cannon's Point Plantation, 1794–1860: Living Conditions and Status Patterns in the Old South.* New York, NY: Academic Press.

Shackel, Paul A.
    2013   Changing the Past for the Present and the Future. *Historical Archaeology* 47(3):1–11.

Singleton, Theresa
    1990   The Archaeology of the Plantation South: A Review of Approaches and Goals. *Historical Archaeology* 24(4):70–77.

Sodaro, Amy
    2018   *Exhibiting Atrocity: Memorial Museums and the Politics of Past Violence.* Rutgers, NJ: Rutgers University Press.

Spencer-Wood, Suzanne
    1987   *Consumer Choice in Historical Archaeology.* New York, NY: Plenum Press.

United States Federal Population Census
    1850   Fredericksburg, Virginia. Federal Population Census Schedule. Washington, D.C. National Archives and Records Administration. Electronic document, www.ancestry.com, accessed November 2018.

Upton, Dell
    2015   *What Can and Can't Be Said: Race, Uplift, and Monument Building in the Contemporary South.* New Haven, CT: Yale University Press.

4

"Each Soldier's Grave a Shrine"

Confederate Cemetery Monuments

JEFFREY SMITH

The last shots of the Civil War had not even been heard when the specter of death and remembrance haunted families on both sides. In the South, the initial focus centered on bringing remains of the fallen back home to new Confederate cemeteries or newly created sections in existing local burial grounds. As the last third of the nineteenth century unfolded, the focus of commemoration in cemeteries went through a metamorphosis from memorializing the local dead to crafting a Southern identity based on the Ideology of the Lost Cause; death—and its monuments, memorials, and cemeteries—was a defining tool in the collection of methods Southerners used to reinforce the ideas that interwove Southern identity and all that the Lost Cause stood for. After the Civil War, sectional differences took a new turn with the use of public spaces and monuments in them. Prominent examples are familiar in the debate over Confederate monuments across the South—stately Jefferson Davis, heroic Stonewall Jackson, Robert E. Lee astride his horse, and obelisks to fallen Confederate soldiers on the town square or courthouse grounds are common examples. Organizations like ladies memorial associations and, later, the United Daughters of the Confederacy (UDC) raised money and funded these monuments as part of a broader agenda to promote the Ideology of the Lost Cause by erecting constant reminders, and they built some of them in large urban cemeteries that already existed. It was here, in places where the mortal remains of fallen soldiers lay, that they sought to wrap the Lost Cause in the shroud of the sacred. This chapter asserts that because of the nature of those cemeteries and the ways the living used and interacted with them, such monuments succeeded in further entrenching the Ideology of the Lost Cause. But the initial effort to commemorate the end of the war and the ensuing Ideology of the Lost Cause was on a far more widespread battlefield, one that sought to combine the memory of the fallen and sanctify-

Figure 4.1. Mount Olivet Confederate Monument. When the monument on Confederate Circle in Mount Olivet Cemetery was dedicated in Nashville, it was a citywide celebration. At some 45 ft. tall, it is among the largest Confederate monuments in a cemetery. Photo by Jeffrey Smith.

ing the message through the use of the rhetoric of mourning and the sacred space of cemeteries.

The Rural Cemetery Movement

Even before the Civil War, Americans in both the North and the South understood the power of cemeteries and their particular role in articulating collective memory that dated to the 1830s with the advent of the Rural Cemetery Movement. Cemeteries like Mount Auburn in Cambridge, Laurel Hill in Philadelphia, Hollywood in Richmond, and Magnolia in Charleston introduced a new way of thinking about burial spaces. No longer merely places to bury the dead, they became city amenities not unlike parks, libraries, or museums that people visited. Cemeteries became a critical weapon in the arsenal of weapons to advance the Ideology of the Lost Cause because of this pre-established role of burial grounds in shaping collective memory. This role came from national trends in cities on both sides of the Mason-Dixon divide predating the Civil War.

Groups placing Confederate monuments in larger cemeteries stood on a national tradition that emerged in the 1830s, the rural cemetery movement. Antebellum Southern cities shared much with their northern counterparts in terms of the cultural amenities that comprised a great city, such as libraries, athenaeums, opera houses—and cemeteries. Unlike older burying grounds, they were large "rural cemeteries," spaces that combined burial and commemoration with collective memory. Southerners built on ideas about cemeteries and cultural values that were already well established by the start of the Civil War. Notions about cemeteries as more than merely places to bury the dead emerged in the 1830s, starting with the opening of Mount Auburn Cemetery in Cambridge, Massachusetts, in September 1831, the first institution in the rural cemetery movement. Others followed in other cities, responding to many of the same needs and cultural priorities. Paradoxically, these "rural" cemeteries were anything but rural in our context; they were almost exclusively an urban phenomenon, albeit located in suburban areas or just outside cities in the adjacent countryside. Within a decade or so, the remaining ten largest cities in the United States (and a number of the smaller ones as well) had similar burial sites—Laurel Hill in Philadelphia, Green-Wood in Brooklyn, Green Mount in Baltimore, and Mount Hope in Rochester opened such cemeteries by decade's end, and the five largest cities in slaveholding states at mid-century (Baltimore, Charleston, Richmond, St. Louis, and Wilmington) all opened such cemeteries, all with similar ends in mind that responded to similar emerging urban needs.

Visitors to Confederate cemeteries after the Civil War stood on this tradition of visiting burial sites. The cemetery at Resaca, Georgia, for example, "was regarded by the country people as a sort of pleasure ground in the midst of a devastated land," recalled Mrs. E. J. Simmons in 1904. "It was a great resort for rustic lovers of Sunday afternoons, and many a troth was plighted there." (*History of the Confederated Memorial Associations of the South* 1904:149) In such spaces, monumentation took on a new kind and level of importance. Markers evolved into ways to communicate ideas about more earthly concerns such as social position, family status, economic status, and real or perceived importance in these cemeteries nationally. Grave markers and family monuments became larger, more elaborately decorated with portraits of the deceased, flowers, and other popular Victorian mourning symbols, offered more information about the deceased, and were located in places that suggested status and convenience to be viewed. Confederate cemeteries and Confederate monuments embedded in larger burial grounds stood on this accepted role of cemeteries. Despite a rhetoric of cemetery monuments' role of preserving history (and to an extent they do preserve a version of history), it is a highly mediated history that reflects desires about personal and community remembrance; they are, as rhetorician Elizabethada Wright asserts, a kind of invention (Wright 2003:28). That is to say, collective memory and history are not necessarily two sides of the same coin, despite the fact that the makers of them believe "that they embody *history,* defined as objective reality, not an interpretation of a memory" (Upton 2015:21). Once we see them as a product of a creative process rather than recording information or contributing to the mourning process alone, cemeteries and their markers, monuments, mausoleums, and other structures take on new importance as a prism through which we can understand the values and attitudes of the people and communities that erected, visited, and supported them. Collective memory and monuments that reflect the values of both the creators of the monuments and those who interact with them, both at the time of creation and at every subsequent moment, and their responses may not be the same, but are based on their own values and pasts. By the time memorial associations began the work of collecting Confederate remains and marking their graves locally, the role of cemeteries to articulate collective memory and conspicuously and intentionally express a set of social values was generally accepted. Laurel Hill Cemetery founder John Jay Smith sent an article to the daily newspapers in Philadelphia in 1839 about his having recently received the new visitor's guide to Mount Auburn—some 250 pages long with sixty engravings, he noted—observing that "thus does a rural cemetery ensure a double chance for good or great names being remembered first on a stone tablet, and next on the ever more enduring page" (Smith 1839:n.p.).

The key here has to do with the definition of "good or great names," of course. Such a cemetery was firmly established in every Southern city before the first shots were fired at Fort Sumter, and their residents understood the role those institutions played in their communities. Small wonder, then, that they turned to those very institutions when seeking to craft a new collective memory around the Lost Cause. In short, Southerners began recrafting their definition of what constituted "good or great names" starting at war's end to align with their ideas about the Ideology of the Lost Cause.

Sanctifying the Lost Cause

Cemeteries were the first places where messages of the Lost Cause were literally etched in stone. Even before the final shots were fired, women in the former Confederacy began the process of identifying the burial locations of local men who had died in the war and consolidating and collecting those remains in local burial grounds. When the war ended, the collection and commemoration of these dead in the South focused on commonly accepted mourning practices with the cemetery, whether pre-existing or one created for the purpose, at the center. Like much of the South, the Confederate cemeteries erected in the immediate years after the end of the war were strapped for cash, which meant that the cemeteries were often modest affairs at first, sometimes with little more than a lone shaft or obelisk, but that changed radically in the last quarter of the nineteenth century. Women across the South created Ladies' Memorial Associations to bury Confederate soldiers or have their remains relocated nearer to home, either in existing burial grounds or in new Confederate cemeteries (Mills 2003:xvi). A year after the war, the constitution of an Association in Raleigh, North Carolina, thundered that "we may be poor, but enough is left to prove our hearts to be still rich in treasures of gratitude and affection" despite their inability to afford the "storied urn or sculptured pillar" (Bishir 2003:5). Others continued to apologize for erecting only modest monuments for what they saw as such a glorious cause due to financial restraints. The Confederate Relief and Historical Association took over a monument project in Memphis in the mid-1870s when the Ladies Memorial Association had raised just over $1,100 (*Memphis Daily Appeal,* 1878). It raised enough extra money through collections "plus other 'schemes'" to erect the monument and dedicate it in June 1878. Apologetic but proud, the committee spoke to the design, lamenting that it was "not such a monument as Memphis should erect to its Confederate dead, nor does it express as fully as we could wish the taste and sentiment of our people" (Memphis *Daily Appeal,* 1878). But better to erect a smaller monument now than wait, the committee decided in 1878:

> We preferred their simple and modest design to further delays, in the hope of more prosperous times and a more costly and elaborate monument. We are also mindful that the material monuments erected to commemorate virtue or evidence affection are not always the best reflection of the taste or sentiment of the people. Circumstances of distress or poverty often control these, but the shrines and temples most indicative and most lasting are the memory and heart of the people. Marble and brass decay; the pillar, the shaft, and the mausoleum crumble; the material monuments of taste, evidences of skill and characteristics of genius, pass away; but when these are gone then *tradition* and *Letters* built their monuments, more enduring than the pyramids. (Memphis *Daily Appeal* 1878)

Consider the McGavock Confederate Cemetery in Franklin, Tennessee, near Nashville. In the spring after the Battle of Franklin in late November

1864, the makeshift burial site was already deteriorating, with hastily installed wooden headboards disappearing as people used them for heating wood over the winter. John McGavock donated two adjacent acres next to his family graveyard as a more permanent resting place. A year after the war ended, McGavock and others raised money to reinter bodies to the Confederate cemetery and mark the graves. Visitors came to the graveyard, administered by McGavock's wife Caroline, until 1890, when the John L. McEwen Bivouac of Veterans headed fundraising efforts for granite markers to replace the wooden ones. When the newly created McGavock Confederate Cemetery Corporation took over control in 1911, it included funding for widened roads and easier access for visitors (McGavock Cemetery Trustees 2014:n.p.).

The experience in Franklin was fairly typical—a small group, often of women, began raising money for re-interment and modest markings in the years right after the war, then expanded commemoration efforts as more money became available. Similarly, women in Raleigh, North Carolina, worked for two years before raising enough money for a monument in 1869 (Bishir 2003:10). The graveyard near the hospital at Summerville, South Carolina, was "the last resting place of many of the heroes of our 'lost cause,'" until the Irvine Walker Chapter of the United Daughters of the Confederacy began raising money in 1899 to fence in the space, plant oak trees, erect "a simple memorial stone on the spot," and rename it Oak Grove Cemetery as "a fit resting place for the dear ones who have consecrated the cause and this spot by their lives" (Confederate Veteran 1899:84). The UDC expressed similar sentiments in *Confederate Veteran* about the organization in New Orleans in 1911, discussing the origins of Green-wood Cemetery, organized in 1866 as an outgrowth of a Soldiers Aid Society created in 1861 with the monument dedicated in 1874 (*Confederate Veteran*, 1899:84). Later, the United Daughters of the Confederacy and others noted the modest beginnings of these cemeteries. Noting the cliché about Virginia being "once a great battlefield, [that] is now a great graveyard," *Confederate Veteran* noted in 1903 that women who had cared for the wounded took on the mantle of collecting remains into Confederate cemeteries, remembering that "in many instances they were only able to enclose such with a simple plank fence; occasionally a monument to our heroic dead arose" (Confederate Veteran 1903:69).

Monuments commemorating Confederate dead at burial sites fell into several broad categories. In the years immediately following the war, women's groups across the South began the task of collecting both records and remains of the fallen from their communities. In some cases, they organized separate cemeteries for this purpose, often called "Confederate cemeteries." Not all groups or communities established new spaces, but rather relied on existing

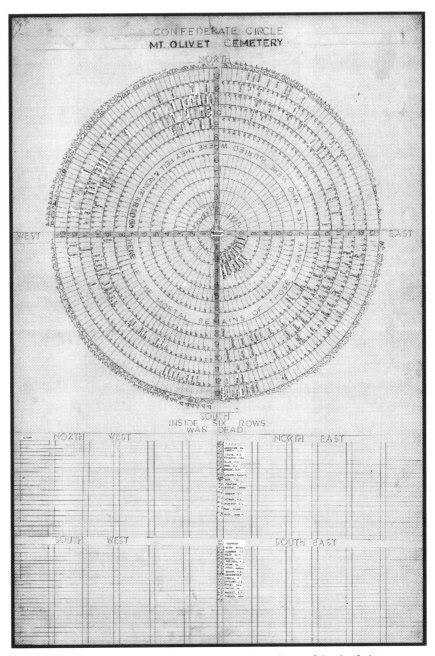

Figure 4.2. Plan for Confederate Circle. The United Daughters of the Confederacy planned to move and reinter a great number of soldiers, as this plan indicates. Note that the inscription around the inside of the circle refers to "brave" men. Courtesy of the Tennessee State Library and Archives.

burial grounds, often creating a separate space for the war dead. In both cases, it was common for local groups to erect monuments on those burial grounds. Those installed right after war when money was scarce were smaller, while those created later were larger and more lavish, reflecting trends in monument design and construction in the Gilded Age. The fact that these monuments stand at graves in cemeteries gives them a different kind of power, both at the time they were constructed and today as we view them, than those created for other public or civic spaces. They are monuments to those who have died and mark their places, and as such, are akin to gravestones, but there is more to the story than that. Cemeteries were (and still are, for many) sacred spaces, which gives both the spaces themselves and everything inside them a kind of reverence reserved for the commemoration of the dead.

Divisions between North and South were also divisions of victors and vanquished as Southerners tried to come to grips with having lost not just the war but an epic battle over what they came to consider a just and noble cause. Starting in the late 1880s, the next generation of Southerners built on those ideas of death and collective memory as they pursued a broader agenda that included lionizing Confederate leaders and war dead. This new group sought to use cemeteries to articulate and advance the Ideology of the Lost Cause in a more far-reaching way. Starting during the late nineteenth century, organizations such as the United Confederate Veterans (UCV), Sons of Confederate Veterans (SCV), and the United Daughters of the Confederacy (UDC) strove to guide the narrative about the Civil War in ways that justified their having fought and lost the conflict. This included strengthening ideas about white supremacy. They used a number of mechanisms to confirm white supremacy, especially among poor White Southerners and youngsters, further solidifying the social order of both class and race from the antebellum period. This included a number of tools, including efforts to have a more "balanced" treatment of the South in textbooks, referring to the Civil War as "The War Between the States," framing the cause of the war as not about slavery but "states' rights" and defending the Constitution, and casting slavery as benevolent and favorable to African Americans. Indeed, their arguments echoed antebellum slaveholders who argued that the South boasted a stable social order in which all were in their proper role ordained by God, including the status of slaves at the bottom of the heap; now, they sought to create that social order anew, including the racial order, even if slavery had been banished from the nation.

Leaders of these organizations understood well that memorializing the war dead and doing so in cemeteries was more than part of the process of grief and healing and that it was also a fundamentally political act. The Confederate cemeteries and monuments in larger cemeteries conveyed not just collective memory, but a particular cultural and political message as well. Burial spaces for the war dead carried more "symbolic capital" because they used the memory of those who died for a particular cause as a way of shaping awareness and internalizing a particular social order and identity (Doss 2010:2–10). And when people internalize those ideas, monuments take on power. Kelly McMichael's observation that "when a war memorial is erected, the stakes are always high" is even more true when collecting the war dead in a cemetery dedicated to them or erecting a monument inside the sacred space of a cemetery (McMichael 2009:2).

Among those was the Confederate Circle at Mount Olivet Cemetery in Nashville—the same city where the United Daughters of the Confederacy organized themselves on a national level. Mount Olivet was a typical cemetery of the period, founded in 1856 about two miles outside town in response to a rapidly growing Nashville. A generation after the end of the Civil War, Mount Olivet became home to a monument on Confederate Circle, a section in the Bolivar *Bulletin* referred to its including "a vast assemblage" with "floral offerings [that] were magnificent and profuse" (*Bolivar Bulletin,* 1889:1). Another from McMinnville observed that "the latter half of the day was generally observed as a holiday in Nashville" (McMinnville *Southern Standard,* 1889:4). The monument is immense—45 ft. tall overall, with a 9 ft. tall Confederate marble soldier on top with "the countenance and general appearance of the statue that is of a typical Confederate soldier standing at parade rest" (Memphis *Daily Appeal,* 1889:2). Most telling are the inscriptions on the sides of the base of this granite marker:

> This shaft honors the valor, devotion, and sacrifice unto death of Confederate soldiers of Tennessee. The winds of heaven kissing its sides, hymn an everlasting requiem in memory of the unreturning brave.... The muster roll of our dauntless dead islets and their dust dispersed on many fields. This column sentinels each soldier's grave as a shrine. (*Memphis Daily Appeal* 1889:2)

Each soldier's grave a shrine. The phrasing drove home the intent to speak to subsequent generations through the sacred space of cemeteries that were second in reverence only to churches. The rhetoric of burial changes the status of Confederate monuments just as their location in sanctified space—even the use of terms like "shrine" elevated them from mere grave markers to a representation of a larger cause. The power of that memory and its rationalization of participation in a losing war—the Lost Cause—became the powerful message of the era.

Confederate Cemetery Monuments · 65

Figure 4.3. Confederate Pyramid, Hollywood Cemetery, Richmond. The women of Richmond, Virginia, wasted little time in raising funds to erect this massive pyramid to commemorate the Confederate dead. It includes several Confederate relics—and was constructed using nearby prison labor. Today, it is part of Hollywood Cemetery. Photographs in the Carol M. Highsmith Archive, Library of Congress, Prints and Photographs Division.

The early efforts to commemorate the dead included Ladies' Memorial Associations gathering soldiers' remains for reburial and commemoration on Confederate Decoration Day. Others raised the sacred nature of the spaces beyond the remains alone to new levels by including other relics of the Lost Cause, and the one relic that every cemetery possessed by its very nature were the remains of fallen soldiers. Perhaps the earliest example came just three years after war's end in the former Confederate capital of Richmond. Women in Richmond organized the Ladies' Memorial Association in 1866 to take care of the graves of Confederates in Hollywood Cemetery and remove the remains of others from distant graves and raised enough money to start construction of a 90 ft. granite pyramid in late 1868 (Oakley 1872:1). Other cemeteries included similar relics. Just three years after the dedication of the giant pyramid in Richmond, the Ladies' Memorial Association in Wilmington, North Carolina, dedicated the Confederate section in Oakdale Cemetery in June 1872 and laid under the monument a copper box with the names of the interred both there and throughout the cemetery, the Association's records and officers' names, a newspaper, a Confederate flag, and "other mementos of our fallen, but most righteous cause" (Oakley 1872:1). Almost a decade later, the Confederate monument in Elmwood Cemetery in Memphis was described as a "spot of hallowed ground" and noted in its coverage of the dedication of the Confederate monument that the cornerstone included an envelope containing Confederate currency, a small Confederate battle flag, photos of Confederate leaders, an autographed letter by Jefferson Davis, and an assortment of Civil War–era newspaper clippings (*Memphis Daily Appeal* 1878).

Commemoration of the ultimate relic, the bodies of the war dead, was heightened by the sheer numbers of dead on both sides, leaving virtually no family untouched by the death of a father, brother, son, or other relative by war's end. Thus, collecting the remains of the fallen and marking their graves became a high priority; these burials brought closure and mourning, but they also gave subsequent generations something more. Initially, these burial sites were the focus of Memorial Day commemorations, but they evolved into lasting symbols of patriotism and the principles of the Lost Cause that recognized Confederates not as traitors but as heroes to what they considered a valiant cause (Cox 2003:66–67). By the late nineteenth century, the rhetoric of heroism and the Lost Cause at cemeteries with Confederate burials and monuments was common. For example, later memorials would "perpetuate the memories of the glorious struggle of the South for Constitutional rights," noted a call in the *Confederate Veteran* in 1895 for a Confederate Memorial Association, "to pay deserved tribute to the heroic deeds of their fallen comrades, to furnish an inspiring object lesson to their descendants, and to leave to posterity enduring proofs of the courage, loyalty and devotion to day of the Confederate soldier" (*Confederate Veteran* 1895:8).

New Cemeteries and Established Cemetery Design

Members of memorial associations understood the role of cemeteries in preserving collective memory, and therefore their symbolic role as well, "so continued to emphasize the aesthetic nature of these cities of the dead" while also preserving the memory of the fallen dead (Janny 2008: 140). Women established as many as 100 Ladies Memorial Associations (LMAs) throughout the South, with the most in Virginia—there were more than two dozen by 1868, with fifty or more members in each, creating a movement that involved more than 1,300 of the state's white women from elite or middle-class families (Cox 2003:66–67).

It was these women who crafted the initial narrative for preserving the memory of not just the fallen dead, but of Southern White solidarity in mourning the cause of the Confederacy (Cox 2003:2). Even into the 1880s, the combination of idyllic setting and Lost Cause narrative attracted White Southern visitors, reflecting their understanding that cemeteries were potent forces in articulating collective memory (Cox 2003:140). Dolly Lamar later wrote of her memories of growing up in Georgia after the war and roaming the cemetery in Macon while her father reinforced the Lost Cause message: "Sometimes I took a Sunday afternoon stroll with Papa to Rose Hill Cemetery at the other end of College Street, a three-mile round trip. Papa, at his conversational and forensic best, would read me the tombstone inscriptions and discourse on the dead with considerable pomp and oratory. This was a wild and wonderful treat on Sunday" (Lamar 1952:35). By the 1880s, these newly created Confederate cemeteries attracted "white southerners of every generation, providing a tranquil and contemplative setting for them to reflect on the heroic deeds of the war dead" (Janney 2008:140).

Such monuments to the Confederate war dead embodied the principles of the Lost Cause, messages that were amplified by the construction of larger and larger monuments in existing cemeteries. Of the Confederate monuments erected in the two decades after the Civil War, some seven in ten were placed inside cemeteries (Janney 2008:141–142). In some cases, Confederate sections already existed in cemeteries due to proximity to battlefields or hospitals. As many as several hundred bodies were buried in large pre-existing cemeteries during the war, providing a platform for memorial associations to build larger sites for public commemoration. The year after the war ended, for example, the Memorial Association in Wilmington, North Carolina, began the effort of removing soldiers who had died in nearby battles to Oakdale Cemetery; the LMA installed an iron gate to the lot in 1866 identifying it as a Confederate Cemetery, and Oakdale donated the site to the Association the following year (*Wilmington Daily Journal*, 1868:1). Eventually, some 366 unidentified bodies were reinterred there. Starting in 1868, the Association began to raise almost $8,000 to enclose the lot with an iron fence, saying it wanted the lot "*immediately* enclosed with proper material" and, eventually, to construct "a suitable monument to the memory of these departed participants in that strife which will live in history. Let their [the ladies of the Association] solicitations be cheerfully, encouragingly met," begged the *Daily Journal,* "and let us open our hearts to a cause in which *honor* tells us we are most deeply interested" (*Wilmington Daily Journal,* 1868:1).*** Two days later the paper referred to it as "the narrow trace [that] is rich with sacred dust—so precious to all of our hearts," promising both improvements to make it "an ornament to the Cemetery" and a monument with the names of those interred. Dedication ceremonies and the unveiling of the monument were held on Memorial Day, 10 May 1872—the anniversary of the death of Stonewall Jackson (Wilmington *Daily Journal,* 1868:1). The granite pedestal was some 7.5 ft. tall with profiles of Robert E. Lee and Jackson and topped by a bronze soldier holding a musket that was described by the *Wilmington Morning Star* as "a size known as 'heroic,' the intermediate between the colossal and life-size, or about eight feet in height" ("The Confederate Monument," *Wilmington Morning Star,* June 5, 1872:1).

Two years earlier, the *Wilmington Daily Journal* had offered the Ladies Memorial Association some unsolicited advice on the design of the forthcoming monument, which its members apparently did not take. Noting that a reporter had recently visited the local marble yard of James Walker and seen some sculptures that were "not inferior in appearance to the Italian" white marble, he suggested that the work "lays high claim to being a piece of art, and . . . apropos of the fact we would suggest to the Ladies' Memorial Association the propriety of conferring with this gentleman as to the monument which they propose to erect to the Confederate dead" (*Wilmington Daily Journal* 1872:3). Perhaps, the paper thought, "the Association could commission a sculpture based on a series of photos of the Lost Cause featured in a local bookstore" (*Wilmington Daily Journal* 1872:3). People in other cities had similar ideas, though. The Ladies' Memorial Association in Fairview Cemetery in Bowling Green, Kentucky, had a similar notion about including a notable artwork for its Confederate monument completed in 1876. Fairview, a city cemetery, had opened just a decade previous when its Pioneer Cemetery was filled with war dead. Efforts to erect a monument to fallen Confederates started in 1875 in a town with a complicated relationship to the Civil War and its history. While Kentucky never seceded from the Union, it briefly had a Confederate capital in Bowling Green early in the war. The monument in Fairview is a striking one, a limestone tower with cannon barrels at the corners and cannonballs around it. But perhaps most arresting is the bronze relief on the front, a casting of Henry Mosler's painting, "The Lost Cause." Former Confederate officer Albert Berry commissioned the painting in 1866, which was quickly and widely reproduced as a chromolithograph (The Johnson Collection 2021).

Figure 4.4. Confederate Monument, Fairview Cemetery. The Confederate monument in Fairview Cemetery in Bowling Green, Kentucky, includes a copy of this immensely popular engraving of Henry Mosler's "The Lost Cause," depicting a returning Confederate soldier, seeking to associate the Lost Cause with everyday veterans as well. Photo by Jeffrey Smith.

Unlike many popular images of the former Confederacy, Mosler's painting harkens to the postwar experience of enlisted men, portraying a returning Confederate soldier bent in grief in front of a destroyed small farmhouse as a commentary on the impact of the war's destruction on everyday people.

By the late 1880s, monuments in cemeteries had taken a new turn, with some, such as that in Mount Olivet in Nashville or Elmwood in Memphis, looking more toward the giant monuments that were soon to sprout in civic spaces. Among the most grandiose of those, the "Lion of the Confederacy" (also known as the "Lion of Atlanta") was unveiled in Atlanta's Oakland Cemetery in 1894. Like a number of its Southern urban counterparts, Oakland grew during the Civil War due to both its proximity to military hospitals and, after the war, the removal of war dead from the Atlanta campaign. The first commemoration of these graves came on Memorial Day of 1874 (the tenth anniversary of Gen. Joseph Johnston's surrender of Atlanta) with the dedication of 65 ft. obelisk, at the time the tallest structure in Atlanta. After the dedication, the Ladies' Memorial Association continued to raise money to pay off the remaining $350 for it by selling photos of it, both larger prints (at $2.50 each) and *cartes de visit* (for a quarter) (*Atlanta Constitution* 1874:8). "The pictures will make quite an ornament for a parlor or sitting room," promised the *Atlanta Constitution,* "and will have a speedy sale." (*Atlanta Constitution* 1874:8) But by the time Memorial Day arrived in April 1894, the installation of huge Confederate monuments was in full swing, both in and beyond cemeteries. The Ladies Memorial Association commissioned T.M. Brady, a sculptor who owned the Georgia Marble and Finishing Works in nearby Canton, to create the work from marble quarried in northern Georgia ("Unknown Confederate Dead," *New Orleans Times-Picayune*, 1894). The "Lion of the Confederacy" portrays a wounded lion lying on a Confederate flag as a memorial that was based on a huge lion in Lucerne designed by Bertel Thorvaldsen and completed in 1821 in memory of the Swiss Guards who were massacred in the 1792 storming of the Tuileries in Paris (Gravely Speaking 2021). The Lion of Lucerne had previously served as inspiration for other memorial lion monuments, including the monumental Sphinx designed by Jacob Bigelow and dedicated as a monument to Union soldiers in Mount Auburn Cemetery in 1872 (Giguere, 2013:62–84). The dedication in Atlanta lasted much of the day. The parade to the cemetery "served as an inspiration to patriotism" for the thousands watching. The Rev. I. S. Hopkins started the ceremony with an opening prayer that correlated the Lost Cause with the Godly and the sacred space of the cemetery, praying, "May the time never come when the cause for which they died will be less sacred in the hearts of their comrades and their children. May their memory be an enduring benediction and their consecration to duty a ceaseless inspiration" (*Atlanta Constitution* 1894:1, 5–6). Col. John T. Milledge, marshal for the event, whose wife Fannie headed the Association that orchestrated the monument's construction, noted that the soldiers commemorated (many of whom were unknown) had died in a just cause, then wondered, "Why this righteous cause should have failed, God in His wisdom only knows" (*Atlanta Constitution*, 1894:5) Notably, Henry H. Carlton reinforced the connection between sacred and secular, fallen dead and Lost Cause. Referring to the place as a "southern Mecca," the monument was for "the heart of every human being who aspires to the higher, nobler spheres of life, who loves his country, aye, and who loves his God, and the cause of truth and right." It was, he said, a "sacred occasion, upon this hallowed ground" (*Atlanta Constitution* 1894:5–6). The Confederate Lion and the Confederate obelisk in Oakland Cemetery suggest the complicated nature of these monuments. In November 2017, the Confederate Monuments Advisory Committee appointed by Atlanta Mayor Kasim Reed recommended transferring ownership of both the Lion and the Confederate obelisk in the cemetery to the Historic Oakland Foundation, an organization founded in 1976 to help preserve and maintain the cemetery (*Atlanta InTown* 2017). The City dodged the controversy, now able to claim no control over the monument or its removal, since it is now privately controlled, not unlike other cemeteries. Confederate monuments inside cemeteries make commemoration and its politicized nature today an even thornier issue once they are embedded in a sacred space.

Conclusion

Cemeteries were not the only public spaces where Southerners memorialized the dead to reinforce ideas about the Lost Cause, although they were the first. Southerners used them in the first years after the war since federal restrictions on expressions of support for the Confederacy precluded many overt activities. However, cemeteries were generally overlooked by federal commanders in the South during Reconstruction since they were the spaces dedicated to memorializing the dead; thus, cemeteries became the initial venue for melding death and the Lost Cause. In the last third of the nineteenth century, commemorations of the dead expanded in both scale and venue. When federal troops withdrew from the former Confederacy, they left Southerners to commemorate the end of the war and its "heroes" as they saw fit, without having to worry about appearing to be traitorous. As a result, memorialization moved beyond the exclusive venue of cemeteries to the civic sphere. Public monuments appeared in town squares, courthouse grounds, and public parks. More importantly, they also appeared in cemeteries all over the South. Each and every one of them carried the message of the Lost Cause—the heroism of their troops, who they said defended democracy but, in fact, fought to retain a sociopolitical system built on the foundation of enslaving people of African descent. As such monuments appeared in existing cemeteries, they wrapped those messages in the robe of the sacred as well. Existing cemeteries were not just for the war dead, but also for everyone else, so people visited them to honor ancestors and others. They were sacred spaces, so those monuments sanctified their messages by association. By the time organizations like the United Daughters of the Confederacy, the Sons of Confederate Veterans, and United Confederate Veterans began their work to fund memorials in and elsewhere, they knowingly and intentionally associated their message with the sacred. Those civic and seemingly secular monuments were as inextricably linked to death as were those in cemeteries, tying the entire Southern landscape to the Lost Cause through death.

References

Atlanta Constitution
    1874   The Confederate Monument, 26 April 26: 8.
    1894   "Lion of Atlanta. The Spirit of the Southern Soldier Symbolized in Marble. Thousands Witness the Unveiling. Hon. Henry H. Carlton Delivers the Oration of the Day. Graves Bedecked with Flowers. Gentle Hands Tenderly Lay Fragrant Blooms on the Last Resting Places of the Sleeping Heroes," 26:1.

Atlanta InTown
    2017   Nov. 2017, vol. 23, no. 11. https://issuu.com/reporter_newspapers/docs/110117_atlantaintown_web, accessed March 28, 2024.

Bishir, Catherine W.
    2003   "'Strong Force of Ladies': Women, Politics, and Confederate Memorial Associations in Nineteenth-Century Raleigh." In *Monuments to the Lost Cause: Women, Art, and the Landscapes of Southern Memory*, Cynthia Mills and Pamela Simpson, eds. Pp. 10. Knoxville, TN: University of Tennessee Press, Knoxville.

Bolivar Bulletin
    1889   Southern Gleanings 10 May, 24:40.

Confederated Southern Memorial Association
    1904   *History of the Confederated Memorial Associations of the South*. New Orleans, LA: Graham Press.

Confederate Veteran
    1895   No Title:8.
    1899   Caring for our Dead 7:84.
    1903   Monuments in Cemeteries in Virginia 11:69.
    1911   Ladies Memorial Association, New Orleans 10:149.

Cox, Karen L.
    2003   *Dixie's Daughters: The United Daughters of the Confederacy and the Preservation of Confederate Culture*. Gainesville, FL: University Press of Florida.

Doss, Erika
    2010   *Memorial Mania: Public Feeling in America*. Chicago, IL: University of Chicago Press.

Giguere, Joy M.
    2013   The Americanized Sphinx: Civil War Commemoration, Jacob Bigelow, and the *Sphinx* at Mount Auburn Cemetery. *The Journal of the Civil War Era* 3:1.

Gravely Speaking
    2021   Lion of Atlanta. *Gravely Speaking*. https://gravelyspeaking.com/2012/01/20/lion-of-the-confederacy/, accessed 15 May 2021.

Janney, Caroline E.
    2008   *Burying the Dead but Not the Past: Ladies' Memorial Associations and the Lost Cause*. Chapel Hill, NC: University of North Carolina Press.

Johnson Collection
    2021   Henry Mosler. *The Johnson Collection*. https://thejohnsoncollection.org/henry-mosler/, accessed 15 May 2021.

Lamar, Dolly Blount
   1952   *When All Is Said and Done*. Athens, GA: University of Georgia Press.

McGavock Cemetery Trustees
   2014   *McGavock Confederate Cemetery: Minute Book of the Original Trustees*. Franklin, TN: McGavock Confederate Cemetery Corporation.

McMichael, Kelly
   2009   *Sacred Memories: The Civil War Monument Movement in Texas*. Denton, TX: Texas State Historical Commission.

Memphis Daily Appeal
   1878   Our Dead Heroes 6 June 6, 37:4.
   1889   "A Column of Granite," 49:2.

Mills, Cynthia
   2003   Introduction. In *Monuments to the Lost Cause: Women, Art, and the Landscapes of Southern History*. Cynthia Mills and Pamela H. Simpson, eds. Pp. XV-XX. Knoxville, TN: University of Tennessee Press.

New Orleans Times-Picayune
   1894   Unknown Confederate Dead. Atlanta Will To-Day Unveil a Unique Monument to Their Memory, 26 April.

Oakley, Julia E.
   1872   Ladies Memorial Assn. *Wilmington Morning Star* 5 June, 10:1.
   1872   Ladies Memorial Assn. *Wilmington Morning Star* 6 May, 10:1.

McMinnville Southern Standard
   1889   [No title], 18 May, 10:4.

Smith, John Jay
   1839   Rural Cemeteries—Mount Auburn. Philadelphia: Laurel Hill Cemetery Records, Laurel Hill Archives.

Upton, Dell
   2015   *What Can and Can't Be Said*. New Haven, CT: Yale University Press.

Wilmington Daily Journal
   1868   Memorial Bazaar 12 May, 17:3.

Wilmington Morning Star
   1872   The Confederate Monument.

Wright, Elizabethada
   2003   "Reading the Cemetery, 'Lieu de Memoire par Excellence.'" *Rhetoric Society Quarterly* 33:2.

5

Remembering, Reconciliation, and Forgetting

Monuments of Northern Cemeteries for Confederate Prisoners of War, Especially Elmira

SHERENE BAUGHER

The 150th anniversary of the Civil War in 2011–2015 brought remembrances of heroic battles, such as Gettysburg, and the unfortunate and tragic events associated with them. Andersonville is a familiar name to Americans because of the South's brutal treatment of Union prisoners during the Civil War. In a camp built to house no more than 10,000 prisoners, over 32,000 Union soldiers were imprisoned at the same time, and 12,920 died (Andersonville National Historic Site 2021). After the war, the land of the Andersonville prisoner of war camp reverted to farmland, but veterans and other citizens continued to make pilgrimages to the site. In 1890, the Georgia Division of the Grand Army of the Republic purchased the site. It then sold the campsite for one dollar to the Women's Relief Corps, an auxiliary of the Grand Army of the Republic, which managed the site (Andersonville National Historic Site 2021). In 1910, the Women's Relief Corps turned over the control and ownership of the camp to the U.S. Department of the Army, and in 1970, the site was given to the National Park Service, which operates the site as Andersonville Historic Site (Roberts 2000:240).

The National Park Service has expanded the narrative at Andersonville to encompass all wars. The National Prisoner of War Museum at the site tells the stories of all American prisoners of war (United States National Park Service 2022). This change could be seen as an example of a reconciliation effort with the South to deemphasize the causes of the Civil War and instead place this prisoner of war (POW) camp within a larger context of all POW camps. This change in the narrative of a Civil War prisoner of war camp and cemetery is not unique to Andersonville. The focus of this chapter is not on Andersonville but on the cemeteries of Union-run Civil War camps for Confederate prisoners. The chapter examines the monuments at these cemeteries and discusses the efforts to alter the narratives of the Civil War through reconciliation efforts.

There were a total of 16 major Civil War POW camps, seven in the South (Confederate-run) and nine in the North (Union-run). After the war, most of the POW camps were dismantled, and the buildings were often sold. Most of the POW campsites were developed, and today, the only reminders of these sites are city or state historic site markers. The focus of this chapter is on the cemeteries associated with these camps and not on the campsites. Both in the Northern and Southern camps, bodies were usually buried near the POW camps. Many prisoners died at all these camps. The average death rate in Northern prisons was 12 percent, while the average death rate in Southern prisons was 15.5 percent, with Andersonville having the highest death toll at 29 percent and Elmira at 24 percent (Cloyd 2010:14). This chapter focuses only on Northern POW cemeteries, especially the Elmira Prisoner of War Camp cemetery. A discussion and comparison of Northern POW cemeteries, their monuments, and the changing narratives are provided. This comparison provides a context for the Elmira POW cemetery.

Elmira is located in the southern tier of New York State near the border with Pennsylvania. The POW camp and cemetery are mainly unknown, even for residents in Central New York State. However, the cemetery remains intact. The role of John Jones sexton of Elmira POW cemetery, is examined. A single monument to John Jones highlights the heroic work of a former slave who gained his freedom, was involved in the Underground Railroad, and his significant contributions to the unique preservation of the Elmira cemetery. The Northern POW camp cemeteries and their monuments, including Elmira, reveal the changing meanings and messages of the monuments regarding reconciliation, the causes of the Civil War, the "Lost Cause," slavery, and racism.

Background on Cemeteries for Civil War Soldiers

After the war, battlefields were still covered with many bodies of Union and Confederate soldiers in shallow graves or mass graves, and Union prisoners lay buried often in hastily dug graves near the POW camps (Blair 2004:52, Speer 1997:297–311). In 1865, Andersonville National Cemetery was established (Cloyd 2010:164). In 1866, Congress authorized funds to create national cemeteries for all Union soldiers in the South, including those in POW camps (Blair 2004:53). These national cemeteries were modeled after the national cemetery at Gettysburg with individual headstones of equal size and the bodies separated into state sections (Janney 2008:44). Bodies of Union soldiers who died in battle or in prison were exhumed from their temporary graves and placed in these new national cemeteries (Janney 2008:44). An example is the national cemetery in Fredericksburg, Virginia, with graves laid out state by state. This Southern reburial project was a massive effort, and within four years, 73 national cemeteries had been created in the South containing the bodies of over three hundred thousand Union soldiers (Janney 2008:45).

During this period of Reconstruction, no funds were provided for the graves of Confederate soldiers, and the bodies of Confederates in Northern prisoner of war camps received no marble gravestones. As mentioned in other chapters, throughout the South, upper- and middle-class women formed Ladies Memorial Associations to create Confederate cemeteries and rebury the Confederate soldiers from battlefields in the South (Janney 2008:11). The cemeteries were sometimes a Confederate section of an existing cemetery such as the City Cemetery in Fredericksburg, Virginia. But with limited funds and overwhelming numbers of deceased Confederate soldiers, the LMA focused its attention on the local battlegrounds and not on the Confederate dead in Northern prisoner of war camps. Historian William Blair (2004:78) notes that these Southern women (LMA), through their memorial work, "provided a means for rebel resistance to continue in a form of guerrilla warfare through mourning" and "protected the memory of the Confederacy from oblivion." When their cemetery work was completed, the Ladies Memorial Associations focused on promoting the "Lost Cause" with monuments in town squares and Memorial Day celebrations (Janney 2013:156). White Southerners continued to vehemently assert that the Confederacy fought to defend states' rights. They "denied slavery as a cause of the war" while "celebrations of white supremacy escalated" (Janney 2013:8).

Ironically, the Constitution of the Confederacy, article I, section 9.1, states that Confederate states can buy and sell slaves to one another. Article IV, section 2 clarifies the importance of slavery to these states, that slavery will be allowed in any new territory acquired by the Confederacy, that escaped slaves will be returned to their owners, and slave owners can travel with their slaves from one Confederate state to another with the knowledge that "the right of property in said slaves shall not be impaired" (Commager 1973a:379, 383). Furthermore, in Jefferson Davis's address to the Confederate States Congress in April 1861, he asserted the continuing importance of slavery to the South and added that with the production of cotton, rice, sugar, and tobacco in the South, "the labor of African slaves was and is indispensable" (Commager

1973b:391). Thus, there was a disconnect between historical facts and the presentation of history by the LMA.

By 1890, a younger generation of women formed the Daughters of the Confederacy (later renamed the United Daughters of the Confederacy, UDC) with broader goals. They continued raising monuments in public spaces, influencing what was presented as Southern history in schools, publishing pro-Confederate accounts, and perpetuating the "Lost Cause" (Cox 2003). The UDC was more active than the Ladies Memorial Association in erecting Confederate monuments in public places; in fact, 93 percent of those monuments were built after 1895, with half of them erected between 1903 and 1912 (Cox 2003:50). They also became involved in funding monuments for some Confederates in POW cemeteries in the North (to be discussed later in this chapter).

National Reconciliation Efforts

Attempts at commemoration and reconciliation started in the 1870s and increased in the 1880s and 1890s with so-called Blue and Gray reunions at battlefields. For Union veterans, praising the courage of their enemies "served to boost Union veterans claims of bravery and triumph," and for Confederates being reassured of their courage, they could attribute their defeat to Northern resources and that they had fought against a worthy adversary (Janney 2013:167). But veterans on both sides resisted, even though some were willing to meet at these events. In the last quarter of the nineteenth century, both sides funded monuments for town squares and courthouse lawns. African Americans celebrated Emancipation Day. Soldiers penned memoirs. Books were written about battles and the war, and both sides wrote about the terrible conditions in the prisoner of war camps.

As early as 1871, Fredrick Douglass expressed his concerns about forgetting the causes of the Civil War:

> We are sometimes asked in the name of patriotism to forget the merits of this fearful struggle, and to remember with equal admiration those who struck at the nation's life, and those who struck to save it; those who fought for slavery and those who fought for liberty and justice. I am no minister of malice, I would not repel the repentant, but may my tongue cleave to the roof of my mouth if I forget the difference between the parties to that bloody conflict. I may say if this war is to be forgotten, I ask in the name of all things sacred what shall men remember? (Janney 2013:4)

The monuments in Northern cemeteries for Confederate POWs showed that Frederick Douglass was justified in his concerns about forgetting the causes of the war.

By the late nineteenth century, reconciliation efforts emphasized the bravery and courage of the soldiers, overlooking the real causes of the war, growing white supremacy, and the lynching of Blacks in the Jim Crow South. Economic and political motivations for reconciliation may have been motivated by Northern and Southern eagerness to participate in the growing market economy, by White Southerner's desire to regain political power, and by the need for Southern soldiers in America's efforts at expansionism to take American Indian lands, and territories in the Caribbean and the Pacific. The North faced its own issues with labor unrest, unionism, and discrimination against immigrants. Karen Cox (2003:5) writes that the "cult of Anglo-Saxonism" in the North as a push-back against ethnic diversity "provided a supportive climate for a movement that celebrated white heroes." A focus on reconciliation had profound impacts on the memorialization at Northern POW cemeteries.

Northern Cemeteries for Confederate Prisoners of War

By 1870, all Union dead had been interred in national cemeteries, most of which were battlefield cemeteries (MacCloskey 1968:26–37). In March 1873, a Congressional law allowed the creation of more national cemeteries for the burial of all honorably discharged Union veterans and allocated $1,000,000 to purchase gravestones to be placed on each grave in these cemeteries (MacCloskey 1968:37). In some of these Northern national cemeteries, there was a Confederate section for the deceased prisoners from the POW camps, such as the Confederate sections of Rock Island National Cemetery in Rock Island, Illinois, Camp Butler National Cemetery in Springfield, Illinois, and Woodlawn National Cemetery in Elmira, New York. In the national cemeteries, the government provided marble headstones only for Union soldiers.

The Confederate graves had wooden markers. The exception was the POW camp for Confederate officers at Johnson Island, Sandusky, Ohio. In 1889, a group of politicians and citizens from Georgia raised funds to have Georgia marble headstones carved, inscribed, and placed on every grave of the 206 officers and a few enlisted men in the Johnson Island POW cemetery (Downer 1962:112–113). They also paid for an iron archway and iron fence to enclose the cemetery. The owner of Johnson Island refused to sell the cemetery to the federal government. In 1904, the UDC purchased the cemetery and erected a statue of a soldier called "The Lookout" who gazes away from the cemetery looking to Sandusky Bay, and in 1931, the UDC donated the cemetery to the U.S. government (United States Department of Veterans Affairs 2019). Ironically, this statue is of an enlisted man at a cemetery for Confederate officers. Perhaps the choice was to cover the fact that this was the only cemetery the UDC was protecting and preserving. Class differences mattered to the Southern women regarding what Confederate prisoner of war graves they were willing to protect and commemorate in the North. In 1925, the UDC erected two more memorials, not to deceased soldiers, but to celebrate their own UDC women in preserving the Johnson Island cemetery (U.S. National Park Service 2021a).

In 1898, in hopes of generating Southern support for the Spanish–American War and gathering support for American expansionism, President William McKinley announced that the federal government would provide gravestones and maintain graves of all "fallen" from the Civil War—including Confederate soldiers (Blair 2004:179, 181). The Spanish–American War demonstrated that Northerners and Southerners could fight together on the same side against a common enemy. However, some African Americans felt that McKinley's offer regarding Confederate graves "was selling out to the white South to head off anti-expansionist efforts by Democrats" (Blair 2004:185). At the end of the war, the U.S. gained possession of Puerto Rico, Guam, and the Philippines.

Before placing marble gravestones on Confederate graves, Congress in 1900 allowed the bodies of 262 Confederate soldiers that were in graves in the Washington D.C. area to be reburied in Arlington National Cemetery on the former property of Robert E. Lee (Arlington National Cemetery 2021). In 1906, the UDC was allowed to erect a Confederate monument at Arlington. They raised funds, hired Moses Ezekiel to create it, and President Woodrow Wilson of Virginia unveiled it in 1914 (Cox 2003:53–55, 60–70). The monument contains scenes of an idealized South, including gallant soldiers going to fight against the Union and two controversial vignettes of a slave following his owner into war and a Black female slave holding a White child. The unveiling of the monument was on Jefferson Davis's birthday, and Woodrow Wilson declared the monument, with its defiant images of slavery and rebellion, an "emblem of a reunited people" (Janney 2013:263). But what was the price of this reuniting, and the changing of the narrative? At the time Wilson was celebrating the Confederate monument, the graves of Black Union soldiers were denied burial with White Union soldiers at Arlington (Arlington National Cemetery 2021).

In 1906, Congress authorized the funding of marble tombstones to mark the graves of Confederate soldiers and sailors who were buried in Northern POW cemeteries and funding for monuments for mass graves (Gray 2001:162). The Secretary of War created a Commission for Marking the Graves of the Con-

Figure 5.1. The 85 ft. granite monument at Finn's Point Cemetery, New Jersey. The memorial is for the 2,436 Confederate soldiers who died in the Fort Delaware Prisoner of War Camp. Photo by Richard Veit, 2022.

federate Dead and evaluating the monuments to be placed on the sites of mass graves (Crankshaw et al. 2016:13, 15). Congress authorized the same marble markers for Confederate headstones as the headstones for Union soldiers. But Congress wanted to distinguish the design for the Confederates, so the top of the Confederate gravestones was pointed instead of rounded, and a military shield was omitted (United States Department of Veterans Affairs 2012).

However, locating individual graves proved to be a problem. During the war, the camp doctor had to record "the individual's name, rank, regiment and company, date and place of capture, and date and cause of death," but there were no mandated procedures for burying the Confederate prisoners (Crankshaw et a1. 2016:3). In many of the POW cemeteries, the Confederate soldiers were not placed in individual coffins but put in mass graves, so it was impossible to place individual grave markers. For example, in 1910, at Finn's Point Cemetery (Figure 5.1) in New Jersey, the federal government erected an 85 ft. granite monument in memory of the 2,436 Confederate soldiers who died at Fort Delaware POW Camp and are buried in a mass grave (Finn's Point National Cemetery 2015). Similar federal government obelisks mark Confederate POW Camp mass graves at Point Lookout in Maryland, at North Alton Confederate Cemetery in Alton, Illinois, and at Greenlawn Cemetery in Indianapolis. The inscription on the Greenlawn obelisk, "Erected by the United States to mark the burial place of 1616 Confederate soldiers who died here while prisoners of war and whose graves cannot now be individually identified," became almost the standard text for these mass gravesites (Crankshaw et al. 2016:15).

Separate from the words, the monument itself conveys meaning to the viewer. The commission chose obelisks for these mass graves. The obelisk is the most common monument found in nineteenth-century cemeteries. In ancient Egypt, it represented Ra, the sun god, as in a ray of the sun (Cooper 1978:121). But it also symbolizes eternal life; thus, it is an appropriate image for use in cemeteries (de Vries 1974:348). In the nineteenth century, many obelisk monuments were erected at Revolutionary battlefield sites, such as at Bunker Hill, Oriskany Battlefield, Newtown Battlefield, the Bennington Monument, and even the Washington Monument. In the United States, obelisks became a "cultural symbol for memorializing significant men and events" (Giguere 2014:92). The monuments were also used to mark victories and heroes and were associated with democracy (Crankshaw et al. 2016:16). To choose an obelisk as an image of victory and heroes to remember men who were secessionists is an example of how monuments represent the social and political messages their producers want to convey. The commission that chose these obelisks was made up of all Southerners and Confederate veterans (Crankshaw et al. 2016:13).

Over time other monuments were placed on Northern POW cemeteries. For example, in the 1890s, two Northerners, William Knauss and Henry Briggs, cleaned up Camp Chase in Columbus, Ohio, and Mr. Briggs placed a boulder that he carved "2260 Confederate Soldiers of the war 1861–1865 buried in this enclosure" (Crankshaw et al. 2016:13). In 1902, Knauss and friends raised funds to erect a memorial arch topped by a statue of a soldier at rest with his rifle, and the arch had the words "Americans" (Cloyd 2010:98). The simple words "Americans" reflect this mood of reconciliation.

In Chicago, a Confederate men's group, United Confederate Veterans, received permission from the U.S. military to place a monument in the military-owned portion of Oakwood Cemetery. They dedicated the monument in 1895, where over 4,000 Confederate bodies were placed in a mass grave (Crankshaw et al. 2016:10–11). Over 40 ft. tall, the monument is capped with a statue of a soldier "standing aggressively, arms crossed in unrepentant defiance," and for the South, its heroism was recognized, and slavery was forgotten (Cloyd 2010:73). In 1911, the federal Commission for Marking the Graves paid to have the monument lifted and set upon a base of red granite with bronze plaques inscribed with the names of Confederate prisoners buried in the mass grave (U.S. National Park Service 2021b). The statues at the POW cemeteries are diverse examples of the efforts at reconciliation and changing the narrative.

Elmira Cemetery and John Jones

In Elmira, New York, there is a large, well-kept, rural cemetery known as Woodlawn. The most famous burial is that of Samuel Clemens, also known as Mark Twain. Next to the rural cemetery is the Woodlawn National Cemetery. In 1874, Congress allocated funds to establish a national military cemetery in Elmira (Horigan 2002:182). The cemetery is open for the burial of veterans of any wars. The land next to the rural cemetery was owned by the City of Elmira and contained the two-and-a-half-acre Confederate POW burial ground (Gray 2001:95). The federal government purchased this property, and the site became part of the national military cemetery. Over time, more land was purchased, and today, the cemetery is 10½ acres and contains the graves of over 9,000 veterans from the Civil War through the Vietnam War (Horigan 2002:194). One example is the stone for Lula Tuttle, a World War I army nurse. But off in a distant section is the Confederate section containing the graves of the soldiers who died in the Elmira POW camp. The Confederate markers are white marble stones laid out in long, orderly rows. In walking through the Confederate section, one notices the sheer number of stones, just under 3,000. While the cemetery is serene and peaceful, the numbers suggest that this landscape conceals another, perhaps darker, story.

Elmira was called the Andersonville of the North. The Elmira death rate, like Andersonville's, was incredibly high. The death rate in Elmira was 24 percent and was shockingly close to the death rate at Andersonville, which was 29 percent (Horigan 2002:180, 193). In July 1864, when the prison opened, the army leased a half-acre from Elmira city-owned Woodlawn Cemetery for the burial of prisoners, and because of so many deaths, an additional half-acre was leased in January 1865 (Gray 2001:95). John Jones, the sexton of Woodlawn Cemetery, was hired to handle all the Confederate burials. Jones, born in 1817, was a slave on the Elzy family plantation in Leesburg, Virginia, and in 1844, Jones, along with his two half-brothers and two other slaves, escaped and made their way to Elmira, New York, an abolitionist city (Holmes 1912:140–142). Jones was actively involved in the Underground Railroad, harboring escaped slaves that were sent from Philadelphia by abolitionists such as William Sill and working with Elmira abolitionists, such as Jervis Langdon, Mark Twain's father-in-law (Ramsdell 2003). During his nine years of work in the Underground Railroad, Jones is credited with saving over 800 slaves, who made their way to St. Catherines, Canada (Holmes 1912:144). Jones was not only the sexton of Woodlawn Cemetery, but he was also in charge of the Baptist Burial Ground in Elmira and was the sexton, usher, and general helper of the First Baptist Church in Elmira (Ramsdell 2003:5410). By 1854, he had saved up enough money to buy his own house for $500, and two years later, he married Rachel Swails (Ramsdell 2003:5410). In 1863, the 54th Massachusetts Volunteer Infantry (the Black Regiment depicted in the film *Glory*) was formed. Jones was 46 years old, but as a prominent member of the Black community, he may have helped recruit volunteers for the army. Twenty-three young Black men from Elmira joined the 54th Massachusetts, including Jones's 31-year-old brother-in-law, Lieutenant Stephan A. Swails, who served with distinction and survived the war (Emilio 1995:336, 359, 364–368, 376). Jones's war work also involved the burials of Confederate prisoners in Elmira.

Jones was very meticulous in keeping records of the decreased Confederates. Their name, company, regiment, and date of death were recorded for each body; this information was written onto the coffin lid, was also placed in a bottle in the coffin, and was recorded in a ledger that Jones kept recording the exact location of each burial (Gray 2001:96–97). In addition, Jones "made sure that the wooden headboards had the correct information written on them in white lead paint, and then placed them over the appropriate plot" (Gray 2001:97). The wooden grave markers survived for decades until they were replaced with marble tombstones in 1907. For many of these Northern POW camp cemeteries, connecting bodies to individuals was extremely difficult, if not impossible. However, at Elmira, the task was easy because of the work of John Jones. Ironically, it was a former slave who kept such careful records when some of the other Northern POW camps had incomplete records. It would be easy for a former slave to feel resentful and hostile to the Confederates fighting to maintain slavery. Still, his humanity is seen in the care he took with recording the burials.

Elmira Monuments

The cemetery is a poignant reminder of this landscape of conflict. While a few families had their relatives exhumed and reburied in their community in the South, most families left the graves in Elmira. However, eight Southern families did erect their own stones (Gray 2001:162). Two examples are still in good condition. In 1905, a son erected a granite stone for his father, T. John Smith, who died at age 34 in the POW camp. Both the father and son were from Alabama. On another stone is a scroll with the name W.B. Le Quenx, a twenty-year-old man who died in Elmira. The broken bud or seedpod carved on the stone symbolizes that the soldier was cut off in the flower of his youth (Keister 2004:43).

The wooden markers made by John Jones survived until 1906, when preparations for the new marble markers were made with each grave staked out, and Grave Commissioner William Elliot "had the old headboards collected and burned" (Gray 2001:162). By 1907, marble gravestones were placed over all the Confederate graves (Horigan 2002:194). Grave Commissioner Elliot used the meticulous data kept by Jones on the wooden markers and in his ledger to mark the graves with marble gravestones (Gray 2001:97, 162). In visiting the cemetery in the twenty-first century, what immediately stands out to the viewer is that the Confederate stones are pointed while stones for Union soldiers have rounded tops. The legislation simply required that the gravestone contain the grave number, the individual's name, rank, regiment, and state, if known (Gray 2001:162). The Blue Ridge Marble Company produced the Confederate stones in Nelson, Georgia (Gray 2001:163). Perhaps the decision to use a Southern company rather than a marble company in Vermont, which was much closer to Elmira, was to assure the Southern families that great care was being taken in creating these Confederate tombstones. Years later, in 1930, the War Department implemented new regulations for Confederate headstones that also allowed the inscription of the Confederate Cross of Honor in a small circle on the top front face of the stone (United States Department of Veterans Affairs 2012). A small number of families requested that their 1907 stone be replaced with a marble stone with the Confederate Cross and those newer stones are visible in the cemetery.

In 1912, Congress paid for another monument for the Elmira cemetery (Gray 2001:165). It is a monument to the Confederate prisoners of war and the Union soldiers guarding them who died in a train wreck in Shohola, Pennsylvania. These men were traveling to Elmira in the summer of 1864. The remains of all these men were initially buried in Pennsylvania in 1864 but were reinterred in the Elmira cemetery in 1911 (Gray 2001:164–165). The

Figure 5.2. The photo on the left is a monument to the victims of the Shohola train wreck. This side of the monument lists the names of the 49 Confederate prisoners who died in the accident. The monument faces the Confederate side of the cemetery. Notice the Union gravestones with the rounded tops in the background facing the Union side of the monument. Photo by Sherene Baugher, 2011. The photo on the right depicts the Union side of the monument dedicated to the Union victims of the Shohola train wreck. This side lists the names of the 17 Union soldiers (guards) who died in the accident. The monument faces the Union side of the cemetery. Notice the Confederate gravestones in the background with pointed tops facing the Confederate side of the monument. Photo by Brant Venables, 2019.

notion of reconciliation would suggest having all the names on the front of the monument, but that is not how this monument was carved. On one side of the monument, the Confederate side lists the names of the forty-nine dead Confederate prisoners (Fig. 5.2a). The other side is the Union side, which lists the names of the seventeen Union soldiers who were the guards on the prison train (Fig. 5.2b). The monument was erected so the Union inscription faces the Union graves, and the Confederate inscription faces the Confederate graves. The sense of North and South separation was still strong in 1912 in Elmira.

After 1890, the United Daughters of the Confederacy erected many memorials throughout the South. However, it was not until 1937 that they erected a monument at Elmira. They chose Frederick William Sievers, who created the controversial Virginia Memorial of Lee at Gettysburg, to sculpt a Confederate memorial for Elmira (Crankshaw et al. 2016:9). A bronze figure of a common soldier is set in a niche in a granite monument (Fig. 5.3). There were

Figure 5.3. Confederate Monument erected in 1937 by the United Daughters of the Confederacy in the Elmira Prisoner of War Camp Cemetery. Photo by Sherene Baugher, 2011.

no officers sent to the Elmira POW camp, so the figure of the enlisted man is appropriate, unlike the UDC monument of a common soldier at Johnson's Island cemetery for Confederate officers. The Elmira image is what some art historians call "the sentinel," a figure of an infantryman at parade rest (Panhorst 1988:213). In the late nineteenth century, the solemn image of a soldier in uniform with a hat in hand was often used for mortuary monuments in both the North and the South (Panhorst 1988:215). The UDC chose to use this nineteenth-century style for their memorial at Elmira. At the bottom of the monument, the text is: "In memory of the Confederate soldiers in the War Between the States who died at Elmira prison and lie buried here erected by

Figure 5.4. A modest memorial erected in 1997 to John W. Jones, a former slave, and the sexton of the Elmira Prisoner of War Camp Cemetery. Photo by Sherene Baugher, 2011.

the United Daughters of the Confederacy November 6, 1937." The term *War Between the States* rather than *Civil War* has been used in material promoted by the UDC and is still a term used on their website in 2021 (United Daughters of the Confederacy 2021). The UDC website also notes that their goals include "To collect and preserve the material for a truthful history of the War Between the States," ignoring that this was a war about secession from the Union and the right to maintain slavery. Historian Karen Cox (2003:2) notes that as part of the "Lost Cause" symbols and ideas, "Confederate soldiers are remembered as heroes, in spite of military defeat, because they fought to defend states' rights. Consequently, they were also heroes for fighting to sustain white supremacy." The Elmira memorial and its text offer the viewers reminders of the Southern view of the war.

A final monument was erected in the Elmira POW camp cemetery in 1997. This monument was not to one of the Confederate prisoners but to John Jones, the former slave and sexton of the POW cemetery (Fig. 5.4). The modest monument is a gray granite stone with a bronze tablet with dedication. The text on the monument states:

> Confederate soldiers were buried here with kindness and respect by John W. Jones, a runaway slave. They have remained in these hallowed

grounds of Woodlawn National Cemetery by family choice because of the honorable way in which they were laid to rest by a caring man.

High school students from Elmira raised funds to create this memorial to Jones (Horigan 2002:194). This monument subtly reminds the viewers of slavery and its connection to the war. Another Jones memorial, while not a monument, is the John Jones House, located a block away from the national cemetery and opposite the former entrance to Woodlawn Cemetery. The house sits on farmland owned by John Jones. In 1997, the house was condemned by the City of Elmira, was purchased by a group of concerned citizens, moved to its present location, preserved and is open to the public as a museum on African American history and abolition in Elmira, as well as highlighting the life of John Jones (John Jones House 2020).

Conclusion

Historian Edward Linenthal (1991) has written how military sites with monuments and commemorative ceremonies create a patriotic past. Paul Shackel (2001) notes that collective memory can be about forgetting the past. The patriotic history is seen in Civil War monuments in both the North and South. But the United Daughters of the Confederacy certainly took significant steps through their monuments, commemorations, and publications to create a collective memory that is at odds with the actual historic facts about the war and slavery.

Through the separation of these Union and Confederate cemeteries in both the North and South, today, we have a permanent landscape of symbols that reflect the bitter memories and regional divisions that have existed since before the Civil War. The focus on states' rights of the Confederacy continues with the rhetoric of right-wing politicians in the twenty-first century in their moves against a strong federal government and pro-states' rights regarding voter suppression and support of repressive state laws against minorities, immigrants, women, and the LGBTQIA communities. While slavery was ended in December 1865 with the thirteenth amendment to the Constitution, racism did not end. Systemic racism is seen in the many nineteenth- and twentieth-century lynchings in the South, school segregation, Jim Crow laws, contemporary voter suppression, and the multiple twenty-first-century police killings of Black men and women in both the North and South, especially the murder of George Floyd.

Heritage scholar David Lowenthal (1985) has written extensively about the theme of exclusionary memory and how some people and subordinate groups are written out of history and out of a community, a state or province, or even a nation's collective memory. Selective amnesia about the causes of the war, the brutality of slavery, and the fact that Confederates were fighting against the United States are evident in many of the monuments erected in the late nineteenth and early twentieth centuries, especially those in POW cemeteries. As much as government officials wanted to believe in reconciliation, the refusal to confront the reasons for the Civil War did not produce a united country. The insurrectionists' takeover of the capital on 6 January 2021, sadly demonstrates the continued divisions in the country.

Monuments convey powerful messages about those divisions. Christopher Gwinn (2020:10) notes that monuments "are not neutral, nor are they unbiased." These monuments often reflect an exclusionary memory. Perhaps, the monument to John Jones at Elmira cemetery is a glimmer of hope that we will see new monuments being erected on battlefields and on POW cemeteries to challenge the traditional heritage narrative and reveal the contributions of other Americans.

References

Andersonville National Historic Site
    2021   Learn About the Park. https://www.nps.gov/ande/learn/index.htm, accessed 9 February 2021.

Arlington National Cemetery
    2021   Confederate Memorial. https://www.arlington cemetery.mil/Explore/Monuments-and-Memorials/Confederate-Memorial, accessed 17 February 2021.

Blair, William
    2004   *Cities of the Dead: Contesting the Memory of the Civil War in the South, 1865–1914*. Chapel Hill, NC: University of North Carolina Press.

Cloyd, Benjamin G.
    2010   *Haunted by Atrocity*. Baton Rouge, LA: Louisiana State University Press.

Commager, Henry Steele, ed.
    1973a   The Constitution of the Confederate States of America, March 11, 1861. *Documents of American History*. 9th edition. Englewood Cliffs, NJ: Prentice-Hall.
    1973b   Davis' Message to Congress, April 29, 1861. *Documents of American History, Ninth Edition*. Englewood Cliffs, NJ: Prentice-Hall.

Cooper, J. C.
    1978   *An Illustrated Encyclopedia of Traditional Symbols*. London, UK: Thames and Hudson.

Cox, Karen L.
    2003   *Dixie's Daughters: The United Daughters of the Confederacy and the Preservation of Confederate Culture*. Gainesville, FL: University Press of Florida.

Crankshaw, Ned, Joseph E. Brent, and Maria Campbell Brent
   2016   The Lost Cause and Reunion in the Confederate Cemeteries of the North. *Landscape Journal* 35 (1):1-21

de Vries, Ad
   1974   *Dictionary of Symbols and Imagery*. Amsterdam: North-Holland Publishing Company.

Downer, Edward T.
   1962   Johnson's Island. *Civil War History* 8(2), 202-217. https://doi.org/10.1353/cwh.1962.0059, accessed 10 February 2021

Emilio, Luis F.
   1995[1894]   *A Brave Black Regiment: The History of the 54th Massachusetts, 1863–1865*. With a new introduction by Gregory J. W. Urwin. New York, NY: De-Capo Press.

Finn's Point National Cemetery
   2015   Civil War Era National Cemeteries, Finn's Point. https://www.nps.gov/nr/travel/national_cemeteries/New_Jersey/Finns_Point_National_Cemetery.html, accessed 15 February 2021.

Giguere, Joy M.
   2014   *Characteristically American: Memorial Architecture, National Identity, and the Egyptian Revival*. Knoxville, TN: University of Tennessee Press.

Gray, Michael P.
   2001   *The Business of Captivity: Elmira and its Civil War Prison*. Kent, OH: Kent State University Press.

Gwinn, Christopher
   2020   The War for Memory. *Preservation & Progress* 31(3):10–12.

Holmes, Clay W. A.M.
   1912   *The Elmira Prison Camp*. New York, NY: G.P. Putnam's Sons.

Horigan, Michael
   2002   *Elmira: Death Camp of the North*. Mechanicsburg, PA: Stackpole Books.

Janney, Caroline E.
   2008   *Burying the Dead but not the Past*. Chapel Hill, NC: University of North Carolina Press.
   2013   *Remembering the Civil War: Reunion and the Limits of Reconciliation*. Chapel Hill, NC: University of North Carolina Press.

Keister, Douglas
   2004   *Stories in Stone: A Field Guide to Cemetery Symbolism and Iconography*. Salt Lake City, UT: Gibbs Smith.

Linenthal, Edward Tabor
   1991   *Sacred Ground: Americans and their Battlefields*. Urbana, IL: University of Illinois Press.

Lowenthal, David
   1985   *The Past is a Forgotten Country*. New York, NY: Cambridge University Press.

MacCloskey, Monro
   1968   *Hallowed Ground: Our National Cemeteries*. New York, NY: Richards Rosen Press.

NPS (National Park Service)
- 2022 Camp Sumter Military Prison, Andersonville National Historic Site. NPS Civil War Prisons. https://www.nps.gov/ande/learn/historyculture/npsprisons.htm, accessed 25 September 2022.
- 2021a Confederate Stockade Cemetery, Johnson's Island, Ohio. https://www.nps.gov/nr/travel/national_cemeteries/ohio/Confederate_Stockade_Cemetery.html, accessed 10 February 2021.
- 2021b Confederate Mound at Oak Woods Cemetery, Chicago, Illinois. https://www.nps.gov/nr/travel/national_cemeteries/illinois/confederate_mound_oak_woods_cemetery.html, accessed 16 February 2021.

Panhorst, Michael Wilson
- 1988 *Lest We Forget: Monuments and Memorial Sculpture in National Military Parks on Civil War Battlefields, 1861–1917.* Ph.D. Dissertation, Department of Art History, University of Delaware.

Ramsdell, Barbara S.
- 2003 The John W. Jones Story and his Connection with the First Baptist Church and Area Abolitionists. *The Chemung Historical Journal* 49(2):5307–5424.

Roberts, Edward F.
- 2000 *Andersonville Journey*. Shippensburg, PA: Burd Street Press.

Shackel, Paul A., ed.
- 2001 *Myth, Memory and the Making of the American Landscape.* Gainesville, FL: University Press of Florida.

Speer, Lonnie R.
- 1997 *Portals to Hell: Military Prisons of the Civil War.* Mechanicsburg, PA: Stackpole Books.

United Daughters of the Confederacy
- 2021 History of the United Daughters of the Confederacy. https://hqudc.org/history-of-the-united-daughters-of-the-confederacy/, accessed 12 February 2021.

United States Department of Veterans Affairs
- 2012 History of Government-Furnished Headstones and Markers: Confederate Markers. https://www.cem.va.gov/cem/history/hmhist.asp, accessed 18 February 2021.
- 2019 Confederate Stockade Cemetery. https://www.cem.va.gov/cems/lots/confederate_stockade.asp, accessed 19 February 2021.

6

Race, Gettysburg Memory, and the Jenkins Monument in Pennsylvania, 1990s–2020

HILARY N. GREEN

On 20 November 1999, readers of the *Sentinel* (Carlisle, PA) learned of a new Civil War monument planned for the area (*Sentinel* [Carlisle, PA] 1999). Honoring Confederate Brigadier General Albert Gallatin Jenkins, the Camp Curtin Historical Society had commissioned Gary Casteel, a noted Gettysburg sculptor, to design a 9 ft. granite obelisk with a bronze portrait of the general and tablets detailing the Confederate advance into Pennsylvania during the Gettysburg campaign of 1863. Placed where the Jenkins had established his headquarters outside the Rupp House, the Camp Curtin Historical Society president hoped that the expected $35,000 monument could bring attention to local history: "In fact, it is often forgotten that Harrisburg was the target of (General Robert E.) Lee's 1863 invasion of Pennsylvania and Jenkins's troops were the vanguard of Lee's army (*Sentinel* [Carlisle, PA] 1999)." Reports of the proposed monument encouraged fundraising as the organizers desired, but the pronouncement spurred the resurrection of another memory of Jenkins's role in the Confederate invasion. For Black Franklin County residents whose roots as free people predated Gettysburg, Jenkins did not deserve the bronze and granite monument. He was responsible for the largest seizure and enslavement of free African Americans throughout south-central Pennsylvania during the Civil War. Memories of the trauma, names of the individuals enslaved, and consequences for United States Colored Troops (USCT) enlistment from the county persisted even after the nation encouraged collective forgetting at the turn of the twentieth century.

For current Franklin County residents and living Civil War–era descendants, the announcement and final unveiling in 2005 felt like another attack. The monument again erased the history of the enslavement of Black Pennsylvanians and celebrated a Confederate general responsible for civilian trauma in the Gettysburg campaign in a reconciliation attempt rooted

Figure 6.1. Photograph of the Jenkins Monument, ca. 2005. Courtesy of the Cumberland Valley Visitors Bureau.

in anti-Blackness. It also ignored how the Civil Rights Movement gains set the stage for a new generation of African Americans committed to removing these divisive symbols (*Sentinel* [Carlisle, PA] 2005a; [Carlisle, PA] 2005b; Robinson, 2017; Cox 2021:129–134). During the second of three Confederate raids on the border of Pennsylvanian County, the Confederate military policy of "gathering up" terrorized whole communities. Scholars have provided some discussion of the seizure and enslavement of free Blacks in relation to the Gettysburg campaign and the wartime destruction of Chambersburg (Ayers 2003, 2017; Alexander 2001, Coddington 1984; Neely 1999, and Smith 2013). Developed in response to the Confiscation Acts and the Emancipation Proclamation, the Confederate policy transformed soldiers into slave catchers who indiscriminately seized and enslaved free-born African Americans and re-enslaved any individuals who secured freedom for themselves during the war (Alexander 2001; Ayers 2003, 2017). Many fled for safety. Others witnessed the forced removal of African American neighbors and the military occupation of the communities. Rescue attempts proved futile. Few returned. As their removal became permanent losses, the effects reverberated throughout Franklin County. Hence, Franklin County residents collectively remembered the strong emotions associated with loss, forced separation, and military occupation. They voiced their discontent (Green 2019). This chapter is in conversation with the works of other scholars but offers careful attention to the experiences and memories of Black Pennsylvanians and county residents.

Instead of praise, the monument had the opposite effect desired by the Camp Curtin Historical Society builders. Reconciliation had been the goal. "The monuments remind us that even as a red state/blue state divide is loudly proclaimed, there are Americans still working to bind the wounds from the great civil conflict that tore the nation apart 140 years ago," according to one Sunbury, Pennsylvania, journalist commenting on the monument dedication ceremonies honoring Jenkins and the White federal general who prevented the advance into the Harrisburg (Swift 2005). But it did not heal as hoped. Certain "descendants of the occupied" rejected the newly erected "monument to the occupier (Swift 2005)." Collective memories countering this Civil War narrative resurfaced. Developed during the Gettysburg invasion of 1863, the sustained counter-memory formed the basis of a movement ultimately contributing to its removal following the murder of George Floyd and national summer of 2020 reckoning.

Local historians, residents, and individuals, like the author, who are descended from the Civil War communities targeted during the Gettysburg raid, coordinated in an effort that rejected the whitewashed historical narratives of Jenkins, the Gettysburg campaign, and memory. After a discussion of the consequences of the Gettysburg invasion, I hope to show how Black Franklin County residents and their White allies could not forget the Civil War military experience or the civilian trauma over the nineteenth and twentieth centuries. This resurfaced Civil War history ultimately contributed to its removal while obscuring the dedication of another public monument that advanced a more inclusive commemorative understanding of the Black Civil War experience and transformative legacy.

Origins of Jenkins Monument Protest

In the weeks before the Battle of Gettysburg of 1–3 July 1863, General Albert G. Jenkins's arrival in Franklin County, a border county in south-central

Pennsylvania, became unforgettable. Jenkins and his men began the massive search and seizure of free Black Pennsylvanians and self-emancipated persons on 15 June 1863. For over two weeks, Jenkins became one of many Confederate officers and soldiers who reduced Black residents to enslaved captives and White residents to bystanders throughout the county (Coddington 1984:160). One Twenty-Third North Carolina Infantry major recounted the process in a letter to his brother about his exploits in two Franklin County communities: "We have also captured thousands of horses and many hundred slaves. I have several negroes, free and slave, in my hands but negroes are worth nothing at all. No kind of negroes will sell for more than one hundred dollars" (Blacknall 1863). Despite the low financial return, the Confederate raiders continued the practice as citizens remained "shut up in their houses and frightened nearly to death" (Blacknall 1863). This Confederate soldier's letter reveals the scope of practice in an unfiltered letter to his brother. Such accounts had no place in subsequent Gettysburg commemorations. Lost Cause and Blue and Gray reunion proponents intentionally forgot this publicly acknowledged practice and shaped the original placement of the Jenkins Monument on private land in the late twentieth century (Blight 2001; Janney 2013; Levin 2019).

In contrast, Franklin County residents captured their emotions and accounts of the Gettysburg invasion during the summer of 1863. Their memory work actively remembered Gettysburg and the other raids for the civilians removed and enslaved. They also promoted accounts acknowledging their traumatic civilian experiences while dismissing ones that did not.

Historians Edward L. Ayers (2003:405 and 2017:65–67) and Ted Alexander (2001:85) extensively employed the Rachel Cormany diary in their respective works. Rachel Cormany and her diary offer a window into the seizure and enslavement of Black residents and self-liberating African Americans in Chambersburg. The Canadian-born wife of Samuel Cormany, a Sixteenth Pennsylvania Cavalry officer, vividly described the frantic pre-arrival of self-liberating African Americans and refugees, seizures, and military occupation over the course of several diary entries. In the 16 June 1863 entry, she wrote that the Confederates

> were hunting up the contrabands and driving them off by droves. O! How it grated on our hearts to have to sit quietly and look at such brutal deeds—I saw no men among the contrabands—all women and children. Some of the colored people who were raised here were taken along—I sat on the front step as they were driven by just like we would drive cattle. Some laughed and seemed not to care—but nearly all hung their heads. (Cormany 1863)

Helpless to prevent the seizure of Black townspeople and refugees, the raiders reduced Cormany to the role of a spectator. With her own husband serving in the federal army, she could not have effectively mounted any resistance. She might have pleaded with the raiders. However, fear paralyzed her. She only found her voice through private contemplations in her diary. Her feelings of pain and vulnerability were equally echoed in the surviving journal accounts.

In a few instances, several White civic leaders and residents moved beyond inaction and actively attempted to rescue the seized Black Pennsylvanians. Often pleading with Confederate raiders, Mrs. Jemima Cree, Jacob Hoke, and other individuals attempted to prevent their removal, but to no avail (Turner 1940; Schaff 1894). Benjamin S. Schneck, a prominent Reformed Church theologian, would have a distinct place in the shared collective memory for successfully negotiating the return of Esque Hall, Henry Dietrick, and Samuel Claudy. Schneck persuasively appealed directly to Jenkins at his headquarters and secured their release (Ayers 2003; Hoke 1884).

African American residents' reports emerged only when the perceived threat to their freedom abated. Many free Black residents exploited locales on the area Underground Railroad network. Joseph R. Winters composed the song titled "About Ten Days After the Battle of Gettysburg" (Winters 1863). Like the White Franklin County diarists, Winters showed his disgust toward the dishonorable Confederate soldiers who employed force and destruction on a civilian population. Winters revealed the terror experienced by free Black residents. Many simply fled. Winters noted in the fifth stanza:

> The colored people all ran away,
> Likewise the composer of this song, they say–
> For if I hadn't, I don't know
> But I'd been in the South a'working the hoe (Winters 1863)

Winters and others understood the threat to their freedom posed by the Confederate raiders. Rather than endure possible enslavement, they hid. They only resurfaced after the military engagement at Gettysburg had ceased. For Winters, his song title signaled his own emergence after ten days. The threat of slavery proved too great. Sold as a song sheet, Winters gave voice to the Black experience unmediated by White Franklin County residents (Winters 1863).

Others were not as fortunate. Neither negotiations nor armed rescues occurred for individuals like Alexander Lewis, who was captured and enslaved in the kitchens of Castle Thunder, a Confederate prison in Richmond, Virginia. Confederate military officials granted him parole in late March 1865.

He eventually returned and secured employment at a Chambersburg hotel. For other enslaved Pennsylvanians at Castle Thunder, their fates remained unknown (Franklin Repository 1865; Neely, Jr. 1999:139–140). The sights and sounds of men, women, and children left invisible scars on surviving Franklin County residents who were forced to bear witness to the abductions.

The return of Amos Barnes, a free Black resident seized during Jenkins's Raid, renewed hope and positively shaped an inclusive Civil War countermemory. The *Franklin Repository* secured an interview with Barnes that provided the most detailed account of his experiences in its 23 December 1863 edition (Franklin Repository 1863). Confederate soldiers seized and enslaved Amos Barnes on 2 July 1863. He made the long trek to Richmond, Virginia, with other free and self-emancipated persons captured. Barnes labored around Castle Thunder and Camp Winder (Mercersburg Journal 1863). After negotiations between White Mercersburg leadership, Rev. J. V. Moore of Richmond, and Confederate officials, Confederate Major J. H. Carrington released the "free negro, resident of Pennsylvania who was brought off by our troops" on account of a lack of "charges against him" (File C [WD] 1025 1863). Seen as an early Christmas present to a community still reeling from the effects of the Gettysburg campaign, the newspaper coverage of Barnes's return and account of his brief enslavement only motivated young Black men to become USCT liberators of both the enslaved men, women, and children of the Confederacy and of the border Pennsylvanian communities.

Black men enlisted within days of Barnes's reported return. On Christmas Day 1863, Joseph Lane, my own Civil War ancestor, enlisted in the Twenty-Second USCT. He and other Franklin County men joined USCT Regiments at Chambersburg (Pension File of Joseph Lane n.d.). For them and the other Black Franklin County men who enlisted following the eventful summer of 1863, Amos Barnes's harrowing narrative most likely influenced their actions. Rather than remain passive bystanders forced to hide, they chose to wear the blue uniform and become liberators of enslaved Black Pennsylvanians and their Southern brethren. These Franklin County enlistees joined other Black volunteers for training at Camp William Penn outside of Philadelphia before leaving for the battlefront in one of eleven USCT units (Green 2019).

After the Civil War, these Civil War USCT veterans returned home, established families, and formed strong community organizations. As franchised veterans, they transformed their military service and communal collective memories of their wartime sacrifices into advancing civil and political rights. As parents and community leaders, they educated the next generation to remember and not forget the services and sacrifices of the Civil War generation. They shared their collective memories of enlistment, war, and the Gettysburg invasion in their homes and in other segregated safe spaces. They used Memorial Day, the dates of the preliminary and final Emancipation Proclamation (22 September and 1 January respectively), and Fourth of July celebrations to advance the local Black Civil War memory. In segregated cemeteries, they built monuments and connected past and present generations through parades that began and ended at their sacred spaces. The author is the product of this memory work. She grew up hearing these stories on her childhood visits to her maternal grandparents and family whose ties to the county as free people of color date to the 1820 census. Porch stories and community memory traditions confirmed traditional archival sources and findings of academic scholarship on the Civil War. This memory work and these academic understandings contributed to outrage surrounding the Jenkins Monument but also the collective celebration at its quiet removal.

Jenkins Monument, 2005–2020, and the Future of Civil War Monuments

Unveiled in June 2005, the Jenkins Monument prompted swift rejections by many who questioned its placement in the post–Civil Rights Movement nation. As one journalist surmised, "Controversy has dogged the Jenkins monument, one of the few dedicated to Confederates north of the Mason-Dixon Line, from the start" (Miller 2020).

The criticism was not unique. Late twentieth-century Confederate monuments received similar responses. The location of the central Pennsylvania monument and its honoree marked a major difference. The nation had changed in terms of Civil War memory. Lost Cause and whitewashed Reconciliationist attempts no longer represented the dominant views of the Civil War commemorative landscape. The academic profession also changed and promoted more nuanced understandings. Scholars, like myself, pushed back at this monument in our classrooms, professional meetings, and community outreach work. The 2015 Charleston Massacre changed everything (Cox 2021).

On 17 June 2015, when Dylann Roof murdered nine African American parishioners at Emmanuel African Methodist Episcopal (AME) Church, a national conversation began over the Lost Cause commemorative landscape. Twelve memorials fell. Some communities chose contextualization over removal. But the American public began listening to African Americans who had never accepted this landscape (Cox 2021; Green 2021:488). Removal was not seriously considered for the Jenkins Monument. Camp Curtin Historical

Figure 6.2. Before (*left*) and after (*right*) photographs of the Jenkins Monument by Shippensburg University Professor John Quist, 2020. Courtesy of PennLive.com.

Society placed several wayside markers contextualizing the Gettysburg campaign. These markers helped to neutralize any local discontent.

In the wake of the violent Charlottesville's Unite the Right 2017 rally, a shift occurred both nationally and in Pennsylvania. This 2017 event and the murder of Heather Heyer revealed the failure of post–Charleston Massacre removals and discussions over contextualization in resolving the ongoing Civil War culture war. Eighty-five removals occurred. Several state legislatures responded by adopting heritage preservation laws (Green 2021; Cox 2021). In Pennsylvania, a heightened awareness over the Jenkins Monument renewed discussions over its fate. PennLive.com journalist Wesley Robinson shed light for contemporary newspaper readers of the Jenkins Monument. He remembered how the Jenkins Monument was one of several non-battlefield Confederate monuments in the state. The Confederate monument debate extended beyond the former Confederate states and affected Pennsylvanians. And Robinson felt that his readers should care (Robinson 2017).

By the time of George Floyd's murder in May 2020, the Jenkins Monument's fate had been sealed. The Pennsylvania monument became one of over 250 monuments to the Confederacy, slavery, and colonialism removed globally (Green 2021). Announced on the 157th anniversary of the Battle of Gettysburg's final day, PennLive.com informed readers how the Jenkins Monument quietly came down.

Shippensburg University professor John Quist provided the before and after photographs of the site and offered context for the removal. "Aside from

Figure 6.3. Photograph of *A Gathering at the Crossroads* monument. Photo courtesy of the Pennsylvania Heritage/Pennsylvania Historical and Museum Commission, 2020.

Jenkins's act of treason in embracing armed rebellion against the very government he had sworn to uphold as a member of the U.S. Congress, Jenkins's cavalrymen became notorious for kidnapping every African American in Pennsylvania they could overtake—all of whom were free—and forcibly removing them to the Confederacy where they became enslaved," Quist explained (Miller 2020). The Jenkins Monument only inflamed tensions. It never resolved them. Welcoming the news, Quist questioned the monument builders: "It struck me as just an inappropriate way to remember the Civil War" (Miller 2020). Indeed, the monument celebrated a sanitized history and continued to perpetuate the erasure of the African American enslavement during Gettysburg. Whiteness undergirded the twentieth-century reconciliation attempt. And it failed. Removal brought the intended healing and fuller understandings of the Civil War experience.

Unfortunately, the extensive coverage of the removals of Jenkins and other Lost Cause monuments diverted attention from another Pennsylvania monument dedicated in 2020. *A Gathering at the Crossroads* is a Civil War monument that served as a corrective to the removed Jenkins Monument.

The life-size, immersive monument featuring William Howard Day, Thomas Morris Chester, Frances Ellen Watkins Harper, and Jacob Compton, a Twenty-Fourth USCT veteran, now stands at the Pennsylvania Capitol Complex in Harrisburg. Three of the four honorees participated in the November 1865 reception honoring returning USCT soldiers in response to the exclusion of Black soldiers at the May 1865 Grand Review of Armies (Zander 2020; Jordan 2014; Janney 2013). The COVID-19 pandemic affected the dedication. Two ceremonies unveiled the powerful Civil War monument. A 26 August 2020 event saw the unveiling of the pedestal with a map of the Old Eighth Ward and the names of one hundred Black Harrisburg residents on the sides. Flanking the pedestal, life-size statues of William Howard Day and Frances Ellen Watkins Harper appear in conversation. The dedication of Thomas Morris Chester and Jacob Compton statues occurred on 16 November 2020, amid the backdrop of the ongoing pandemic and active contestation of the 2020 Presidential Election results (Mealy 2021; Benscoter 2020; Marroni 2020).

While coinciding with the Summer of 2020 Confederate monument removals, plans began four years earlier for this new Harrisburg monument. Lenwood Sloan, Jeb Stuart (a city historian who shares the name with the Civil War Confederate general), and Kelly Summerford hosted a series of community roundtable events over the spring and summer of 2017 at a local university (Mealy 2021). These community meetings encouraged the formation of the Harrisburg Peace Promenade Monument Project, an alliance of organizations and institutional partners, which transformed the city Riverfront Park into one of the D'Amore's International Institute for Peace through Tourism (IIPT) Global Peace Parks. While achieving this commemorative change, Sloan and other group members felt that something else was needed. The new plaques and markers proved insufficient to achieve the desired peace, reconciliation, and healing (Mealy 2021).

Sloan and his group quickly planned a new public monument celebrating Black Pennsylvanians' Civil War–era contributions. They successfully petitioned city officials and state legislators. They secured the funding and location for the Crossroad Monument. Seeing their work as "an act of reparation as well as a place-making initiative," Sloan and the Harrisburg alliance selected the final design honoring Black Pennsylvanians' contributions to the Civil War era, specifically the Underground Railroad, USCT recruitment, USCT military service, and major participants in November 1865 reception for returning USCT soldiers (Mealy 2021; Sloan 2020). Calobe Jackson Jr. and a team of "history detectives" selected the one hundred names placed on the pedestal and developed a companion book profiling Black Harrisburg individuals who made significant contributions between 1850 and 1920 (Sloan 2020:x). From the life-size figures to the pedestal, the final monument corrected the previous exclusion of Black Pennsylvanians to the Civil War and its transformative legacy and squarely countered the Jenkins Monument of the late twentieth century. These Black activists deserved honor and recognition as the pathway forward to reconciliation and healing. Jenkins Monument and its 2020 removal reflected its regulation of the past and one no longer essential for shaping the future of the city, state, and nation. Sculpted by Becky Ault, the rare Civil War monument made a powerful statement.

In the final style and pose, Ault took immense care with the wax casting method used for crafting each life-size figure in three sections before applying the patina finish (Ault 2021). She realistically captured the four individuals' likeness and character. For Chester, she used his pose, features, and clothing to communicate that he was a "man of strong moral character with gentle eyes that have seen the world and understand its knowledge and affect. His posture is strong, with good shoulders to demonstrate determination" (Ault 2021:227–228). Less refined fabric clothing marked the real difference between the Day and Chester statues. Ault still conveyed Day's expression as one of "compassion while his wide eyes demonstrate knowledge and strength." Relying on historical photographs and images, Ault captured Harper's "beautiful, gentle, glowing face with expressive, strong, determined eyes." Depicted holding a copy of the Fifteenth Amendment, Ault sculpted her posture to "express joy . . . and her determination for another fight ahead, to gain her right to vote" (Ault 2021:228). Unlike the other figures, Compton's statue emphasized a specific monument in Civil War history. Ault did not depict him as either a Civil War veteran or one of the African Americans mobilized in defending Harrisburg against the threat posed by Jenkins (U.S., Civil War Draft Registrations Records, 1863–1865 2010; U.S., Civil War Pension Index: General Index to Pension Files, 1861–1934 2000). Rather, she highlighted his bravery shown during an assassination attempt of Abraham Lincoln during his visit to the city in 1861. She and her team "chose to design him as a true hero, the carriage driver who whisked Abraham Lincoln to safety" (Ault 2021:228). The monument showed Compton dressed as a typical Civil War–era coachman. Ault sculpted him with "the expression of a gentle soul with inner strength, a sign that he is also determined and accomplished" (Ault 2021:228).

While appearing in casual conversation discussing the passage of the Fifteenth Amendment, Ault's design allowed for an immersive experience. "Their eyes will follow the spectator and yet appear to be looking at each other," according to Ault (Ault 2021:226). In between the four individuals, she placed a pedestal with a map of the historic Black Eighth Ward community and the selected names of 100 individuals. The elevated names prevented visitors from walking over them and forced them to see them for their contributions. The map featured important locations, including Wesley Union AME Church, schools, businesses, hotels, and neighborhood locales (Ault 2021).

With an equally detailed pedestal in between the life-size figures, this monument does more to educate and invite spectators to learn the underappreciated history of the Civil War. Each figure and name on the pedestal corrected previous silencing of the Civil War past. The final monument, as Ault hoped, introduced new heroes and heroines who shaped the "history of the city, county, commonwealth and nation" (Ault 2021:232). To date, it has.

Coda

Few removed monuments caused me as much satisfaction as the Jenkins Monument. As a descendant of the Civil War communities affected by Jenkins's actions, I found comfort that neither other descendants nor future generations of Black Pennsylvanians had to experience the "know your place aggression" of the Lost Cause and Reconciliationist traditions intentionally placed into the American landscape (Mitchell 2020:4–5). Removal represented an acknowledgment. Both-sideism, whitewashed myths, and top-down solutions no longer had a place in defining how the Civil War should be commemorated in twenty-first-century Pennsylvania non-battlefield locales. Unfortunately, Confederate removal received much more airtime, ink, and public debate than the newly placed Civil War monument in Harrisburg. The recognition of ordinary Black Pennsylvanians' contributions in an immersive bronze statuary in a central location on the State Capitol grounds and in the accompanying companion book for the individuals named on the pedestal is the pathway forward to reconciliation and healing. Unlike the Jenkins Monument, this monument represents the future and possibilities of Civil War commemoration in the state and nation.

And, therefore, I celebrate these 2020 events in Pennsylvania.

References

Alexander, Ted
    2001   "A Regular Slave Hunt": The Army of Northern Virginia and Black Civilians in the Gettysburg Campaign. *North and South* 4(7):82–89.

Ault, Becky
    2021   The Commonwealth Memorial: A New Sculpture for the Capitol Grounds. *Pennsylvania History: A Journal of Mid-Atlantic Studies* 87(1):225–232.

Ayers, Edward L.
    2003   *In the Presence of Mine Enemies: The Civil War in the Heart of America.* New York: Norton and Company.
    2017   *The Thin Light of Freedom: The Civil War and Emancipation in the Heart of America.* New York, NY: W. W. Norton and Co.

Benscoter, Jana
 2020 Harrisburg Monument Recognizes the Old 8th Ward Who 'Believed in Active Citizenship.' *PennLive.com*, 26 August 2020, https://www.pennlive.com/news/2020/08/harrisburg-monument-recognizes-those-from-old-8th-ward-who-believed-in-active-citizenship.html, accessed 26 March 2024.

Blacknall, Charles
 1863 Letter to Brother George, June 18, 1863, printed in the *(NC) Carolina Watchman,* 13 July, accessed in Gettysburg Library File V7-NC23, Gettysburg National Park Library and Research Center, Gettysburg, PA.

Blight, David W.
 2001 *Race and Reunion: The Civil War in American Memory*. Cambridge, MA: Belknap Press of Harvard University Press.

Sentinel (Carlisle, PA)
 1999 Monument to Recognize Confederate General, 20 November:A1 and A4.
 2005a Two Civil War monuments to be Dedicated on Saturday, 21 June:B9.
 2005b Monuments Dedicated, 27 June:B3.

(Chambersburg, PA) *Franklin Repository*
 1863 Discharged from Richmond, 23 December:8.
 1865 Paroled, 5 April:3.

Coddington, Edwin B
 1984 *The Gettysburg Campaign: A Study in Command*. New York, NY: Charles Scribner's Sons.

Cormany, Rachel
 1863 Diary, in Valley of the Shadow. Charlottesville, VA: University of Virginia, Charlottesville. http://valley.lib.virginia.edu, accessed 26 March 2024.

Cox, Karen L.
 2021 *No Common Ground: Confederate Monuments and the Ongoing Fight for Racial Justice*. Chapel Hill, NC: University of North Carolina Press.

Green, Hilary
 2019 The Persistence of Memory: African Americans and Transitional Justice Efforts in Franklin County, Pennsylvania. In *Reconciliations After Civil Wars: Global Perspectives*. Paul Quigley and James Hawdon, eds. Pp. 131–149. London, UK: Routledge.
 2021 2 Shifting Landscapes and the Monument Removal Craze, 2015–20. *Patterns of Prejudice* 54(5):485–491.

Hoke, Jacob
 1884 *Historical Reminiscences of the War: Or, Incidents which Transpired in and about Chambersburg, During the War of the Rebellion*. Chambersburg, PA: M. A. Foltz.

Janney, Caroline E.
 2013 *Remembering the Civil War: Reunion and the Limits of Reconciliation*. Chapel Hill, NC: University of North Carolina Press.

Jordan, Brian Matthew
 2014 *Marching Home: Union Veterans and Their Unending Civil War*. New York, NY: Liveright Publishing Company.

Levin, Kevin M.
   2019   *Searching for Black Confederates: The Civil War's Most Persistent Myth*. Chapel Hill, NC: University of North Carolina Press.

Marroni, Steve
   2020   Old 8th Ward Monument Completed, Commemorating Historic Harrisburg Neighborhood. *PennLive.com*, https://www.pennlive.com/news/2020/11/old-8th-ward-monument-completed-commemorating-historic-harrisburg-neighborhood.html, accessed on 17 November 2020.

Mealy, Todd
   2021   A Gathering at the Crossroads: Memorializing African American Trailblazers and a Lost Neighborhood in Harrisburg. *Pennsylvania Heritage* (Spring 2021), http://paheritage.wpengine.com/article/a-gathering-at-the-crossroads-memorializing-african-american-trailblazers-and-a-lost-neighborhood-in-harrisburg/, accessed 26 March 2024.

Mercersburg Journal
   1863   Just from Dixie. 25 December:2.

Miller, Matt
   2020   Another Confederate Monument Falls, This Time on the West Shore. *PennLive.com,* 3 July 2020, https://www.pennlive.com/news/2020/07/another-confederate-monument-falls-this-time-on-the-west-shore.html#:~:text=As%20controversy%20swirls%20around%20Confederate,Trindle%20Road%20in%20Hampden%20Township, accessed 26 March 2024.

Mitchell, Koritha
   2020   *From Slave Cabins to the White House: Homemade Citizenship in African American Culture*. Urbana, IL: University of Illinois Press.

Neely, Mark, Jr.
   1999   *Southern Rights: Political Prisoners and the Myth of Confederate Constitutionalism*. Charlottesville: University Press of Virginia.

Pension File of Joseph Lane, Twenty-Second USCT
   n.d.   Department of Veterans Affairs, Washington, DC, released under the Freedom of Information Act to the author who is a direct descendant.

Robinson, Wesley
   2017   Local Confederate Monument Marks the Farthest North the Army Held Territory. *PennLive.com,* 17 August 2017, https://www.pennlive.com/news/2017/08/confederate_monument_in_hampde.html, accessed 26 March 2024.

Schaff, Philip D.D.
   1894   The Gettysburg Week. *Scribner's Magazine* 16(1):21–30.

Sloan, Lenwood
   2020   Foreword. In *One Hundred Voices: Harrisburg's Historic African American Community, 1850–1920*. Calobe Jackson, Jr., Katie McArdle, and David Pettegrew, eds. Pp. ix-xii. Grand Forks, ND: The Digital Press at the University of North Dakota.

Smith, David G.
   2013   *On the Edge of Freedom: The Fugitive Slave Issue in South Central Pennsylvania, 1820–1870*. New York, NY: Fordham University Press.

Swift, Robert B.
    2005   Statues Symbolize Efforts to Heal Conflict. *Daily Item* (Sunbury, PA), 3 July:B1.

Turner, J. D. Edmiston
    1940   *Civil War Days in Mercersburg as Related in the Diary of the Rev. Thomas Creigh.* Kittochittiny Historical Society, Chambersburg, PA, 29 February 1940.

U.S., Civil War Draft Registrations Records, 1863–1865
    2010   Ancestry.com Operations, Inc., Provo, UT.

U.S., Civil War Pension Index: General Index to Pension Files, 1861–1934
    2000   Ancestry.com Operations, Inc., Provo, UT.

Winters, Joseph R.
    1863   Vertical File—Winters, Franklin County Historical Society, Chambersburg, PA.

Zander, Cecily N.
    2020   'Victory's Long Review': The Grand Review of Union Armies and the Meaning of the Civil War. *Civil War History* 66(1):45–77.

7

Confronting Confederate Narratives

Archaeology at the Judah P. Benjamin Confederate Memorial at Gamble Plantation Historic State Park

S. Matthew Litteral and Diane Wallman

History buffs and tourists alike in the greater Tampa Bay area may be tempted to spend a balmy afternoon exploring the site of a former sugar plantation in Ellenton, Florida. The antebellum plantation is now a state park, where you can opt to tour the still-standing Greek Revival plantation mansion (Figure 7.1). A volunteer tour guide, often a member of the United Daughters of the Confederacy (UDC), will greet you on the mansions colonnaded front porch. They will most likely begin the tour by highlighting the accomplishments of Major Robert Gamble, the original owner of the plantation. Your guide will then regale you with several swashbuckling stories of the McNeill family, who inhabited the home during the Civil War, culminating in the harrowing tale of Judah P. Benjamin. Benjamin was the Confederate Secretary of State, who took brief refuge at the site during his escape from federal troops in 1865. The guide will also inform you of how the UDC graciously saved the mansion from ruin in 1925 by raising the funds to purchase both the house and 16 acres of surrounding land, which was subsequently donated to the state for preservation. Today, the state park still bears the name proposed by the UDC upon donation in 1925, Judah P. Benjamin Confederate Memorial at Gamble Plantation Historic State Park. The entire park remains a memorial to this former Confederate cabinet member.

What you will not hear on your tour, however, is a discussion of the nearly 200 enslaved peoples who lived and labored on the plantation. There may be a brief mention of "servants," "cooks," or "workers," language referring directly to enslavement at the site carefully withheld. You may hear stories of the "whistle walk" from the detached kitchen to the dinner table; they will explain a charming Southern tradition in which "Young enslaved laborers were made to whistle while carrying food from the kitchen to the mansion, because you

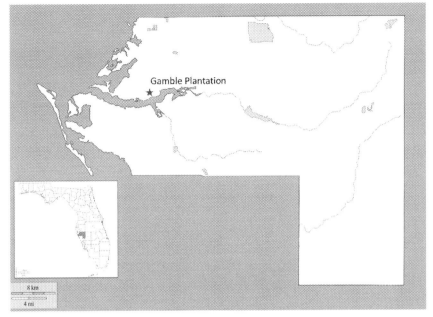

Figure 7.1. Location of Gamble Plantation. Map by Diane Wallman.

can't whistle with food in your mouth." Used as an ice-breaker joke by the guides, this quick anecdote has severe, but unacknowledged, implications regarding the oppressive system of control and food insecurity associated with enslavement. Further, the guides will unanimously fail to explain that those enslaved at Gamble Plantation cleared thousands of acres of thick forest, dug 16 miles of drainage canals, sowed and harvested fields of sugar cane, built a sophisticated sugar mill complex, *and* constructed the very beautiful Greek Revival mansion, tabby brick by tabby brick.

This story is not unique to Gamble Plantation, as the censorship of dark or uncomfortable histories is a common occurrence at historical sites across the nation, particularly in the South, where plantation sites serve as physical reminders of institutional slavery on American soil (Jackson 2012). The omission of enslaved laborers from plantation narratives is largely a result of the "Lost Cause" movement and its lasting social impact. Developed during the Reconstruction period in the South, the Lost Cause movement gained momentum in the 1920s and 30s with the passage of Jim Crow segregation, the publication of Gone with the Wind, and many other popular books and films (Hartley 2021:68). The narratives offered in these works of fiction attempted to re-write history, and negate the horrors of enslavement, focusing solely on the gentility of an antebellum lifestyle "swept away by war."

Gamble Plantation, however, is not typical of the Confederate monuments and memorials that have been the focus of recent national debates on remembrance. It is not comprised of a single commemorative statue—the entire landscape (plantation house and grounds)—has been designated as a memorial that honors a single individual who had a fleeting historical presence at the site. Further, the site was preserved due to the actions of the UDC, whose perspective, while sometimes problematic, prejudiced, and specious, cannot be completely ignored. It is important to understand the UDCs role in the history of Gamble Plantation State Park as part of the varied biographies and politics surrounding this built environment.

Memorials, as an act of remembrance, are imbued with political and historical struggle. As cultural geographers Alderman and Inwood (2013) suggest, by studying sites of memory, we can explore: What is said and not said about the past? Whose history is remembered or forgotten? What does the differential treatment of histories and identities tell us about power relations and patterns of inequality within historical and contemporary societies? As archaeologists, we ask how can we offer a more complete and nuanced understanding of the past through our work, and try to shift the narrative of such "imagined landscapes" to a more inclusive, and more accurate version of history? What are our moral and ethical responsibilities in working with organizations or groups whose actions or beliefs conflict with our principles as anthropologists?

These are the questions we address in this chapter. Our objective is to review ongoing research and community engagement at Gamble Plantation, presenting recommendations that will be submitted to Florida State Parks for a new interpretive focus at the site. First, we outline the history of the Gamble Plantation, and detail how the current interpretation at the site developed through the lens of the Lost Cause. We then discuss our archaeological project, which also includes community and descendant engagement. Based on our research and outreach, we argue, as many anthropologists and historians have, that by examining the plantation landscape through the lens of the enslaved experience, archaeologists can challenge and aim to reform the revisionist narratives of antebellum life that are the very foundation upon which racist memorial landscapes were built (Jackson 2012; McDavid 1997).

Florida as a Slave State

Florida often gets left out of discussions of slavery in the U.S., and this is likely due to the liminal position of the peninsula as a Spanish and British colony and then an independent territory until 1845. Middle Florida held the vast majority of enslaved peoples, and by 1860, Florida's population was 140,424, with 44 percent of the population enslaved (Tebeau 1991:181). In South Florida, plantation agriculture was limited and relatively short-lived, with mixed success. After Spain ceded Florida to the United States in 1821, however, a wave of wealthy planters from Kentucky, Maryland, Virginia, North Carolina, South Carolina and Georgia moved into Middle Florida (Tallahassee area) (Landers 2003). They brought with them plantation culture and the intention of building a society akin to the one they had left behind (Baptist 2002:17).

In 1842, the Armed Occupation Act prompted the movement of many White settlers into South Florida, in support of Indian Removal. This act granted 160-acre homesteads to the head of any family who resided on their designated lands for five years. Hundreds of incoming settlers made their homesteads along the Manatee River, in the central Gulf Coast of Florida, in this government-sanctioned appropriation of Native American land (Matthews 1983). Gamble, along with several other mid-Florida White elites, were convinced sugar would become a lucrative industry in southern Florida, avoiding the short growing seasons and frost of northern Florida (Rivers 2000). In 1841, Gamble purchased his land from the U.S. government (Wiggins 2003). In 1844, efforts to clear the property began, and by 1847, Gamble held 69 enslaved laborers at his Manatee plantation (later dubbed Gamble Plantation), with numbers increasing to 151 individuals by 1855 (Schene 1981). At peak production, Gamble owned approximately 3,500 acres with nearly 200 enslaved people (Silpa 2012). As with the rest of Florida's sugar cane agriculture, however, the success of sugar production at the plantation was short-lived and erratic.

In 1856, due to debt and family concerns, Gamble's brother-in-law Allan MacFarlane assumed ownership of the plantation. MacFarlane sold the plantation along with 185 enslaved individuals, 41 of whom were from one of the Gamble plantations in Leon County, for $190,000 in 1858 to New Orleans bankers, John Calvin Cofield, and Robert McGuinn Davis (Manatee County Public Library 1859). In 1859, Cofield and his wife Ann moved into the Gamble Mansion and managed the plantation for the following two years (Silpa 2012).

After several years of disappointing profit margins, the banks foreclosed on Cofield and Davis, and the Cofields returned to New Orleans. In the spring of 1862, the Confederate government seized the property and sold what remained of the processed sugar (1972). Captain Archibald McNeill was placed in charge of the plantation and lived in the mansion until 1873 with his wife and children (Silpa 2012:83). It is unclear exactly what happened to the enslaved people, but evidence suggests that most were transported to Louisiana, with some individuals remaining at Gamble.

Because of the pivotal moment in history during which the McNeills inhabited the mansion, they have become romanticized in the site's current historical narrative. Public presentations given by the UDC, and observed by the authors, portray Archibald as a cavalier sea captain. His wife is similarly revered as a powerful matriarch holding down the fort, so to speak, as her husband was often called away on wartime exploits. At the end of the Civil War (1865), the U.S. Government ordered Confederate cabinet members arrested, and it was this moment in history that the site would come to memorialize.

Confederate Secretary of State, Judah P. Benjamin, took brief refuge with the McNeills at Gamble Plantation in May 1865 while escaping pursuit by the Union troops (Baker 1987; Matthews 1983; Silpa 2012). From Gamble, Benjamin found passage on a ship headed for Bimini, and later went on to become a successful barrister in England (Schene 1981). Benjamin's brief sojourn at the mansion prompted the United Daughters of the Confederacy to work to preserve the site in the mid-1920s (Baker 1987:7).

In December 1873, a Georgia farmer and former slaveholder, George Patten, bought the property (Clerk of the Circuit Court 1873:418–423; Matthews 1983). The mansion was occupied by his rather extensive family until 1895, and most of the lands were divided among Patten's children after his death. By 1920, the mansion was in complete disrepair. The Judah P. Benjamin Chapter of the UDC began raising money for the purchase and restoration of the mansion in 1923, and in 1925, they donated the site to the state for preservation as a memorial to Judah P. Benjamin (Baker 1987:7). The mansion was listed on the National Register of Historic Places on 12 August 1970, and contains the only standing plantation house in South Florida. The site is now a state park, consisting of the 13-acre parcel with the mansion, as well as an additional 19-acre parcel surrounding the sugar mill ruins purchased by the park in 2002.

The "Lost Cause" and the Confederate Memorial at Gamble Plantation

During reconstruction, the White plantocracy in the Southern states remained fearful of the Union government and military, as well as emancipation, citizenship, civil rights, suffrage and equality for African Americans. Southerners needed a way to come to terms with their failure, portraying themselves as the aggrieved party, calling the conflict the "War of Northern Aggression" (Weitz 2009:81). The movement of the "Lost Cause" developed from these fears, and was cultivated and maintained by the White elite class. Gaines Foster (1987:2) defines the movement as the "postwar writings and activities that perpetuated the memory of the Confederacy" through organizations.

Various organizations developed in the late nineteenth century with the goal of memorializing local Confederate soldiers killed in battle. Ladies' Memorial Associations were the first organizations formed by elite Southern women to protect Confederate burials, and support narratives of the Lost Cause (Cox 2003:2). In 1890, many of these groups merged, forming the "Daughters of the Confederacy," followed by the formal founding of the UDC in 1895 to "honor and vindicate their Confederate ancestors" (Cox 2003:2). This organization has since utilized its political and economic power to defend the Lost Cause and Confederate history.

The Gamble Plantation was purchased and donated to the State by the UDC in 1925 as a memorial to Benjamin. Upon donation to the State, the associated statute codified into law that the state shall "restore and preserve the [Gamble Plantation lands] as an historical monument of the flight and Escape of Judah P. Benjamin, Secretary of State of the Confederate States, after the fall of the Confederacy" (State of Florida 1925). The Florida Department of Natural Resources would "own the building and be solely responsible for the maintenance, protection and management as a Confederate shrine and museum." While there has been some reinterpretation of the mansion over the years, the narrative at the mansion foregrounds Benjamin, the Confederacy, and Robert Gamble.

The UDC had near complete control of this narrative until the late 1970s. During this time, the mansion served solely as a museum of Confederate history, with little emphasis on the history of the site, with the notable exception of Judah P. Benjamin's stay (Litteral 2019). The UDC's influence at the state park remained unchecked until 1977, when State Naturalist Major Jim Stevenson created a new narrative for Gamble Plantation. He actively sought to dismantle the Confederate museum and refocus interpretation on the history of the site and those who lived there, especially enslaved laborers. He wrote a new, more inclusive, tour guide script that was fit for post–Civil Rights Movement America. The script emphasized the daily lives and tasks of enslaved laborers (Litteral 2019).

Stevenson faced severe backlash from the UDC, who were outraged that the mansion would no longer be represented as a true Confederate museum and memorial. After reviewing the changes Stevenson proposed, the UDC sought council from conservative senator and attorney Tom Gallen, who in turn wrote to the Director of Florida State Parks and Recreation backing the UDC. Pressure was placed on Stevenson to compromise with the UDC. In the end, the back two rooms of the house were left to commemorate Benjamin and Confederate heritage. Many edits were also made to Stevenson's original tour script by members of the UDC, and in the end, almost all mentions of slavery were omitted (Litteral 2019).

Archaeological Research

In 2017, we initiated archaeological research at Gamble Plantation, through two successive field schools, to better understand the nuanced history at the site. We were specifically interested in learning more about the enslaved laborers at Gamble, their stories, and their continued legacy. Focused on community engagement, we shared our findings with interested communities (local residents and historical societies) in Ellenton as well as the greater Tampa Bay area through public days, talks, social media, and meetings.

Because the location of the slave village remains elusive (likely on inaccessible private land), our archaeological investigations focused largely on the 13-acre tract around the mansion, with a small amount of survey near the site of the former sugar mill. Based on artifact density maps from surveys in the 1970s and 1980s (Baker and Peterson 1978; Baker 1987), we judgmentally placed trenches and test units behind the mansion, north of the detached kitchen and cooks' quarters. In so doing, we hoped to capture the archaeological signature of the antebellum occupations. However, excavation recovered primarily postbellum nineteenth- and early twentieth-century deposits associated with the Patten family's occupation of the estate. The lower levels did contain some mid-nineteenth-century material, along with cast iron cooking implements and faunal remains. The materials are currently under analysis.

To locate potential archaeological features in the landscape surrounding the mansion and grounds, we used LiDAR data collected from the National Ocean Service survey of the Florida coastline to create a digital terrain model (Figure 7.2). This model represents a 2 km by 1 km rectangular area; 1,457,196 points were collected in this area with a vertical accuracy of 5.7 cm and a horizontal accuracy of 115 cm compiled to meet accuracy at a 95 percent confidence level. From this model, we identified potential archaeological features in a field northeast of the plantation, consisting of multiple raised circular areas (possibly historic structures) linked by depressed linear pathways. Aerial photography confirmed the existence of these features as far back as 1940 (Litteral 2019). The features are situated in a location to the east of the sugar mill, an area vaguely indicated in historical records as a possible site of the slave village.

114 · S. Matthew Litteral and Diane Wallman

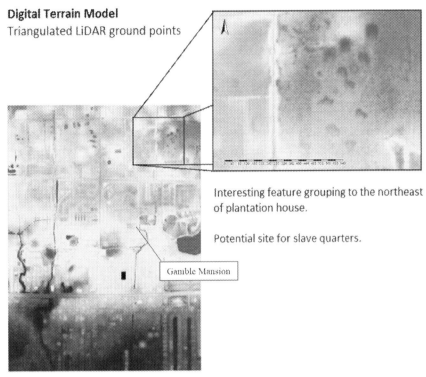

Figure 7.2. Digital Terrain Model (DTM) of Ellenton highlighting landscape features. Model created by Matt Litteral.

Public Engagement and Descendant Outreach

Although our current efforts have recovered material associated primarily with the postbellum period, we have been using this project as a platform to complicate and challenge the longstanding narrative at the park, which highlights the perceived accomplishments of Robert Gamble and the escape of Benjamin. The very publicly oriented nature of the site and our fieldwork allowed us to interact with a plethora of communities and stakeholders, including but in no way limited to, visitors, volunteers, state park employees, field school students, members of the UDC, local teachers, elementary school students, local business owners, local residents, social media followers, and descendants of the enslaved. Our efforts have involved public events with a collective of artists, academics, policymakers, and descendants, focusing on issues of memorialization and monuments. Though few tangible materials associated with the enslaved were uncovered archaeologically, by carefully shifting the conversation and by presenting a new and exciting historical narrative, we were able to avoid instigating conflict between the various groups with a vested interest in the site.

Over the course of the field schools, we held 12 public days at the site, which invited community members to excavate, screen, and tour the site. On these days, we gave informal and alternative "tours" of the grounds, emphasizing the history and lives of the enslaved. Our information for these tours came from a combination of archival research, insights from local residents and historians, geospatial data, and our excavations. Informal discussions with Ellenton residents during these events suggested that this community, though predominantly White, is very interested in the history of enslavement at the site. Visitors ranged from the elderly to elementary school groups. A common theme among visitors and participants was the desire to know more about the slave cabins and the general organization of the plantation.

We also launched a Facebook page, which currently has over 900 followers. Our social media presence allowed individuals with an interest in our work to voice their thoughts and opinions as comments on our posts. Through social media, we engage with a community comprised of a diverse range of individuals from many different states; however, local residents are the majority, and are often the most vocal. Over the past few years, we have responded to several comments that had rather racist undertones, including one that suggested the enslaved laborers were "paid for" and "proud of" their labor. It was clear that these individuals felt personally affronted by our attempts to challenge the age-old narrative of enslavement at the site. We responded to these individuals with resources and articles that may encourage growth and broadened understanding of the insidious nature of enslavement.

In addition, we have identified and are working with descendants of the enslaved community to develop an inclusive perspective on research questions and interpretation. In particular, we have been working closely with one descendant of the plantation, Chandra Carty. Ms. Carty is the representative for a larger local family descended from Nelson Burton, an enslaved laborer at Gamble Plantation. While our discussions are ongoing, her primary concern is the inclusion of the enslaved people and their lives in the plantation's story at the site. She has advised that the family wishes for the installation of interpretation and signage that explicitly focuses on the history of their ancestor and the other enslaved families. She, along with her family, also wish to be directly included in decisions about how their heritage is presented at the site. We are currently advocating for this perspective and the inclusion of descendant voices in our conversations with Florida State Parks.

Finally, in 2021, we directed our efforts toward a multivocal and community-oriented series of discussions to pressure the State of Florida to change the narrative at the site. With the support of a Florida Humanities Community Project grant, we held a series of four free virtual public symposia entitled the Monuments, Markers, and Memory Symposium Series (https://www.facebook.com/monumentsandmemorycollective/).

The events, which involved hundreds of virtual attendees, critically explored power, politics, and activism around public monuments and memorials. This series united artists, academics, activists, politicians, organizations, institutions, descendant and local communities to address public memory, heritage, and memorialization, and promote restorative justice, social equity, and legislative action. The series centered on the Gamble Plantation, with one of the events held at the site to challenge the State of Florida to transform the narrative at the park to focus on the history of the enslaved community, to install a public memorial to these individuals, and to change the name to remove the memorial to Benjamin.

A new community of individuals interested in reframing the narrative at Gamble Plantation was created from these efforts and stands in direct opposition to those who are committed to the maintenance of the Lost Cause narrative. At present, however, these two groups have had limited interaction, existing primarily in separate spheres. Conflicts have primarily arisen via comments on our social media platforms. As the UDC currently controls the narrative at the park, which is codified in Florida law, efforts toward restorative justice have largely been stifled, but we continue to seek avenues to remove the law and change the interpretive focus at the plantation.

The vital interactions and discussions from the public days, outreach to local communities, work with descendants, and the *Monuments* series have allowed us to produce a community-focused and inclusive narrative for the site, which focuses on the lives of enslaved laborers. While change is slow, we are in conversation with Park management and Florida State Parks to develop a revised history for the site, offering them the following suggestions based on our research and experience.

Transforming the Narrative: A Landscape Biography of Enslavement at Gamble Plantation

As it stands, the entire physical space of this plantation exists as a monument to Judah P. Benjamin. We argue, in line with most contemporary academic and activist perspectives on plantation spaces (Jackson 2012; McDavid 1997), that the site should instead be established as a memorial to the enslaved at the site. While the final report is currently in progress, we are recommending the following narrative to the State of Florida. Based on archaeological and his-

Table 7.1. Gamble Plantation Enslaved Laborer Demographics, from 1850 and 1860 United States Census Slave Schedules

	1850			1860		
AGE (YEARS)	MALE	FEMALE	TOTAL	MALE	FEMALE	TOTAL
0–5	6	1	7	14	25	39
6–10	4	2	6	12	13	25
11–15	8	4	12	4	7	11
16–20	6	8	14	16	5	21
21–25	0	2	2	10	14	24
26–30	1	8	9	4	11	15
31–35	4	3	7	4	4	8
36–40	3	0	3	5	1	6
41–45	2	0	2	5	3	8
46–50	1	2	3	2	7	9
Over 50	4	0	4	19	5	24
Total	39	30	69	95	95	190

torical research, along with the knowledge generated through community engagement, our proposal to the state centers the plantation landscape through the embodied history of the enslaved families who inhabited this space. The remaining plantation structures and ruins are, of course, visible and clear reminders of those held in bondage at the site, but there remain other, more subtle patterns on the landscape that are legacies of slavery at Gamble Plantation. The drainage canals dug by enslaved laborers, for example, continue to alter the ecology of the area to this day. In addition to impacts on the ecological landscape, there were also impacts on the archaeological landscape. The vast quantity of raw material needed for construing tabby brick suggests that shells were likely resourced from Native American midden mounds in the vicinity of the plantation.

In the remaining pages, we present the reader with a landscape biography, the story of the enslaved as told through the built environment of the site, as a way to re-integrate the lives and experiences of the enslaved into the history of Gamble Plantation. Demographic information about the enslaved population was tabulated from the 1850 and 1860 federal census slave schedules, which list each person's age, sex, and race (Table 7.1). The average age of all individuals was 23 years old. Individuals between the ages of 11 and 20 made up 38 percent of the total population. According to the 1860 federal census, 21 children were born between the sale of the plantation to Cofield and Davis in 1858 and the time the census was recorded. The total number of enslaved people increased from 69 in 1850 to 190 in 1860. Based on our analysis of these documents, the population of Gamble Plantation was comprised predominantly of many young families. The 1860 slave schedule lists 52 cabins on the Gamble property. It is likely, therefore, that each cabin housed an individual family, likely nuclear, with some extended family members. The location of the slave village remains unknown, although the historical record provides some clues. Documentary accounts, including a purported reproduction of a hand-drawn map by Gamble, indicate that the cabins were situated several hundred meters east of the Sugar Mill. The results of the LiDAR suggest there are some potential features in this location (Figure 7.2).

Unfortunately, the land is currently private and inaccessible for testing. The village, however, would have been the central space of community building for the enslaved. Historians characterize slavery in Florida by the maintenance of durable family units, localized and internal economies, and self-sufficiency (Landers 2003). The remote location of the plantation, along with Gamble's records, suggest that the enslaved grew a variety of crops for the plantation, many likely in gardens in and around the cabins. Livestock pens and chicken coups may have lined the village as well. Battle-Baptiste (2011, 48) suggests that the "captive household" is the primary unit of analysis in the archaeology of enslavement, and that these domestic systems allowed enslaved communities to "create, structure and maintain a cohesive and nurturing domestic space." Here, while we do not have access yet to enslaved households, we are proposing that Florida State Parks change the interpretation at the site by memorializing the enslaved community.

Land Clearance and Modification

We estimate that the enslaved laborers were tasked with clearing approximately 1,600 acres of dense Florida hammock (Figure 7.3a). This land was primarily transformed into canefields, but also contained additional agricultural grounds and living areas (Gamble 1888). Gamble's (1888) own words depict the intensive labor involved in this process:

> I carried down an additional force . . . and continued from year to year to increase the laborers. The labor of clearing these lands and fitting them for cultivation exceeded any of my past experience in clearing the primeval forests of Middle Florida.

At Gamble's command, the enslaved also dug 16 miles of canals to create drainage, forever altering the marshy landscape along the river. These canals are still visible and functioning to this day. Enslaved laborers turned what was once a swamp into well-drained and productive farmland.

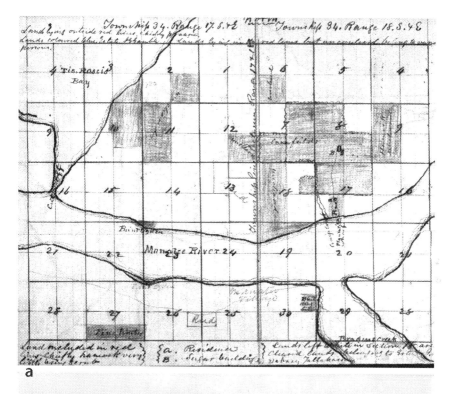

Figure 7.3. *A*, Robert Gamble's map of the Gamble plantation on the Manatee River. Courtesy of Manatee County Public Library Historical Digital Collections. *B*, Gamble mansion before restoration, ca. 1915–1917. Courtesy of Manatee County Public Library Historical Digital Collections.

The Plantation Mansion

The Greek Revival mansion was built by the labor of the enslaved between 1844 and 1850 (Figure 7.3b). It is a massive two-story structure, measuring 41 × 93ft, with an attached cistern. The opulent structure was meant to display the wealth and class of Gamble to any visitors to the site. Along the northern edge of the structure is a detached section, with a kitchen and additional room on the first floor, and two rooms on the second floor. The enslaved cooks and domestic servants occupied these spaces, but are not mentioned during the mansion tour or in the museum. Regrettably, this is typical of many plantations in the South (Deetz 2017).

Sugar Mill and Sugar Processing

In the 1850s, Gamble received large bank loans to construct a massive steam-powered sugar mill (Figure 7.4). According to Gamble (1888), bricks were made on site by enslaved workers from both locally sourced yellow clay, and tabby. Unfortunately, skilled Black laborers are too often overlooked in histories of plantation architecture (Jackson 2012; Vlach 2014). Gamble (1888) described the brick construction of his sugar mill:

> The mill-house 40 × 40, walls 18 feet high; boiling-house 40 × 40, walls 16 feet high; cooling-house 40 × 40, walls 12 feet high; draining-house 40 × 60, walls 8 feet high. All of these bricks were made on the spot and by my own force, and with the exception of one White workman, as boss bricklayer, they were all laid by my own negroes; the most intelligent being selected and under the tuition and guidance of Mr. Godard, who was one of the "armed occupationists" and a master workman, they did good and loyal work.

Enslaved African Americans cleared the fields, planted and harvested the sugar cane that was brought to the mill, and processed the cane into molasses. Processing sugar requires a number of labor-intensive steps: chopping the cane, grinding, and then heating the resulting liquid until sugar crystallization occurs. The labor cost of producing sugar would have been astronomical had Gamble, or other plantation owners, actually paid their laborers.

Gamble's sugar mill was powered by cutting-edge steam technology. He had two 50 horsepower steam engines to drive the cane mill. Boilers were used to evaporate cane juice with steam pans for granulating the sugar. A separate steam engine ran his grist and sawmill and supplied water to the boilers (Schene 1972). These early steam technologies, operated by the enslaved laborers, were very dangerous and ran the risk of explosion, due to a lack of

Figure 7.4. Drone image of the Gamble plantation sugar mill ruins. Created by Steven Fernandez, 2019.

airtight engineering. The working conditions inside the mill were noted by Gamble in a newspaper article (1888):

> While the mill was in motion a solid mass of cane five feet wide and 14 in. high passed continuously between rollers, and was so effectually crushed that the bagasse as it passed from the rollers was nearly as dry as tinder, cut in two at every joint, and if applied to the mouth while inhaling would produce partial suffocation by its dry impalpable powder.

The enslaved laborers would have worked in extreme heat, with explosive machinery, in a building full of tinder, all while being suffocated by an "impalpable powder." There is no doubt that these conditions would have had a huge impact on the health of the enslaved. Archaeological work is ongoing at the sugar mill to better understand the lived experiences of the enslaved whose labor is embodied in the factory ruins.

Conclusion

In the nearby cities of Bradenton and Tampa, the removal of Confederate memorials in public spaces has been a controversial issue since 2017. The chapter of the UDC at Gamble, have been staunch advocates against the "erasure of southern heritage," and are frequently at the forefront of rallies attempting to "save" Confederate monuments. We are faced with the task of challenging many of the falsehoods presented through the narrative of the Lost Cause. The current master-slave narrative at the plantation site is designed to uphold systems of power that benefit Whites and perpetuate the status quo (Jackson 2012). As McGuire (2008:8) notes, "Archaeology entails a practice that can be used to advance the interests of many communities through a range of endeavors from the technical to the interpretative, from the practical to the creative."

To date, we have faced significant challenges in pushing for changes to the park's interpretation. We have noticed some progress, however, within the park's infrastructure. The park's Citizen Support Organization, the Gamble Plantation Preservation Alliance, for example, recently installed a sign with an outline of a generalized slave cabin. This group is comprised mostly of UDC members. While the design is based loosely on depictions from historical accounts, and not informed by archaeology at the site, it is a positive step. Further, due largely to public pressure, our *Monuments* series, and recommendations based on our work, Park management is working with a consulting agency (the name of the agency has not been disclosed) to hold community meetings to hear public opinions on the future of the park.

At Gamble Plantation, archaeology can be a medium through which the historical narrative at Gamble can become more inclusive, based on the realities of the experiences of those who lived there. We know little about what life was like for enslaved peoples in this region of Florida, which was extremely isolated and sparsely populated in the nineteenth century. Moving forward, we are working to conduct additional archaeological testing adjacent to the sugar works, an area that has had minimal survey or testing. This parcel of land likely holds information regarding the labor and daily experiences of the enslaved at Gamble. We also suggest further archaeological research of areas we have identified as possible slave quarters. Of course, this continued research is completely dependent upon when, or if, access is ever granted by private landowners. An archaeological investigation of the homes of the enslaved workers would be invaluable for shedding light upon their daily lives at Gamble Plantation, including how the houses and village were organized, questions concerning subsistence, the structure of labor, and more.

References

Alderman, Derek H., and Joshua F. J. Inwood.
    2013   Landscapes of Memory and Socially Just Futures. In *The Wiley-Blackwell Companion to Cultural Geography*. Nuala Christina Johnson, Richard H. Schein, and Jamie Winders, eds. Pp. 186–197. Hoboken, NJ: Wiley-Blackwell.

Baker, Henry A.
    1987   *An Archaeological Auger Survey at the Gamble Plantation State Historic Site*. Bureau of Archaeological Research. Submitted to Florida Department of Natural Resources. Copies available from Florida Master Site File.

Baker, Henry, and Curtiss Peterson
    1978   *An Archaeological Survey of The Gamble Plantation, Manatee County, Florida*. Bureau of Archaeological Research. Submitted to Florida Department of Natural Resources. Copies available from Florida Master Site File.

Battle-Baptiste, W.
    2011   *Black Feminist Archaeology*. New York, NY: Routledge.

Clerk of the Circuit Court
    1855–1889   Manatee County Deed Book A. Clerk of the Circuit Court, Manatee County Courthouse, Bradenton, FL.

Cox, K. L.
    2003   *Dixies Daughters: The United Daughters of the Confederacy and the Preservation of Confederate Culture*. Gainesville, FL: University Press of Florida.

Deetz, K. F.
    2017   *Bound to the Fire: How Virginia's Enslaved Cooks Helped Invent American Cuisine*. Lexington, KY: University Press of Kentucky.

Foster, Gaines

1987   *Ghosts of the Confederacy: Defeat, the Lost Cause and the Emergence of the New South.* New York, NY: Oxford University Press.

Gamble, Robert, Jr.
1888   Florida as a Sugar State. *Tallahassee Floridian,* 28 September: 8.

Hartley, R. C.
2021   *Monumental Harm: Reckoning with Jim Crow Era Confederate Monuments.* Columbia, SC: University of South Carolina Press.

Jackson, Antoinette
2012   *Speaking for the Enslaved: Heritage Interpretation at Antebellum Plantation Sites.* New York, NY: Routledge.

Landers, Jane
2003   African Contributions to Florida's Northeastern Plantations. *The Florida Anthropologist* 56(3):183–88.

Litteral, S. Matthew
2019   "An Archaeological Investigation of Enslavement at Gamble Plantation" Unpublished Master's Thesis, Department of Anthropology, University of South Florida.

Manatee County Public Library,
1859   Cofield and Davis's Deed to Gamble Mansion, Manuscript, Historical Digital Collections, M01-04835-A-M01-04843-A, Bradenton, Florida.

Matthews, Janet B.
1983   *Edge of Wilderness: A Settlement History of Manatee River and Sarasota Bay.* Sarasota, FL: Coastal Press.

McDavid, Carol
1997   Descendants, Decisions, and Power: The Public Interpretation of the Archaeology of the Levi Jordan Plantation. *Historical Archaeology* 31(3):114–131.

McGuire, Randall H.
2008   *Archaeology as Political Action.* Berkeley, CA: University of California Press.

Rivers, Larry
2000   Slavery in Florida: Territorial Days to Emancipation. Gainesville, FL: University Press of Florida.

Schene, Michael
1972   *Gamble Mansion Project Paper.* Unpublished manuscript, Division of Recreation and Parks. Tallahassee, Fl.
1981   *The Daring Escape of Judah P. Benjamin.* Manatee County Clerks Archives. Bradenton, Fl.

Silpa, Felicia Bianca
2012   Reflections of Virginia on the Manatee River. *Historical Archaeology* 46(1):74–93.

State of Florida
1925   General Laws of Florida, Chapter 10293, No. 271. Legislature of Florida, Tallahassee, FL.

Tebeau, Charlton W.
1991   *A History of Florida.* Miami, FL: University of Miami Press.

Vlach, John Michael

2014 The Witness of African American Folkways. In *The Oxford Handbook of the African American Slave Narrative*. John Ernest, ed. Pp. 133. Oxford, UK: Oxford University Press.

Weitz, Seth
2009 Defending the Old South: The Myth of the Lost Cause and Political Immorality in Florida, 1865–1968. *The Historian* 71(1):79–92.

Wiggins, Jim
2003 *Ellenton: Its Early Years.* Jim Wiggins. Manatee County Clerks Archives. Bradenton, FL.

8

Hidden in Public

The Power of the Memorial Landscape and the Archaeology of a Cornerstone Deposit from Louisville's Confederate Monument

M. Jay Stottman

There are thousands of Confederate monuments in America, with most being in the communities that comprised the former Confederacy (Widener 1982). Such monuments reside in the memorial landscapes of cemeteries, public streets, and the lawns of government buildings, standing as a reminder of the South's "Lost Cause" and as a symbol of the power structure that ensued (Winberry 1983; Leib 2006). In the wake of recent political rhetoric and racial tensions, communities are removing these monuments and sparking a national discussion about race, history, and heritage. Within this context, the City of Louisville, Kentucky removed its only dedicated Confederate monument in 2016. During its disassembly, a metal box was found sealed in its base. In this chapter, I examine the history of this monument and its public role in the battle for the memorial landscape and in normalizing the revisionist "Lost Cause" movement. An archaeological analysis of the box and its contents tells a more personal story about the women responsible for its construction and the motivations behind it. I believe that a deeper understanding of the purpose of such monuments and the story of how they came to be can help society in the present grapple with how to reconcile memorial landscapes.

Post–Civil War Louisville

When one examines the dates of when most Confederate monuments were erected, the period between 1890 and 1920 was the most prolific, especially for those established on public property (Widener 1982). This pattern prompts the question of why there was such an effort to create these monuments more than 30 years after the Civil War. It is important in our analysis to understand what was happening in cities like Louisville during this time.

Louisville had conflicted identities during the Civil War, being a major base of operations for the Union's Western theater, but also being a pro-slavery community. It was culturally a Southern city with a Northern economy (Yater 1987). After the war, Louisville became a major manufacturing center, but its Southern sympathies held Louisville back politically and culturally. Although the South had lost the war, ex-Confederates had a secure hold on Louisville's political landscape, as prominent families and business leaders exerted their influence. Race relations in post–Civil War Louisville would follow the struggles that many Southern cities experienced during that time (Yater 1987; Kleber 2001:798).

In the thirty years after the Civil War, Louisville saw a dramatic increase in its African American population as formerly enslaved people sought work and to connect with families (Wright 1985). The influx of African Americans, a tradition of slavery, and the domination of local politics by ex-Confederate Democrats led to an environment that strained race relations and stoked the fears of Whites. Many Whites feared that African Americans could gain more power by taking jobs, swinging elections, infiltrating traditionally White housing, or just by becoming educated. Up until the 1880s, these fears were largely unwarranted, as the traditional racial positions within society held consistent, and racial segregation practice was rather inconsistent. However, by the 1890s, Whites made a more concerted effort to institutionalize segregation with the establishment of Jim Crow laws and policies (Wright 1985; Kleber 2001:798).

Although African Americans had the right to vote, they were unable to disrupt the Democrat's stranglehold on politics and racist policies. However, African Americans occasionally fought back against segregation through the court system, eventually winning cases in housing during the early 1900s. Despite those victories, Whites in Louisville asserted their control in less overt ways through the economy and education, which historian George Wright (1985:48) has dubbed "Louisville's polite racism." It is within this racially charged time of Louisville's history, where ex-Confederates controlled the politics and shaped public opinion, that the Confederate monument was conceived and constructed. As we have recently seen, many of the fears that set the stage for Confederate monument building still exist and are used to help fuel racist attitudes and policies that are part of the debates about these monuments today.

Creating Louisville's Confederate Monument

In the twenty years following the end of the Civil War, local women's monument associations had the task of honoring the soldiers who died for the Confederacy. Later, national organizations, such as the United Daughters of the Confederacy (1896), took the lead in this effort (Janney 2008). In Louisville, a local group looked to honor the Confederacy in grand public style.

Susan Preston Hepburn led the effort to form and presided over the Kentucky Women's Confederate Monument Association, which raised the money to build Louisville's Confederate monument (Kleber 2001:261). Hepburn had many ties to the Confederacy, as her brother was a general, and her nephew, William Preston Johnston, was personal aid to the president of the Confederacy, Jefferson Davis. The women of the Monument Association were well connected to the ex-Confederates who wielded power in Louisville and used that power in their effort to erect Louisville's first and largest public monument. The idea of creating a monument to honor Confederate soldiers in Louisville began in 1887 during a meeting for decorating the graves of Confederate soldiers (Kleber 2001:261). However, there were at least some efforts to raise money for honoring Confederate soldiers in Louisville as early as 1882 (Courier-Journal 1895a:8).

It is unclear how the effort to decorate graves transformed into the construction of a public monument, but it appears that the Monument Association noticed what was happening elsewhere in the South. From that first meeting, a nearly ten-year effort began to raise money and construct a monument. The success of this effort was a testament to Louisville's Southern sympathies and the power that ex-Confederates wielded in Louisville's politics. The members of the Monument Association held social events, including theater productions, music concerts, boat excursions, lectures, and auctions to raise the $12,000.00 needed to construct a monument (Courier-Journal 1890:6, 1891a:6, 1892:12).

Having raised most of the funds for the construction of the monument, a competition for its design was held in 1894, which was won by Enid Yandell. Yandell was a Louisville native and a pioneering female sculptor. Although she had already won prestigious art awards, her selection to design Louisville's monument was very controversial (Baird 1988). It spurred accusations of favoritism by the Monument Association's leadership, which included Yandell's mother. However, the controversy was less about nepotism and more about the choice of a woman to design a war memorial and the design itself, which featured a statue of Lady Liberty rather than a soldier. Yandell's contract was revoked and shortly afterward, she moved to Paris, France, where she became a successful and recognized sculptor (Baird 1988).

Eventually, the contract for the monument was awarded to Michael Muldoon, a local maker and supplier of monuments and headstones (Courier-Journal 1894:6). At the time, Muldoon had just completed a design for the Confederate monument on the State Capitol grounds in Raleigh, North Carolina (Kleber 2001:261). Muldoon aggressively pursued work for Confederate monuments, advertising in veteran's magazines and other publications. He went on to win contracts to erect several large Confederate monuments throughout the country. Muldoon's design for the Louisville monument was nearly identical to Raleigh's, with only some slight variation in column shape. The monument featured a large granite base with a 70 ft. tall granite column on top of which is a bronze statue of an infantry soldier. On either side of the base are bronze statues of an artilleryman and a cavalryman. Muldoon created the granite portions of the monument, while the bronze statues were sculpted and cast in Germany by Ferdinand Von Miller (Figure 8.1) (Kleber 2001:261).

Unlike many other Confederate monuments, which were erected in cemeteries and on courthouse lawns, the place desired for Louisville's monument was a busy street where it would be most visible. Ultimately, a street in an undeveloped part of the city near the House of Refuge, a home for juvenile delinquents, was selected. Although this location seemed remote, the Monument Association recognized that it had great potential because it served as the entranceway to a new park designed by famed landscape architect Frederick Law Olmsted (Yater 1987).

The cornerstone for the monument was laid during a ceremony on 25 May 1895 and it was dedicated on 30 July 1895, about two months after Muldoon's other monument in Raleigh. Within ten years of the dedication, the area surrounding the monument was fully developed, fulfilling its promise as the busy visible site that the Association had desired. However, as automobile traffic became more commonplace, motorists complained that the monument was a traffic hazard. Also, it was expensive to maintain, and thus, the City unsuccessfully attempted to remove the monument in the 1930s and 1950s (Kleber 2001).

A significant change to the area occurred in 1923 when the University of Louisville moved its main campus to the city's old House of Refuge property. Over time, the university expanded around the monument. By the late 1990s, the monument's prominent location on campus drew the attention of students and faculty, who pointed out its contradiction to the university's mission of

Figure 8.1. Photograph of the monument just after dedication in 1895. Image ULPAP_0036 R.G. Potter Collection, Photographic Archives, University of Louisville, Louisville, Kentucky.

diversity. Soon discussions began as to how to address the issue. Because the university did not own the monument, it could not remove it, so in 2002, the university approved a plan to contextualize it. The result of that effort was the Charles H. Parrish Jr. Freedom Park, constructed in 2012. The park's design used the monument as a discussion piece about race and the history of African Americans in Louisville. Despite the attempt to contextualize the monument, it still commanded a prominent place on campus. However, by

2016, a rise in racial political rhetoric and racially motivated violence by white supremacists across the country spurred a movement to remove Confederate monuments. As political pressure grew to remove Louisville's monument, the City made plans to disassemble the monument and give it to the small rural community of Brandenburg, Kentucky.

Confederate Monuments and the Battle for the Memorial Landscape

Although the initial idea behind Louisville's Confederate Monument was to honor those who fought and died for the Confederacy, there is much more to this monument and others like it. Scholars have suggested that such memorials were about control over public memory and power (Shackel 2003a; Leib 2006). They discuss such memorials in reference to the relationship of public memory and identity to the landscape (Dwyer and Alderman 2008). The landscape, its physical elements, and the performances or actions that take place there can create, maintain, and normalize public memory and cultural identity (Bodner 1992; Schein 1997; 2003). Thus, those who shape the landscape can create or change public memory and then normalize that memory. Control over the message of the landscape seizes power for those it represents.

The effort of ex-Confederates to rewrite the narrative of the South during the Civil War as a chivalrous and gallant society that defended its home and honor has been called the "Lost Cause" movement (Wilson 1980; Foster 1987). Conspicuously absent from this narrative are the uglier aspects of the South's legacy, such as slavery. Typically, history is written by the winners of the war, but ex-Confederates not only rewrote the history of their past, but they also used the landscape to create the heritage of their present and future. Thirty years after the Civil War, ex-Confederates were engaged in a battle for the memorial landscape not only to remember their dead, but also to promote their revisionist narrative and display their political power. They took to this cause by creating memorial landscapes, as evidenced by the preponderance of Confederate monuments erected after 1890 and their proliferation into the public spaces of many communities across this nation. However, the creation of these landscapes was dependent on attaining sufficient power to assemble public and political support for the efforts; thus, it is important to understand the relationship of power dynamics to such landscapes (Savage 1994). The public and political climate of Louisville at the time was conducive to a battle for the memorial landscape.

The battle for the memorial landscape played out in a variety of ways as both Confederate and Union veterans, such as the Grand Army of the Republic, sought to memorialize their fallen. Both built monuments at famous battlefields and in cemeteries. Union veteran groups focused more on performative memorials, such as holding parades, encampments, band concerts, and events honoring their dead and their victory, while the Confederates focused on monuments (Courier-Journal 1895b: C3). The Confederate Women's Monument Association and the local chapter of the Grand Army of the Republic engaged in a battle for the coveted gateway of the new park. The Association petitioned the Parks Commission in January 1891 for the site of their monument. Just a month later, the Grand Army of the Republic petitioned to build a memorial arch honoring Union soldiers at the same location. Eventually, the Monument Association's petition won over the selection committee, which included some prominent ex-Confederates and friends of its members (Courier-Journal 1891b:8).

The Confederates may have lost the war, but they won the battle for the memorial landscape in Louisville and all throughout the South due in large part to the power and influence that ex-Confederates wielded in many communities (Savage 1994). The monument was a symbol of power that was manifested in a racially unequal political and economic environment amid segregation laws, and it communicated that power to the public (Wright 1985). It served not only to memorialize soldiers, but also to remind the public in the present and the future of who had power and control over the narrative of history and of society in the present.

Although it can be assumed that because the Grand Army of the Republic's arch was never built, the challenges for the memorial landscape ended there, this was not the case. The landscape is never static; it evolves and changes, and so do its meanings, such as is the case with the Confederate Monument (Schein 1997). Although the monument itself had changed little up until its dismantling, the landscape surrounding it had changed, mainly with the construction of Freedom Park. Despite these changes, it survived and remained on the landscape, delivering its message.

The end of the twentieth century saw a significant change to the nation's memorial landscape, with the erection of memorials to the Civil Rights Movement honoring the events and people associated with this pivotal struggle for race equality. These monuments represented a direct challenge to the dominance of Confederate memorials on the landscape (Upton 2015). These new additions to the memorial landscape challenged the racial narratives of Confederate monuments. Despite the changing landscape, the power of these monuments to deliver their message persisted until recently, when power finally began to shift, and Confederate narratives began to be challenged and dismantled. The battle for public memory speaks to the importance that the materiality of the landscape has compared to less permanent performance memorials like that favored by the Grand Army of the Republic who lost the battle for Louisville's memorial landscape.

Archaeology of Louisville's Confederate Monument

Archaeologists have long been interested in monuments and landscapes, as they have studied their materiality and meanings (Shackel 2001; 2003b). Although some have written and blogged about the recent efforts to remove them, one could ask how an archaeologist becomes involved in the removal of one of these monuments (Lees and Gaske 2014; Mullins 2017; Saitta 2017). My experience with the archaeology of these monuments began with a small brass box recovered from the cornerstone of Louisville's Confederate Monument.

While doing research at the City's archives months after the monument was taken down, I was approached by the archivist who asked if I would like to see the box. I was presented with a copy of an 1895 newspaper article that listed the items that were reportedly placed in the box on the day of the cornerstone ceremony and a badly damaged brass box (Courier-Journal 1895a:8). Inside of the box was a brownish mass. The archivist asked if I would examine the box's contents, which I gladly did.

The condition of the box was very poor. There was mortar adhering to it, some of which conformed to the shape of the large dents in the thin metal. It was clear that the box had been crushed when it was sealed in the stone base of the monument on that day in 1895. Thus, the box was compromised from day one, allowing the infiltration of water, which severely deteriorated its contents. Fortunately, the newspaper article provided an extensive listing of the items intended to be placed in the box. Unfortunately, most of the items listed were made of paper and textiles, resulting in the mass that occupied the bottom of the box.

Carefully excavating through this mass, I was able to sort through the objects and verify that most listed in the article were present (Table 8.1). However, some objects listed were not there, mainly Confederate money and colors. Despite the poor condition of the paper, I was able to see enough of the text to verify that nearly all listed in the article were present. No photographic images were identified, but heavy bond paper with a border indicated the presence of photographs. Most of the textile objects listed in the article were identified, though in poor condition.

Metal and broken flat glass objects were also found, including some not listed in the article. U.S. coins minted in the 1890s were the only metal objects found that were listed in the article. Other objects not listed in the article

Table 8.1. Objects Found in Box by Category

Category	Object
Context	U.S. copper penny (1895)
	U.S. copper 5-cent piece (1890s)
	U.S. silver dime (1892)
	U.S. silver quarter dollar (1894)
	U.S. silver half dollar (1894)
	U.S. silver dollar (1892)
	Silver spoon commemorating Daniel Boone
	English language local newspapers
	German language local newspapers
Personal	Photo of Susan Preston Hepburn, Monument Association president (probable)
	A metal and glass photo stand
	A card by Rosa Johnson Robinson
	Monument fundraiser badges
	Oxford Bible given by Mrs. Howard Griswold
Message	Poem by Mrs. Sophie Fox Sea with photo of Jefferson Davis
	William Preston Johnston's mourning scarf
	A brass tube containing Jefferson Davis's cigar
	A likeness of Gen. Robert E. Lee (probable photograph)
	A Vicksburg newspaper from 1863 on wallpaper
	The story "Who's the Patriot" by Mrs. Flora McDonald

included a sealed brass tube, a silver spoon, and parts of a glass and metal picture stand. The spoon commemorated Daniel Boone and was made by local jewelers Rodgers and Pottinger (Figure 8.2). They had donated a *jardinière* to be auctioned at one of the Monument Association fundraisers (Courier-Journal 1892:12). The brass tube was 10 in. long and enclosed on each end with a screw cap (Figure 8.2). Unfortunately, it could not be opened without damaging the tube and potentially damaging the object inside. Based on the size and shape of the tube, it likely held the cigar belonging to Jefferson Davis listed in the article.

After I examined the box, its contents, and the context of its creation, it was clear that it was a "foundation deposit," "cornerstone repository," or what I refer to as a cornerstone deposit (Jarvis 2003:263). Such deposits are ceremonial objects used to commemorate a building or site, such as during the cornerstone ceremony known to have taken place for the monument. The choices made for what was included in the deposit often speak for and about the people who built the structure. Such is the case with the objects recovered from the Confederate Monument's cornerstone deposit. When coupled with an examination of the history of the monument itself and of its context, these

The Archaeology of a Cornerstone Deposit from Louisville's Confederate Monument · 135

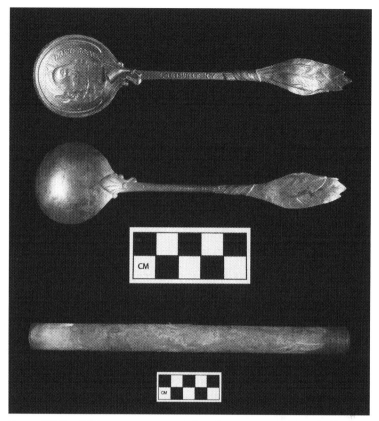

Figure 8.2. Daniel Boone commemorative silver spoon and a sealed brass tube likely containing a cigar lit by Jefferson Davis. Photos by Heyward Wilkinson.

objects can provide a better understanding of the meaning and intent of the monument and the women who had it constructed.

Analysis and Interpretations

My analysis of the objects from the deposit included the development of categories that facilitate an understanding of what they represented to the Monument Association members and the "Lost Cause" movement. I devised three categories based on the typical characteristics of such deposits: context, personal, and message (Table 8.1). The context category represents the objects that are indicative of the time and place of the cornerstone deposit. These objects are typical of such deposits, which seek to transfer knowledge through time and inform people in the future (Jarvis 2003). The personal cat-

Figure 8.3. Ribbon from a badge printed with "CONFEDERATE ASSOCIATION OF KY May 11, 1891." Photo by Christina Pappas.

egory represents items that are related to the Monument Association members responsible for the cornerstone deposit and the monument. The message category represents items that speak to the purpose of the monument and its intended message, as were described in the newspaper article: "The corner stone box . . . will contain many relics connected with the South's great men and her Lost Cause" (Courier-Journal 1895a:8).

Context category items include contemporary newspapers, U.S. coins from the 1890s, and a silver spoon with the image of famous Kentuckian Daniel Boone and stamped with "Louisville, Kentucky," which are reflective of the time and place of the monument's construction. Like other such cornerstone deposits, they commemorate the time and place of the monument's context.

Personal category items include the fundraising badges, a photograph, bible, and card. The badges commemorate the extensive effort of the members of the Association needed to plan and construct the monument (Figure 8.3). The remnants of a photograph and stand were likely associated with Susan Preston Hepburn, the president of the Association. Its inclusion speaks to her importance and leadership in the effort to build the monument. The presence of Mrs. Griswold's bible is indicative of the importance of religion to the Monument Association members and that their mandate to honor the Confederate "Lost Cause" narrative and perpetuate that their political power was perhaps of divine purpose (Wilson 1980). The card placed in the box by Rosa Johnson Robinson, the youngest member of the Association, suggests that the support of a new generation was important for reproducing the narrative of ex-Confederates and ensuring that it was perpetuated.

The Message category items are connected to famous Confederates and the "Lost Cause" narrative. The poem by Monument Association member Mrs. Rosie Fox Sea honoring Jefferson Davis at the time of his death, along with his accompanying photo, shows that the members desired to connect their effort directly to important Confederates. This also was the case for the brass tube containing a cigar reportedly lit and left by Jefferson Davis during his last visit to Louisville and William Preston Johnston's mourning scarf that he wore to Jefferson Davis's funeral, which established a connection between the monument and the leader of the South and its cause (Figure 8.2).

The memoirs of Dr. Hobson, who was General John Hunt Morgan's chaplain, represent a connection to a Kentucky native and a revered general of the Confederacy. The inclusion of "a likeness of Gen. Robert E. Lee," likely a photograph, also sought to connect the monument to the most famous general of the Confederacy (Courier-Journal 25 May 1895a). The presence of the manuscript, "Who's the Patriot," by Mrs. Flora McDonald, who held the first monument fundraising event, speaks volumes about the intent of the monument as a purveyor of ex-Confederate revisionist narratives, which portrays the South's cause as just and patriotic. The presence of an 1863 Vicksburg newspaper about the battle is the only item related specifically to an event where soldiers were lost in battle.

The items found in the box and those reported to have been placed in the box show a deep connection with important leaders of the Confederacy and the "Lost Cause" narrative. Thus, the cornerstone offerings do reveal a meaning that extends beyond the memorialization of the regular soldiers of the Confederacy to the perpetuation of the "Lost Cause" narrative. These items clearly represent and support the Monument Association's role in this narrative and speak to the effort to create the monument as a symbol of that movement. However, the placement of items in the cornerstone box directly related to the Monument Association's effort and the women who made it happen exposes the role of gender in the Confederate monument movement and in the new Southern identity.

There is no doubt that women were the driving force behind monument building and the crafting of the "Lost Cause" movement (Gulley 1993; Janney 2008; Cox 2019). Although their efforts in this movement have long been acknowledged, women are largely invisible on the memorial landscape that they created. Scholars have debated the effects of the Civil War and the proceeding rebranding of Southern identity on the role of women, such that these events expanded women's roles to more prominent leadership positions in Southern society. However, such roles were temporary, and ultimately, the patriarchal traditions of the South reinforced the existing perceptions of women as supporting or propping up the men of the Confederacy. This role is perhaps most evident in the Enid Yandell controversy over the design of Louisville's monument, where it was seen as appropriate that women could lead the effort to create the monument, but not so for a woman to design or be featured on it. Furthermore, women could help create the memorial landscape, but not be memorialized in it. Although invisible in the memorial landscape, the women of the Association chose to memorialize their efforts with the objects hidden within the monument.

The cornerstone deposit was seen by these women as a space where they were equal to the men they honored. Susan Preston Hepburn is given nearly equal recognition as Robert E. Lee. The poem and patriotic story written by Monument Association women also speak to their unheralded role in the perpetuation of the "Lost Cause" narrative through literature and education. Women not only were responsible for the erection of monuments but also the production of much of the "Lost Cause" literature that was used to educate the youth about this revisionist history (Robins 2003). Through their analysis of battles and commander's actions in their writings, women reinforced their position within the patriarchal Southern society by protecting the reputations of the South's leaders and creating the gallant, heroic, and patriotic underpinnings of the "Lost Cause" narrative. Such writings had an impact on how children viewed the war and understood the South's cause (Robins 2003).

What is also interesting about the cornerstone deposit is what was reported to be in the box, but not found, especially the Confederate colors and money, which represents the sovereignty of the Confederacy. No evidence of these items was found in the box, and it can be concluded these particular items were not placed there as planned, which leads to questions of why?

The contemplation of placing the Confederate colors and money perhaps suggests some debate about their inclusion and their meaning. It is impossible to know why the items were excluded, but it does not seem coincidental that both were the only ones on the list related to the Confederacy's sovereignty and nationalism during the Civil War. An explanation for their exclusion may be related to Foster's (1987) discussion of the South's acceptance of defeat and minimal interest in creating a nation during the war. Foster suggests that the result of the war was not important to most ex-Confederates, and instead, they were focused on the future and creating a new identity. For symbols of a sovereign Confederate nation to be included in the commemoration of a monument intended to help create a new identity, members of the Monument Association could have seen them as detracting from its purpose to espouse a new Southern identity and remind the public who held the power in Louisville. Or perhaps, because ex-Confederates had such a stranglehold on politics in the South that their focus was on controlling the current Republic rather than building a new nation. This is not to say that Confederate colors or money did not have symbolic value to ex-Confederates at the time, but their omission from the monument's cornerstone deposit could suggest that they did not have the symbolic importance that they would later for Southern identity.

We may never know why these items are missing, but it is clear from the contents of the cornerstone box that the "Lost Cause" narrative and the effort to build the monument, which cements that narrative on the landscape, were of primary importance to those who commemorated the monument. They represented a contemporary battle for the landscape that looked to the future of creating a Southern revisionist narrative. The items from the cornerstone deposit reflect the ideals of perpetuating a new Southern identity in the reality of postbellum America, but they also reflect the role of women in this identity that is not evident on the monument itself despite their effort to create it.

The current disposition of the cornerstone deposit objects is unknown, although they are believed to be in the possession of the City. Though all but the paper has been cleaned and conserved, they are not likely to be seen on display anytime soon, as the political climate will not allow it. They are likely to be hidden away as they were that day in 1895 when they were first placed in the monument. However, their display could become a vehicle for telling the story of the intent and motivations behind the monument's construction.

Conclusions

For over 120 years, Louisville's Confederate monument has been a fixture on the landscape, anchoring the power of the South's "Lost Cause" narrative. Although the political and social context of the 1890s spurred the monument's creation and the messages it communicated, more recently, challenges to its power ultimately led to its dismantling. The call to remove the monument illuminated a variety of perspectives about its present-day meaning. For African Americans, it was a symbol of a painful past and a reminder that White privilege still held power. For many on the University of Louisville campus, it was a confusing mix of history and contradiction within its academic context. Preservationists saw the monument as an historical artifact that can inform the present about the past so as not to repeat it. Some saw it for what it was intended, a symbol of the "Lost Cause" narrative, and they used it to exacerbate current racial tensions and embolden traditional power structures.

These meanings and the arguments to remove or save the monument have been and will continue to be debated as there is a new battle for the memorial

Figure 8.4. The monument's new landscape in Brandenburg, Kentucky. Photo by M. Jay Stottman.

landscape and control over the narrative of history. Through an analysis of Louisville's Confederate Monument's cornerstone deposit and the materiality and power of the landscape, archaeologists have a role in this battle (McGuire 2008; Stottman 2010). Their perspectives on the past and culture and at least this analysis of a cornerstone deposit provides insight into the intent of the women responsible for the conception and construction of the monument. The analysis of the cornerstone deposit clearly shows that creating and perpetuating the "Lost Cause" narrative was very much at the forefront of the effort to build the monument. Furthermore, this analysis also exposes the gendered reality of the new Southern identity and the relegation of the memorialization of women who created it to unseen objects hidden in the public monument.

Regardless, the Confederate Monument no longer dominates the landscape that it once presided over. Its former landscape is more conducive to the university context and safe traffic flow. Perhaps the act of dismantling the monument relieved some of the pain of those who felt oppressed by its messages, but it has done little to shift the power and privilege of those who control the narrative. While the discriminatory inequality within most of our laws has largely been eradicated, the hard work of exposing and equalizing the more obvious and implicit privileges and biases that work against those gains has yet to be realized. The fact that Louisville's Confederate monument was relocated is a testament to that privilege as it now communicates its message over a new landscape in Brandenburg, Kentucky (Figure 8.4). It was recommemorated with new cornerstone offerings during a ceremony that is a modern reinterpretation of the original, complete with Confederate reenactors. The items placed in the monument included business cards, pens, and trinkets from people who wanted to be a part of the monument and perhaps its cause. These items are reflective of a new time, place, and context, but reaffirm the message that the monument's original creators hoped it would. Its relocation demonstrates the power of the memorial landscape and that we still have a long way to go toward achieving social justice for those oppressed by it. Studies such as this analysis of a monument and its cornerstone deposit can change how the public sees monuments and inspire us to question the purpose and motives of why they exist. We can look deeper into how public monuments reflect who we are and where we came from and use the memorial landscape to communicate messages of who we want to be.

References

Baird, Nancy D.
 1988 Enid Yandell: Kentucky Sculptor. *The Filson Club History Quarterly* 62(1):5–31.

Bodner, John
 1992 *Remaking America: Public Memory, Commemoration, and Patriotism in the Twentieth Century*. Princeton, NJ: Princeton University Press.

Courier-Journal
 1890 Confederate Monument Association. *Courier-Journal,* 8 February:6. Louisville, KY.
 1891a Arch or Monument: The Women's Confederate Association Monument Not Yet Agreed Upon, Another Entertainment to be Given for the Fund. *Courier-Journal,* 5 January:6. Louisville, KY.

1891b The Park Board. *Courier-Journal,* 8 April:8. Louisville, KY.

1892 A Pretty Jardiniere: Gift of Messrs. Rodgers & Pottinger to the Confederate Monument Association. *Courier-Journal,* 3 September:12. Louisville, KY.

1894 Mr. Muldoon Says a Word. *Courier-Journal,* 5 October:6. Louisville, KY.

1895a For the Monument, Interesting Relics to be Placed in the Corner-stone. *Courier-Journal,* 25 May:8. Louisville, KY.

1895b Honor to Them: Strong Contingent from Columbia Post No. 706. *Courier-Journal,* 11 September:C3. Louisville, KY.

Cox, Karen L.

2019[2003] Preface to *Dixie's Daughters: The United Daughters of the Confederacy and The Preservation of Confederate Culture.* Gainesville, FL: University Press of Florida.

Dwyer, Owen J., and Derek H. Alderman

2008 Memorial Landscapes: Analytic Questions and Metaphors. *GeoJournal* 73(3): 165–178.

Foster, Gaines M.

1987 *Ghosts of the Confederacy: Defeat, The Lost Cause, and The Emergence of the New South 1865 to 1913.* New York, NY: Oxford University Press.

Janney, Caroline E.

2008 *Burying the Dead but Not the Past: Ladies Memorial Associations and the Lost Cause.* Chapel Hill, NC: University of North Carolina Press.

Jarvis, William E.

2003 *Time Capsules: A Cultural History.* Jefferson, NC: McFarland and Company.

Kleber, John, ed.

2001 *Encyclopedia of Louisville.* Lexington, KY: University Press of Kentucky.

Lees, William B., and Frederick P. Gaske

2014 *Recalling Deeds Immortal: Florida's Monuments to the Civil War.* Gainesville, FL: University Press of Florida.

Leib, Jonathon

2006 The Witting Autobiography of Richmond, Virginia: Arthur Ashe, the Civil War, and Monument Avenue's Racialized Landscape. In *Landscape and Race in the United States.* Richard Schein, ed. Pp. 187–211, New York, NY: Routledge.

McGuire, Randall H.

2008 *Archaeology as Political Action.* Berkeley, CA: University of California Press.

Mullins, Paul

2017 Memory, Monuments, and Confederate Things, Contesting the 21st Century Confederacy: Archaeology and Material Culture. Blog posted 16 June 2017 https://paulmullins.wordpress.com/, accessed 20 September 2020.

Robins, Glen

2003 Lost Cause Motherhood: Southern Women Writers. *Louisiana History: The Journal of the Louisiana Historical Association* 44(3):275–300.

Saitta, Dean

2017 Confederate Statues, Archaeology, and the Soul of Community: Intercultural Urbanism, Blog posted 24 August 2017 http://www.interculturalurbanism.com/, accessed 20 September 2020.

Savage, Kirk
   1994   The Politics of Memory: Black Emancipation and the Civil War Monument. In *Commemorations: The Politics of National Identity*. John R. Gillis, ed. Pp. 127–149. Princeton, NJ: Princeton University Press.

Shackel, Paul A.
   2001   Introduction. In *Myth, Memory, and the Making of the American Landscape*. Paul A. Shackel, ed. Pp. 1–16. Gainesville, FL: University Press of Florida.
   2003a   Archaeology, Memory, and Landscapes of Conflict. *Historical Archaeology* 37(3):3–13.
   2003b   Heyward Shepherd: The Faithful Slave Monument. *Historical Archaeology* 37(3):138–148.

Schein, Richard H.
   1997   The Place of Landscape: A Conceptual Framework for Interpreting an American Scene. *Annals of the Association of American Geographers* 87:660.
   2003   Normative Dimensions of Landscape. In *Everyday America: Cultural Landscape Studies after J.B. Jackson*. Chris Wilson and Paul Groth, eds. Pp. 199–218. Berkeley, CA: University of California Press.

Stottman, M. Jay, ed.
   2010   *Archaeologists as Activists: Can Archaeologists Change the World?* Tuscaloosa, AL: The University of Alabama Press.

Upton, Dell
   2015   *What Can and Can't Be Said: Race, Uplift, and Monument Building in the Contemporary South*. New Haven, CT: Yale University Press.

Widener, Ralph W., Jr.
   1982   *Confederate Monuments: Enduring Symbols of the South and the War Between the States*. Washington, D.C.: Andromeda Associates.

Wilson, Charles R.
   1980   *Baptized in Blood: The Religion of the Lost Cause 1865–1920*. Athens, GA: University of Georgia Press.

Winberry, John J.
   1983   "Lest we Forget": The Confederate Monument and the Southern Townscape. *Southeastern Geographer* 23:107–121.

Wright, George C.
   1985   *Life Behind a Veil: Blacks in Louisville, Kentucky, 1865–1930*. Baton Rouge, LA: Louisiana State University Press.

Yater, George
   1987   *Two Hundred Years at the Falls of the Ohio: A History of Louisville and Jefferson County*. Louisville, KY: Filson Club Historical Society.

9

Pullman

A Model Town Becomes a National Monument

MARK CASSELLO

The Town of Pullman was not constructed as a monument to George Pullman—although his name was etched into the landscape in front of his iconic factory. Instead, it is a model factory town that *became* a monument.[1] The Pullman National Monument memorializes the surviving "historic designed landscape" (Birnbaum and Capella Peters 1996:5) of the model Town of Pullman (1880–1907) and the historical events linked to industrialist George M. Pullman and the "Pullman's Palace Car Company."

How does public memory function within Pullman, a memory-site[2] that is both a material remnant of a mythical past and a contemporary urban community? Pullman is an apt example of "how societies . . . reconstruct their pasts rather than faithfully record them, and . . . do so with the needs of contemporary culture clearly in mind—manipulating the past in order to model the present" (Kammen 1991:3). Various and competing histories of Pullman exist and have been regularly invoked to advance local, state, and national interests since the town's construction.

Memory at Pullman can be understood in terms provided by Kammen and Bodnar. Kammen (1991:10) distinguishes between "collective memory" and "popular memory." He defines the former broadly as "what is remembered by the dominant civic culture" and the latter as what is remembered by "ordinary folks." For this study, I will prefer Bodnar's (1992:13–14) terminology. He differentiates between "official culture" and "vernacular culture."

---

[1] This chapter does not explore questions about physical monuments, what James Young (1993:4) describes as "the material objects, sculptures, and installations used to memorialize a person or thing." Instead, it focuses on the memory practices enacted in Chicago's Pullman community over the past century.

[2] My use of the term *memory-site* derives from Young (1993:4), who "treats all memory-sites as memorials, the plastic objects within these sites as monuments."

For Bodnar, official culture acts to subsume difference within a unifying—but often distorted, incomplete or otherwise problematic—consensus. In Bodnar's (1992:14) view, "public memory" is an "ideological system" with "special language, beliefs, symbols, and stories" that can be used "as a cognitive device to mediate competing interpretations and privilege some explanations over others" (Bodnar 1992:14). Public memory attempts to reconcile conflicts between official culture and vernacular culture or between collective memory and popular memory to produce a durable and dominant account of historical events.

When U.S. presidents establish national monuments, they act as spokespersons of official culture. Their purpose is to "create a sense of shared values and ideals" and "create common loci around which national identity is forged" (Young 1993:6). If this is the case, it should be clear that these constructions of public memory by the state must, to an extent, diminish, disregard, or silence those sites or stories that may compete, contradict, or otherwise complicate the accounts favored by official culture. As such, presidential proclamations of historic sites as national monuments are fertile ground for the study of how this mediation between the official culture and vernacular culture is articulated and later enacted. This study examines the place and cultural factors that have influenced which narratives are told in Pullman and the implications of President Obama's attempt to reconcile Pullman's vexed history into a single, unifying nationalistic narrative through his establishment of the Pullman National Monument.

An Evolving Landscape: Model Town to Urban Neighborhood

The model Town of Pullman gained notoriety in the late nineteenth century for the beauty of its cohesive design and landscape, the amenities afforded to its residents, and its technological achievements. Industrialist George Pullman built the town for the workers who produced his luxurious railroad "Palace Cars." These sumptuously furnished and elegantly appointed rail cars revolutionized travel. Anyone with a little extra money could experience comfort and service usually reserved only for the wealthy (Buder 1967:22–24). Service on these cars was provided by Pullman porters, who were exclusively African American men (Walikainen Rouleau et al. 2019:4). Pullman chose to lease his cars to the railroad, thereby maintaining complete control of every facet of his business and maximizing his profits.

As demand for his cars surged, Pullman built a new factory fourteen miles south of downtown Chicago. With the factory, Pullman constructed a beautiful, state-of-the-art model town for his workers. The homes, commercial, and

Figure 9.1. Historic Pullman rowhouses along South Langley Avenue (formerly Fulton Street) in the Pullman National Monument, Chicago, Illinois. Photo by Mark Cassello, 2021.

industrial buildings were replete with "all modern conveniences" (Walikainen Rouleau et al. 2019:48) of the day. The town featured a variety of housing types meant to accommodate workers of all income levels. The managers and executives lived in large, ornate homes close to the factory and the commercial buildings. Other workers lived in tidy rowhouses (Figure 9.1). The poorest workers lived in densely populated tenement block houses lining the east side of Fulton Street (Carwardine 1971:22–23) and in "brickyard cottages" to the south of town (Buder 1967:58–59). The town's fame grew. It was featured prominently as a satellite site of the World's Columbian Exposition in 1893 and was proclaimed the "World's Most Perfect Town" in 1896 (Walikainen Rouleau et al. 2019:45–48).

But Pullman's social experiment ultimately failed after a punishing national strike in 1894 damaged the reputation of the man and his town. A recession in 1893 collapsed demand for Pullman's rail cars. Workers' wages were slashed, but Pullman refused to lower rents in his town (Walikainen Rouleau et al. 2019:6). On 11 May 1894, Pullman's manufacturing workers walked off the job. Eugene V. Debs and his fledgling American Railway Union joined with the Pullman workers, sparking a national strike. By early July, the strike turned violent (Kelly 2018:191–208). President Grover Cleveland called in the National Guard and broke the strike, defeating the workers. Afterward, George Pullman's reputation was tarnished, and his dream of a utopian town that could end the strife between labor and capital crumbled. The town was incorporated into the City of Chicago in 1889 (Bachin 2004:17). A later Illinois Supreme Court decision in 1898 ruled that the company could not "hold real estate beyond the necessities of its manufacturing business" (Taylor 1915:35). By 1908 the residential and commercial structures had been sold off to private interests (1915:35).

As the homes became privately owned, residents took pride in them as their means would allow. Although the town had a "forlorn air of faded glory" in the early 1900s (Taylor 1915:37) and some efforts were made to "modernize" the homes in the 1930s, (*Chicago Daily Tribune* 1936a:B10, 1936b:S3), by the 1950s it was reported that the homes were "as good as new" (Merrill 1952:N A4) and "still highly valued" (Fuller 1955:A9). One resident declared that it was the hard work and creativity of the community that made Pullman "one of the most attractive [communities] in the area" (Merrill 1952:A4). But in 1960, proposed economic development threatened to destroy Pullman. The town was to be demolished "brick by brick" to make way for an "industrial estate to support the local Calumet Harbor" (Avignone 1984:21). About 4,000 residents, nearly half of whom were Italian Americans (1984:21), defended the community by reactivating a World War II–era "Civil Defense Organization" that was the forerunner of today's Pullman Civic Organization (Beberdick and HPF 1998:126). The work of the Pullman Civic Organization and its "Beman Committee," named in honor of Pullman's architect, contributed to securing the community's status as a City of Chicago Landmark District (1969, 1993), National Historic Landmark District (1970), and eventually, a National Monument (2015).

At the same time, racial divisions became more pronounced in the community. As early as 1909, shifts in Pullman's demographics led to the enactment of restrictive racial covenants. These were designed to keep African Americans out of Pullman and nearby Roseland (Reiff 2000:20). The departure of manufacturing in the 1970s, coupled with "white flight" to the suburbs, polarized the racial demographics of the community (2000:10). Today, the section north of the factory, "North Pullman," is populated mostly by African Americans (93 percent). The section south of the factory, "South Pullman," consists of a mixture of White (37 percent), African American (34 percent), and Hispanic (21 percent) residents (U.S. Census Bureau 2019a, 2019b). The geographical and racial division of the community has contributed to treating these areas as two distinct communities, even though historically there was only one Town of Pullman.

These demographic patterns have, in part, influenced where certain historical narratives are commemorated. With some exceptions, South Pullman has generally commemorated George Pullman's model factory town and the figures most closely associated with it. These narratives have been commemorated in its visitors' center and on its walking tours consistently since the 1970s. By contrast, North Pullman has commemorated the contributions of the Pullman porters and A. Philip Randolph and the Brotherhood of Sleeping Car Porters. These narratives have been commemorated in the National A. Philip Randolph Pullman Porter Museum since 1995. Attempts to bridge this interpretive and racial divide became more visible in the 1990s. Residents in both parts of the community worked to include North Pullman as part of the City of Chicago Landmark District (Reiff 2000:9). Efforts to reunify the community continue today.

In addition to the demographic shifts, the historic designed landscape of Pullman has been substantially altered since its construction in the 1880s. With the death of George Pullman in 1897, the company took a more utilitarian approach to the factory site. Massive industrial buildings were constructed in the early 1900s to accommodate the production of steel train cars (IHPA 1990:18; Walikainen Rouleau et al. 2019:8). Scenic "Lake Vista" was filled in to become a parking lot. Modern landfill and construction of the Calumet Expressway in 1962 moved Lake Calumet to the east, severing its historical relationship to the town. The once grand Arcade was demolished in 1929 (*Vicinity News* 1929) as was the Pullman Water Tower in 1957 (Pullman History 2021). The tenement block houses of Fulton Street were mostly erased from the landscape. Fire claimed the Market Hall twice, once in 1892 and again in 1973—it is still in ruins today (Beberdick and HPF 1998:122). In 1998, an arson fire gutted much of the Factory Administration Building, Rear Erecting Shops, and adjacent industrial buildings (National Park Service [NPS] 2013:21). With funding from the State of Illinois, the north wing and central portion of the Factory Administration were reconstructed. Today the "clock tower" portion of the building is owned by the National Park Service and has been converted into a new visitors' center for the national monument (Maynez 2020). Relatively little remains of Nathan F. Barrett's landscape architecture, which was integral to the aesthetic charm of the community. Like the shifts in Pullman's racial demographics, these physical changes to the landscape have also influenced which sites and stories are commemorated and which are silenced.

Making Memory at Pullman

A recent historical study of the Pullman community commissioned by the National Park Service identified a "disjuncture between the heritage resources, published research, and public memory in Pullman" (Walikainen Rouleau et al. 2019:14). They noted that "the existing stories told in and about this place often sidestep the centrality and interconnectedness of race, class, nationality, and gender to the town's history" (2019:14). The authors suggest that "the true significance" of President Obama's monument designation is the project of restoring the interconnectedness of this siloed history. However, I argue that such an aim will be complicated by the place and cultural factors that contributed directly to the development of these parallel and often competing narratives over the past century.

The Annual Pullman House Tour

Surprisingly, few traditional stone monuments or historical markers can be found in the Pullman National Monument. Commemoration is the preferred form of memorialization in Pullman. The longest-running and most popular commemorative event in the community is the annual Pullman House Tour. It exemplifies the vernacular culture of the community and is unique in that it promotes a generic, commercial consumption of "history" rather than a specific narrative about George Pullman, his workers, or the town. Its emphasis appears to be on ensuring that visitors enjoy themselves rather than that they leave with a particular understanding of Pullman's history.

The Pullman Civic Organization (PCO), which operates in South Pullman, manages the Pullman House Tour. The first Pullman House Tour took place on 12 October 1974 (Reynolds 1974) and has been held annually since. Each year about nine Pullman homes are opened for visitors to walk through and view (Figure 9.2). A few of Pullman's larger buildings, such as the Hotel Florence or Greenstone Church, are usually open to the public, too. An ever-changing cast of volunteer docents are stationed at each house and around the community to direct visitors from one site to the next. The docents receive index cards with information about their assigned house to convey to the visitors (Jasmont 1984). Guests receive a pamphlet with a map and short informational passages about each home on the self-guided tour. Visitors can choose to see some or all of the houses, as their time and interest permit.

Although a peek inside the Pullman houses is the main event, a bevy of other attractions draw visitors from the main streets into the alleys and other spaces in the community. In the alleys, residents fling open their garages and hawk their wares and bits of Pullman memorabilia to passersby. Local artists

Figure 9.2. Visitors attend the annual Pullman House tour. Photo by Mark Cassello, 2014.

hang their paintings along chain link fences, looking for consumers with a discerning eye. A blues band echoes through the brick ruins of the Market Hall. Proud owners arrange their vehicles for an antique car show on the lawn of the visitors' center. In nearby Arcade Park, the Pullman Morris & Sword (2021) dancers present the "century old tradition of Morris in Chicago." Like other sanctified sites, Pullman attracts many unique and interesting examples of ritual commemoration, which may or may not be related to its past (Foote 2003:9).

It could be argued that the annual Pullman House Tour is one of the most unifying events in the community precisely because it does not advance any specific version of the Pullman story. Rather, it celebrates the idea of community itself. The narratives that are told mostly arise from interpersonal communications between visitors and those "Pullmanites" they encounter. House Tour also provides the occasion and space for "intergenerational" dialogue. At the same time, a commemorative house tour is a logical outgrowth of the designation of the community as a city, state, and national historic landmark. These designations articulate an official expression of the past that vernacular interests can draw upon as needed. The material past of Pullman, available in the form of privately owned historic residential properties, is accessible to everyone living there. Thus, the House Tour democratizes commemoration and affords expressions of vernacular culture.

A Tale of Two Histories

Since before Pullman's designation as a National Historic Landmark District in 1970, the Pullman Civic Organization (PCO), the Historic Pullman Foundation (HPF), and the Illinois Labor History Society have been active "cultural leaders" (Bodnar 1992:15) in Pullman. The PCO was established in 1960. It "consists of residents and homeowners . . . who have banded together to promote the general welfare of the community, to preserve its historical significance, and to educate and promote the significance of the area" (PCO 2021). The PCO often operates in tandem with the Historic Pullman Foundation (HPF). The HPF was established in 1973 (Beberdick and HPF 1998:122) to "promote and sponsor restoration projects within the Pullman Historic District" (HPF 1980:7.1). In addition to owning property, throughout its existence the HPF has developed tours and prepared publications "to make the lessons and values of Pullman better understood" (Beberdick and HPF 1998:122). The PCO and HPF have remained intertwined to varying degrees over the past 50 years.

The Illinois Labor History Society (ILHS) was established in 1969 with the assistance of labor attorney Joseph H. Jacobs (ILHS 2021). The mission of the ILHS is "to encourage the preservation and study of labor history materials of the Illinois Regions, and to arouse public interest in the profound significance of the past to the present" (ILHS 2021). Since its inception, the organization has worked to protect sites related to labor history in Illinois, including a consistent involvement in the preservation and interpretive efforts in Pullman. These efforts were led, in part, by Professor William Adelman, who provided "labor history programs and tours for thousands of union members, students, teachers and . . . the general public" (ILHS 2021). Adelman also authored *Touring Pullman* (1972). The thick pamphlet includes a self-guided walking tour of sites related to the Pullman Strike of 1894. This guide has been reprinted several times and is still used by visitors to the district who find it online or through other "unofficial" channels. The ILHS is not located in the Pullman community but remains an active participant in all major developments within the community, including efforts to secure its designation as a national monument.

These organizations republished two out-of-print books central to understanding Pullman's past. In 1971, the ILHS reprinted a facsimile edition of Rev. William H. Carwardine's *The Pullman Strike* (1894), which had been out of print since its initial publication in the waning days of the famed railroad strike (Bech-Meyer 2019:ii). Carwardine arrived in Pullman at 37 years old as pastor of the Pullman Methodist Episcopal Church. He was there in 1894 and witnessed the suffering caused by the strike to the workers and their families first-hand. Consequently, Carwardine became an "unapologetic critic" (2019[1894]:ii) of George Pullman. In *The Pullman Strike*, Carwardine rebuts claims made by George Pullman and his managers. He decries their "misrepresentations, half-truths, and outright lies" (2019[1894]:iii). Carwardine's fiery, worker-centered account of the strike is highly critical of Pullman and his company and favors the strikers whom he lived and preached alongside.

In 1974, the PCO republished a facsimile edition of an out-of-print book of their own, *The Town of Pullman: Its Growth with Brief Accounts of Its Industries* (1893), by Mrs. Duane Doty. The 250-page tome is an incredibly exhaustive account of the model town, its technical innovations, its industrial facilities, landscape features, and more. It documents in wonderful, but at times excruciating detail, every facet of the operation of the town and its manufacturing facilities. More importantly, Doty's account, published a year before the Pullman Strike of 1894, is highly laudatory of George Pullman and his town. Doty (1974:4) describes the company as "the most remarkable business enterprise of the age, or any age." She proclaims George M. Pullman has shown the world that "the interests of capital can be amply provided for while operatives . . . are made sharers in the results of good work" (Doty 1974:4). Her detailed account of the town's facilities and its operations was integral to the formation of early interpretive narratives centering on the industrial history of the factory and life in the model town.

These opposing historical accounts exemplify how competing narratives have been literally reproduced in Pullman. Bodnar explains that "cultural leaders" within a community work to promote "interpretations of the past and present reality that reduce the power of competing interests that threaten the attainment of their goals" (Bodnar 1992:13). In the case of the PCO and the HPF, it does not serve their interests to promote a negative depiction of the town. It becomes harder to achieve their aims of restoring historic properties and building community when Pullman is tainted by an association with a failed social experiment. The controversy surrounding the strike, they argue, has "often ignored the town in its effort to portray the *more infamous* Pullman Strike of 1894 [emphasis added]" (HPF 1979). Likewise, the ILHS has an incentive to venerate the labor struggles associated with the Pullman company as heroic to advance a pro-labor agenda in the present.

The Pullman Porters: "It's Complicated"

Conspicuously absent from both of the above accounts is the Pullman porter. No figure—aside from George M. Pullman himself—is arguably more central to the Pullman story than is the Pullman porter. Yet their contributions

Figure 9.3. National A. Philip Randolph Pullman Porter Museum, Pullman National Monument, Chicago, Illinois. Photo by Mark Cassello, 2021.

have often been overlooked in the day-to-day commemorative practices of the community, particularly in South Pullman. The invisibility of the Pullman porters has been the focus of increased scrutiny in the wake of President Obama's national monument designation. In the lead up to the designation, the Pullman porters were regularly cited as a justification for Pullman's national significance. Studies of the Pullman National Historic Landmark District from 2010 to its designation as a national monument in 2015 point to the Pullman company's status as "the largest employer of African Americans in the nation" (ULI 2011:6), noting that the porters made up 44 percent of the workforce of Pullman's railcar enterprise (NPS 2013:3, 17–18). Also frequently mentioned are the efforts of the Pullman porters and A. Philip Randolph to establish the Brotherhood of Sleeping Car Porters, which brokered the first labor agreement between an African American labor union and a major U.S. corporation (2013:18). Despite this, many in the Pullman community have rationalized the exclusion of the porters with the refrain, "but the porters did not live here."

To remedy this historical silencing, the National A. Philip Randolph Pullman Porter Museum was founded in 1995 (NPS 2021) by Dr. Lyn Hughes. The museum is located in a three-story, red-brick Pullman building dating from the 1880s (Figure 9.3). It "remains the only black history museum in the country to focus specifically on labor history" (Good 2016). Hughes was motivated to establish the museum after attending a walking tour in the community that featured no discussion of African American participation in the Pullman story (Good 2016). The museum's mission is "to promote, honor and celebrate the legacy of A. Philip Randolph, Pullman Porters, the Brotherhood of Sleeping Car Porters and contributions made by African Americans to America's labor movement; with a significant focus on the African American Railroad Employee" (Crawford 2015). The museum houses an extensive archive and has developed a "National Registry" of Pullman porters. In addition to its historical work interpreting the Pullman porter experience, the museum advances the concept of "cultural economic development" aimed at leveraging African American history and culture to improve the lives of African Americans. By foregrounding the African American experience, the museum reminds visitors that George Pullman's model town was "predicated on the exclusion and exploitation of the black workers" (Good 2016). This is a vivid counterpoint to other narratives that portray George M. Pullman as a flawed but benevolent industrialist.

In the year following Pullman's national monument designation, controversy erupted surrounding remarks made about including the Pullman porters' story at the site. On 6 November 2016, at the Chicago Humanities Festival, Lynn McClure of the National Parks Conservation Association (NPCA) moderated a discussion titled "Pullman: Past and Future." During the discussion portion, McClure remarked that the inclusion of the Pullman porters' story "*presents challenges to the Chicago site* [emphasis added]" (Johnson 2016). She explained that "The A. Philip Randolph Pullman Porter Museum is in the Pullman district, but Randolph's work organizing and guiding the union was done largely out of Harlem, in New York City" (Johnson 2016). She added, "*It's complicated* because it actually all didn't happen right in the community [emphasis added]" (Chicago Humanities 2016). McClure's remarks seemed to imply that the Pullman porters story somehow did not belong at the site.

Lyn Hughes published a response to McClure's comments in the *Crusader*, a weekly African American newspaper serving Chicago. Hughes pointed out that "EVERY piece of marketing material distributed, stories written, all documents, suggestions, etc." and President Obama's designation speech all repeatedly invoked "the Pullman Porters" (Hughes 2016). She questioned why now, after the monument has been established and development is taking place, the "story of the Porters has mysteriously become 'challenging to the site'" (Hughes 2016). After all, much of the Pullman story takes place outside the confines of the real or imagined boundaries of the model town. It seems strange then, as Hughes suggests, to single out the story of the porters as particularly difficult to interpret at the site.

The preceding exchange offers a glimpse into the conflicts of public memory at Pullman. David Blight explains that "deflections and evasions, careful remembering and necessary forgetting, and embittered and irreconcilable versions of experience are all the stuff of historical memory" (2001:5). Pullman is no exception. The Pullman House Tour rallies the community around civic pride and a benign version of Pullman's past. The homes are presented as art objects or works of architecture and interior design for public consumption. The obligatory pamphlet and map offer historical information, but visitors are free to develop their own understanding through their subjective encounters with the community and its material past. At the same time, competing narratives are literally reproduced as texts. This is exemplified by the dueling publications produced by the PCO and the ILHS. Last, the "challenge" of integrating the African American experience in historical accounts and interpretative efforts at Pullman remains. McClure's comments and Hughes's response offer insight into the subtle ways the pasts of marginalized groups can be diminished, de-emphasized, or silenced, even when official culture—or the U.S. President—asserts their centrality to a memory-site.

Proclamation 9233 and the Official Culture of President Obama

Under the authority of the Antiquities Act of 1906 (Antiquities Act), presidents can declare by public proclamation lands "owned or controlled" by the federal government to be national monuments (U.S. Congress 2014). The Antiquities Act also gives presidents the power to "reserve parcels of land as a part of the national monuments" so long as the size of these parcels is "confined to the smallest area compatible with the proper care and management of the objects to be protected" (U.S. Congress 2014). Monuments can be established to protect "historic landmarks," such as the Pullman National Historic Landmark District, as well as "historic and prehistoric structures, and other objects of historic or scientific interest" (U.S. Congress 2014). For over a century, presidents have used the act to protect a broad array of sites at their discretion.

President Obama established the Pullman National Monument on 19 February 2015 through an act of formal consecration (U.S. President 2015:10315). President Obama arrived in the Pullman community, spoke before an audience assembled in a high school gymnasium, and publicly signed Presidential Proclamation 9233, the executive order establishing the Pullman National

Monument. An act of formal consecration, such as this, is a "prerequisite of sanctification" (Foote 2003:8). For a site to be transformed into a monument, "there must be a ceremony that includes an explicit statement of the site's significance and an explanation of why the event should be remembered" (Foote 2003:8). Such ceremonies transform places "into monuments that serve as reminders or warnings, the function indicated by the Latin root of the word *monument*" (2003:8). The text of President Obama's proclamation is the "explicit statement" (2003:8) of Pullman's significance and explains how the events associated with George Pullman and his model town are integral to a national narrative of progress toward greater economic and social justice. "This place," President Obama affirmed, "is a milestone on our journey toward a more perfect union" (Obama 2015). He featured the Pullman porters prominently in the text of the proclamation, mentioning them nine times—nearly as many times as he mentions the district itself. He binds the events at Pullman inextricably to the broader industrial, labor, and social history of the U.S.

By situating Pullman's history within this broader, national ideal, President Obama tries to reconcile the tensions between the competing interests and narratives at the site. He breaks precedent, weaving the labor struggles of the Pullman company's White factory workers and its African American porters into a single, unified history. The actions of both groups exemplify how *all workers* can organize to be an effective and necessary check on abuses of corporate power. Woven together, this singular history becomes a fundamental expression of a collective, national interest in achieving a "more perfect union," a phrase rooted in the origins of the nation itself. But as I have already illustrated, a range of underlying cultural tensions and historical disagreements persist about the meaning of these specific narratives and of Pullman more generally. Bodnar (1992:17) suggests that these "local, regional, class, and ethnic interests" are likely to persist in some form but will together tend to serve a "dominant meaning" that is often "nationalistic." In the case of a national monument, the tendency for histories to accrete around a central, national narrative will be viewed by many to be an obvious and organic sign of "progress" for the site. But in fact, the imposition of a "dominant meaning" for a memory-site as sprawling, layered, and complex as Pullman may act to silence other histories that are no less important but that may lie somewhat outside the prescribed scope of the monument's legislated purposes.

Conclusion

Although the concept of a Pullman National Monument enjoys broad-based support, its implementation has disrupted the traditional relationships within the community and between local, state, federal, and private interests in the monument. The nature and extent of these disruptions merit further study. In addition to redefined relationships within the community, reformulations of Pullman's past have appeared as a means to advance particular political and economic interests. Such an outcome should have been anticipated. As early as 2011, the Urban Land Institute (2011:10) noted that "there are multiple identities for the site due to its diversity of significant themes . . . and conflicting visions of small-scale use versus aspirations of national and international prominence." If the meaning of Pullman's past is contested, visions for its future are even more so. Groups working in and around Pullman mine its history for usable pasts that can be deployed to advance their interests in the present.

This practice of manipulating the past has become even more pronounced in the years following Pullman's national monument designation. Adjacent commercial development has invoked Pullman's past industrial and transportation history as a means to market the area as a hub of "green and sustainable development" (Henderson 2020). The construction of an affordable housing complex catering to artists was described as a "chance to propel historic Pullman's legacy of artistry into the future" (Flynn 2021). These narratives fit well within a larger attempt to portray Pullman as a "Model for Neighborhood Revitalization" (Guthmann 2020) or an "economic engine" (NPCA 2013). The practice has gone so far as to suggest that the construction of a fast-food restaurant is a "milestone for the neighborhood's revitalization" (REjournals 2020), recalling President Obama's remarks at the dedicatory ceremony for the Pullman National Monument that "This place has been a milestone on a journey toward a more perfect union" (Sullivan and Eilperin 2015). How the mighty have fallen.

The landscape of the monument itself has already begun to be transformed. The National Park Service opened a new visitors' center in the restored Factory Administration "Clock Tower" Building on Labor Day 2021 (Figure 9.4). A reconstruction of the original Pullman Factory Gate through which the striking workers walked in May of 1894 has been rebuilt upon its original foundation (Figure 9.4). At the same time, the controversial construction of a modern apartment building on the site of "Poverty Row," a historic site with consequential historical associations to the Pullman Strike of 1894, destroyed in situ archaeological remains and diminished the integrity of design, feeling,

Figure 9.4. Pullman National Monument Visitors Center under construction in the Pullman Factory Administration Building. Photo by Mark Cassello, 2021.

and association of the site. But as Kammen (1991:13) suggests, "memory is more likely to be activated by contestation, and amnesia is more likely to be induced by the desire for reconciliation." With its contested past and a convergence of local, national, class, and ethnic interests, Pullman will remain a fascinating site for scholars of public memory for generations to come.

References

Adelman, William
    1972   *Touring Pullman: A Study in Company Paternalism.* Chicago, IL: Illinois Labor History Society.

Avignone, Mario
    1984   *Petals from Roseland. Fra Noi.* April:21. Friends of the Pullman State Historic Site. DOI:12913: PFS.11.01.08.48. https://www.pullman-museum.org/pshs/pshsFullRecord.php?collection=pshs&pointer=15805, accessed 1 March 2021.

Bachin, Robin F.
    2004   *Building the South Side: Urban Space and Civic Culture in Chicago, 1890–1919.* Chicago, IL: The University of Chicago Press.

Beberdick, Frank, and the HPF (Historic Pullman Foundation)
    1998   *Images of America: Chicago's Historic Pullman District.* Charleston, SC: Arcadia Publishing.

Birnbaum, Charles A., and Christine Capella Peters
    1996   *The Secretary of the Interior's Standards for the Treatment of Historic Properties with Guidelines for the Treatment of Cultural Landscapes.* Washington, DC: U.S. Department of the Interior, National Park Service.

Blight, David W.
  2001   *Race and Reunion: The Civil War in American Memory.* Cambridge, MA: The Belknap Press of Harvard University Press.

Bodnar, John
  1992   *Remaking America: Public Memory, Commemoration, and Patriotism in the Twentieth Century.* Princeton, NJ: Princeton University Press.

Buder, Stanley
  1967   *Pullman: An Experiment in Industrial Order and Community Planning, 1880–1930.* New York, NY: Oxford University Press.

Bech-Meyer, Nico
  1894[2019]   *A Story from Pullman-Town.* Chicago, IL: Charles H. Kerr, Chicago. Reprinted by Pullman National Monument Preservation Society, Chicago, IL.

Carwardine, William H.
  1894[1971]   *The Pullman Strike.* 4th edition. Chicago, IL: Charles H. Kerr. Reprinted 1971 by Illinois Labor History Society, Chicago, IL.

Chicago Daily Tribune
  1936a   Old Pullman Houses to Be Modernized: Two Completed Units Are Open Today. 5 January 1936:B10. https://www.proquest.com/docview/181689601/8DA44D94C5424C8BPQ/1, accessed on 22 March 2016.
  1936b   Pullman Homes of 50 Years Ago Are Modernized: 2 Units Transformed by Improvements. 12 January 1936:S3. https://www.proquest.com/docview/181718169/1C6B508B72C34C98PQ/1, accessed 22 March 2016.

Chicago Humanities Festival
  2016   Pullman: Past and Future. 6 November 2016. https://www.youtube.com/watch?v=dgzrynzPauc, accessed 5 April 2021.

Crawford, T. J.
  2015   David Peterson Jr. and Pullman Porter Museum preserving Blacks' labor history. *Rollingout* 19 February. https://rollingout.com/2015/02/19/david-peterson-jr-pullman-porter-museum-preserving-blacks039-labor-history/, accessed 15 April 2021.

Doty, Mrs. Duane [Margarita Jane Richards]
  1893[1974]   *The Town of Pullman: Its Growth with Brief Accounts of Its Industries.* Pullman, IL: T. P. Struhsacker. Reprinted facsimile edition, Pullman Civic Organization, Chicago, IL.

Flynn, Carol
  2021   Pullman Project Combines Historic Preservation, Promotion of the Arts in One Project. *Daily Southtown* 4 January. https://www.chicagotribune.com/suburbs/daily-southtown/ct-sta-pullman-artspace-lofts-st-0105-20210104-pv7ehg2rjbbtp02th7474mf704-story.html, accessed 20 December 2020.

Foote, Kenneth E.
  2003   *Shadowed Ground: America's Landscapes of Tragedy and Violence.* Austin, TX: University of Texas Press.

Fuller, Ernest
  1955   Old Pullman Homes Still Highly Valued. *Chicago Daily Tribune* 29 May:a9. https://www.proquest.com/docview/179428348/6C7DFD25F2BE4C13PQ/1#, accessed on 22 March 2016.

Good, Christopher
   2016   Speaking Truth to Power. *South Side Weekly* 22 November. https://southsideweekly.com/speaking-truth-to-power/, accessed 15 April 2021.

Guthman, Andrea
   2020   Chicago's Pullman: A Model for Neighborhood Revitalization? *WTTW* 29 January. https://news.wttw.com/2020/01/29/chicago-s-pullman-model-neighborhood-revitalization, accessed 7 April 2021.

Henderson, Audrey
   2020   A Sustainable Refocus Helps a Historic Chicago Community Rebuild. *Energy News Network*, 2 December. https://energynews.us/2020/12/02/a-sustainable-refocus-helps-a-historic-chicago-community-rebuild/, accessed 1 April 2021.

HPF (Historic Pullman Foundation)
   1979   Pullman Tours. Harold Washington Public Library Archives. Historic Pullman Foundation, Chicago, IL.
   1980   *The Historic Pullman Center: A Proposal for Restoration.* Harold Washington Public Library Archives. Chicago, IL: Historic Pullman Foundation.

Hughes, Lyn
   2016   Hidden Agenda to Remove the A. Philip Randolph Pullman Porter Museum from the Pullman National Monument. *Crusader* 18 November. https://chicagocrusader.com/hidden-agenda-remove-philip-randolph-pullman-porter-museum-pullman-national-monument/, accessed 15 April 2021.

IHPA (Illinois Historic Preservation Agency), Historic Sites Division
   1990   *Pullman State Historic Site Prospectus.* 2nd edition. Springfield, IL: IHPA.

ILHS (Illinois Labor History Society)
   2021   *Mission & History.* Illinois Labor History Society. http://www.illinoislaborhistory.org/mission-history, accessed 7 April 2021.

Jasmont, Pat
   1984   *House Tour 1984 Confirmation Letter.* Friends of the Pullman State Historic Site. DOI: 11644: pfe.07.28.06.66: File. https://www.pullman-museum.org/pshs/pshsCompoundObjectWebPage.php?collection=pshs&pointer=20593&root=20594, accessed on 29 September 2022.

Johnson, Steve
   2016   Planning an Ambitious Future for Pullman. *Chicago Tribune* 7 November. https://www.chicagotribune.com/entertainment/museums/ct-pullman-future-humanities-fest-ent-1108-20161107-story.html, accessed 12 April 2021.

Kammen, Michael
   1991   *Mystic Chords of Memory: The Transformation of Tradition in American Culture.* New York, NY: Alfred A. Knopf.

Kelly, Jack
   2018   *The Edge of Anarchy: The Railroad Barons, The Gilded Age, and The Greatest Labor Uprising in America.* New York, NY: St. Martin's Press.

Maynez, Maria
   2020   Work to Begin on Visitors Center in Pullman's Historical Clock Tower. *Block Club Chicago* 3 February. https://blockclubchicago.org/2020/02/03/work-to

-begin-on-visitors-center-in-pullmans-historic-clock-tower/, accessed 10 April 2021.

Merrill, Betty Jane
    1952   Pullman Town Pulls "Sleeper" on Its Critics. *Chicago Daily Tribune* 25 December. http://www.newspapers.com, accessed 15 January 2021.

NPCA (National Parks Conservation Association)
    2013   *Economic Engine: An Analysis of the Potential Impact of a Pullman National Historical Park*. Chicago, IL: NPCA.

NPS (National Park Service)
    2013   *Pullman Historic District: Reconnaissance Survey*. Chicago, IL: National Park Service, Midwest Region.
    2021   *National A. Philip Randolph Pullman Porter Museum*. https://www.nps.gov/places/national-a-philip-randolph-pullman-porter-museum.htm, accessed 15 April 2021.

Obama, Barack H.
    2015   President Obama's Designation Address. *Pullman National Monument Preservation Society*. http://www.pnmps.org/the-monument/establishment/, accessed 9 December 2020.

PCO (Pullman Civic Organization)
    2021   *About the Pullman Civic Organization*. http://www.pullmancivic.org/, accessed 7 April 2021.

Pullman History
    2021   *The Water Tower*. https://www.pullman-museum.org/theCompany/waterTower.html, accessed 1 April 2021.

Pullman Morris & Sword
    2021   http://pullmanmorris.org/, accessed 12 April 2021.

REjournals
    2020   Culver's Coming to Pullman in Latest Milestone for Neighborhood's Revitalization. 2 July. https://rejournals.com/culvers-coming-to-pullman-in-latest-milestone-for-neighborhoods-revitalization/, accessed 1 April 2021.

Reiff, Janice L.
    2000   Rethinking Pullman: Urban Space and Working-Class Activism. *Social Science History* 24(1):7–32. http://www.jstor.org/stable/1171651, accessed 21 January 2021.

Reynolds, Barbara
    1974   Pullman Opening Doors to History—and to You. *Chicago Tribune*, 10 October. Friends of the Pullman State Historic Site. DOI: 12934:pf2008.27.13. https://www.pullman-museum.org/pshs/pshsFullRecord.php?collection=pshs&pointer=16558, accessed 5 April 2021.

Sullivan, Sean, and Juliet Eilperin
    2015   Obama Declares Three National Monuments, Including One in Chicago. *Washington Post* 19 February. https://www.washingtonpost.com/politics/obama-declares-three-national-monuments-including-one-in-chicago/2015/02/19/3c62bca8-b84e-11e4-a200-c008a01a6692_story.html, accessed 29 September 2022.

Taylor, Graham Romeyn
 1915 *Satellite Cities: A Study of Industrial Suburbs.* New York, NY: D. Appleton and Company.

U.S. Census Bureau
 2019a American Community Survey 5-year Estimates. Retrieved from *Census Reporter Profile Page for Census Tract 5002, Cook, Illinois.* http://censusreporter.org/profiles/14000US17031500200-census-tract-5002-cook-il/, accessed 12 April 2021.
 2019b American Community Survey 5-year Estimates. Retrieved from *Census Reporter Profile page for Census Tract 5003, Cook, Illinois,* http://censusreporter.org/profiles/14000US17031500300-census-tract-5003-cook-il/, accessed 12 April 2021.

U.S. Congress
 2014 54 USC § 320301. Chapter 3203—Monuments, Ruins, Sites, and Objects of Antiquity. *Public Law 113—287,* 19 December. https://www.govinfo.gov/content/pkg/PLAW-113pub1287/pdf/PLAW-113pub1287.pdf, accessed on 28 September 2022.

U.S. President
 2015 Establishment of the Pullman National Monument, Proclamation 9233 of 19 February 2015. *Federal Register* 80, no. 37, 25 February 2015:10315. https://www.govinfo.gov/content/pkg/FR-2015-02-25/pdf/2015-04090.pdf, accessed 20 February 2021.

ULI (Urban Land Institute)
 2011 *A Technical Assistance Panel Report: The Pullman State Historic Site, Chicago, IL, October 17–18, 2011.* Chicago, IL: ULI.

Vicinity News
 1929 Old Arcade Is Wrecked. 10 February. Friends of the Pullman State Historic Site. DOI: 7884: PFS.05.07.05.186. https://www.pullman-museum.org/pshs/pshsFullRecord.php?collection=pshs&pointer=11788, accessed 15 April 2021.

Walikainen Rouleau, Laura, Sarah Fayen Scarlett, Steven A. Walton, and Timothy Scarlett.
 2019 *Historic Resources Study of Pullman National Monument, Illinois.* Report for the National Park Service. https://digitalcommons.mtu.edu/michigantech-p/14692, accessed 10 February 2021.

Young, James
 1993 *The Texture of Memory.* New Haven, CT: Yale University Press.

10

A Feminist Intersectional Perspective Addressing the Dearth of Statues of Women and Minorities Resulting from the Great Predominance of Racist Patriarchal Public Statues in the United States

Suzanne Spencer-Wood

Statues are more than the materialization of important historic persons to keep their memory alive. Statues are usually larger-than-life on high pedestals to be looked up to literally and figuratively, made of durable materials to last through the ages as exemplary historic individuals embodying and promoting dominant cultural narratives, values, and beliefs. In Europe, its colonies, and descendant nations, White men historically held the positions of power and the funds that allowed them to predominantly decide who deserved statues, resulting in the great preponderance of statues of White men that ideologically legitimate and materially support intersecting racist–patriarchal cultural beliefs, viewpoints, values, and behaviors. Racist patriarchy is a White-male-controlled and dominated society that subordinates women and minorities through intersecting sexist and racist oppression and discrimination.

This research is conducted from my feminist intersectional theoretical perspective, which draws on, and goes beyond, Black feminist intersectionality theory that has developed since 1971 (Spencer-Wood 2022) and was named by Kimberlé Crenshaw (1989) for the combination of racism and sexism that makes the identity category of Black women invisible in the American legal system. In contrast to Crenshaw's (1989) dichotomy between invisible Black women as opposed to White women as the visible category of identity assumed in anti-sex-discrimination law, Spencer-Wood's (1991a:237; 2022:75) feminist inclusive *both/and* theoretical approach critiques such *either/or* binary-oppositional thinking that Deetz (1988) considered innate, and instead considers the intersections of supposedly opposed dichotomous identities to explain the relative invisibility of *both* White *and* minority women in American statues. Minority women are more invisible in statues than White women, whose sexual invisibility is mitigated by racial privilege. This research further expands Black feminist intersectionality theory with evidence that statues often materialize the patriarchal–racist subordination of women, and especially intersectional women of color, by depicting them in embodied subordinate poses.

The length of this chapter does not allow it to be comprehensive, so examples are provided. First, statistics are provided showing the severe dearth of statues of women, and especially minority women, in America. Next, this discriminatory pattern is explained as the result and reification of patriarchal gender ideology. The next two sections critically analyze three common types of statues that exemplify the embodiment of patriarchal, racist, colonialist beliefs, including 1. Confederate generals, 2. European conquerors/colonizers, and 3. European priests/missionaries. Black Lives Matter and indigenous groups have protested, defaced, toppled, or caused the removal of some of these three types of statues. In contrast, subsequent sections analyze statues that have predominantly been recently erected that re-enfranchise Americans of historically accomplished women to empower achievements by *both* White *and* minority women, and patriarchal resistance to one historical empowering statue of women. Finally, brief proposals are made for the placement of a few new statues of remarkable historic women to begin to counteract the predominance of racist patriarchal statues and the lack of statues of accomplished historical women.

The Lack of Statues of Women

A 2017 survey of the 5,575 American public statues listed in the Smithsonian American Art Museum online inventories catalog found only 559 (10 percent) were of women, many of which were erected in the last twenty-five years (Peled 2017). Of the statues on American city landscapes, 88–95 percent are of White men, and at most a few are of historic women. Several cities, including Chicago, have had no statues of women, at least until recently (Stingl 2019). Of 115 statues on the landscape of our nation's capital, only 6 (5 percent) are of women, and only one of these is a woman of color: the first statue of an African American woman, erected in 1974 in Capitol Hill's Lincoln Park, of educational reformer and civil rights activist Mary McLeod Bethune (Lefrak 2019). The other real women's statues in D.C. are of Whites: Joan of Arc, Olive Risley Seward, who authored primarily children's books, Crown

Princess Märtha of Sweden, and Eleanor Roosevelt (Capps 2016). Out of 200 statues inside the Capitol building, 11 (6 percent) are of women (Workman 2001:62). More statues of minorities and women are needed in the national and state capitals to remind legislators to serve the interests of the diversity of people who elected them and stop taking away voting rights and women's right to bodily autonomy.

On New York City's landscape statues were erected in 1770 of King George III and his adviser William Pitt, which were torn down during the Revolution, followed by 145 additional statues of real men in the nineteenth and twentieth centuries. Only 5 (3 percent) of the 150 statues in New York City were of real women until 2019. In 1915, the first statue of a real woman erected in the city was of the legendary Joan of Arc, followed in 1984 by Golda Meir, in 1992 by Gertrude Stein, in 1996 by Eleanor Roosevelt, and in 2008, Harriet Tubman, the first African American woman's statue in the city. Only Roosevelt's statue represented a historic resident of New York City. Of the 23 statues of historic individuals in Central Park, none were of real women prior to the 2020 women's rights statue (Carlson 2020).

It is extraordinary that 11 more statues of women have recently been added to New York City's landscape. On 26 August 2019, Women's Equality Day, in front of sponsor RXR Realty's office at 1285 6th Avenue, Australia's most prolific and successful public sculptors, the married couple Gillie and Marc, unveiled their 10 larger-than-life bronze statues of modern women that New Yorkers voted for, including 4 (40 percent) African Americans: Oprah Winfree (actor), Janet Mock (writer), Gabby Douglas (gymnast) and Tererai Trent (Zimbabwe women's rights activist); and 6 Whites (60 percent): Jane Goodall (primatologist), Tracy Dyson (chemist and astronaut), P!nk (singer), Nicole Kidman, Cate Blanchett (actors), and Cheryl Strayed (memoirist) (Gillie and Marc 2021). Some of these women are not Americans or New Yorkers, although they do provide girls with role models in several professions. By 2021, these statues were moved to other venues in New York City, except two that were shipped to a hotel in San Francisco (Gillie and Marc 2021), increasing the number of statues of women in that city to 5 (6 percent) compared to 85 (94 percent) statues of men (Quaglia 2019). In March 2021, a statue of Supreme Court Justice Ruth Bader Ginsberg, by the same sculptors, was installed at the City Point building, 336 Flatbush Extension, Brooklyn (Gillie and Marc 2021). These and the new statues in Central Park of suffragists Elizabeth Cady Stanton, Susan B. Anthony, and African American Sojourner Truth (Levenson, Tambou, and Brunswick 2020) increase statues of real women to 12 percent of the statues in New York City.

For intersectional groups no overall statistics have been published, but research on the top 50 individuals honored with the most statues, totaling 1684, 89 percent (1491) have the intersectional identity of White men. Therefore, Americans very predominantly see statues of White men that legitimate and sanctify racist patriarchy. The 50 individuals with the most American statues only include three women, totaling 67 statues (4 percent of 1684). The intersectional identity of Native American men has one more statue than the intersectional identity of Native American women. Of the 126 statues of African Americans, Harriet Tubman has 21 (17 percent), while men have 105 (83 percent). Of the 74 statues of French people, Joan of Arc has 26 (35 percent), while Frenchmen have 48 (65 percent). Of the 41 statues of Native Americans, Sacagawea has 20 (49 percent), while the warrior Tecumseh has 21 (51 percent), closer to gender equality than the other racial/ethnic groups that include a statue of a woman. These statistics on the 50 people with the most American statues show that women within every intersectional racial and ethnic group have fewer statues than men in those groups (Allen et al. 2022).

Why There Are So Few Statues of Real Women

The first question raised by this research is why are there so many fewer statues of real women than men? From a structural feminist theory perspective, patriarchy is legitimated and promoted by the lack of statues of powerful, accomplished women and minorities, making their achievements invisible by erasing them from the past and materially constructing the false patriarchal narrative that women have not made, and are incapable of making, important contributions to society and culture, thus disenfranchising women of their powerful heritage and legitimating the subordination of women by disempowering them from trying to achieve anything. In Western patriarchal binary-oppositional gender ideology, only supposedly rationally superior culture-generating men are considered capable of actively making public achievements worthy of commemorating with statues, while women are devalued as domestic, passive, irrational/emotional, bestial for giving birth, inferior and therefore justifiably subordinate, so it is impossible for them to make important public contributions deserving statues.

Historic men misogynistically enforced their false beliefs by excluding supposedly inferior women, by law and practice, from public positions in the government and military, which are the subjects of the vast majority of statues. Wives were subordinated by men's laws that made them nonpersons, dependent minors, and chattels akin to slaves of their husbands. In all public matters, husbands legally represented their wives, who had few civil rights and no public roles under the law. By the late nineteenth century, a minority of states gave wives legal rights to keep their earnings, own land, conduct business, divorce for adultery by husbands, and have custody of their children (Spencer-Wood 2013:176–7). Despite ideologies and rhetoric valorizing the moral superiority of domestic women to keep them content to be limited to their sphere, the lack of statues of real women materializes the overriding patriarchal ideology and practices of excluding women from men's public sphere and the belief that domestic-feminine moral influence was supposed to be invisible, especially in the public sphere (Ginzberg 1990:15, 19, 53, 64).

Domestic accomplishments, whether by women or men, have never been considered important enough to commemorate with public statues. Only public accomplishments of individuals have been considered potentially worthy of commemoration with statues, a bias that needs to be reconsidered. Despite the ideological and legal limits placed on women's public actions, my both/and feminist inclusive theoretical perspective reveals that women made important contributions to *both* the domestic *and* public spheres (Spencer-Wood 1991a:237–8), as demonstrated by many machines patented by women (Macdonald 1992). In the early nineteenth century, reform women began creating public institutions that socialized time-consuming domestic work, such as childcare and cooking meals (Spencer-Wood 1991b:259).

Racist Patriarchal Meanings of Public Statues of White Men

Platt (2020), who teaches a course titled "Statues and Public Life" at Cornell University, argues statues are "ideological powerhouses: physical objects that compress whole systems of authority into bodies of bronze or marble." Loewen (1999:43–4) contends that "The grandeur of monuments intrinsically includes an element of consecration, which not only sanctifies the past but sanctions future actions. Their very existence implies that the person or event portrayed is worth emulating or the cause symbolized is worth forwarding. They embody a moral imperative: go thou and do likewise." For instance, dominant White men created the most pedestalled statues of larger-than-life, powerfully clothed White male politicians and military men, often elevated on horses, to embody, sanctify, and valorize the intersectional racist, patriarchal cultural values, power dynamics, and narratives that legitimate and promote the dominance of militaristic masculinity and the militarization of American society.

Nearly all of the 50 individuals with the most American statues were involved in colonial conquest or serving the military in some way, including declaring war and recruiting soldiers, totaling 1476 statues (88% of 1684), including 11 presidents totaling 606 statues (36% of 1684), 12 generals and four leaders of the confederacy totaling 135 statues (8% of 1684). Of the 89%

(1491) of statues that are of White men, 50% were slave owners (746 statues, 44% of 1684). The only individuals who had no military connection were two women, four priests or missionaries, and Shakespeare, totaling 208 statues (12% of 1684) (Allen et al. 2022). The majority of public statues that Americans have to physically look up to as models to emulate are powerful symbols glorifying White male slave owners and oppressors of minorities and women; legitimating, sanctifying, and promoting the persistence of White supremacist, racist and patriarchal values supporting the persistence of discrimination and the lack of justice for subordinated minorities and women.

An example of the past and current effects of statues on cultural beliefs and social actions are the many statues throughout the U.S. sanctifying and glorifying the treasonous failed secession by Whites in Southern states, including some statues of named generals and male leaders, such as President of the Confederacy Jefferson Davis, as discussed by Shackel (2003:37–9). Confederate statues were intended to powerfully intimidate African Americans as their segregation and subordination were violently enforced after Reconstruction in the Jim Crow South from c. 1875–1965. Confederate statues ideologically legitimate, support, and glorify the widespread White Southerners' framing of their treasonous secession as the Second Revolution against the tyranny of President Lincoln and the North over the South (Jameson 2024, personal communication). This framing provides insight into the meaning and importance of White supremacists chanting "1776" while waving Confederate and Trump flags in following former President Trump's instructions to "fight like hell" in violently attempting an illegal coup/insurrection/sedition at the U.S. Capitol building on 6 January 2021. Confederate statues and flags also ideologically supported and sanctified the erection on the Capitol's west front lawn of a makeshift gallows with a noose that was built for lynching Mike Pence and Nancy Pelosi, a plan openly discussed on social media, in a modern echo of the lynchings that terrorized African Americans in the Jim Crow South. More statues of accomplished women working for social justice and civil rights are needed to counteract statues that legitimate, sanctify, and promote modern racist and sexist White supremacists, especially leaders such as ex-president Trump.

My feminist intersectional perspective reveals the importance of women of color who founded and have led the global Black Lives Matter movement after George Zimmerman murdered Black teen Trayvon Martin in 2013. The resulting protests sometimes deface, topple, or remove statues that sanctify White men who oppressed Black, Indigenous, or immigrant women and men in the past, thus legitimating and supporting the modern persistence of intersecting racist and sexist oppressions marginalizing minorities and women.

Black Lives Matter protests have led to the removal of 160 Confederate statues through 2020. On 12 July 2021, statues of Confederate generals Robert E. Lee and Stonewall Jackson were removed from public squares in Charleston, South Carolina, as voted by residents following the "Unite the Right" White supremacist rally that centered on these statues on 11 and 12 August 2017 (Pavior 2021). Since at least 1995, Native American protests, later supported by Black Lives Matter, have led to the removal of oppressive racist-colonialist statues of Spanish conquistador Don Juan de Onates in New Mexico, priest Junipero Serra in Los Angeles and San Francisco, and a symbolic statue of Indian men assaulting a White colonial woman in Chicago. However, 20 statues of Junipero Serra remain (Spencer-Wood, forthcoming).

Patriarchal Colonialist Messages in Statues of Women

Feminist post-colonial theory argues that women are the last colony because of their continued exploitation by men (Lorber 2001:61), who have erased women's achievements and made them invisible by not commemorating them with statues, or by making statues of women in subservient positions to men, reinforcing patriarchal male domination of women. Minorities and women are oppressed and marginalized by statues that predominantly portray them in subordinate positions, and sometimes nearly naked, which is legitimated as art while actually reducing minorities and women to the status of subhuman animals. In hierarchical statues, the patriarchal dominance of White men is symbolized by elevating them physically above White women, while the ideology of racial inferiority of minorities is symbolized predominantly by statues of Native American men in loincloths attacking White women or lying fallen at the feet of Spanish priests or conquistadors; and by partially clothed African American men who crouch at the feet of a powerfully clothed White man, most often President Lincoln, who is symbolized as their liberator by showing broken chains (Spencer-Wood, forthcoming).

A colonialist perspective is evident in statues celebrating the cultural assimilation of Native Americans to supposedly superior European culture, symbolized by White male conquerors, priests, or teachers standing over subordinate Native Americans in bodily racist and sexist intersectional domination. For instance, the U.S. Capitol includes an intersectional statue of Native American Pocahontas kneeling for baptism by a White patriarchal priest standing over her (Workman 2001:62). Some colonialist statues of Pocahontas and Sacagawea (the first statue erected 1905) further celebrate Native Americans, most often women, who assisted White men in colonizing America (Chernick 2020), in some cases marrying them, exemplified by Pocahontas. These statues promote and sanctify the obliteration of Native American culture through assimilation to Anglo-American culture as an ideal to be emulated, by valorizing women who left their native villages to live with the English or Anglo-Americans. A 1919 statue in Charlottesville, Virginia, of Lewis and Clark with Sacagawea cowering at their feet, is being removed by the city council after Sacagawea's female descendants visited and voiced their shame and humiliation over the position of their ancestor in the statue. One descendant said she had seen every statue of her ancestor, and this one was the worst. Unfortunately, the statue is only being moved 20 ft. southwest from its central position on West Main Street to an area that will be made into a pocket park (Stout 2019). A plaque needs to be added to raise consciousness and reflection about the inequalities Native American women have suffered historically and today.

Empowering Statues of Real Women

Statues of historic suffragists are empowering for modern women seeking equal rights, but are threatening for men who want to dominate women. This explains why the powerful men in the U.S. Congress shamelessly supported patriarchy and sought to suppress feminism and women's rights by physically disappearing *The Woman's Movement* statue of busts of three White leaders of the women's rights movement emerging from a rough block of Italian marble, carved by Adelaide Johnson in 1920 after 70 women's organizations raised funds that barely covered the cost of materials. In 1921, the donated statue, with the gilt inscription "Woman first denied a soul, then called mindless, now arisen, declaring herself an entity to be reckoned," was installed in the Capitol Rotunda. Two days later, the Congressmen misogynistically ordered that the inscription be painted over and the statue moved (disappeared) into a basement broom closet. Congressmen voted down three bills that sought to return the statue to the Rotunda, arguing it weighed too much, or was too big and ugly, mockingly calling it "women in a bathtub." In 1963, the statue was moved to the basement crypt along with other statues, where it was disrespectfully displayed facing a wall and still without an inscription, so it would not be recognized by many visitors. Not until 1997 was the statue returned to the Rotunda, as a result of rapidly increasing the number of Congresswomen (9 percent of the Senate and 12 percent of the House) and a year of activism and fundraising by women's groups to celebrate the 75th anniversary of the woman suffrage amendment (Figure 10.1; Workman 2001).

The next statue of a suffragist was erected in Wyoming in 1953, followed by the Women's Rights National Park that was created in 1980, with an interpre-

Figure 10.1. The 1921 *Woman's Movement* (aka Portrait Monument) in the Capitol Rotunda, Washington D.C. Emerging from a rough eight-ton block of Italian marble are (*left to right*) busts of suffragists Elizabeth Cady Stanton, Susan B. Anthony, and Lucretia Mott, with an unfinished stone column behind them representing future women fighting for gender equality. Photo by Suzanne Spencer-Wood, 2016.

tive center on the site of the Wesley Chapel where the 1848 predominantly White Women's Rights Convention was held, which is portrayed with statues in the 1998 First Wave Exhibit (Figure 10.2). The park also includes a statue of Amelia Bloomer introducing Susan B. Anthony to Elizabeth Cady Stanton (Crozier et al. 2018:4, 6, 10, 46). Two cities in Tennessee, the last state to ratify the nineteenth amendment, erected group statues: in 2006 in Knoxville to three Tennessee suffragists (TWSM 2020) and in 2020 in Nashville to five

Figure 10.2. The 1998 First Wave Statue Exhibit at the Women's Rights National Historic Park, Seneca Falls, New York. The 19 bronze statues are mostly generically representing the 300 attendees of the 1848 Women's Rights Convention who did not sign the "Declaration of Sentiments." Statues of signers of the declaration, *in front from left*, are Elizabeth Cady Stanton, Frederick Douglass, and Martha Wright; *in the rear*, are Mary Ann and Thomas M'Clintock, Lucretia and James Mott, and Jane and Richard Hunt (Crozier De-Rosa and Mackie 2018:4, 6, 10, 46). Photo by Suzanne Spencer-Wood, 1998.

Tennessee suffragists (Staff 2020). In 2020, five silhouettes of suffragists were erected in Lexington, Kentucky (Collins 2020). In 2020, a statue of suffragist and doctor Martha Hughes Cannon was unveiled at the Utah State Capitol (Stauffer 2020). She became the first elected woman state senator in the U.S. in 1896 and worked for protective legislation for working women, the *Pure Food and Drug Act*, and welfare for disabled people, among other reforms. This statue will be moved to become only the tenth statue of a woman among the 100 statues in the National Statuary Hall at the U.S. Capitol (Deseret News 2018). This statue may have been inspired by, and also empowers, the recent increase in women legislators. These statues of suffragists powerfully legitimate and sanctify continuing the fight for the Equal Rights Amendment to the U.S. Constitution and provide role models for women to be activists and political leaders.

My feminist intersectional research found the fewest historical markers and statues memorializing subordinated minority women. Racism-sexism resulted in few statues of African American women. The 2020 Women Pioneers Monument in New York City's Central Park is the only statue to include *both* White suffragists *and* African American suffragist Sojourner Truth (Levenson et al. 2020), although there are several statues of Truth alone, who, like many Northern White suffragists, was also an abolitionist. The creation of Boston's Women's Heritage Trails (1990–99), which include 17 sites mapped by Spencer-Wood (1987, 1996), led to the erection in 2003 of the Boston Women's Memorial, with statues of two White feminists and enslaved Phillis Wheatley, who was the first African American poet (Bergmann 2005; Figure 10.3a). There has recently been an increase in empowering statues of historic African American women, who led movements for social justice, resonating with the modern Black Lives Matter movement.

My feminist intersectional research found that although there are some symbolic statues of immigrant mothers and families, there are practically no statues of real immigrant women and men due to xenophobic anti-immigrant sentiment in the dominant historical narrative that considered non-Anglo-Americans to be inferior races, legitimating their subordination and marginalization (Spencer-Wood 2022; forthcoming). In 2020, in New York City's Battery Park, facing Ellis Island, a larger-than-life bronze statue was dedicated representing the Italian American nun called Mother Cabrini, who was sent by Pope Leo XIII in 1889 to educate children in a series of Catholic church schools. In front of her statue are two symbolic statues, in a fantasized large bronze paper boat, of a little girl holding a small book and an older boy holding a piece of paper with writing on it. Mother Cabrini was known for making paper boats and releasing them into bodies of water. She was renowned for her work teaching immigrant children English and other skills and was the first American canonized by the Catholic church. Although this statue received the most votes from New Yorkers, it was excluded from the list of new statues planned by the initiative "She Built NYC" program to honor prominent historic women, which was headed by Mayor DiBlasio's African American wife, Chirlane McCray. This action indicates some sort of discrimination, either against immigrants, Italians, or Catholics, all of whom have a long history of being discriminated against by the protestant-American "nativist" movement. Ultimately, New York Governor Cuomo, who is of Italian descent, obtained state funds for the statue. The year-long controversy over the statue outraged the Italian American community, and the fallout included the exclusion of the statue-blocker's husband, Mayor DeBlasio (who also has Italian ancestry), from being featured in Columbus Day celebrations (Hogan et al. 2020). The recent revival of anti-immigrant prejudice may be the political reason for excluding this statue from the "She Built NYC" program, but diminishing this prejudice is a strong reason for creating more statues of immigrant women who have made important contributions to American society and culture.

The dominant heterosexism in Western culture usually leads people to

Figure 10.3. *A*, The 2003 Boston Women's Memorial on the Commonwealth Avenue Mall includes three bronze statues of renowned Boston women: the nineteenth-century abolitionist and suffragist Lucy Stone (*left*), and from the eighteenth century: the first African American poet, slave Phillis Wheatley (*right*), and her contemporary, Abigail Adams (*center*), who famously, but vainly, asked her husband John to "Remember the Ladies" and grant them freedom in the new nation's laws. Photo by Suzanne Spencer-Wood, 2008. *B*, The 1999 Harriet Tubman Memorial entitled Step on Board. Columbus Ave. at Warren Street, Boston's South End. Two 10 ft. bronze statues and bas reliefs in an arched slab, showing Tubman, Bible in hand, leading a group of escaped captives, while the back of the slab has a map of the route she took on the Underground Railroad, and several quotes about and by her. Photo by Leila Alciere, 2017, Wikipedia Commons. https://commons.wikimedia.org/wiki/File:Harriet_Tubman _Memorial,_Boston_(front,_uncropped).jpg.

assume that statues represent heterosexual individuals, since sexual orientation is not identifiable from statues. However, historical and forensic research has identified some statues that represent non-heterosexuals. Three statues represent reform women who were lesbians and renowned founders of social settlements (Cook 1979:417, 420–1): the statue of Jane Addams' helping hands in Chicago (Stingl 2019) and the busts of Jane Addams and Lillian Wald in the Hall of Fame for Great Americans in New York (Wikipedia 2022). The term *Boston marriage* was used to describe the prevalent practice of reform women homosocially living together, because it was so common in that city (Spencer-Wood 2004). In New York's Central Park, the statue of an angel alighting on top of the Bethesda Fountain actually depicts the famous actor Charlotte Cushman, who was sculpted by her lover Emma Stebbins (Capps 2016). There is also a bust of Cushman in the Hall of Fame for Great Americans (Wikipedia 2022). Across America, 51 statues have been erected of Polish general Casimir Pulaski, who organized and led the cavalry in the Revolution (Allen et al. 2022). He was forensically and historically identified in 2015 as intersex—a hermaphrodite who identified as male (Schoenberg 2019). The sexuality of the individuals represented in these statues needs to be noted in their inscriptions in order to re-enfranchise LGBTQIA communities of their powerful heritages.

A greater diversity of statues of real women is needed to counteract the repetition of statues of the same accomplished women, which gives the impression only very few women attained important achievements, such as Joan of Arc, Eleanor Roosevelt, Elizabeth Cady Stanton, and Susan B. Anthony for White women; Sacagawea, Pocahontas, and more recently Sarah Winnemucca for Native American women; and Harriet Tubman, Sojourner Truth, and Rosa Parks for African American women. Most of the statues of real women are duplicates that have been erected in the last 25 years. For instance, identical statues of Harriet Tubman by Jane DeDecker were placed in Mesa, Arizona, in 1995; in Gainesville, Florida, in 1997; in Little Rock, Arkansas, in 2004; and in Ypsilanti, Michigan, in 2006. Two statues of Tubman by other artists were placed in Boston in 1999 (Figure 10.3b); and in Bristol, Pennsylvania in 2006 (Geltzer 2015:ii). In 2009, a bust of Sojourner Truth was the first sculpture of an African American in the U.S. Capitol building, in the Visitor Center Emancipation Hall (Jones 2009). Following statues of her in a number of cities, in 2013 Rosa Parks was the first statue of an African American woman in the Capitol building, although some feminists protested that her passive, tired demeanor in her seated pose misrepresented her activism in the Civil Rights Movement (Amer and Theoharis 2013). While these are all worthy of statues, there is a greater diversity of women who deserve statues so that modern people can understand and be inspired by the great diversity of women's achievements and contributions to society and culture.

Recently, the number and diversity of new statues of women have rapidly increased. For instance, the Virginia Women's Monument in Capitol Square in Richmond was opened in 2019, to correct the lack of statues of women in the state by etching the names of 230 accomplished Virginia women on a glass wall, although it would be more empowering to also list their achievements. Seven of the following 12 planned statues of women have been unveiled: Cockacoeske, eighteenth-century chief of the Pamunkey tribe; Jamestown English colonist Anne Burras Layton; White *Virginia Gazette* publisher in colonial Williamsburg Clementina Bird Rind; White pioneer Mary Draper Ingles; White suffragist and arts leader Adele Goodman Clark; White Laura Lu Sherer Copenhaver, Lutheran lay leader and founder of Rosemont Industries; White Sarah G. Boyd Jones, the first woman physician in Virginia; Elizabeth Keckley, the slave who freed herself and became Mary Todd Lincoln's seamstress; Maggie L. Walker, the first African American woman to charter an American bank; and African American education pioneer and leader Virginia Randolf. Controversy has arisen over the planned statues of slave owners Martha Washington and Civil War Confederate hospital administrator Sally Louisa Tompkins (Curran 2019). Of the 12 statues, 8 (66 percent) were planned for White women, materializing continuing racism.

On the 26th of August 2020, the most comprehensive monument, called Gathering at the Crossroads, was erected on the site of what was the eighth ward of Harrisburg, Pennsylvania, which was destroyed in 1912 to expand the grounds that now include what was ironically named Equality Circle in front of the state Capitol. The monument includes statues of African Americans Frances Ellen Watkins Harper, a poet, abolitionist, and suffragette; William Howard Day, an educational reformer and civil rights pioneer; and military men Thomas Morris Chester and Jacob Compton, in conversation around a pedestal listing 100 important residents, including abolitionists who operated stations on the Underground Railroad, with a 3D model of the eighth-ward streets and buildings on top and bas relief street views of buildings on the sides. A book titled *100 Voices* details the achievements of the people named on the monument (Digital Harrisburg 2020). Half of the names are of military men and only one is of a woman.

Proposed Future Statues of Real Women

More statues are needed of the diversity of remarkable historic women and minorities to re-enfranchise Americans of their powerful, inspiring past and empower social movements for equality that counteract the vast majority of statues symbolically legitimating and sanctifying the persistence of intersecting racist, patriarchal values, beliefs, and behaviors. There are few statues honoring and sanctifying women who have worked for social justice and equality for women and minorities, which shows that these values in our Constitution are not being upheld in reality. There are too many accomplished women who deserve statues to name them all here. *Notable American Women* alone provides short biographies of 1,359 accomplished women who deserve statues. Length limits on this chapter have led me to focus on four women who worked for social justice and deserve statues, including a Native American, an African American, an immigrant woman, and a White Anglo-American.

A statue is needed of the Native American Sarah Ahauton for resisting colonialist, racist patriarchy in the Ponkapoag Praying Town of converted Christian Native Americans, founded south of Boston by Puritans in 1654 and named for a subtribe of the Massachusett Indians. Documents record that Sarah was accused of adultery by her husband William, and although she denied it and accused him of adultery and beating her, only she was arrested by the English Supervisor of Indians, imprisoned in Boston and displayed on a public "lecture day" with a noose around her neck at the city gallows. A feminist analysis reveals this resulted from the fact that adultery was defined as a crime by a man damaging the property of another man in his wife. Men, including husbands, who had sex with unmarried women only committed fornication, not adultery, and at most, were fined. Further, husbands could legally beat their wives "moderately." And wives could not divorce their husbands except for lack of financial support, in contrast to Sarah's matrilineal tribe that allowed wives to easily leave their husbands. In Sarah's "translated" testimony, she repeated that she was innocent and stated that she was pregnant with her fifth child by her husband and acknowledged "her duty to suffer and pray for her husband and to love him still." She was sentenced to pay court costs and be whipped at least 30 times by the Native American constable after she gave birth. Although there are no more written records about her, oral history has passed down the story that Sarah resisted being whipped into submission to patriarchy by jumping off a cliff and bashing her head on a rock (Clements 2011:104–6; Spencer-Wood 2013:176). The standing statue of Sarah Ahauton, with her face raised to heaven for justice, would be visible to the most people if erected in the Rotunda of the Massachusetts State House in Boston, below the mural showing John Eliot, the "apostle of the Indians" who founded Ponkapoag, preaching to convert Indians (Boston 2022). A plaque on the base of Sarah Ahauton's statue would counteract the mural's narrative of peaceful English-Indian relations with information about how English patriarchal laws allowed Native American men to be adulterous and physically abuse their wives with impunity, in contrast to the Ponkapoag tribal practice of permitting wives to leave abusive husbands.

A Black civil rights activist who deserves a statue is Sarah Elizabeth (called Lizz) Ray, who joined the Great Migration of African Americans from the South to the North, migrating to Detroit in the 1940s. When she graduated in 1945 from secretarial school, her class decided to celebrate by taking the ferry from the dock at the intersection of Clark and Jefferson Streets to Boblo amusement park on Bois Blanc Island in the Detroit River, but Lizz was escorted off the boat for being Black. She threw her refunded fare of 85 cents (now worth over $12.24) at the boat and went to the National Association for the Advancement of Colored People (NAACP), which hired Thurgood Marshall, who won her case at the U.S. Supreme Court in 1948, upholding the Michigan Constitution forbidding discrimination in public accommodations (Cooper 2006). A statue of Lizz Ray exerting her social agency by throwing change at the Boblo boat would be erected in front of the land side of the surviving building of the Boblo boat company on the Detroit River in downtown Detroit (Figure 10.4a).

A statue is warranted of Polish immigrant Dr. Marie E. Zakrzewska, who, in 1857, co-founded the first American hospital run by and for women in New York City. In 1862, Dr. Zakrzewska founded the second American women's hospital, the New England Hospital for Women and Children, which was a teaching hospital to train women doctors and nurses, at 55 Dimock Street, on the northeast corner of Columbus Avenue in Roxbury, in Greater Boston (Blake 1971:702–3). Then, in 1885, Dr. Zakrzewska instigated women of the Massachusetts Emergency and Hygiene Association's playground committee to found the American playground movement by establishing the first supervised playground in the yard of Parmenter Street Chapel, a mission at 20 Parmenter Street in Boston's North End. Ellen H. Tower and other reform women spread the playground movement to cities across America (Dickason 1983; Spencer-Wood and Blackburn 2017:945). The statue of Dr. Zakrzewska holding hands with a mother and child would be placed in front of the hospital building that is named for her (Figure 10.4b).

A statue is also needed of suffragist, reformer and philanthropist Clara Arthur of Detroit. She led the successful campaign that won women's suffrage in Michigan in 1918. Starting in 1901, Clara also led the playground movement in Detroit, which by 1926 had 36 supervised playgrounds in schools and parks, attended by eight million children and adults annually. Clara also led the establishment of shower baths in public schools and led the antituberculosis movement in Detroit. A statue of Clara Arthur would be seen

Figure 10.4. *A*, Surviving Boblo Boat company dock building on the Detroit River. A statue of Sarah Elizabeth Ray throwing her ferry fare at the river where the boat was docked would be placed in front of the building next to the intersection of Jefferson and Clark Streets. Photo by Notorious4life 2020. Wikipedia Creative Commons. Accessed September 30, 2022. *B*, Surviving Zakrzewska building of the New England Hospital for Women and Children, founded by Dr. Marie Zakrzewska in 1862. In 1969, it became the Dimock Community Health Center, at 55 Dimock Street, Roxbury, MA. A statue of Dr. Zakrzewska holding hands with a mother and child would be placed in front of the entrance to the building. Photo by User Magicpiano 2013, Wikipedia Creative Commons, accessed September 30, 2022.

by the most people if it were placed in the only surviving playground still used for its original purpose at Duffield Public School, now called the Bunche Preparatory Academy, located at 2715 Macomb Street (Spencer-Wood and Blackburn 2017:956, 961–2, 964–5).

These are just a few of the women and minorities who deserve statues to sanctify and promote the American values of justice and equality with examples of real people who worked for these ideals. This chapter intersectionally focuses on women and minorities because their valuable accomplishments and contributions to society are most overlooked, with most statues of real women only erected in the last 25 years, and especially in the last few years. Statues of historic women and minorities are erected to empower us today to work on improving society through greater equality, as exemplified by the statues of women reformers and civil rights leaders. Statues celebrating women's public achievements are needed to generate pride and inspire girls and women to reach beyond sexist stereotypes that devalue women as domestic and incapable of accomplishing anything significant, to realize their aspirations to achieve contributions that make a difference in society and culture.

References

Allen, Laurie, Paul Farber, and Sue Mobley (directors)
    2022   National Monument Audit. Monument Lab and Andrew W. Mellon Foundation Landmark Monuments Project. https://monumentlab.com/audit, accessed on 1 August 2022.

Amer, Marwa, and Jeanne Theoharis
    2013   Honoring Rosa Parks Requires More Than a Statue. *The Nation*, 28 February. https://www.thenation.com/article/archive/honoring-rosa-parks-requires-more-statue/, accessed 10 January 2021.

Bergmann, Meredith
    2005   The Boston Women's Memorial. *American Arts Quarterly* 22(3): 24-29, accessed 8 August 2022, at the Newington-Cropsey Cultural Center. https://web.archive.org/web/20160407005057/http://www.nccsc.net/essays/boston-women%E2%80%99s-memorial

Blake, John B.
    1971   ZAKRZEWSKA, Marie Elizabeth (Sept. 6, 1829–May 12, 1902). In *Notable American Women: A Biographical Dictionary*. Edward T. James, Janet Wilson James, and Paul S. Boyer, eds. Pp. 702–4. Cambridge MA, USA: The Belknap Press of Harvard University Press.

Capps, Kriston
    2016   The Gender Gap in Public Sculpture. There is Almost No Public Art Commemorating History-making Women in America. We Need to Change That. *Bloomberg City Lab Design*, 24 February, New York. https://www.bloomberg

.com/news/articles/2016-02-24/the-gender-gap-in-historic-sculptures-and-public-art, accessed 5 January 2021.

Carlson, Jen
  2020   NYC's First Female Historical Statue Was Unveiled 105 Years Ago. The 6th Just Arrived This Week. *Gothamist, News and Entertainment,* 26 August. https://gothamist.com/arts-entertainment/nycs-first-female-historical-statue-was-unveiled-105-years-ago-6th-was-unveiled-week, accessed 2 May 2021.

Chernick, Karen
  2020   The Complicated History of the First Monument to Sacajawea, Funded by Suffragists and Designed by a Woman. *The Art Newspaper,* 26 August. https://www.theartnewspaper.com/2020/08/26/the-complicated-history-of-the-first-monument-to-sacajawea-funded-by-suffragists-and-designed-by-a-woman, accessed 8 August 2022.

Clements, Joyce M.
  2011   Sarah and the Puritans: Feminist Contributions to New England Historical Archaeology. In Special Issue: The Impact of Feminist Theories on Archaeology, guest editors Suzanne M. Spencer-Wood and Laurajane. Smith. *Archaeologies* 7(1): 97-121.

Collins, Katherine
  2020   'Stand' Statue Honoring Suffragists Unveiled in Lexington. *Lex 18 NBC,* 20 August, Lexington, Kentucky. https://www.lex18.com/news/covering-kentucky/stand-statue-honoring-women-suffragists-unveiled-in-lexington, accessed 28 January 2021.

Cook, Blanche W.
  1979   Female Support Networks and Political Activism. In *A Heritage of Her Own.* Nancy F. Cott and Elizabeth H. Pleck, eds. Pp. 412–45. New York, NY: A Touchstone Book, Simon and Schuster.

Cooper, Desirée
  2006   Long Journey Ends Injustice: Detroiter Fights Bob-Lo in Supreme Court and Wins. *Detroit Free Press* 28 February:18–19.

Crenshaw, Kimberlé W.
  1989   Demarginalizing the Intersection of Race and Sex: A Black Feminist Critique of Antidiscrimination Doctrine, Feminist Theory and Anti-Racist Politics. *University of Chicago Legal Forum* 140:139–67.

Crozier De-Rosa, Sharon, and Vera Mackie
  2018   *Remembering Women's Activism.* Abington, UK: Routledge.

Curran, Colleen
  2019   "A Monumental Day": Seven Statues Unveiled at Virginia Women's Monument in Capitol Square. *Richmond Times-Dispatch,* 14 October. https://richmond.com/news/local/government-politics/a-monumental-day-seven-statues-unveiled-at-virginia-women-s/article_ca7c3e3e-2bf4-52ed-a078-5b3f450684ec.html, accessed 1 February 2021.

Deetz, James F.
  1988   Material Culture and Worldview in Colonial Anglo-America: Historical Archaeology in the Eastern United States. In *The Recovery of Meaning.* Mark P.

Leone and Parker B. Potter, Jr., eds. Pp. 219–35. Washington, D.C.: Smithsonian Institution Press.

Deseret News
    2018   In our opinion: Martha Hughes Cannon goes to Washington. *Deseret News, Opinion*, 7 April, Salt Lake City, Utah. https://www.deseret.com/2018/4/7/20642998/in-our-opinion- martha-hughes-cannon-goes-to-washington, accessed 2 May 2021.

Dickason, Jerry G.
    1983   The Origin of the Playground: The Role of the Boston's Women's Clubs 1885–1890. *Leisure Sciences* 6(1):83–98.

Digital Harrisburg
    2020   *Commonwealth Monument Project*. https://digitalharrisburg.com/commonwealth/, accessed 22 July 2021.

Geltzer, Elise A.
    2015   *Variations on a Theme: Contemporary Memorials to Harriet Tubman*. MA Thesis, City College of the City University of New York.

Gillie and Marc
    2021   *Statues for Equality*. https://statuesforequality.com/, accessed January and July 2021.

Ginzberg, Lori D.
    1990   *Women and the Work of Benevolence: Morality, Politics and Class in the 19th-Century United States*. New Haven, CT: Yale University Press.

Wikipedia
    2022   Hall of Fame for Great Americans. *Wikipedia, the free encyclopedia*. https://en.wikipedia.org/wiki/Hall_of_Fame_for_Great_Americans, accessed 8 November 2022.

Hogan, Bernadette, Carl Campanile, and Rachel Green
    2020   Mother Cabrini Statue Dedicated in Battery Park. *New York Post*, 12 October. https://nypost.com/2020/10/12/mother-cabrini-statue-dedicated-in-battery-park- overlooks-ellis-island/, accessed 10 January 2021.

Jameson, John H
    2024.   Personal communication that Confederates considered their secession to be the second American Revolution against the tyranny of President Lincoln. Email 31 March.

Jones, Joyce
    2009   Sojourner Truth Celebrated with a Bust at the Capitol. *50 Black Enterprise*, 28 April. https://www.blackenterprise.com/sojourner-truth-celebrated-with-a-bust-in-the-capitol/, accessed 10 January 2021.

Lefrak, Mikaela
    2019   Most of D.C.'s Statues Are of White Men. A New Bill Could Add More Women and Locals to The Mix. npr station *WAMU 88.5 American University Radio*, 2 April, Washington D.C. https://wamu.org/story/19/04/02/most-of-d-c-s-statues-are-of-white- men-a-new-bill-could-add-more-women-and-locals-to-the-mix/, accessed 3 January 2021.

Levenson, Eric, Tawanda S. Tambou, and Deborah Brunswick
  2020   Central Park is Unveiling a Statue of Women's Rights Pioneers. It's the Park's First Statue of Real Women. *CNN Style.* https://www.cnn.com/style/article/central-park-womens-rights-statue/index.html, accessed 3 January 2021.

Loewen, James W.
  1999   *Lies Across America: What Our Historic Sites Get Wrong.* New York, NY: The New Press.

Lorber, Judith
  2001   *Gender Inequality: Feminist Theories and Politics. Second Edition.* Los Angeles, CA: Roxbury Publishing Co.

Macdonald, Anne L.
  1992   *Feminine Ingenuity: Women and Invention in America.* New York, NY: Ballantine Books.

Peled, Shachar
  2017   Where are the Women? New Effort to Give Them Just Due on Monuments, Street Names. *CNN*, March 8. https://www.cnn.com/2017/03/08/us/womens-monument-project-trnd, accessed 8 August 2022.

Platt, Verity
  2020   Why People are Toppling Monuments to Racism. *Scientific American*, 3 July. https://www.scientificamerican.com/article/why-people-are-toppling-monuments-to-racism/, accessed 3 January 2021.

Quaglia, Sofia
  2019   Cracking the Bronze Ceiling: The US has Fewer Than 400 Statues of Women—But That's Changing. *QUARTZ*, 24 April. https://qz.com/1732974/new-york-citys-central-park-will-get-its-first-statue-of-women/#:~:text=Across%20the%20US%2C%20there%20are,150%20statues%20are%20real%20women, accessed 3 January 2021.

Schoenberg, Nara
  2019   "It's a Woman. It's not Pulaski": New Documentary Argues Revolutionary War Hero was Intersex. *Chicago Tribune*, April 3. https://www.chicagotribune.com/lifestyles/ct-life-casimir-pulaski-intersex-040319-story.html, accessed 13 August 2022.

Shackel, Paul A.
  2003   Memory in Black and White: Race Commemoration and the Post-Bellum Landscape. Lanham, MD: AltaMira Press.

Spencer-Wood, Suzanne M.
  1987   Survey of Domestic Reform Movement Sites in Boston and Cambridge, c. 1865–1905. *Historical Archaeology* 21(2):7–36.

Spencer-Wood, Suzanne M.
  1991a Towards a Feminist Historical Archaeology of the Construction of Gender. In *The Archaeology of Gender: Proceedings of the 22nd [1989] Chacmool Conference.* Dale Walde and Noreen D. Willows, eds. Pp. 234–44. Calgary, AB: University of Calgary Archaeological Association.
  1991b Towards an Historical Archaeology of Materialistic Domestic Reform. In *The*

Archaeology of Inequality. Randall M. McGuire and Robert Paynter, eds. Pp. 231–86. Oxford, UK: Basil & Blackwell.

1996   Feminist Historical Archaeology and the Transformation of American Culture by Domestic Reform Movements, 1840–1925. In *Historical Archaeology and the Study of American Culture.* L. A. De Cunzo and B. L. Herman, eds. Pp. 397–446. Knoxville, TN: Winterthur Museum and University of Tennessee Press.

2004   A Historic Pay-for-Housework Community Household: The Cambridge Cooperative Housekeeping Society. In *Household Chores and Household Choices: Theorizing the Domestic Sphere in Historical Archaeology.* Kerri S. Barile and Jamie C. Brandon, eds. Pp. 138–58. Tuscaloosa, AL: University of Alabama Press.

2013   Western Gender Transformations from the Eighteenth Century to the Early Twentieth Century: Combining the Domestic and Public Spheres. In *Historical and Archaeological Perspectives on Gender Transformations: From Private to Public.* Suzanne M. Spencer-Wood, ed. Pp. 173–215. New York, NY: Springer.

2022   Empowering Social Justice and Equality by Developing a Feminist Intersectionality Framework to Increase the Inclusiveness of Detroit Historical Markers. *Archaeologies* 18(1):72–131.

Forthcoming   The Social Agency of Statues in Materially Symbolizing Ideological Messages: Intentions and Interpretations of Multiple Meanings. *International Journal of Historical Archaeology.*

Spencer-Wood, Suzanne M., and Renée Blackburn

2017   The Creation of the American Playground Movement by Reform Women, 1885–1930: A Feminist Analysis of Materialized Ideological Transformations and Gender Power Dynamics, in a special issue entitled "Archaeology of Reform/Archaeology as Reform," co-edited by Megan Springate and Kim Christiensen. *International Journal of Historical Archaeology* 21(4):937–977.

Staff

2020   Dedication of Tennessee Woman Suffrage Monument. *Tennessee Tribune*, 13 August, Nashville. https://tntribune.com/dedication-of-tennessee-woman-suffrage-monument/, accessed 24 January 2021.

Stauffer, McKenzie

2020   Dr. Martha Hughes Cannon Statue Unveiled at the Utah State Capitol. *2KUTV*, 15 September, Salt Lake City. https://kutv.com/news/local/dr-martha-hughes-cannon-statue-unveiled-at-the-utah-state-captiol, accessed 5 May 2021.

Stingl, Jim

2019   Like Most Cities, Milwaukee has Precious Few Statues of Real Women. *Milwaukee Journal Sentinel*, January 10. https://www.jsonline.com/story/news/columnists/jim-stingl/2019/01/10/milwaukee-has-precious-few-statues-real-women-like-most-cities/2529982002/, accessed 10 January 2021.

Stout, Nolan

2019   City Council Votes to Remove Lewis-Clark-Sacagawea Statue. *Daily Progress*, 15 November. Charlottesville, VA. https://dailyprogress.com/news/local/city-council-votes-to-remove-lewis-clark-sacagawea-statue/article_50f35095-a8c9-55b9-98f3-fc6a92c535f6.html, accessed 2 January 2021.

TWSM (Tennessee Woman Suffrage Memorial)
　2020　*Honoring the Past and a Legacy for the Future.* http://tnwomansmemorial.org/, accessed 24 January 2021.

Workman, Courtney
　2001　The Woman Movement: Memorial to Women's Rights Leaders and Perceived Images of the Women's Rights Movement. In *Myth, Memory and the Making of the American Landscape.* Paul A. Shackel, ed. Pp. 47–66 Gainesville, FL: University Press of Florida.

11

Three Ways of Remembering World War I

The Sledmere Memorials, Yorkshire, England

Harold Mytum

World War I memorials were erected in large numbers across Britain and its colonies and comprise highly visible and socially significant features of urban and rural landscapes. Erected in the years following the armistice, they take a range of forms, with internal wall panels being complemented with external structures varying from monuments with crosses or statuary through to utilitarian structures such as village community halls and churchyard lychgates (Moriarty 1995:2008). The monuments vary greatly not only in form but also in the content and emphasis of their inscriptions. Although most listed all in the relevant community who lost their lives, some also celebrated those who participated but survived.

The development of commemoration of the fallen from wars—and doing so by naming them individually—reveals a change in attitude to military deaths. Earlier memorials to battles were to victory and national success rather than remembering losses. The greater recognition of the diversity of loss is represented in the numerous memorials. The War Memorials Register, administered by the Imperial War Museum, already contains records for 84,000 memorials. Some are for individuals, and others are for other wars, though the vast majority are for World War I. Many were augmented with the names of those who died fighting in World War II, though a few additional memorials were erected. An analysis of the 57,000 war memorials cataloged in 2002 revealed that two-thirds are for World War I, with plaques for World War II added to many of these (Furlong et al. 2002). The analysis considered the popularity of different memorial forms by conflict and allows a quantifiable background that can be set against the memorials discussed here.

This chapter considers three communal memorials, all found in one English village. Due to limited access because of the COVID-19 epidemic, the internal memorial—an illuminated book that names and has a short entry for each individual created in a Gothic revival style of the manuscript—is not analyzed in detail. Edmund Thomas Sandars produced the volume over a period of two years, listing the names of local men who died in the war from the Wolds Wagoners[1] and the Green Howards, a local regiment of the British army. Sir Mark Sykes, who shall be shown to be instrumental in the design and construction of all the memorials discussed in this chapter, had served with this regiment in the Boer War and was commanding officer of the 5th battalion of the regiment at the start of World War I. The volume is still on display in a glass case within the parish church. Rolls of honor set within a picture frame were classed with books of remembrance by Furlong et al. (2002, Table 1.1) and only comprised 5.5 percent of World War I memorials, and personal experience indicates that the rolls of honor are far more frequent, so a book was a rare form of commemoration. It was, however, at least part of a recognized tradition, whereas the other two external memorials were unique expressions of the conflict. They are considered in more detail below.

The Setting

Sledmere is a village on the estate of Sledmere Hall, home of the Tatton Sykes family, set in the Yorkshire Wolds in East Yorkshire, England (Neave and Neave 2008). The family descends from seventeenth-century Hull merchants who became wealthy through strategic marriages and then, once established on the Wolds, by espousing agricultural improvement as the chalkland landscape was converted through enclosure from extensive grazing to arable farming. Villages such as Sledmere were also improved with the construction of estate housing for the agricultural workers, with successive generations of the Sykes family taking a paternal attitude to their workforce and tenants.

The memorials under discussion here are set on the B1251 Bridlington Road that curves around the periphery of the Sledmere House grounds and through the estate village. The external memorials are set equidistant c.50m from the gateway that leads down a drive to the parish church, within which the illuminated memorial book can be found. The Eleanor Cross is close to a road turning off the B1251 to North Grimston, and the Wagoners' Memorial lies next to the junction with the road to Kirby Grindalythe (Figure 11.1).

---

1 The spelling *Wagoners* is one used for the organization on their membership badges and celebrated on the memorials, and it was used at the time for a category of agricultural employee. It is spelled thus on the memorial inscription. It is still used for the small museum housed at Sledmere House, so it is used consistently in this chapter.

The Commissioner

Sir Mark Sykes, 6th baronet, is central to the three memorials discussed in this chapter, as he commissioned them all and was involved with the design of two. He was in a line of Sykes landowners who settled on the Yorkshire Wolds in the eighteenth century after effective mercantile enterprises and strategic marriages into landed wealth, which included Sledmere House (Mytum 2007).

Sir Tatton Sykes, 4th baronet, developed the estate to create a profitable landscape with a concentration on cereal production. On his death, an impressive, eye-catching memorial tower paid for by public subscription was placed outside the village (Historic England 1987, Mytum 2007). His son, Sir Tatton Sykes Jr., 5th baronet, showed his benevolence to his estate villages by having estate cottages constructed, and he also invested heavily in rebuilding the churches in the estate villages, including Sledmere church tower in 1893 (Pevsner 1984). He also erected a limestone monument at a road junction in Sledmere opposite the church, a version of the 1291 Eleanor Cross at Hardingstone, Northamptonshire, which was later adapted to become a war memorial that is discussed below (Banbury 2000; Mytum 2007, Historic England 2016a). This was not the only Eleanor Cross-style memorial erected in England in the nineteenth century (Davies 2018:89–93). By the time Sir Mark Sykes inherited the estate, there was already a monumental landscape within the village that, combined with Sledmere House and the estate housing, created a physical environment in which the landowning family were celebrated.

Sir Mark Sykes was a soldier, civil servant, and diplomat, as well as continuing to manage his family estates. Born in 1879, he served in the Second Boer War in the Green Howards regiment (Adelson 1975:71–89). He then became private secretary to the chief secretary of Ireland, George Wyndham, but he did not find the role satisfying (Adelson 1975:99). Sir Mark subsequently spent a considerable time in Turkey (then the Ottoman Empire) and was fascinated by the culture of the region. He became a military attaché in Constantinople from early 1905 until returning to Britain in 1906 (Adelson 1975:108–114). For Sir Mark, 1911 was a tumultuous year—he was elected MP for Central Hull, but the family home, Sledmere House, was badly damaged by fire. A Catholic chapel was also built in the house as he had followed his mother in being a committed Roman Catholic, though he was buried, as were his ancestors, in the graveyard of the Anglican parish church next to Sledmere House and across the road from the Eleanor Cross.

Sir Mark was well aware of the skills of his agricultural workforce, and as he anticipated a major conflict between Britain and Germany, began to

Three Ways of Remembering World War I: The Sledmere Memorials, Yorkshire, England

Figure 11.1. Eleanor Cross (*left*) and Wagoners' Memorial (*right*). Photo by Harold Mytum.

prepare his male workforce to use their horse transport skills to support the impending war. The family was able to move back into the house in 1915, but Sir Mark was from this time more involved with the War Office and then Foreign Office, using his Middle Eastern experience in diplomatic and intelligence work (Adelson 1975:175–195). Sir Mark was active in the negotiations that led to the Sykes-Picot agreement (secretly concluded in 1916) by which the current Middle Eastern states, including Iraq and Syria, were constructed (Berdine 2018). He was also influential in the drafting of the Balfour Declaration, which led to the establishment of Palestine for the Jews (Bloom 2011). The allied powers planned an allocation of the region to British, French, and Russian spheres of influence, following the anticipated fall of the Ottoman Empire. Sir Mark died in Paris in early 1919 from the Spanish influenza, during ongoing negotiations to implement arrangements for the Middle East, developing from the original Sykes-Picot agreement (Adelson 1975:290–295).

Plans for the memorials at Sledmere, already well advanced, were completed after the death of Sir Mark Sykes, with his own memorial added to the Eleanor Cross even though his was not a war death. There is no doubt that both external memorials were conceived, designed, and planned by the 6th baronet, with correspondence and drawings in his hand that attest to his intimate level of involvement (Mark Sykes Papers 1879–1919. Hull History Centre archives, DDSY2/6/32). The resulting monuments represent individuals in the case of the Eleanor Cross and a community with the Wagoners' Memorial, but the messages they give out are heavily mediated through the mind and hand of Sir Mark Sykes. The two monuments each reflect their designer's attitudes to his friends, estate employees, and their culture. Together, they reveal Sir Mark's romantic notions linked to both popular bucolic culture on the one hand and chivalric values necessary to protect this world in the face of Teutonic threat on the other.

The Eleanor Cross

The cross erected by the 5th baronet was already an established feature in the estate landscape, and visible to those passing through the village. Why it was constructed is nowhere stated in its commissioner's surviving correspondence, but Sir Mark appropriated it to give it an explicit commemorative function and build on any associations a Gothic monument might communicate to the early twentieth-century viewer.

The reuse of the cross, with its Gothic revival style, may have been inspired by Sir Mark's familiarity with the memorial to those from Yorkshire who died in the Second Boer War in which he had served. The York Boer War memorial was erected in 1905, close to York Minster, and had several features that may have influenced the adaptation of the Eleanor Cross. Inset panels of slate on the York monument list the names of all the deceased, with carved figures including a sailor, cavalryman, artilleryman, infantryman, and nurse set in niches above the panels. The brasses show the deceased in uniform, though medievalized to be appropriate when depicted on a medieval-style brass and inset in the panels of the monument like the slate tablets on the York memorial.

The Sledmere Eleanor Cross memorial has been studied from an art historical perspective (Banbury 2000; Meara 1996) and has been considered from an archaeological landscape context (Mytum 2007) (Figure 11.2). What is notable, however, is the way in which this is a selective representation of certain individuals, their facial likenesses based on photographs and with families' approval (Mark Sykes Papers 1879–1919. Hull History Centre archives, DDSY2/6/32). While there is no list of names, each of the 22 World War I casualties commemorated is identified and has a specific inscription on the relevant brass. Sir Mark took a very active interest in their correct design and in the associated text, as evidenced in extensive correspondence with families and the makers of the brasses.

Most war memorials list names, but they are seen as communal monuments—where the regiment, employer, or place is seen as the commu-

Figure 11.2. The Boer War Memorial in York. Photo by Harold Mytum.

nity that is united in its loss. Rank and manner of death, previous occupation, or individual characteristics are deliberately suppressed in that united loss. In contrast, the Eleanor Cross is one of separate individuals, each in their own panel; the one image that commemorates three soldiers combines officers who were not related but whose relatives wished to contribute to their brass. Unlike the identical treatment of names on the typical war memorial, with no difference in font size and usually with names arranged alphabetically by surname, here the individuals vary greatly in size and have unique descriptive texts and even symbols that may indicate their civilian occupation. There is no simple correlation between size of a depiction and status, nor in the nature of their war service. Sir Mark has created a monument that looks different in the arrangement of brasses from every direction; uniformity is only through the medium of the brasses and their style. The commissioner was then also commemorated in similar fashion on the one previously unfilled panel.

The Wagoner's Memorial

Sir Mark foresaw the impending confrontation with Germany, and that this would require enormous logistic support. Looking across his estates and at his tenants and their skills, he recognized that a particular group of employees across the Wolds could provide a particular skill set to enable the military. This group were the wagoners, those involved with the horses and carts extensively used across the farms. Some aspects of mechanization had affected agriculture by the early twentieth century, with threshing machines powered by steam traction engines a well-established seasonal change to the traditional work pattern during harvest (Long 1963).

Agriculture in the early twentieth century was labor-intensive, and it involved teams of workers whose members could gradually progress up the ladder of responsibility over time and with increased experience. The wagoner was, among other skills, an expert in not only managing the horses and their needs, but also driving the wagons or carts that were the main method of moving people and materials around the farm, and indeed off to market. Given that the military would require supply of rations and armaments, Sir Mark saw that this could be a distinctive contribution from this workforce when others could act as infantry soldiers and in other roles in the armed forces.

Sir Mark wished to hone the skills of the Wagoners and also foster a group identity and esprit de corps, ready for when any call might come. As stated in one of the inscriptions on the monument, he established "the Wolds Wagoners Reserve A corps of 1000 drivers raised by him on the Yorkshire Wolds Farms in the year 1912." They became part of the Territorial Army as a Special Reserve and were rapidly introduced to the battlefield setting during 1914, by which time over 1,200 men were in the corps.

The memorial was designed in detail by Sir Mark Sykes, who commissioned the noted sculptor Carlo Magnoni to carve the monument, which was then erected by Alfred Batt, mason, and Thomas Scott, supervisor. They are acknowledged on the memorial, which was carved from pale cream Portland stone (Historic England 2016b). The octagonal base with five steps supports the central column on which the main carved sculptural panels are set on three horizontal bands. The conical roof is carved with an imitation of fish scale slates, and beneath this is an entablature that displays an inscription. It is supported by four columns, each with a distinct geometric design reminiscent of Romanesque and Carolingian architecture. Each capital for the columns displays animal heads within the design: sheep, cattle, horses, and pigs. These represent the livestock aspect of mixed farming in the agricultural economy of the Wolds, with some of the main panels depicting the harvesting of cereals.

The Sykes family papers contain sketches revealing early stages in the design of the panels, and also a detailed set of drawings that set out the three registers of carved scenes on the four faces of the central column drum (Mark Sykes Papers 1879–1919. Hull History Centre archives, DDSY2/6/32). From the start, Sir Mark had a clear idea of the story to be told, and the way the monument would tell of the origin and raising of the Wagoners, with some representation of their efforts in France. There are several inscriptions, including a long poem (Figure 11.3, Panel D), but there is no list of Wagoners who served, or even those who lost their lives. This is different from most war memorials, which do list those involved.

The Wagoners Memorial is a communal monument with only those involved in its design and construction named, and the founder Sir Mark the only person named on the panels themselves. The monument was set up nearer to village estate housing and the entrance to Sledmere House than the Eleanor Cross, and at a road junction which made several sides easily visible.

The Wagoners' Memorial Narrative Panels

The central column contains three horizontal bands of carved sculptural panels. On one side, the top panel is framed by a background of Romanesque arcading, in front of which the enlisting into the Wagoners Special Reserve is displayed. On the far right, a short, apparently incomplete, text is incised: "CAPTN SYKES / OF THE A.S.C. / Attested / one thous / and Farm / hands / Between / Martimas." The scene has a central figure in uniform sitting at a table and holding a Bible out to the wagoner to the left. Accompanied by his seated dog, the wagoner grasps the Bible with his right hand and holds up his left while swearing his loyalty. A standing figure in uniform looks on from the right. The wagoners were subsequently officially incorporated into the Army Service Corps (A.S.C.) by the War Office.

The middle panel is inscribed along the bottom of the panel: "this was the course of the Annual competition held in Fimber Field." The Wolds Wagoners corps held an annual competition on a course that was laid out with a figure-of-eight track around which the wagons had to be steered on a timed run. This is portrayed as a plan on the panel, with arrows that indicate the direction by which the course was negotiated, and with the barriers that ensured the competitors kept to the track and could negotiate the equivalent of gateways. The annual competition became a significant social event on the Wolds and was successful in generating interest in the corps and encouraging skills development among the Wagoners.

The bottom panel depicts the Wolds wagon and its driver (the Wagoner), as a load of full grain sacks are pulled by two horses, one also carrying the Wagoner with saddle and stirrups, and accompanied by his dog running alongside. The wagon has two axles, the rear with larger 12-spoke wheels and smaller front wheels that enable the vehicle to change direction. This was a heavy vehicle that required well-trained horses managed by an experienced Wagoner. Such vehicles were locally made, such as by East Yorkshire and Crosskills Cart and Waggon Co of Beverley (Baggs et al. 1989).

On the second side, the top panel is inscribed with the single word "mobilization" with a scene of harvest taking place. As one man uses a pitchfork to load the stooks of corn into the wagon, another—presumably the Wagoner—stands holding his pitchfork, ceasing his labors, while the postman delivers an envelope containing his call-up papers. Between the two sits a flagon, no doubt containing cider or beer, to sustain the harvesters in their labor. Into this idyllic scene of agricultural labor intrudes the shadow of wartime.

The middle panel is an external scene of Wagoners heading off from home. A house with a gabled roof on the left has a hooded grandmother and child, both waving farewell, with the wife handing over a bag with food for the journey and his stick, all slightly smaller than the Wagoners. The married Wagoner faces his family, his dog jumping up, barking concern at his owner leaving without him. A second Wagoner has turned and faces right, already walking past a roadside milestone inscribed "DRIFFIELD / VIII MILES / York / XXIV MILES." The family's faces display a worried look, while the Wagoners seem more serene and phlegmatic, a carefully constructed image of sacrifice and loyalty to king and country.

The bottom panel has a background of Romanesque arcading, with the Wagoner arriving holding his stick and bag over his shoulder and showing his paper to an officer seated at a desk, probably the same location where he had enrolled in the Special Reserve. The officer points to the right, showing the way to a line of Wagoners who had already been kitted out in uniform, standing to attention and in the process of being checked off a list by an officer holding a pen and scroll. Here is the transformation from civilian to military life. The Wagoners received limited military training, and they were rapidly sent off to the Front to contribute with the skills they already had honed. They were non-combatants, but intimately associated with conflict.

One the third side, the top panel depicts the dramatic portrayal of the voyage to France. The choppy waters are hazardous—two naval mines laid by the Germans to impede British shipping lurk in the water. The fleet of steam ships, all with two funnels belching smoke and with the Royal Ensign flag at the stern, would have been carrying the Wagoners to be given their horses and carts in France.

The next scene shows the Wagoners marching in single file down the gangplank, all firmly holding onto the rail with the ocean waves beneath them and carrying standard packs on their backs. The first Wagoner is just stepping onto foreign soil, the quay being in front of a Romanesque arcaded, crenelated ashlar stone town wall with the upper floors of houses and a church visible beyond. Incised onto the arcading is "LIBERTÉ, EGALITÉ and FRATERNITÉ," emphasizing the French context.

Details of select panels: *Panel A* (Figure 11.3a) shows a very damaged tree to the left, with a Romanesque-style church with a square tower and door and nave with round-topped windows, out of which smoke is billowing. The roofs are tiled. A large figure of a German infantry soldier stands holding a burning torch, presumably having started the fire as he is watching on with a satisfied grin. To the right is another German facing the opposite direction, holding the long hair of a woman who lies on the floor, hand outstretched, and is about to be beheaded by the soldier who wields a sword above his head.

It is likely that this panel represents scenes from the burning of Louvain, Belgium, by German forces in August 1914. In reprisals for civilian resistance to occupation, the German forces destroyed the town and killed a large number of civilians, including women and children (Williams 2018). These events were seized upon by the British press (Goebel 2012), and they helped create the strong anti-German sentiment that led to the internment of German civilians and promoted recruitment to the armed services. A major theme of the propaganda—both in text and image—was the threat to women and families, and the undermining of knowledge and religion by the barbarous Germans (Bennett and Hampton 2007; Robertson 2014). This panel is one of the most overt statements of Sir Mark's sentiments on either of the monuments, but it forms part of the repertoire of symbolism that relates to this feeling.

Panel B (Figure 11.3b) represents the repulsing of a German attack. To the left is a line of German infantry, snarling and grimacing, as they march forward in step with serrated bayonets ready. Despite shells flying overhead from the German artillery barrage fired from behind the lines, a British infantry soldier stands firm, his legs braced, ready to hold the attackers off while the Wagoners load the wagon. The scene here is the retreat from Mons, with the signpost that the Germans are passing pointing toward the left to "MONS" while the wagon and the retreating British will be withdrawing along the road

a

b

c

d

Figure 11.3. Panel scenes *A*, *B*, *C*, and *D* on the Wagoners' Memorial. Photos by Harold Mytum.

signposted prominently to "AMIENS." The Wagoners played an important role in this retreat (Robertshaw n.d.).

Panel C (Figure 11.3c) is a second scene of warfare. Here, the multi-arched bridge across the substantial river is depicted in a naive style, allowing paving to be displayed with "MARNE" incised above. With British shells representing a barrage to support the infantry advance, the central figure on the bridge is a charging British infantry soldier, rifle with bayonet held horizontally and ready for use, as he chases a retreating German soldier, running away with his rifle at an angle. The casualties of war are represented by a German helmeted head and hand emerging from the flowing waters of the river and, to the right, a burning house in the background. The Wagoner faces away from the conflict, quietly holding the reins of his horse as it stands by a tree trunk, signs of new growth sprouting from the ground.

The crossing of the Marne by British troops took place on 9 September 1914, part of a major counterattack following massive German territorial gains earlier in the month. The Wolds Wagoners had been a key part of the earlier withdrawal, but also contributed to the response.

The Wagoner looking serene and untroubled, but traveling so far from home, seeing foreign lands, and, of course, the shocking scenes of battle and loss of both people and horses, would have influenced those who served. The memorial may have served as a focus of remembrance—of friends lost but also of exciting times for the young who went off to use their skills to contribute to the war effort (Giles and Giles 2010).

Panel D (Figure 11.3d) shows another Romanesque arcade but has no figurative scene. Instead, the arcades define panels onto which a poem composed by Sir Mark is set. It describes the story of the Wagoners Special Reserve and its role as seen by its author, a celebration of service and sacrifice by local men for a loyal and Godly cause.

Discussion

The two monuments together reveal Sir Mark Sykes's character and feelings about his Roman Catholic faith, his hatred of the Germans, and his love of the native Yorkshire Wolds (and his British heritage). These attitudes and beliefs are expressed both iconographically and textually on the memorials.

The original Eleanor Crosses were erected by the grieving King Edward I, marking the resting places of Queen Eleanor on the route taken by her corpse and her entourage as they traveled back to London in 1290 from the place of her death (Davies 2018:70). These came from a time when England followed the Roman Catholic faith, and with services in Latin. Roman Catholic services in the early twentieth century were also in Latin and so would have been familiar to Sir Mark, whose Catholic mother encouraged him to change his allegiance from the traditional Anglicanism. This familiarity with Latin contrasted with the wider community, as Protestant (Anglican, Episcopalian) services in the parish church so close to the memorials and Sledmere House were completely in English. Although most inscriptions on the monument were Anglican, several of the quotations on the brasses reflect Catholic sentiments.

Sir Mark despised the Germans, and he framed World War I as a battle of good against evil, where the British character was displayed through a chivalric code and sacrifice. On the Eleanor Cross brasses, the German Eagle and a fierce Teutonic soldier in horned helmet are vanquished and in effect trampled underfoot, and a Moor representing Germany's Ottoman allies is similarly prostrate beneath Sir Mark's figure which carried on his imagery in panel 7, designed to remember his untimely death (Meara 1996). In contrast, his love of the Middle East is displayed by both a representation of the Jerusalem skyline and the phrase "Jerusalem rejoice" in Latin, though this also has a Roman Catholic association. The poem on the Wagoners' Memorial (Panel D) emphasized the fight for right over wrong and protecting the weak from the strong, though Germany is not explicitly mentioned. The German forces, though, are clearly portrayed in their distinctive uniforms and helmets conducting atrocities (Panel A) and being belligerent (Panel B), though eventually defeated (Panel C).

The Green Howards, which was Sir Mark's regiment and whose dead are recorded on the Eleanor Cross, was a Yorkshire regiment with a distinguished record and the one to which many local recruits signed up. The heraldry painted on the shields above the brasses relates either to the families of the men commemorated, or to Yorkshire entities. The Yorkshire association is perhaps even more obvious on the Wagoners Memorial, with local names on milestones and the regional wagon type depicted. The poem (Panel D), composed by Sir Mark, emulated local dialect—a form of speaking alien to the commissioner but common to those who served in the corps. Mechanization is not depicted in the local scenes—Sir Mark emphasizes the bucolic timelessness of the Wolds' agricultural order, but the sacks of grain produced by steam-powered threshing machines are to be seen on the wagon.

Conclusion

Sir Mark provided a selective representation of early twentieth-century East Yorkshire, a romantic portrayal of Britishness where estate workers are happy in their social and economic position, supported by loving families and living within a benevolent estate environment. World War I threatened this social order; all three monuments attempt to maintain that status quo, anticipating a return to a world that, unbeknownst to Sir Mark, would inevitably be changed by the war, the Great Depression, and which would be threatened within decades by another German threat that, in contrast, is not so publicly commemorated at Sledmere. These unique monuments have been, and continue to be, accepted and celebrated by the local community, but they were uniquely created by the mind and will of one man—Sir Mark Sykes. They are therefore not like other war memorials across Britain and its colonies that were designed by committee and avoided any confrontational propagandist elements (Royal Society of Arts 1944). Most war memorials across Britain were unemotional and non-judgmental and largely hid the dead's class and occupational differences. The Sledmere monuments show elements of civilian identities not shown elsewhere, and may reflect an underbelly of xenophobic emotions that were erased and hidden from public art. Their divergence from the norms of war memorial sentiment may indicate the feelings only of Sir Mark, but the contemporary lack of criticism and indeed exultant reception of these monuments by local people and local press suggests that they may have been more in tune with public opinion than might at first appear today.

References

Adelson, Roger D.
    1975   *Mark Sykes: Portrait of an Amateur.* London, UK: Jonathan Cape.
Baggs, A. P., L. M. Brown, G.C.F. Forster, I. Hall, R. E. Horrox, G.H.R. Kent, and D. Neave
    1989   Modern Beverley: Economy, 1835–1918. In *A History of the County of York East Riding: Volume 6, the Borough and Liberties of Beverley.* Keith J. Allison, ed. Pp. 136–141. London, UK: Victoria County History. *British History Online* http://www.british-history.ac.uk/vch/yorks/east/v016/pp136-141, accessed 3 March 2021.
Banbury, P.A.J.
    2000   The Sledmere Cross. *Yorkshire Archaeological Journal* 72:193–216.
Bennett, Jessica, and Mark Hampton
    2007   World War I and the Anglo-American Imagined Community: Civilization vs. Barbarism in British Propaganda and American Newspapers. In *Anglo-American Media Interactions, 1850–2000.* Joel H. Wiener and Mark Hampton, eds. Pp. 155–175. London, UK: Palgrave Macmillan.
Berdine, M. D.
    2018   *Redrawing the Middle East: Sir Mark Sykes, Imperialism and the Sykes-Picot Agreement.* London, UK: Bloomsbury Publishing.
Bloom, Cecil
    2011   Sir Mark Sykes: British Diplomat and a Convert to Zionism. *Jewish Historical Studies* 43:141–157.

Davies, J.
- 2018 *Visions and Ruins: Cultural Memory and the Untimely Middle Ages.* Manchester, UK: Manchester University Press.

Furlong, Jane, Lorraine Knight, and Simon Slocombe
- 2002 "They Shall Grow Not Old": An Analysis of Trends in Memorialisation Based on Information Held by the UK National Inventory of War Memorials. *Cultural Trends* 12(45):1–42.

Giles, Kate, and Mel Giles
- 2010 Signs of the Times: Nineteenth—Twentieth Century Graffiti in the Farms of the Yorkshire Wolds. In *Wild Signs: Graffiti in Archaeology and History. Studies in Contemporary and Historical Archaeology.* J. Oliver and T. Neal, eds. Pp. 47–59. Oxford, UK: Archaeopress.

Goebel, Stefan
- 2012 Britain's "Last Crusade": From War Propaganda to War Commemoration, c. 1914–1930. In *Justifying War. Propaganda, Politics and the Modern Age.* Jo Fox and David Welch, eds. Pp. 159–176. London, UK: Palgrave Macmillan.

Historic England
- 1987 Sir Tatton Sykes Memorial Tower. List Entry for Grade II Listed Building. https://historicengland.org.uk/listing/the-list/list-entry/1346480, accessed 26 January 2021.
- 2016a Eleanor Cross. List Entry for Grade I Listed Building. https://historicengland.org.uk/listing/the-list/list-entry/1083806, accessed 26 January 2021.
- 2016b Wagoners' Memorial. List Entry for Grade I Listed Building. https://historicengland.org.uk/listing/the-list/list-entry/1161354, accessed 26 January 2021.

Hull History Centre archives
- 1879–1919 Mark Sykes Papers 1879–1919. Hull History Centre archives, DDSY2/6/32.

Long, W. Harwood
- 1963 The Development of Mechanization in English Farming. *The Agricultural History Review* 11(1):15–26.

Meara, David
- 1996 Sir Mark Sykes and The Sledmere Brasses. *Transactions of the Monumental Brass Society* 15:486–98.

Moriarty, Catherine
- 1995 The Absent Dead and Figurative First World War Memorials. *Transactions of the Ancient Monuments Society* 39:7–40.
- 2008 Christian Iconography and First World War Memorials. *Imperial War Museum Review* 6:63–76.

Mytum, Harold
- 2007 Monuments and Memory in the Estate Landscape: Castle Howard and Sledmere. In *Estate Landscapes: Design, Improvement and Power in the Post-Medieval Landscape.* Jonathan Finch and Kate Giles, eds. Pp. 149–174. Boydell & Brewer, Society for Post-Medieval Archaeology Monograph 4, Woodbridge.

Neave, David, and Susan Neave
   2008   *The Victoria History of the Counties of England. A History of the County of York: East Riding,* vol. VIII: East Buckrose: Sledmere and the Northern Wolds. London, UK: Victoria County History.

Pevsner, Nicholas
   1972   *Yorkshire: York and the East Riding.* The Buildings of England. Harmondsworth, UK: Penguin.

Robertshaw, Andrew
   n.d.   *Retreat to Victory.* Sledmere, UK: Wagoners Special Reserve Museum Trust, Wagoners Lecture Evening 1 Transcript Booklet.

Robertson, Emily
   2014   Propaganda and "Manufactured Hatred": A Reappraisal of the Ethics of First World War British and Australian Atrocity Propaganda. *Public Relations Inquiry* 3(2):245–266.

Royal Society of Arts
   1944   *War Memorials: A Survey Made by a Committee of the Royal Society of Arts and Published by the War Memorials Advisory Council.* London, UK: Royal Society of Arts.

Williams, John P.
   2018   "The Flames of Louvain: Total War and the Destruction of European High Culture in Belgium by German Occupying Forces in August 1914." In *The Great War in Belgium and the Netherlands.* Felicity Rash and Christophe Declerq, eds. Pp. 35–47. Cham, Switzerland: Palgrave Macmillan.

12

Memorializing Defeat

Remembering Civil Wars in Finland and USA

TIMO YLIMAUNU AND PAUL R. MULLINS

In June 1907, over 100,000 people gathered in Richmond, Virginia, to dedicate a monument to Jefferson Davis. The statue of the Confederate president was unveiled in the former Confederate capital during the United Confederate Veterans' 17th Annual Reunion, just a few days after a monument to rebel cavalryman J.E.B. Stuart was dedicated five blocks to the south. The Davis monument was dedicated near the height of Confederate myth-making that aspired to redeem the secessionists' cause, glorifying the men who had led the rebellion and celebrating the foot soldiers who had gone to war for the Confederacy. Some Northerners certainly resented glorification of the rebellion and remained skeptical of the former rebels' commitment to the restored nation. Yet when the Davis monument rose on Monument Avenue, the White nation was increasingly inclined to reconciliation between former combatants and a willingness to tolerate, accept, or simply ignore Confederate historical fantasies.

Finland also fought an enormously divisive civil war in 1918, and like the American Civil War, the losers in Finland's war eventually established a monumental landscape commemorating their experience. Finland secured its independence from Russia in December 1917, and hostilities broke out in January 1918 between the leftist Reds and the Finnish government troops, dubbed as Whites (compare Seitsonen et al. 2020; Tepora and Roselius 2014). After the revolution in St. Petersburg in March 1917, the Senate and the Parliament of Finland became the central administrative powers in the country; however, they had no military or armed power to rule the country (Haapala 2009; Hoppu 2009). Consequently, there was a power vacuum in Finland in 1917, and the Finnish working class and the bourgeois parties began to form armed guards in fall 1917. The Social Democratic party was supported by the

Russian Bolshevists, and the bourgeois parties who would become known as the Whites pooled their forces against the Social Democratic party during the election campaigns.

Between January and fall 1918, almost 1.5 percent of Finland's population died in battlefield combat, vindictive executions by both sides, and in prisoners of war camps (War Victims in Finland 1914–22 2002). Much like the Confederates a half-century before, the defeated Reds' grief revolved around a sense of victimization following the Civil War, but unlike the Confederates, the Reds were subject to impromptu imprisonment and executions at the hands of victorious Whites following the war. The Whites refused to approve Red memorialization in the 20 years after the war, and Red grief did not assume any condoned public form until the former combatants were united by World War II. Even then, a Red narrative of the Civil War was systematically resisted in national memory and monumental space into the 1960s.

In the hands of vanquished Confederate and Red descendants' monuments acknowledged the trauma of defeat and death, but they ultimately forged distinctive memories of the two defeated causes. In Finland and the United States alike, sentiments over the defeated rebellions transformed in part because of other historical changes. The onset of World War II and Finland's war against the Soviet Union significantly shifted how Finns viewed their national fracture. In the United States, the collapse of Reconstruction in the 1870s and the subsequent national embrace of racial segregation provided traction for a forgiving narrative about the Confederacy's cause. Nevertheless, the ideological tenor Confederate champions took rationalizing insurrection was not mirrored in Finland, where monuments focused overwhelmingly on commemorating the dead. In Finland, the victorious Whites side took control of public memorialization of the Civil War, and the vanquished Reds were not permitted to express their political views of the Civil War's causes or even publicly mourn their deaths during the 1920s and 1930s. In contrast, the Confederate monumental landscape commemorated the dead, voiced unrepentant pride for the defeated cause, honored soldiers' service to the rebellion and to the South, and fantasized about the resurrection of Confederate values. By winning the narrative of the Civil War (Baugher et al., Introduction), the resurrection of a lost cause and that cause's values was given credence through the U.S. Army's 1922 naming of Fort Bragg and Fort Lee after these two Confederate generals. Later, between 1940 and 1942, the U.S. Army named eight camps in the South after other Confederate officers (U.S. Army Center of Military History).

Monumental Landscapes of the Defeated

Our interest is in the ways memories of the defeated causes in these two civil wars were constructed and expressed in the monumental landscape (compare Assmann 2006; Assmann 2008; Dwyer and Alderman 2008; Kattago 2009; Niven 2008). On the one hand, both the Reds and Confederates experienced profound loss in their defeats and the deaths of a significant number of their fellow citizens, and the memorial landscape struggled to negotiate the depth of loss for the defeated forces. On the other hand, the landscapes memorializing the Red and Confederate causes reflected very different approaches to reconciliation and remembering the war experiences of the reunited nations' defeated subjects.

As in the wake of any civil war, the memories of the Confederacy and Reds alike revolved around reconciling former foes to shared citizenship in a post-dissension state. Monuments could, of course, reflect many different state attitudes toward rebellion: in the wake of civil war, victorious states could suppress defeated forces' experiences, strive for communal forgiveness and reunification, or seek anything along that continuum (compare Kattago 2009; Kormano 2014; Koselleck 2002:285–326; Niven 2008). Confederate and Red monuments both acknowledged the sorrow of defeat, but the Finnish and Confederate monumental landscapes were quite different forms of resolution. In the immediate wake of the war, Confederate cemetery memorials acknowledged astounding despair, reflecting the grief of mass mortality and the utter defeat leveled on the South during Reconstruction. However, Confederate monuments eventually romanticized foot soldiers and commanders and aspired to salvage much of the rebellious cause, installing the former Confederacy's values in the most public civic spaces (Savage 1997). Memorials to the Reds, in contrast, provide virtually no testimony to the Red cause and instead focused on foot soldiers' devotion, the profound grief of the war, and the place-based landscape of death and tragedy the war left across much of Finland. The pride many Southern monument artists and benefactors expressed for the Confederate cause contrasts starkly with the grief, tragedy, and even shame that Red monuments expressed for Finland's civil war.

Reconciliation and Reunification: Red Monuments and World War II

Perhaps the most significant evidence of Finnish Civil War reconciliation came in May 1940, when Finnish newspapers proclaimed that 19 May would be spent as "a shared Commemoration Day. It will be dedicated to the war heroes of the recent war and to those who sacrificed their lives for their beliefs at both sides of the crisis year 1918" (*Aamulehti* 1940:1; *Helsingin Sanomat* 1940:8). Finnish commander-in-chief Field Marshal Carl Gustaf Emil Mannerheim introduced the new Commemoration Day for the 1918 Civil War in the wake of the 1939–1940 Winter War against the Soviet Union. In the face of overwhelming Soviet forces, the Finnish military held its own until the Winter War ended with a March 1940 treaty, but more than 26,000 Finnish soldiers died over just three-and-a-half months (Lentilä and Juutilainen 1999). Many of those soldiers hailed from families who had once fought for or been sympathetic to the Red cause, and Mannerheim subsequently ordered that the 19 May Commemoration Day would replace the celebration of 16 May as the victory of the Whites in the 1918 Civil War.

The new May 1940 Commemoration Day was the first time that the veterans, families, and allies of the defeated Red Guards were allowed to publicly grieve and express commemoration. The White soldiers killed during the Civil War had been buried in parish cemeteries and celebrated as heroes with gravestones and memorials for them recognizing their service in the nation's interest (Poteri 2009). Until the first Red memorials were erected during World War II, though, Red grief lingered in covert local memories that imagined a landscape of arbitrary brutality and victimization by victorious Whites. The remote sites where Reds were executed or died as prisoners became concealed places of memory during the post–Civil War years. These places were subterranean spaces of memory where mourners silently, or even secretly, gathered to remember their family members, relatives, and friends.

After 20 years of resistance to Red commemoration, the new Commemoration Day soberly acknowledged that the concession of Red grief was essential for Finland's wartime unification. On 19 May 1940, Parliament Member Aleksi Lehtonen argued that Reds and Whites were now unified as a result of the Soviet Union's Winter War attack, in which "the son of the red guard went, side by side with all others, to defend this country in which his father had been buried in his final resting place more than twenty-years ago" (*Suomen Sosialidemokraatti* 1940a:1, 5). These sentiments were echoed by the head of the Finnish labor union, E. A. Vuori, who spoke at the Hietaniemi War Heroes cemetery in Helsinki, which is the most important military cemetery in Finland: "Those of our comrades, who are resting in the soil of their native country, went into the battle with others to fulfil their duty as citizens. . . . They were fighting for the freedom and national self-determination of this country and people. . . . That blood, which was shed in those terrifying battles and tough combats in the woods of Karelia, Kainuu and Lapland, is precious blood" (*Suomen Sosialidemokraatti* 1940a:5).

Perhaps the first monument reflecting these new attitudes toward the de-

Figure. 12.1. Reds' memorials: *Left*, memorial at Kalevankangas, Tampere, 1941; *Right*, memorial at Ahvenisto cemetery, Hämeenlinna, 1940. Photos by Timo Ylimaunu, 2018.

feated Reds was unveiled in June 1940 at a mass grave in the town of Hyvinkää in southern Finland. The mass grave held 147 Reds who were originally buried in several burial sites in Hyvinkää, most of whom were executed (*Suomen Sosialidemokraatti* 1940b:1). The dead soldiers had been exhumed and reburied in a single mass grave during 1939 in preparation for a planned unveiling of a memorial in October 1939 that was delayed by the Winter War. A member of Parliament, Aleksi Lehtonen, spoke at the monument dedication in Hyvinkää, and he cast the reburial as a prophetic reunification, because immediately after the reburial the entire nation of Finland had to gather together "to seek protection and endorsement from each other and fight for their life and freedom. . . . In our army, sons of the [former] Red guards were as brave and as trustworthy as anyone else sons" (*Suomen Sosialidemokraatti* 1940b:2).

The Hyvinkää monument was among the earliest confirmations of the publicly condoned reconciliation among Finns (Kormano 2014:322–323). In nearby Hämeenlinna, two monuments were erected in September 1940 at mass graves for Reds. These were among seven Civil War mass graves in and around Hämeenlinna. Two memorials were erected and unveiled in a ravine in Ahvenisto behind the cemetery, where Red soldiers had been executed and unceremoniously buried (*Hämeen Kansa* 1940c:3). Several hundred Reds were buried in these five mass graves, which were predominantly execution sites (*Hämeen Kansa* 1940a:3). Parliament member Väinö Kivisalo delivered the unveiling speech for the September 1940 memorial at the Hämeenlinna cemetery, expressing his satisfaction that "We have gained the grave marker for those workers, who fell in the maelstrom of 1918 Civil War and have got their final resting place in the consecrated earth of this burial ground." A memorial had been surreptitiously placed at the site in the wake of the Civil War, and Kivisalo acknowledged that it had been quickly destroyed by White sympathizers: "We erected the memorial for this burial site in 1923, but it was not allowed to rest in peace. Even though it did not have any pictorial motif nor inscription, thus it was not able to hurt anyone, but, nevertheless, it was blown up at one night of June of the same year." Vandalization and removal of 1920s and 1930s Red memorials moved Kivisalo to express concern that "We hope that these markers will be left in peace. The peace of the burial ground should be tended. . . . The grave will redeem all hate, and there are no Reds or Whites at the front of the lord of the death. . . . The dead ones do not belong to any party" (*Hämeen Kansa* 1940b:5–6).

Tampere and the surrounding countryside witnessed some of the most furious battles of the Civil War, with about 2,768 people dying in the town of Tampere. The vast majority, 2,173, were Reds, and 421 were Whites (the remaining victims' affiliations are unknown) (War Victims in Finland 1914–22 2002). The first Red memorial in Tampere was erected at the Kalevankangas cemetery in 1941 at a mass grave holding about 1,000 Reds. The memorial was carved by local sculptor Jussi Hietanen in 1940–1941 (*Aamulehti* 1941a:4; *Suomen Sosialidemokraatti* 1941:1, 7). In contrast to Confederate monuments, Red monuments were not especially clear symbolic invocations of the Red cause, and there was never a tradition of invoking the military leaders or other heroes of the Red rebellion. Whites had adopted foot soldiers and other militaristic symbols in their memorials after the Civil War, so Reds used other motifs and symbols. The Kalevankangas memorial, for instance, depicts a woman mourning with a child (a similar motif was used in a 1940 memorial in the Huittinen Cemetery, in a 1945 memorial in the Nokia Cemetery, and a 1956 memorial in the Akaa Cemetery in Toijala). The memorial in Nakilla (1947) features a tree broken at half-trunk that has no clear link to Red military symbolism. The broken tree motif alludes to the tragedy of a life cut short (a motif also found in American mortuary art). According to Kormano (2014:330–337), most of the broken tree motifs appeared in 1940s Red memorials in places that had high Red mortality by executions and deaths in prisoner of war camps. Sunrays had been featured in post–Civil War Social

Democratic art, the Finnish political party that had represented working-class Red interests in the wake of the Civil War. Sunrays were the main aesthetic motif on the memorials in Hyvinkää and at the Ahvenisto ravine mass grave memorials; the Halikko mass grave holds 50–100 executed Reds beneath a memorial with sunrays (Kormano 2014:326–328). Almost no Red monuments explicitly referred to their cause in the monuments' text, instead memorializing "those who fell for their beliefs," and the majority of monuments feature the year 1918 prominently displayed on the memorial. These symbols and texts were the way to make the deceased's identity meaningful, and mourners were able to get peace for themselves (Koselleck 2002:287–288).

The Kalevankangas memorial was designed by student Jussi Hietanen, who had been among a group of artists that produced a statue of Field Marshal Mannerheim in Tampere (*Aamulehti* 1941b:6; *Uusi Suomi* 1956:3). The Mannerheim statue departed from the symbolism on most Red monuments, portraying Mannerheim as an avenging White Army military commander following the battle of Tampere in 1918. The heroic style of the Tampere monument was similar to many Confederate monuments that depicted the rebellion's military commanders and political leaders. The Mannerheim statue was first scheduled to be erected in downtown Tampere in 1939, but the outbreak of World War II postponed the unveiling, and local resistance to the monument delayed its erection another 11 years after the war, to 1956. The Social Democratic party opposed the Mannerheim statue in a community that was a center for labor activism and the Red military during the Finnish Civil War. The Social Democratic party suggested it would have endorsed the erection of a Mannerheim statue that portrayed him as the Field Marshal for the unified Finnish military forces in World War II, but the party and Red sympathizers opposed commemorating Mannerheim's role as the Civil War's White General. Eventually the statue was erected eight kilometers from downtown Tampere on the ridge from which Mannerheim followed the Civil War battle (*Uusi Suomi* 1956:3). The statue has been repeatedly vandalized since its' unveiling; in 2004 and 2013, for instance, the statue was splashed with red paint and the word "lahtari" (the butcher), which was used by the Reds to describe the Whites during and after the Civil War (YLE 2004; YLE 2013).

When the Kalevankangas memorial was unveiled in 1941, a memorial was also placed at the mass grave of an unknown number of unidentified Reds in Kitula, today known as Akaa. The Kitula monument, now located at the end of a suburban cul-de-sac, marks a mass grave of soldiers killed in action as well as people who had died in a local prisoner of war camp. Three Reds were executed in 1918, and one of them was buried in the Kitula mass grave. The gray granite cobblestone monument has a red granite slab with the text "For

Figure. 12.2. *A*, Memorial with the broken tree motif with inscription "Died for their conviction," with the list of names, Ulvila, 1945. *B*, a memorial with inscription, "In 1918, for those who gave their lives for their conviction" at Kitula mass grave, Akaa, 1941. Photos by Timo Ylimaunu, 2018.

those who gave their lives for their beliefs in the year 1918." The gray cobble stones used for the Kitula memorial differ from the other Red memorials that were erected after 1940. Most of the Reds memorials were made of red granite. Gray granite became associated with Finnish nationalism in the late nineteenth and early twentieth centuries, when the Finnish National Museum and the National Theatre were perhaps the most prominent structures made of gray granite (Aalto and Ylimaunu 2022; Kormano 2014:71, 92–97; Nikula 2000:330–332; Saarikangas 1999:178–179; Ylimaunu 2019). The Kitula memorial was distinctive for apparently hearkening to pre-independence and 1920s and 1930s Finnish nationalism even as it memorialized the Civil War. The memorial was designed by a local factory owner, Erik Estlander, who likely was sympathetic to the White cause, but he may have hoped to contribute to reconciliation by invoking Finnish nationalism in the granite composition of the memorial.

Vindicating the Cause: The Landscape of Confederate Monuments

In the wake of the Civil War Jefferson Davis was denied the adulation showered on field commanders like Robert E. Lee and Thomas "Stonewall" Jackson, but Davis's death in December 1889 triggered a wave of mourning through the South (Figure 12.3). Rather than voice atonement for the rebellion or mourn the scores of foot soldiers who died under his command, memorial ceremonies at the Davis monument in Richmond struck an unrepentant note. During the dedication of the Davis monument, the United Confederate Veterans painted Davis and the South as the victims of distorted Northern historical accounts, exalting that the monument "was a vindication of President Davis, an utter route for the army of slanderers, and above all, a noble tribute to the 'Lost Cause'" (United Confederate Veterans 1907:118). Like the United Confederate Veterans, the monument's sculptor Edward Virginius Valentine also imagined his statue as vindication for Davis. Valentine was perhaps the most prominent sculptor enshrining the Southern cause, and newspaper coverage of his design alluded to Davis's historical rehabilitation when it reported that "the sculptor is a great admirer of Mr. Davis . . . and he predicts that with the lapse of time Americans throughout the country will grow to more and more regard Mr. Davis as a good and a very able statesman" (*Daily Arkansas Gazette* 1906:21).

This romanticization of the Confederacy's leaders was a radical break from post-war Southern memorialization. In the immediate wake of the surrender, memorials rose in Confederate cemeteries, where the Ladies Memorial Associations took charge of preserving wartime cemeteries. These associa-

Figure 12.3. This monument dedicated to Confederate President Jefferson Davis was unveiled in 1907 at the height of Confederate monument building. It was removed in 2020. Photo by Paul R. Mullins, 2018.

tions, composed mostly of middle- and upper-class White women, focused on establishing and maintaining cemeteries throughout the post-war South, and at least 70 of these associations existed a year after the war's end (Janney 2012:39). The first memorials probably rose in 1867, when a Ladies Memorial Association in Cheraw, South Carolina dedicated a cemetery memorial to "the memory of our heroic dead" in July 1867 (*Daily News* 1867:3), and in September a Confederate memorial was dedicated in Romney, West Virginia

(Maxwell and Swisher 1897:692; McLeod 1905:11). This post-war memorialization expressed the South's profound human, material, and social losses, and much of the focus on cemetery memorialization fixed on the dignity of Confederate dead without staking an especially ideological claim to defending the rebellion. In July 1866, for instance, the *Richmond Dispatch* (1866:2) was indignant that a West Virginia newspaper had lobbied to make Confederate memorial associations illegal in the state, calling it a "proposal to persecute surviving relatives and friends for paying honor to their dead."

The mortuary landscape nevertheless rapidly became a stage to perform Southern martyrdom and construct memories of the rebellious cause. In 1869, a memorial service in a North Carolina cemetery acknowledged the South's profound loss, proclaiming, "We are the children of a bereaved and saddened land" (Robbins 1869:3). Yet the speaker sounded a shift in tenor when he vindicated the cause of the cemetery's dead as "a contest for the right of self-government. Ten states and eight millions of men claimed the privilege of governing themselves in their own way, and it was denied them.... Upon the defeat of our armies we lost the privilege of self-government. Strangers now dictate our laws.... Strangers and servants bear rule over us" (Robbins 1869:3).

Perhaps the clearest distinction between Red and Confederate monuments was the placement of Confederate monuments in public spaces without any particular place-based Civil War histories. One of the first Confederate monuments erected in a courthouse or public square came in Bolivar, Tennessee, where a monument commemorating Hardeman County's Confederate dead was erected in January 1873 (*Bolivar Bulletin* 1873:3). The monument's planning had begun in 1865, with one of its first champions indicating it was needed because "thousands of brave men had given their lives for that which in the eyes of the world was an utter failure, with the stamp of treason on it" (McNeil 1901:2). King George County, Virginia erected a Confederate monument on its courthouse square in November 1869, and like the later Bolivar monument it was a rather plain shaft (*Richmond Dispatch* 1869:3). In 1872, a monument was dedicated at the Lancaster County, Virginia courthouse, and in July 1873 a courthouse monument was erected in neighboring Northumberland County (*Alexandria Gazette and Virginia Advertiser* 1873:2).

The placement of a monument in a courthouse square would become very common after about 1895. John T. Winberry (1983:110) concluded that 93 percent of courthouse Confederate monuments were erected after 1895, with fully half of them between 1903 and 1912. Winberry concluded that most of the inscriptions on these courthouse monuments honored Confederate dead and did not explicitly address the Confederacy's cause. However, the 1875

Northumberland County, Virginia, monument had a panel that read, "Go tell the Southrons that we lie here for the rights of their states. They never fail to die in a great cause" (*Richmond Dispatch* 1875:4). By securing prominent civic spaces like courthouse squares, the most visible Confederate monumental memory strategically laid claim on the very institutions the rebellion had been unable to wrest from the nation. The Southern memorial landscape celebrated the persistence, if not victory, of the Confederacy's values and its narrative, even if the war itself had been lost on the battlefield.

Red memorials did not appear in the urban ornamental streetscapes and courthouse squares that were the focus of Confederate memory-making. Red memorials were instead place-based commemoratives scattered across the overwhelmingly rural Finnish countryside in places like roadsides, forests, and fields that were often the scenes of brutal executions. Rather than the public stages of Confederate memory-making, most Red memorials commemorated their dead in cemeteries marking mass graves and the rural landscape where the war had been waged, Reds had been executed, and the dead had been buried in makeshift graves. Reds who were killed in action, executed, or died in prisoner of war camps from disease or starvation were routinely buried in unmarked mass graves without any grave memorials. Much of the post–Civil War memorialization of Finns revolved around securing dignity for those fallen soldiers and victims of the White Terror. Finnish folk beliefs cast this fate as a "bad death" at the hands of executioners in bogs, woods, or haunted spaces like former execution sites, with their bodies consigned to un-consecrated ground. After the war, many Finns believed that only proper Christian burial ritual could allow the dead to enter the underworld and rest in peace (Aalto 2018:335; Fingerroos 2009:309–310; Peltonen 2009:467). Consequently, deceased Reds were doomed to wander in a liminal stage between the living world and the underworld, and their fate imposed an additional punishment on mourning survivors. Many Red corpses buried in remote areas were moved to cemeteries, and other remote places were consecrated when monuments were erected at execution and burial sites. For instance, in 1952, a monument was dedicated at the site of an execution of 66 Reds in Västankvarn, Inkoo, and in June 1953, the space was consecrated. The mass burial at Kitula has also been consecrated as a cemetery and is today maintained by the Akaa parish (Pastell 2019).

Conclusion

Today, many of the place-based Finnish memorials underscore much of the secretive White bloodshed during and after the Civil War, with memorials located along roads, in secluded wooded areas, or in once-rural spaces that have become residential areas. On the one hand, the breadth of White violence is emphasized by the systematic memorialization of a landscape of apparently banal places. The Red memorial landscape materializes grief in the tragic, seemingly random places that witnessed profound Red losses. On the other hand, the Red memorial landscape almost universally avoids expressing Red social and political values and makes none of the Confederacy's efforts to redeem the South's rebellious cause.

The Red memorial landscape focuses on the inexpressible tragedy of death and a national grief that all Finns can claim as their national heritage. That is quite unlike the rationalization and reproduction of neo-Confederate values normalized by their enshrinement in public space. The White privilege at the heart of neo-Confederate ideology has transformed Confederate monuments into galvanizing spaces for White Southern nationalism while simultaneously becoming an increasingly stale artifact of "Southern values." Finnish labor unions still hold ceremonies at Red memorials, but the Red cause and the Finnish Civil War tend to be framed as a national tragedy that inspires less ideological hagiography than the Confederate defense. The Red memorial landscape instead evokes national sadness, if not shame, for the national dissension at the very birth of the Finnish state.

Tepora (2014:489–490) confirms that the Winter War was a unifying event shared between former combatants whose tensions had begun to thaw in the 1930s, accelerating a "healing process [that] was well on its way before the war began." Nevertheless, the World War II–era and post-war Red memorials did not introduce an integrated national history of the Civil War: until the 1960s, the Red narrative remained opposed to a national memory that minimized, if not denied, the White terror and cast the civil war as the victory of freedom over Bolshevik-supported Reds (Peltonen 2009). The reconciliation that Finns imagined in the early 1940s certainly was not a complete resolution of tensions between Red and White combatants just two decades after the Civil War. Facing more than 26,000 deaths in the Winter War (Manninen 1987:319), the state's acknowledgment of Red grief served Finland's strategic national interests in a moment of crisis (Kormano 2014:85–86). Just over a century after the Finnish Civil War, the war is today cast less as a sectarian, class, or regional dispute than a national tragedy.

A half-century after the Confederacy surrendered, the Confederate cause would be largely forgiven or at least ignored by an early twentieth-century White nation whose reconciliation confirmed the North and South's common commitment to Jim Crow segregation. Rather than express repentance, Confederate monuments hoped to cement their imagination of the rebellion's values and cultural heritage with public statuary. The twenty-first-century transformation of that imagination was no clearer than in June 2020, when the Jefferson Davis monument was removed as part of a protest movement against neo-Confederate heritage and its relationship with anti-Black racism. After Davis's statue fell, the neighboring Stonewall Jackson (dedicated in 1919), J.E.B. Stuart (1907), and Matthew Fontaine Maury (1929) monuments were removed as well, following monuments in many other American cities.

For well over a century, the Confederate monumental landscape defiantly clung to a distorted history of the war itself and defended White privilege. Monuments aspired to heroicize the Confederacy and celebrate their values in public places despite the rebellion's defeat. Finland did not engage in an especially transparent public admission of the causes of its Civil War, and the Reds' sense of victimization in the wake of the war was never clearly acknowledged. Nevertheless, the Finnish monumental landscape underscored the tragic grief of the nation's internal war, and memorials placed at graves and execution sites secure their consequence from the sorrow invested in those places.

Acknowledgments

We would like to thank the reviewers and editors of this volume for their help and comments, and we would also like to thank Vesa-Pekka Herva, Titta Kallio-Seppä, Sami Lakomäki, Tuuli Matila, and Roger Norum for their help and discussions during the preparation of this paper. Timo Ylimaunu's travel to the annual conference of the Society for Historical Archaeology was funded by the Faculty of Humanities, University of Oulu.

References

Aalto, Seppo
   2018   *Kapina tehtailla, Kuusankoski.* Helsinki, Finland: Siltala.
Aalto, Sirpa, and Timo Ylimaunu
   2022   Memorializing the Finnish Medieval Past. In *Medievalism in Finland and Russia: Twentieth- and Twenty-First-Century Aspects.* Reima Välimäki, ed. Pp. 85–102. London, UK: Bloomsbury Publishing.
Aamulehti
   1940   Sankarivainajain muistoa vietetään toukokuun 19. pnä. 5 May:1.
   1941a   Punaisten puolella kaatuneiden hautamuistomerkki. 24 May:4.
   1941b   Kuvanveistäjä Jussi Hietanen kaatunut. 28 August:6.
Alexandria Gazette and Virginia Advertiser
   1873   Untitled. 31 July:2.

Assmann, Aleida
    2006   Memory, Individual and Collective. In *The Oxford Handbook of Contextual Political Analysis*. Robert E. Goodin and Charles Tilly, eds. Pp. 210–224. New York, NY: Oxford.

Assmann, Jan
    2008   Communicative and Cultural Memory. In *Cultural Memory Studies; An International and Interdisciplinary Handbook*. Sara B. Young, Ansgar Nunning, and Astrid Erll, eds. Pp. 109–118. Berlin, Germany: Walter de Gruyter.

Bolivar Bulletin
    1873   History of Hardeman County's Confederate Monument. 24 January:3.

Daily Arkansas Gazette
    1906   South's Famous Sculptor. 2 December:21.

Daily News
    1867   Dedication of a Memorial Monument in Cheraw. 2 August:3.

Dwyer, Owen J., and Derek H. Alderman
    2008   Memorial Landscapes: Analytic Questions and Metaphors. *GeoJournal* 73:165–178.

Fingerroos, Outi
    2009   Viipurin punaiset kuolemat. In *Sisällissodan Pikkujättiläinen*. Pertti Haapala and Tuomas Hoppu, eds. Pp. 309–319. Helsinki, Finland: W. Söderström.

Haapala, Pertti
    2009   Vuoden 1917 kriisi. In *Sisällissodan Pikkujättiläinen*. Pertti Haapala and Tuomas Hoppu, eds. Pp. 58–89. Helsinki, Finland: W. Söderström.

Hämeen Kansa
    1940a   Muistomerkki jo kuluvana kesänä. 4 July:3.
    1940b   Kuoleman majesteetin edessä ei ole punaisia eikä valkoisia. 1 October:5–6.
    1940c   Hämeenlinnan toverihaudoille. 19 November:3.

Helsingin Sanomat
    1940   Toukokuun 19:s vietetään yhteisenä muistopäivänä. 5 May:8.

Hoppu, Tuomas
    2009   Sisällissodan puhkeaminen. In *Sisällissodan Pikkujättiläinen*. Pertti Haapala and Tuomas Hoppu, eds. Pp. 92–111. Helsinki, Finland: W. Söderström.

Janney, Caroline E.
    2012   *Burying the Dead but Not the Past: Ladies' Memorial Associations and the Lost Cause*. Chapel Hill, NC: University of North Carolina Press.

Kattago, Siobhan
    2009   War Memorials and the Politics of Memory: the Soviet War Memorial in Tallinn. *Constellations* 16(1):150–166.

Kormano, Riita
    2014   Sotamuistomerkit Suomessa: Voiton ja tappion modaalista sovittelua. Ph.D. dissertation, University of Turku, Finland.

Koselleck, Reinhart
    2002   *The Practice of Conceptual History: Timing History, Spacing Concepts*. Stanford, CA: Stanford University Press.

Lentilä, Riitta, and Antti Juutilainen
1999 Talvisodan uhrit. In *Talvisodan Pikkujättiläinen*. Jari Leskinen and Antti Juutilainen, eds. Pp. 816–828. Porvoo, Finland: WSOY Press.

Manninen, Ohto
1987 Suomi toisessa maailmansodassa. In *Suomen Historia 7*. Paula Avikainen, Ilari Hetemäki, Eero Laaksonen, and Erkki Pärssinen, eds. Pp. 274–416. Espoo, Finland: Tietoteos Press.

Maxwell, Hu, and H. L. Swisher
1897 *History of Hampshire County, West Virginia from its Earliest Settlement to the Present*. Morgantown, West Virginia: A. Brown Boughner.

McLeod, B. D.
1905 The First Confederate Monument. *Confederate Veteran* 13(1):11.

Nikula, Riita
2000 Klassismi maailman sotien välisen ajan suomalaisessa arkkitehtuurissa. In *Kivettyneet ihanteet? Klassismin nousu maailmansotien välisessä Euroopassa*. Marja Härmänmaa and Timo Vihavainen, eds. Pp. 330–332. Jyväskylä, Finland: Athens.

Niven, Bill
2008 War Memorials at the Intersection of Politics, Culture and Memory. *Journal of War and Culture Studies* 1(1):39–45.

Pastell, Paula
2019 Electronic communication with Timo Ylimaunu, 11 June 2019.

Peltonen, Ulla-Maija
2009 Sisällissodan muistaminen. In *Sisällissodan Pikkujättiläinen*. Pertti Haapala and Tuomas Hoppu, eds. Pp. 464–473. Helsinki, Finland: WSOY.

Poteri, Juha
2009 Valkoisten kaatuneiden hautaaminen. In *Sisällissodan Pikkujättiläinen*. Pertti Haapala and Tuomas Hoppu, eds. Pp. 297–308. Helsinki, Finland: WSOY.

Richmond Dispatch
1866 The Proposition of a Renegade. 6 July:2.
1869 Virginia News. 10 November:3.
1875 Warrenton. 3 September:4.

Robbins, W. M.
1869 Address Delivered Before the Memorial Association of Raleigh. *Sentinel* (Carlisle, PA) 13 May:3.

Saarikangas, Kirsi
1999 Wood, Forest and Nature. Architecture and the construction of Finnishness. In *Europe's Northern Frontier: Perspectives on Finland's Western Identity*. Tuomas M. S. Lehtonen, ed., Pp.165-207. Jyväskylä, Finland: PS-Kustannus.

Savage, Kirk
1997 *Standing Soldiers, Kneeling Slaves: Race, War, and Monument in Nineteenth-Century America*. Princeton: Princeton University Press.

Seitsonen, Oula, Paul R. Mullins, and Timo Ylimaunu
2020 Public Memory, National Heritage, and Memorialization of the 1918 Finnish Civil War. *World Archaeology* 51(5):741–758.

Suomen Sosialidemokraatti
    1940a   Kansan kunnianosoitus sankarivainajilleen. 20 May:1, 5.
    1940b   Ensimmäinen kansalaissodassa tuhoutuneiden työläisten muistomerkki paljastettu Hyvinkäällä. 4 June:1–2.
    1941   Tampereen veljeshaudan muistomerkki. 24 May:1, 7.

Tepora, Tuomas
    2014   Coming to Terms with Violence: Sacrifice, Collective Memory and Reconciliation in Inter-war Finland. *Scandinavian Journal of History* 39(4):487–509.

Tepora, Tuomas, and Aapo Roselius, eds.
    2014   *The Finnish Civil War 1918: History, Memory, Legacy.* Leiden: Brill.

United Confederate Veterans
    1907   *Seventeenth Annual Meeting and Reunion of the United Confederate Veterans Held at Richmond, Va.* New Orleans, LA: United Confederate Veterans.

U.S. Army Center of Military History
    n.d.   Naming of U.S. Army Post. https://history.army.mil/faq/naming-of-us-army-posts.htm#Overview, accessed 1 September 2022.

Uusi Suomi
    1956   MANNERHEIMIN patsaan vaiheita. 4 June:3.

War Victims in Finland, 1914–22
    2002 War Victims in Finland, 1914–22. https://sotasurmat.narc.fi/fi/victims/faceted-search/table?page=0, accessed 30 May 2019.

Winberry, John J.
    1983   "Lest We Forget": The Confederate Monument and the Southern Townscape. *Southeastern Geographer* 23(2):107–121.

YLE
    2004   Mannerheimin patsas sai punaista maalia Tampereella. 7 July https://yle.fi/uutiset/3-5194669, accessed 21 June 2021.
    2013   Mannerheimin patsas töhrittiin Tampereella jälleen—puhtaaksi itsenäisyyspäivään mennessä. 25 November. https://yle.fi/uutiset/3-6951324, accessed 21 June 2021.

Ylimaunu, Timo
    2019   Tornion taistelun muistomerkki. Kokemuksia ja muistin tasoja. In *Toinen jalka haudassa. Juhlakirja Juhani Kostetille.* Sanna Lipkin, Titta Kallio-Seppä, Annemari Tranberg, and Tiina Väre, eds. Pp. 28–37. Oulu, Finland: University of Oulu.

13

The Forgotten War Memory Boom

State and Local Korean War Memorials, 1987–2003

Levi Fox

More Americans died in Korea per month than in Vietnam, and the Korean War continues with thousands of troops still stationed along a demilitarized zone. That is why the phrase "The Forgotten War" is both ironic and problematic. It is ironic because while we call the Korean War forgotten, of course it is not, which leads to the question of why it has been so often labeled in this manner. On the other hand, it is problematic because this 'Forgotten War' trope, really a myth of erasure, has enabled the Korean War to be widely recalled in the abstract while the specifics of the conflict are ignored. In this chapter, I discuss the proliferation of the term *Forgotten War* in local and state Korean War Memorials from the late 1980s through 2003, and how these monuments help create a national mythology surrounding the Korean War.

Monuments dedicated to Korean War veterans, or in honor of those who perished in the conflict, today dot the national landscape and vary greatly. Most are built by local and state governments, but many are constructed by churches and schools. Other sites are sponsored by local branches of national veterans' groups, such as the American Legion, Veterans of Foreign Wars, and Korean War Veterans Association. While city monuments are usually found inside parks or town greens, county monuments are more often on courthouse lawns, and state monuments in a range of locations from capitol grounds to cemeteries. I know all this because I spent several years from 2013 to 2017 visiting Korean War Memorials across the Eastern and Midwestern United States, documenting what was my dissertation research through a blog. For that reason, there are few in-text citations in this chapter, as my first-hand observations constitute the bulk of the data on which I base my conclusions about Korean War public memory in the United States.

Some Korean War monuments consist of simple granite markers listing a few local names next to a small cross, while others are glistening black marble towers including sandblasted images and complex narratives about the history of the Korean War. Some local monuments make use of jets, tanks, or other military machines as part of their displays, while others are built along waterfronts and integrated into the local heritage tourism market. Many Korean War monuments also include extensive iconography or use innovative approaches such as sundials, tunnels, or abstract sculptures. Indeed, while many monuments center around stone slabs or human figures, others use non-human forms or modernist art approaches in order to represent how the Korean War is remembered. Beyond statuary, most Korean War monuments include some combination of engraved images, detailed maps, MIA/POW tributes, and the names of local soldiers who died in Korea during the early 1950s. Moreover, the architecture of many of these Korean War monuments seems to emphasize the unique aspects of the war by including sharp angles and dividing lines, which remind visitors of the still ongoing divide between North and South Korea, as well as hollow forms and empty spaces, both suggesting the fact that the conflict technically remains unresolved today.

State and Local Korean War Monuments, 1987–2000

While Korean War Memorials today dot the national landscape, it was not always that way. From the 1950s through the mid-1960s, the Korean War was widely recalled in monuments—often co-dedicated to those who fought in WWII—but from the late 1960s through the mid-1980s, the Korean War became largely forgotten in terms of U.S. memorials. However, from the late 1980s to 2003, the Korean War was "remembered" as many Korean War Memorials were constructed on the state and local level. Moreover, many of these new memorials used the term *forgotten*, suggesting this period can be considered a "Forgotten War Memory Boom," in line with the scholarly era identified by historian Jay Winter (2007).

Woodside Cemetery in Middletown, Ohio dedicated a marker on 25 May 1987, that concludes "may they never be forgotten." Similarly, the Chicago Korean War Memorial in Kennedy Park, dedicated on 15 September 1988, includes a sculpture of one-quarter of a globe showing a map of Korea and reads, "Those who sacrificed so much in the cause of freedom will never be forgotten." In 1990, a marker noting "132,000 Wisconsinites were involved in this 'Forgotten War,'" was installed near Westfield on Highway 51, which years later would become the state Korean War Veterans Memorial Highway. The Laurens County Korea Memorial in South Carolina, unveiled on Veterans Day 1991, doubles down by noting locals "Shall Never Forget Their Own" on one side, while on the other side it says, "The Forgotten War."

The first official state Korean War Mmemorials were also dedicated in the late 1980s and the early 1990s. In contrast to local memorials, state monuments are more likely to include an extensive narrative describing the war and emphasizing the contributions of that state, and such is clearly the case in Iowa. Iowa's Korean War Memorial was dedicated in Des Moines on 28 May 1989, amid a crowded memorial landscape on the lawn of the Capitol. The text on the front of the memorial pillar describes the invasion of South Korea "with 22 Russian built tanks" and states that it starts "what has been referred to as 'Korea—The Forgotten War.'" The text on the other faces of the pillar discusses a range of topics using the following language that lionizes the Korean War era military: "The Valor Of The Ground Forces," "Mighty Navy Command Of The Sea," and "Superior Was Our Air Power." The narrative on the surrounding stones focuses on the opening months of the war; of the eight stones, six deal with the invasion and Inchon while a seventh discusses the actions of the "X-Corps" and entry of "China into the War." Only the last stone notes events from 1951 to 1953—as years of "Truce Talks"—and the creation of a "Demilitarized Zone."

The Maryland Korean War Memorial in Baltimore also gives short shrift to the armistice in its lengthy narrative. Dedicated on 27 May 1990, in Canton Waterfront Park, on a tiny street named Korean War Veterans Memorial Boulevard, the memorial is a void sunken into the ground with circular walls. In addition, running through the middle of the memorial is a line that on closer inspection bisects a map of Korea where the thirty-eighth parallel divided North from South (Figure 13.1a). Besides this main map, the most prominent site design element is the wall of stones with different pieces of a cohesive narrative on the Korean War, offering a brief background overall and only a single sentence describing the armistice. In addition to the site's interesting design, its location along the water near Fort McHenry and historic Inner Harbor, both shown on a bay map, reinforces the importance of Baltimore's nautical heritage tourist trade.

The New York state Korean War Memorial in Albany—dedicated on 25 June 1990, the fortieth anniversary of the invasion of South Korea—includes a fountain ringed by the flags of nations that fought for the United Nations side (Figure 13.1b). Located in the Empire State Plaza next to the state Women Veterans Memorial and near the State Museum, the memorial also contains plaques noting residents who served and telling a similar version of the war story told in Iowa, but in a more muted tone. This memorial, like many state Korean War monuments, is tied to heritage tourism both by its location and due to "the advent of Percent for Art ordinances in multiple American cities and states" since the 1980s that—as Erika Doss points out—"have funded thousands of public art projects across the country" (2010:31). Moreover, as Mike Wallace notes, early 1990s monument building took place amid cuts in federal funding for historic preservation and was possible due to a belief in the "economic benefits of heritage tourism" (1996:230).

Some memorials use sculpture to represent the war as an unfinished conflict, since technically the 1953 armistice was only a cease-fire and U.S. troops continue to remain stationed along the North Korean border. One such example is the silhouette of a soldier at the center of the New York City Korean War Memorial in Battery Park (Figure 13.2a). Dedicated 25 June 1991, the 15 ft. memorial is surrounded by flags of twenty nations that sent troops or hospital ships. Nearby Castle Clinton National Monument gives the park its name, while adjacent memorials honor Merchant Mariners, 9/11 victims, and immigrants. This location next to other monuments makes it likely visitors who have no interest in the memorial might be exposed to information about the war; in this way, the memorial fosters heritage tourism that then fosters knowledge of the Korean War. In design terms, depending on the angle of view, one can see skyscrapers through the hole in the middle or look out over Ellis Island, with the Statue of Liberty off in the distance.

Many Korean War Memorials include soldier statues. In June 1992, Hauppauge, New York, dedicated a memorial to the Korean War with two statues, one a soldier and one a map of Korea, at an Armed Forces Plaza off a Veterans Memorial Highway. The official Tennessee Korean War Memorial, dedicated 3 July 1992, at the War Memorial Plaza in Nashville, includes a granite sculpture of two soldiers flanking a map as well as a list of all state residents who volunteered, were drafted, and died in Korea. The Evansville, Indiana, Korean War Memorial, dedicated 29 August 1992, consists of two life-size bronze figures aiding a third soldier. Like many Korean War Memorials, the monument is on the water, next to "The Pagoda" (a 1912 building home to the "Evansville Visitor Center"), and near a "Museum of Arts, History, and Science."

The term *forgotten War* also appears in some local multi-war memorials built in the early 1990s, such as a Korean War Monument in Dearborn, Michigan dedicated in 1991 as part of a set also honoring WWI, WWII, and Vietnam martyrs. On 4 July 1993, the City Council of North Augusta, South Carolina, along with the American Legion and the Sons of Confederate Veterans, dedicated the Wade Hampton Veterans Park, with memorials commemorating conflicts from the Revolution to the Persian Gulf War. The Korean War marker is "dedicated to the men and woman who bravely fought in 'The Forgotten War,'" which it asserts was "the first war to end the spread of communist tyranny throughout the world."

Figure 13.1. *A*, The Maryland State Korean War Memorial in Baltimore, built in 1990, uses a line to divide a map of Korea, while, *B*, the New York State Korean War Memorial in Albany, also built in 1990, includes a fountain and several plaques. Photos by Levi Fox, 2014 and 2016.

Figure 13.2. *A*, The New York City Korean War Memorial in Battery Park, built in 1991, uses a hollow figure to show absence, while, *B*, the Berrien County Korean War Memorial in St. Joseph, Michigan, includes instructions for calling in to learn more about the monument, which was built in 1994. Photos by Levi Fox, 2014 and 2016.

The push to create a memorial for those who died under communist regimes makes 1993 a key year in commemorative anti-communism, Kirk Savage notes that "Lev Dobriansky, organizer of the Shevchenko Memorial"—built "as a weapon" against "the Soviet Union"—was the "prime mover behind" the Victims of Communism Memorial, eventually dedicated in 2007, which he says "illustrates the larger cultural drift" from hero monuments to victim memorials (2011:263, 292). Jon Wiener notes the first plan was for a "$100 million building" with a Victims of Communism Museum, including "a recreation of the Gulag" and "200-foot high statue of the Goddess of Democracy," and argues this change is part of a "larger phenomenon of forgetting the Cold War" (2012:29). Still, some Korean War Memorials like the one in Danbury, Connecticut—dedicated on 25 July 1993—do discuss the ideologies underlying the war, asserting "it was the first time a United Nations coalition turned the tide against communist aggression." Similarly, the Korean War monument in Chicopee, Massachusetts, dedicated the very same day, notes that U.S. "Army forces participated in the Forgotten War as part of the U.N. forces to expel the enemy."

The Massachusetts Korean War Veterans Memorial, dedicated on 28 July 1993, near Charlestown Navy Yard in Boston is a roofless gazebo with a choice of audio accompaniment, which can be activated by pressing labeled buttons on silver pillars. The monument has empty walls on five sides along with the open-air roof, adding to its unfinished quality. Moreover, this monument integrates motion activated audio as well. As visitors enter, they are surrounded by a voice telling them they are on solemn ground and detailing the meaning of various parts of the memorial. Meanwhile, the Korean War Memorial at McNeely Lake Park in Louisville, dedicated 7 November 1993, blends global with local. The memorial has a map of the Koreas and a plaque with allied flags, while it notes the names of all Jefferson County men who died in Korea. The monument also has a unique engraved timeline that shows the rise and fall of the United Nations allies' fortunes with peaks and valleys in the wall, while linking specific dates to brief, corresponding narrative captions on the ground—like "Inchon landing" or "Chinese entry into the war."

Some communities offer visitors information that can be accessed via telephone while standing in front of local memorials, providing tourists a kind of immediacy that could encourage more to learn about their site, like at the Kansas City, Kansas, Korea-Vietnam Memorial dedicated on Veterans Day 1988. The Berrien County Korean War Memorial in St. Joseph, Michigan, is especially interesting since the message visitors hear also explains why the monument moved (Figure 13.2b). A plaque in front notes it as part of a "Touch Tone Culture" collection of public monuments administered by the nearby Krasl Art Center, and by calling the number, listed visitors can learn—from the Mayor no less—that when the memorial was dedicated in 1994 it was located in a different place, but later all the war monuments in town were relocated to Bluff Park.

Dedicated in 1994, the Wisconsin Korean War Veterans Memorial in Plover sits on an artificial island in Lake Pacawa with picnic tables and commemorative bricks, still for sale as at many monuments (Figure 13.3a). Built for $600,000 by the state Korean War Veterans Association (KWVA), the memorial has been run by the city since a 2010 Change of Command ceremony. Among design elements are five statues from each branch, led by a nurse, notable for their attempt at racial inclusion—as one figure appears to be African American. The monument is visible from the road, which I realized as I left is the state Korean War Veterans Memorial Highway.

Multiple official state Korean War Memorials are located in cemeteries. The Maine Korean War Memorial was dedicated 29 July 1995, at Mount Hope Cemetery in Bangor. It is shaped like a pagoda and has a list of all those state residents who perished in the conflict, flags from the allied nations that fought with the U.S., a map of the Korean peninsula, and a walkway of stones honoring specific veterans. The Illinois Korean War Memorial, dedicated on 16 June 1996, in Springfield at the Oak Ridge Cemetery near Abraham Lincoln's grave, includes the names of all Illinois residents killed in Korea. The monument consists of a 12 ft. bronze bell that plays war songs every hour on the hour and is surrounded by four larger than life figures to create an immersive experience like at the official Massachusetts memorial.

In July 1998 near the city of Exeter, an official Korean War Veterans Memorial was dedicated at the 265-acre Rhode Island Veterans Memorial Cemetery, home to over thirty distinct memorials. One of many local monuments built in the 1990s and early 2000s to proclaim the message "Freedom Is Not Free," the inside rim of the masthead asserts the monument honors those "Who Served And Returned No Less Than Those Who Served And Paid The Ultimate Sacrifice." The fact this part of the memorial is not visible from the road, along with the language emphasizing the equality of those who lived with those who died, suggests it is a hidden tribute directed primarily at living veterans.

Several more state Korean War Memorials were created in the mid-to-late 1990s, including some using innovative designs such as the Ohio Korean War Memorial at Riverside Park in Dayton, dedicated 9 September 1995, at a cost of $1,000,000. The only Korean War Memorial other than The Punchbowl to list the names of all MIA in Korea, the monument uses a windy walkway to recognize Buckeyes from twentieth-century wars and Korea veterans from other states. It has huge sculpted-shrub lettering naming it and includes a 13 ft. tall granite bas-relief of a soldier. Designed by Architectural Associates Inc. of Dayton, the memorial was a passion project of Architectural Associates Inc. (AAI) founder and Korean War survivor Bryan Choi.

The official state of Minnesota Korean War Memorial uses hollowness as a way of "representing the missing-in-action," whose war remains unfinished, and those Minnesotans who did not survive. The monument, dedicated 13 September 1998—with a crowd of several thousand in attendance, according to one attendee—is larger than life with an 8 ft. bronze soldier and an 18 ft. high hollowed-out column. The grounds of the Capitol Mall in St. Paul are a complex commemorative landscape, including a statue of a soldier returning from Vietnam that seems to be asking, "Why?" In contrast, the Korean War Memorial includes an orientation plaque at the entry explaining how it is to be understood, noting a single "soldier, in winter clothing, is looking for his lost comrades" and "the silhouette image created by the monolith represents Minnesotans who did not return." The monument also includes a list of names of all Minnesotans killed in the war and engravings along stones on the right side of the walkway, interspersing a timeline of major events with the names of the UN Allies, including those that only sent hospital ships.[1]

Perhaps the most powerful visual representation of Korean War loss is found at Florida's official Korean War Memorial, which uses dividing lines and abstract statues to represent the specifics of Korea as few state monuments do. On 2 December 1998, construction started at Cascade Park in Tallahassee, and the memorial was unveiled by Governor Jeb Bush on 11 December 1999. The centerpiece of the memorial is a broken circle with the words "Duty," "Honor," and "Country" while the segment on the ground has the word "Life" as well as listing the names of state residents who died in the conflict. The memorial also includes a map of the Korean peninsula, which is divided at the thirty-eighth parallel by the horseshoe-shaped broken circle, and a "Battlefield Cross" made of a helmet and rifle on a pair of boots.

Local Korean War Memorial building continued in the late 1990s. On 18 May 1996, Staten Island dedicated a memorial with a plaque on a boulder reading "Freedom Is Not Free," with then-Mayor Rudy Giuliani signing a bill in 1997 to expand the monument into a memorial park specifically in honor of Korean War veterans. The Pittsburgh Korean War Memorial, dedicated on

---

[1] "Korean War Memorial," Memorials and Remembrances: A walking tour of the Capitol Mall, Minnesota Historical Society, accessed 7/27/2017, http://sites.mnhs.org/historic-sites/static/msc/state_capitol_walkingTour.htm; "Korean War Veterans Memorial," Minnesota Department of Veterans, accessed 9/12/2024, https://mn.gov/mdva/memorials/memorials/koreanwarmemorial.jsp

Figure 13.3. *A*, The Wisconsin State Korean War Memorial in Plover, built in 1994, includes several figures representing different branches of the military, while, *B*, the Lycoming County Korean War Memorial in Williamsport, Pennsylvania, dating from 2000 is shaped like the county itself. Photos by Levi Fox, 2014 and 2015.

27 July 1999, uses a sundial as part of its design. This well-trafficked site, on the North Shore of the Ohio River near two stadiums, has bronze plaques that note it was dedicated by the Matthew B. Ridgeway chapter of the KWVA.

Many local monuments were created in the year 2000 that recall Korea, such as the "C Battery" Plaque at Union Station in Meridian, Mississippi, (in full view of anyone boarding or leaving a train) and the Lycoming County

Korean War Memorial in Williamsport, Pennsylvania, which seems oddly shaped until one realizes it is designed to mimic the outline of the county itself (Figure 13.3b). The Bucks County Korean War Memorial in Doylestown, Pennsylvania, is one of many that includes a pagoda and the phrase "Freedom Is Not Free." The memorial at Somerville High School in Massachusetts, uses several detailed sculptures of objects such as a shovel, a canteen, and ration cans stamped CRACKERS and JAM, PINEAPPLE as well as text and maps to argue for the idea of the Korean War should be recalled as "The Forgotten Victory."

The Lebanon County Korean War Memorial in Pennsylvania, located in Fisher Veterans Park—home to a tank as well as memorials to several additional conflicts—uses the same bronze plaque as in Monroe, Michigan, and many other towns, but with a different caption. Beneath the plaque in Lebanon the text asserts, "They And The War They Fought Were Soon Forgotten" but their "Sacrifice Will Always Be Remembered And 'Not Forgotten.'" Moreover, etched in granite under the plaque are those two phrases most often found on local Korean War monuments: "The Forgotten War" and "Freedom Is Not Free."

Korean War national memorial sculptor Frank Gaylord also designed one state monument. South Carolina's Korean War Veterans Memorial, at Veterans Memorial Park in Columbia, was unveiled on 25 June 2000, the fiftieth anniversary of the start of active hostilities in Korea. The monument includes a plaque noting "82,000 Palmetto state residents served in what has been called the forgotten war," which has a map with arrows showing the direction of the "Inchon Landing" and "Hungnam Evacuation." The circular monument has markers for separate service branches but is centered on the Gaylord sculpture, which mimics the figures he forged for the National Korean War Memorial. Whether in Columbia or the District of Columbia, they are the iconic image of soldiers in Korea in the minds of many Americans.

Case Study: The New Jersey Korean War Veterans Memorial in Atlantic City

Driving down the Atlantic City Expressway, a sign reminds tourists to visit the official New Jersey Korean War Veterans Memorial at Boardwalk and Park Place in Atlantic City (Figure 13.4a). This most valuable Monopoly property was christened 13 November 2000, as a memorial that includes a statue called "The Mourning Soldier" who is clutching dog tags, while under a bronze flame are the names of hundreds of state residents who died or went missing in Korea. The design also contains smaller statues, including a nurse, a soldier aiding an injured comrade, and a bas-relief of the faces of Congressional Medal of Honor winners from the state. These seemingly disparate elements create an atmosphere of commemoration sans analysis. The process of creating it took several years—and cost millions—but it illustrates how many state Korean War Memorials were built, and why many at the time focused on the living as much as the dead.

"An Act establishing the Korean War Veterans' Memorial Committee" and "creating the Korean War Veterans' Memorial Fund" with an appropriation of $25,000 was introduced by State Senators Bob Singer and Louis Kosco at the start of the 1996 legislative term, after its committee made one amendment to "give preference to Korean War veterans" instead of "members of Korean War veterans organizations" in being assigned to the memorial committee. Singer and Kosco, a Korea veteran, pushed the bill through the Senate, gaining passage 5 February, before Assembly allies passed it on 17 June, allowing Governor Christine Todd Whitman to sign it into law on 22 July, noting the "Committee will ensure that veterans will always be recognized and remembered for their dedication and commitment" (NJ State Law Library 1996).

The bipartisan Memorial Committee included two Republicans, Kosco and Assembly Majority Whip Kenneth LeFevre, and two Democrats, Senator Garry Furnari and Assemblyperson Nilsa Cruz-Perez. LeFevre was elected Assemblyman in 1996 after several terms on the Atlantic County Board of Chosen Freeholders. Fumari was elected to the New Jersey State Senate in 1998, while Cruz-Perez joined them in 2014. The rest of the committee consisted of politically connected veterans from across the state.

Importantly, the committee included three members with close ties to Atlantic City, who would play a role in bringing the monument to the Boardwalk. Richard E. Squires, a sailor on the USS *Wisconsin* in the Korean War, was Atlantic County Executive from 1979 to 1999. Edmund Colanzi served in the Air Force in Korea, then began a career working for Atlantic City government in 1961, while Patrick McGahn was a "Marine second lieutenant" in Korea, then a "Democratic Party leader who helped bring gambling," according to his 2000 obituary, as McGahn died just prior to the monument being dedicated (Peterson 2000).

Beyond committee make-up, there were other factors that led to the Boardwalk location beating out all others. According to Joseph Cassella, a past president of the KWVA of Hudson County, the committee "didn't want to build" the monument in Jersey City at the proposed site of "Washington and Dudley" streets "because it was dead-end" and despite his arguing "that we had the PATH and the light rail, . . . they chose Atlantic City anyway" (Kelly 2002). Another issue was financing since the original legislation charged the

Figure 13.4. *A*, The New Jersey State Korean War Memorial in Atlantic City, built in 1990, is the location of annual veterans' ceremonies. *B*, the Perry County Korea Monument in Elliottsburg, Pennsylvania, dating to 2002, sits in front of the local high school. Photos by Levi Fox, 2014 and 2015.

committee not only with picking the "location for the construction of a Korean Veterans' Memorial" but finding an "appropriate method of financing the construction and maintenance of the memorial." Indeed, the deciding factor was most likely the Committee getting a donation of "$1 Million from the CRDA"—the Development Authority charged with Re-investing funds from Casinos into Atlantic City—in December 1999, which paid for the plurality "of the $2.5 million needed to build the memorial," with the state, veterans' groups, and companies such as Lockheed Martin funding the rest (NJ Korean War Memorial).

State and Local Korean War Monuments, 2001-2003

The pace of Korean War Memorial building slowed after the 50th anniversary. Still, several local Korean War monuments were dedicated in towns, and on college campuses, across the nation in the fall of 2001—only weeks after 9/11—including a two-part memorial in Terra Haute, Indiana, with the names of those from Vigo County killed and a statue honoring Medal of Honor winner Corporal Charles Abrell. On 10 October 2001, the Eastern Mississippi Community College Korean War Memorial in Scooba was dedicated in honor of local students who died in the war, while on 4 November 2001 in East Meadow on Long Island, the Nassau County Korean War Memorial statue was built, although it would be another two years until a set of markers listing locals killed was dedicated. Next to Bierce Library at the University of Akron sits a half globe that shows the 38th Parallel and has the words "The Forgotten War," which was dedicated on Veterans Day of 2001 at a cost of $160,000 that was paid for by a local veteran.

The Perry County Korea Monument, dedicated 24 May 2002, sits in front of the West Perry High School in Elliottsburg, Pennsylvania, and includes the message the war is "Forgotten No Longer." (Figure 13b). On 23 November 2002, following years of fundraising efforts, the Hudson County Korean War Memorial was dedicated in the Paulus Hook section of Jersey City with Ellis Island and the Statue of Liberty in the background, at the site that had been a finalist for the official state of New Jersey Korea memorial. The monument is one of the few I have visited with assigned parking spaces for visitors—important for events like the farmers' market that was concluding as I arrived—which came about as a legislated compromise (Thorbourne 2006).

Philadelphia's Korean War Memorial at Penn's Landing, dedicated 22 June 2002, has four pillars containing the names of the war dead from five counties around the city divided by year. The narrative of the war is broken into four phases—invasion, UN advance, Chinese intervention, and stalemate—

and refers to "Chinese Communist Forces" rather than China, alluding to the ambiguous international legal position of those who crossed the Yalu River. The panels on the other side present a history that starts with Japanese colonialism and includes an analysis of the early Cold War, next to a 2001 speech by George W. Bush commemorating the fiftieth anniversary of the war. The panels disagree on the number of war dead, with the official history listing 33,742 casualties and the president's speech counting 33,665. Such disagreements over details may be one reason Korea continues to be labeled forgotten despite the myriad of monuments recalling those who died in the war. Moreover, one reason the memorial is so complex is the number of stakeholders invested, not only locally but federally, since in 2003 Congress appropriated $1,000,000 to pay off the monument, though this was a modest allocation in a bill directing the Pentagon to spend $8,500,000 for "the Fort Benning Infantry Museum" in Georgia (*Congressional Record* 2003).

Many state Korean War monuments are located on bodies of water, such as the one on Mobile Bay. After a three-year effort, on 25 June 2002, an official Alabama Korean War Memorial was dedicated at the USS *Alabama* Battleship Park near other monuments at a cost of $300,000. Its pagoda-shaped sign has Korean translations of each word and sits next to a walkway called Vickery's Bridge that recalls the actions of Lt. Grady Vickery at Namji-Ri Bridge. The monument consists of granite blocks with the flags of each allied nation next to narratives describing their actions in Korea, five pillars for the U.S. military, and one with a map. The other official Alabama Korean War Memorial, which lists the dead by county, was dedicated in 2003 at the other end of the state. It is located within the first rest stop on I-65 South as you enter from Tennessee, which is the Ardmore Welcome Center located at mile marker 363.

More monuments recalling the Korean War would be dedicated before the end of 2003, such as the Northeast Kansas Korean War Memorial in Topeka, Kansas, dedicated on 27 July, the date of the fiftieth anniversary of the armistice. That memorial includes three stones, the largest of them ornamented with the phrase "Freedom Is Not Free." This phrase, drawn from the National Korean War Memorial appears on many state and local monuments built from the late 1980s to 2003—as I have shown—could be the motto of The Forgotten War Memory Boom. Moreover, the memorials built in this era show a process by which Korea—the so-called Forgotten War—came to be widely remembered across the U.S. landscape.

Analysis of Patterns in U.S. Korean War Monuments, 1987–2003

Three elements of the composition of state and local Korean War monuments display important patterns: Symbolism, Narrative, and Place. Symbolism relates to statuary aspects of any monument and can figure into other uses of signs such as flags or insignia on that monument as well as design elements such as the monument functioning as a sundial. Narrative refers to text or audio aspects of any monument, especially information about the history of the war itself or arguments about the meaning of the Korean War, which are most often found carved into a monument but sometimes also found in pamphlets or on signage adjacent to monuments. Place, especially important when considering official state monuments, includes the location of any monument in absolute and relative terms, the commemorative landscape in which that monument is located, and geographic elements such as the monument's proximity to water.

Several memorials symbolize that the war is ongoing. The Battery Park monument in Manhattan includes a hollowed-out figure similar to the official Minnesota state memorial in St. Paul, referencing the unfinished-ness of the war, while others adopt a roofless design to show the unfinished elements of the war, such as official state monuments in Atlantic City and Boston. Finally, several monuments show the specifics of the Korean War by making use of dividing lines to highlight the continued separation of the Korean peninsula including the memorial in Baltimore, while others include a pagoda as part of their design in order to differentiate Korea from other conflicts such as the monument in Bangor, Maine.

The overarching narrative feature in many monuments seems to be stark anti-communism. The fact that so many monuments from the 1980s onward assert in some way or another that "Freedom Is Not Free" reinforces this notion of sacrifice and serves as a justification for militarism, as well as a comfort to the families of soldiers killed in Korea. The phrase "Forgotten War," which appears the most often of any motto on state and local Korean War Memorials across the country, goes even further in asserting those who fought in Korea have suffered from a lack of public memory, despite the fact any given monument is meant as an act of remembering. Some monuments include multiple variations on the phrase, suggesting the war is "No Longer Forgotten" or is a "Forgotten Victory" rather than a stalemate, in a clear attempt to rewrite our understanding of the Korean War and its position within the arc of modern military memory.

The placement of Korean War monuments, especially official state memorials, is also important in understanding their function. While many local memorials are located at the heart of their respective communities such as courthouses, village greens, or public parks (in most cases in line with the regional character of each place) some local monuments are specifically located in key maritime heritage tourism, spots such as the New York City monument in Battery Park, which is next to several other memorials, or the Philadelphia monument near Penn's Landing, similarly set up to be part of a memorial row. Placement near water is also a characteristic of many state monuments, from Mobile Bay in Alabama to Charlestown Harbor in Boston. Moreover, the state memorial in Baltimore is along the water, while the one in Atlantic City is on the Boardwalk. Even inland monuments are often along rivers, such as the Pittsburgh memorial or the state monuments in Riverside Park in Dayton and at the artificial island in Plover, Wisconsin. If we understand places adjacent to water as being 'liminal' zones of transition, especially for those who died far from their home, then the placement of these monuments adjacent to water is another indication of the unfinished-ness of the Korean War, since these memorials functions as places to commune with the dead.

This idea of communion with the dead also helps explain the timing of The Forgotten War Memory Boom. Several events in the early to mid-1980s explain why The Forgotten War Memory Boom occurred. In 1982, at the dedication of the Vietnam Memorial, Korean War veterans were presented a questionnaire about what kind of monument they might want for themselves. In 1983, the finale of *M*A*S*H* became the highest-rated TV show in history, helping cement the place of the Korean War in the popular mind. In 1985, the Korean War Veterans Association was founded, providing the people who sought to commune with their fallen comrades at the state and local monuments they would build over the next two decades. In 1986 the National Korean War Veterans Memorial was authorized, focusing the attention of veterans on state and local sites, and providing the last piece of the puzzle to spur a Forgotten War Memory Boom.

The state and local memorials I discussed were most often created by the very people who fought in Korea, in remembrance of their fallen comrades but also highlighting their own service. This makes the monuments different from others, such as Civil War memorials. While both are arguments about the past, Korean War monuments operate in an expressly ideological space that does not try to hide its privileging one side over another. Instead, Korean War monuments unapologetically celebrate what they see as their contribution to a global anti-communist struggle, arguing only that their fight has been too long forgotten.

References

Congressional Record
　2003　　*V. 149, PT. 17* (24 September to 3 October)

Doss, Erika
　2010　　*Memorial Mania: Public Feeling in America.* Chicago, IL: University of Chicago Press.

Kelly, Donald M.
　2002　　"After Five years Long-awaited Korean War monument to be dedicated," *Hudson Reporter*, 8 November.

NJ Korean War Memorial
　nd　　"Official Dedication of The NJ Korean War Memorial Pays Tribute To Those Now No Longer Forgotten," NJ Korean War Memorial website, https://www.nj.gov/military/community/civic-engagement/war-memorials/korean-war-memorial.shtml, accessed on 25 November 2017.

NJ State Law Library
　1996　　52: 18A-218, LEGISLATIVE HISTORY CHECKLIST (Korean Veterans Memorial). Trenton, NJ: New Jersey State Law Library.

Peterson, Iver
　2000　　Patrick T. McGahn, 72, Lawyer for Casinos. *New York Times*, 3 August.

Savage, Kirk
　2011　　*Monument Wars: Washington D.C., the National Mall and the Transformation of the Memorial Landscape.* Berkeley, CA: University of California Press.

Thorbourne, Ken
　2006　　Korean Vets Salute Deal to Access Memorial. *Jersey Journal*, 19 October.

Wallace, Mike
　1996　　*Mickey Mouse History and Other Essays in American Memory.* Philadelphia, PA: Temple University Press.

Wiener, Jon
　2012　　*How We Forgot the Cold War: A Historical Journey Across America.* Berkeley, CA: University of California Press.

Winter, Jay
　2007　　The Generation of Memory: Reflections on the 'Memory Boom' in Contemporary Historical Studies. *Archives & Social Studies: A Journal of Interdisciplinary Research* 1(0)(March): 363–397.

14

"Be Assured That . . . All . . . Memorials Will Be Kept Sacred and Beautiful"

The Life Cycle of Memorials at Fort Monmouth, New Jersey

Melissa Ziobro

Why and how are memorials "born," if you will? When do they "die?" Can they survive adaptive reuse if we might borrow a preservation term? What long-term responsibilities do we have to individuals memorialized? This chapter ponders these questions, using as a case study the freestanding monuments and memorials of a now defunct Army base called Fort Monmouth in central New Jersey. The archival records cited in the following text, unless otherwise noted, come from the Tradition Committee/Memorialization Committee Records now in the possession of the United States Army Communications-Electronics (CECOM) Command Historical Office, located at Aberdeen Proving Ground (APG), Maryland. Descriptions of the memorials are largely adapted from the 2009 booklet, *Landmarks, Memorials, Buildings, and Street Names of Fort Monmouth, New Jersey, and the U.S. Army CECOM Life Cycle Management Command (LCMC)*, which the author of this piece helped produce.

Fort Monmouth: An Overview

The U.S. Army needed to expand rapidly following America's entry into World War I. This is where our story begins. The Army's search for land for additional Signal Corps Training Camps eventually led them to a site in Monmouth County, NJ in May 1917. The installation was originally called "Camp Little Silver," based merely on its proximity to that town. The Army renamed Camp Little Silver "Camp Alfred Vail" in September 1917 to honor the New Jersey inventor who helped Samuel Morse develop commercial telegraphy.

This would, after all, be a Signal Corps encampment, and the Signal Corps was charged with all manner of military communications. Ultimately, the camp prepared several battalions for war (Galton and Wheelock 1946:20). In addition to wartime training, the Signal Corps conducted research and development work at the base. The Army wanted its own laboratories, largely independent of the commercial facilities. Much of the laboratories' research focused on wireless communications (Galton and Wheelock 1946:1–23; Phillips 1967:14–23; Rejan et al. 2008:1–6).

Although the site was supposed to be temporary, the Chief Signal Officer authorized the purchase of Camp Vail in 1919. The installation received permanent status and the name "Fort Monmouth" in August 1925. The designation honored the soldiers of the American Revolution who fought in the nearby Battle of Monmouth Court House in 1778 (Galton and Wheelock 1946:1–15; Phillips 1967:14–23; Rejan et al. 2008:1–6).

Fort Monmouth would soon be known as the "Home of the Signal Corps." It held this title until the Vietnam era, when the Signal School gradually moved from Fort Monmouth to Fort Gordon, Georgia. What would remain at Fort Monmouth, primarily, was the research and development piece of the mission first established during the Great War. Famous research projects tied to Fort Monmouth included the first United States' aircraft detection radars, early weather radars, early communications satellites, early weather satellites, early televised weather satellites, early high-capacity communications satellites, night vision technologies, counter improvised explosive device technologies, situational awareness devices, and much, much more (Phillips 1967; Rejan et al. 2008).

The base remained open until 2011, when it closed during one of the Army's Base Realignment and Closure rounds (intended to divest the government of excess real estate, thereby saving money where possible). Those interested in more on the Fort's decades of service to the nation and pioneering research and development should read *A History of Army Communications and Electronics at Fort Monmouth, New Jersey* (Rejan et al. 2008), *Fort Monmouth* (Rejan 2009), *Camp Evans: The Untold Story* (InfoAge Science History Learning Center 2010), or *Fort Monmouth: The U.S. Army's House of Magic* (Ziobro 2024).

The Memorials

Over the years Fort Monmouth became home to over 100 freestanding memorials, monuments, or markers (terms used more or less interchangeably on the base). They are the focus of this chapter. Note that there were also dozens of other "things," such as buildings, roads, outdoor public spaces, and conference rooms, named at the base. This is not uncommon at military installations. Those interested in a comprehensive list of everything named at the Fort can download a copy of *Landmarks, Memorials, Buildings, and Street Names of Fort Monmouth, New Jersey and the U.S. Army CECOM Life Cycle Management Command* from the website of the United States Army CECOM Command Historian. (This internally produced, collaboratively staff-written booklet has existed in some form since the 1960s and has been edited and updated many times).

The Signal Corps Tradition Committee (later known as the Fort Monmouth Tradition Committee and then the Memorialization Committee) installed the bulk of the freestanding memorials, monuments, or markers in the mid-twentieth century. The Committee traces its roots to 1948. That October, officers from across Fort Monmouth began meeting, at the request of Major General Francis Lanahan (Commanding General of Fort Monmouth 1947–1951), "to determine the best method of improving Fort Monmouth as the center of traditions of the Signal Corps . . ." (Memorandum dated 22 October 1948 found in Memorialization and Tradition Committee Records, Box 1, "1945–1949," Folder, "Establishment of Tradition Committee 1948–1951," available via the U.S. Army CECOM LCMC Historical Office, APG, MD).

In a 22 October 1948 memorandum to General Lanahan, Colonel Harrod G. Miller reported on the wide-ranging discussions that these officers had. Ideas included naming buildings and streets, erecting statues, adopting a "new, catchy, inspirational song," "that historical landmarks on or near the post be plainly marked," and "that the slogan 'Get the Message Through' be impressed upon all personnel of The Signal Corps through proper publicity, education and training." Finally, the officers recommended "that an officer be appointed whose primary duty is to carry out this program, and that a board composed of representatives of the Board of Governors of the Fort Monmouth Officers' Club, the Non-Commissioned Officers' Club, and the Civilian Employees, be appointed to implement ways and means of carrying out these recommendations" (Memorandum dated 22 October 1948 found in Memorialization and Tradition Committee Records, Box 1, "1945–1949," Folder, "Establishment of Tradition Committee 1948–1951," available via the U.S. Army CECOM LCMC Historical Office, APG, MD).

General Lanahan knew just the man. A 3 November 1948 memorandum from General Lanahan to one Colonel Terence J. Tully informed him, "You are hereby designated, in addition to your other duties, as Officer-in-Charge of a project to be known as 'The Signal Corps Tradition Program'" (Memorandum found in Memorialization and Tradition Committee Records, Box 1, "1945–1949," Folder, "Establishment of Tradition Committee 1948–1951," available via the U.S. Army CECOM LCMC Historical Office, APG, MD). The records of the Signal Corps Tradition Committee shed little light on General Lanahan's motivations here, other than the fact that he was a longtime Signal Officer. 1948 was not a big anniversary year for the Signal Corps; they would have at that time considered 1948 their 85th anniversary year (while today the Signal Corps counts their birthdays from their 1860 founding as part of the meteorological service, back then they were counting from 1863, when they stood up as a separate branch). And 1948 falls outside the "Two great monumentalizing periods" Dell Upton identifies in his article in the 2013 book, *Commemoration in America,* those being the 1880s–1930s and the 1980s–present (Gobel and Rossell 2013). However, the nation—and the military especially—were still struggling with the great losses of WWII, and memorializing the dead of WWII specifically would be a major focus of the Tradition Committee. It is likely that longtime Signal Officer General Lanahan, inspired by the recent sacrifices of Signalmen in WWII, and those who came before them, simply felt moved to commemorate the Signal Corps, and was in a position to make it happen.

Things moved quickly. By 6 December 1948, a memorandum to the Chief Signal Officer in Washington, D.C., informed him that: "In line with the desires of General Lanahan, a special committee is being set up, to be known as the 'Signal Corps Tradition Committee,' at Fort Monmouth, New Jersey." The memo explains that "The chief objectives of this committee are as follows: a. To insure a better appreciation of all, particularly Signal Corps personnel, of the historical accomplishments of the Signal Corps in the interest of National Defense. b. To extend proper recognition to organizations and individuals of the Signal Corps for their contributions to such accomplishments" (Memorandum found in Memorialization and Tradition Committee Records, Box 1, "1945–1949," Folder, "Establishment of Tradition Committee 1948–1951," available via the U.S. Army CECOM LCMC Historical Office, APG, MD).

By 17 December 1948, Colonel Tully shared "A Plan to Implement the Signal Corps Tradition Program" with General Lanahan. The Tradition Committee would be composed of both military and civilian representatives of major activities at the Signal Corps Center at Fort Monmouth. The plan stressed that no government funds would be earmarked for these memorialization efforts. Instead, the Tradition Committee would be tasked with fundraising, both on post and off. It was suggested, for example, that, on post, officers contribute $1.00, enlisted men, $0.40, and civilians, $0.50 (presumably, this would cover them for the year, although this is slightly unclear) (Memorandum found in

Memorialization and Tradition Committee Records, Box 1, "1945–1949," Folder, "Establishment of Tradition Committee 1948–1951," available via the U.S. Army CECOM LCMC Historical Office, APG, MD). This would translate to donations of almost $11.00, $4.35, and $5.44, respectively, in 2020 dollars. According to *A History of Army Communications and Electronics at Fort Monmouth, New Jersey* (Rejan et al. 2008:31), there were just over 15,000 personnel on base in November 1948, so the potential for this "voluntary" / compulsory fundraising was great. There were also other Signal Corps outposts to tap, and retirees, and civilian partners, and the families and friends of the honored dead. General Lanahan himself sent letters around the globe, tactfully encouraging donations from many. For example, a November 1950 "Type of Letter Sent by General Lanahan to all Army Signal Officers in the United States and to All Key Signal Officers in the Overseas Command" informs the recipient of memorialization actions at Fort Monmouth and contains phrases like, "Thus far, the Post of Fort Monmouth has contributed some $7,500 toward this project, and in addition there have been outside contributions by some officers and civilians. For the completion of this project some $15,000 is needed," and:

> The purpose of this letter is to inform the Signal Officers of major commands of the program which is under way here at Fort Monmouth and to afford the officers and Signal units of these commands the opportunity to participate ... I believe that all members of the Signal Corps will want to have an opportunity to contribute in some measure toward such a project, and I would appreciate very much your help in affording them this opportunity. (Memorandum found in Memorialization and Tradition Committee Records, Box 1, "1945–1949," Folder, "Letters on Implement," available via the U.S. Army CECOM LCMC Historical Office, APG, MD)

While the government is often depicted, fairly or not, as a lumbering bureaucracy, the Tradition Committee within its first year had already started installing markers along the main thoroughfare of the base (first christened Memorial Drive and later, the Avenue of Memories) (Figure 14.1b). These markers would memorialize Signal Corps soldiers who died in World War II. Each marker consisted of a stone base, to which a roughly 4 × 6 bronze plaque was affixed. A tree graced each marker, and flags stood sentry at times. Records show that each marker cost $30.00 ($326.00 in 2020) (Memorandum available in Memorialization and Tradition Committee Records, Box 1, "1945–1949," Folder, "Tradition Committee 1948," available via the U.S. Army CECOM LCMC Historical Office, APG, MD).

a

b

Figure 14.1. *A*, The first Avenue of Memories memorial plaque, dedicated to Edmund P. Karr. Courtesy U.S. Army CECOM LCMC Historical Office, APG, MD. *B*, The Avenue of Memories, ca. 1970s. Can you spot the memorials lining the road? Courtesy U.S. Army CECOM LCMC Historical Office, APG, MD.

The Committee placed the first marker in memory of Major Edmund P. Karr on 6 April 1949. Major Karr, of the 17th Signal Operation Battalion, was killed in action in Liege, Belgium on 6 January 1945 (Figure 14.1a).

Major Karr's family was not at the ceremony, but a 17 April 1949 letter from Fort Monmouth's Lieutenant Colonel A. Helmer to Karr's parents reveals how the memorials were viewed by those responsible for them at the time:

> The memorial tree, monument, and plaque program is . . . the product of the love and affection born here at Monmouth by brother officers and men for our departed friends. We choose a tree as our memorial because it is a living thing of God. It is our hope that as a tree lifts its arms to God in constant prayer, so may we, the living, spiritually do the same . . . we of Monmouth endeavor to give mortality to our departed comrades.
>
> Tens of thousands of young soldiers will pass Edmund's tree throughout the years. We know that in pausing, reading, and contemplating, they will gain of the nobility of his soul. So will . . . Karr's spirit, always live after him.

The letter ends with a promise: "You and Mrs. Karr can be assured that this, our very first memorial, and all other memorials will be kept sacred and beautiful and that in favorable weather the two American flags beside the markers will always be kept flying" (Letter found in Memorialization and Tradition Committee Records, Box 1, "1945–1949," Folder, "Establishment of Tradition Committee 1948–1951," available via the U.S. Army CECOM LCMC Historical Office, APG, MD).

Numerous Avenue of Memories markers would be installed in 1949; that number eventually grew to 117. However, these markers were not all the Committee tackled in 1949, by any means. For example, April 1949 saw the dedication of Greely Field and Myer Park. Greely Field honored Major General Adolphus W. Greely, who led the Signal Corps expedition to the Arctic in 1881 and served as Chief Signal Officer from 1887 to 1906. Myer Park honored Albert J. Myer, the first Chief Signal Officer (Letter found in Memorialization and Tradition Committee Records, Box 1, "1945–1949," Folder "Tradition Committee 1949," available via the U.S. Army CECOM LCMC Historical Office, APG, MD). Even as these first markers were going into the ground, the Committee was formalizing its long-range plans. A memorandum of 19 May 1949 notes that the "essential part" of the Committee's "master plan" was "the development of Fort Monmouth—the home of the Signal Corps—as the center of Signal Corps tradition" (Memorandum found in Memorialization and Tradition Committee Records, Box 1, "1945–1949," Folder, "Tradition

Committee 1949," available via the U.S. Army CECOM LCMC Historical Office, APG, MD).

The Committee identified its first goals as follows:

(1) The continued procurement and dedication of individual memorials to honor Signal men who were killed in action or died of battle wounds in World War II.
(2) The installation of bronze markers and historical plaques in parks, buildings, and parade areas in memory of eminent members of the Corps now deceased.
(3) The installation of historical unit plaques in permanent buildings to commemorate the records of wartime Signal Corps units.
(4) The establishment of a Signal Corps Museum.
(5) The collection of pictures . . . showing the Signal Corps in action. . . . (Memorandum found in Memorialization and Tradition Committee Records, Box 1, "1945–1949," Folder, "Fort Monmouth Memorialization Committee, Men to be Memorialized," available via the U.S. Army CECOM LCMC Historical Office, APG, MD)

For the most part, the Tradition Committee programs do seem to have been well received. There was enough interest, and money, to keep the program going, and Fort Monmouth intended to do so. After all, a 6 January 1949 memorandum had stated that, "The Tradition Committee will be permanent in nature . . . to insure (stet) continuity of effort to the whole program" (Memorandum found in Memorialization and Tradition Committee Records, Box 1, "1945–1949," Folder "Tradition Committee 1949," available via the U.S. Army CECOM LCMC Historical Office, APG, MD). While its work ebbed and flowed over the years, a Tradition Committee, under slightly different names, existed right up until the base closed. But what does *permanent* really mean? Can anything ever really be permanent? As we will see in a moment, the military's presence at Fort Monmouth certainly would not be, and we are still tracking what that means for the memorials and the commitment made to the honored dead (Figure 14.2).

Before we turn to the base closure and the fate of the individual monuments, memorials, and markers, let us consider some commonalities among them. If we were to summarize the memorializations—that is, the naming of "things" at the base—all honored *deceased* individuals (or in one case, animals—specifically hero homing pigeons) for their service to the nation. No big donors funded their names on things, as you might see on a college campus or at a museum. A few of the freestanding memorials that are the subject of this piece covered specific groups of people or events: the Holocaust Me-

Figure 14.2. The World War II memorial viewing stand, the grandest memorial at the base, was too large to move and is one of the memorials that remains in situ. Courtesy U.S. Army CECOM LCMC Historical Office, APG, MD.

morial, the D-Day memorial, and the Purple Heart Memorial, for example. Another commonality among the Fort Monmouth freestanding memorials? All were made of stone. As the authors of *Philosophical Perspectives on Ruins, Monuments, and Memorials* note, "Permanence is important, for stone remains after all else is gone. Perhaps this is why stones seem so suited to connect the living with the dead, to help us resist ruin and loss" (Bicknell et al. 2019:4). Interestingly, none of the Fort Monmouth memorials incorporated military weaponry or equipment, so common in public memorials around the United States. (Who hasn't seen a tank or such displayed in front of a VFW or in a town square as part of a war memorial? Refer to the chapter in this volume by Veit, Cianciosi, and Butchko on this topic.) The only example of military weaponry displayed on base in a commemorative fashion would be a pair of Rodman Guns, given to Fort Monmouth in 1950 by another local base when *it* closed (U.S. Army CECOM LCMC Historical Office Staff, *Landmarks, Memorials, Buildings, and Street Names of Fort Monmouth, New Jersey and the U.S. Army CECOM Life Cycle Management Command*, 2009).

Base Closure

As noted earlier, the Army slated Fort Monmouth for closure following one of its Base Realignment and Closure rounds, in 2005. By 2011, the activities located at Fort Monmouth would all relocate to various other installations across the country, and the land (by this time over 1,000 acres) would eventually be turned over to the Fort Monmouth Economic Revitalization Authority (FMERA). The FMERA included representatives from the state, county, and the local towns of Tinton Falls, Eatontown, Oceanport. It would be responsible for settling the fate of the property (parceling pieces off for private development, public benefit conveyance, etc.) (Army BRAC Program—NJ 2021).

The main entity at the base pre-Base Realignment and Closure was the U.S. Army Communications Electronics Life Cycle Management Command (CECOM LCMC). This Command had previously been (and is now once again) called the Communications-Electronics Command (CECOM; the Army loves both acronyms and name changes). To simplify a rather complicated story, CECOM traces its roots to the Signal Corps research and development laboratories located at Fort Monmouth since World War I. The Command was created at Fort Monmouth around the same time the United States Army Signal School made its gradual departure from Fort Monmouth to Fort Gordon, Georgia.

Anyway—where were we? The bulk of the CECOM LCMC was in 2005 slated to move to Aberdeen Proving Ground, Maryland by 2011. This was incredibly logistically complicated. CECOM LCMC was an installation actively supporting military operations around the globe. Ensuring continuity of operations in support of the "joint Warfighter" was obviously of paramount importance. Minimizing the impact on the base's thousands of civilian employees was also a concern. The local communities dreaded the economic impact the base closure would have on them as thousands of jobs left the area. Despite these pressing issues, the question of the memorials arose again and again, both on post and in the surrounding communities. Would the Command—could the Command—take the memorials that had been on post for decades to Aberdeen Proving Ground with them? If they did not, what would happen to them? In 2005, even as some on the base remained in complete denial about the closure, the first questions about the memorials began to trickle into the CECOM LCMC Historical Office. The Memorialization Committee would ultimately convene to puzzle over these issues. It was not led by the Signal Corps' descendant CECOM LCMC, but rather by the Fort Monmouth Garrison (garrisons are responsible for the development, operation, and maintenance of military facilities). Army Regulation 1–33, *The Army Memorial Program,* guided discussions. It stated, "When an installation closes, the installation commander is responsible for the disposition of memorial plaques. The plaque should be offered to the next of kin of the person memorialized. If the next of kin cannot be located or refuses a plaque, send it to the Commander, Pueblo Army Depot" (Headquarters Department of the Army 2006).

This is not exactly what happened at Fort Monmouth. First, locating the next of kin for over 100 individuals, some of whom died over 60 years ago, would be a massive, unwieldy undertaking. And, as you can imagine, different stakeholders on the Memorialization Committee (and in the local communities) had different visions for what should happen to the memorials and markers. Some thought attempting to locate the next of kin, if logistically daunting, a worthy endeavor. Some thought everything should move to Aberdeen Proving Ground, Maryland, with the CECOM LCMC. Some thought items should be sent to Fort Gordon, Georgia, which, as noted earlier, gradually assumed the mantle of "Home of the Signal Corps." Some thought the memorials should stay in place to commemorate the site's rich military history even after its privatization. Others argued that should be the last possible option, as no one from the military would be able to guarantee their safety in that case. Really the one thing everyone agreed on was the fact that sending these items to collect dust at an Army Depot in Colorado was *not* a good idea. For all the respectful disagreements, reverence for the memorials seemed to drive the conversations at all turns.

So, What Actually Happened?

The CECOM LCMC decided, for sake of ease, that they would *recreate*, rather than move, some monuments. This included the 117 "Avenue of Memories" markers discussed earlier, honoring WWII dead. New bronze plaques in the men's honor now adorn the exterior of a building on the Command's new campus at Aberdeen Proving Ground. Also recreated at Aberdeen Proving Ground was a bronze "Defense of Freedom Monument" listing the names of Signal Corps' Cold War era dead, originally dedicated sometime in the 1960s or 1970s, and the "Wright Memorial" dedicated by the 10th Field Signal Battalion Association and the 7th Division Association of WWI veterans to their founder, E. Frederic Wright on 21 May 1977 (Reilly 2011).

The large bronze plaques marking Greely Field and Cowan Park were physically moved from Fort Monmouth to Aberdeen Proving Ground. As noted earlier, Greely Field honors MG Adolphus W. Greely, Chief Signal Officer from 1887 to 1906. Cowan Park, originally dedicated on 24 June 1961, honored Colonel Arthur S. Cowan, who commanded Camp Alfred Vail from 16 September 1917 to 28 June 1918 and Fort Monmouth from 2 September 1929 to 30 April 1937. COL Cowan consolidated the Signal Corps Laboratories and is remembered for his leadership during the formative years of the Signal School (Reilly 2011).

A few monuments were sent to other Army bases. For example, the Signal Corps Centennial time capsule went from Fort Monmouth to the new Home of the Signal Corps at Fort Gordon, Georgia. The time capsule had been buried at Fort Monmouth on 16 September 1960 to commemorate the first centennial of the Corps. The capsule was not to be opened until 21 June 2060, and sending it to Fort Gordon seemed the best way to ensure this (Spinelli 2012).

The BG Dunwoody / Spanish–American War Memorial (Figure 14.3) accompanied the time capsule to Fort Gordon. Designated 22 September 1950, Dunwoody Park memorialized BG Henry H.C. Dunwoody, who served as the Chief Signal Officer in Cuba from 22 December 1898 to 24 May 1901. Under his leadership, the U.S. Army reconstructed, extended, and modernized the entire Cuban Telegraph System. Dunwoody Park at Fort Monmouth featured the Spanish–American War Memorial. In the March 2012 article "Fort Gordon receives, rededicates monuments," by Fort Gordon Public Affairs Nick Spinelli, Fort Gordon garrison commander Col. Robert A. Barker was quoted as saying, "This historic rededication ceremony is a great day that honors the history and heritage of signal Soldiers" (Spinelli 2012).

Some memorials found new homes in the local communities around Fort Monmouth. The base returned the Breslin War Memorial, for example, to the Borough of Belmar on 9 February 2010. The Memorial is stone, similar to a headstone. Two private citizens, Pat and Sandy Breslin, had originally erected the memorial in 1949 on private property in Belmar. For sixteen years (1941–1957), the Breslins had used their Belmar boating business on Route 35 to support the morale, welfare, and recreation of troops. From the day that the Japanese bombed Pearl Harbor, the Breslins declared their 150 boats, fishing equipment, dock, and food free to anyone in uniform. The couple often allowed servicemembers, many from Fort Monmouth, to call their families at no cost. Pat and Sandy paid special attention to convalescents, hosting regional hospital outings that dedicated the use of their facilities to wounded warriors on certain days of the week. After losing the lease on their business property, the memorial sat in storage until coming to its new home at Fort Monmouth in 1961. In February 2010, the Breslin Memorial was the first to leave the base in advance of its closure. Belmar had been advocating for its return for several years. Today it has a prominent waterfront spot in the town (*Monmouth Message* 19 February 2010).

The Battle of the Bulge Memorial, originally dedicated at Fort Monmouth on 6 May 2001, was given to Thorne Middle School in nearby Middletown. It too is a stone memorial, similar to a headstone. It certainly makes sense that it now lives at a school named for Horace "Bud" Thorne, who died in December 1944 during the Battle of the Bulge. Some 90 Battle of the Bulge Veterans

Figure 14.3. The Spanish–American War memorial at Dunwoody Park was among those that left Fort Monmouth for a new home, in this case, Fort Gordon, Georgia. Courtesy U.S. Army CECOM LCMC Historical Office, APG, MD.

gathered for the 2011 rededication. *Greater Media* staff writer Andrew Davison quoted Principal Thomas Olausen as saying, "There is no doubt in my mind that Thorne Middle School is the proper location for this monument... We are the only school in New Jersey named for a Congressional Medal of Honor recipient" (Davison 2011).

The Holocaust Memorial was relocated to nearby Brookdale Community College, home to the Center for Holocaust, Human Rights & Genocide Education (CHHANGE). The Holocaust Memorial consisted of a tree (planted in 1992) and plaque (added in 1993), dedicated by Jewish War Veterans. A sculpture by local artist Brian Hanlon was added by the Jewish Federation of Greater Monmouth County in 2005. CHHANGE seems the perfect home for these (Rick Harrison, personal correspondence 2020).

It also makes perfect sense that a bronze Vietnam Veterans Memorial and benches originally donated by VFW Post 2226 in nearby Oakhurst returned to them in time to be rededicated in honor of the 50th anniversary of the end of the war in 1975.

Many memorials, though, were in fact left behind on the Fort Monmouth property, initially under the care of the aforementioned FMERA. As parcels of the land change hands, though, so too, do the memorials. Is this practice sustainable?

Over 13 years after the base closed, some of the property has been redeveloped. Some of it is a bit overgrown. However, good faith efforts have been made to maintain the many memorials that remain on site. The Avenue of Memories memorials continue to line the main thoroughfare through the base, as they have done since 1949. As of August 2024, they are well maintained and adorned with flags. Now part of County Route 537, Monmouth County has even installed new interpretive signage to explain the significance of the Avenue of Memories markers to travelers. A FMERA spokesperson pointed out the County's significant involvement in protecting and maintaining the memorials along Avenue of Memories and elsewhere on the Fort, thanks in large part to Monmouth County Freeholder Lillian Burry and Director of Public Works John Tobia (FMERA correspondence 2021).

Off the Avenue of Memories, many of the other "left-behind" monuments have been moved to a publicly accessible Memorial Park, on a well-traveled road adjacent to former Officers' Housing (now privatized and beautifully renovated). Monuments moved to the Memorial Park include the aforementioned Cold War era memorial and the Wright Memorial recreated by the CECOM LCMC at Aberdeen Proving Ground, and a granite Purple Heart Memorial, originally dedicated c. 2004. It honors the recipients of the nation's oldest military decoration.

Another grouping of memorials exists across the former parade grounds from the new Memorial Park, near another section of redeveloped and privatized Officer Housing. There, a large WWII memorial viewing stand has been paired with the following:

(1) The Augenstine Memorial: Originally dedicated in 1951, the stone bench and its plaque originally had a background of three dogwood trees. The bench memorializes Chief Warrant Officer Edwin Daniel Augenstine, a native of West Long Branch, New Jersey with over 17 years of Army service. Augenstine served at Fort Monmouth from 1936 to 1942, and then deployed to Europe and Manila. He died of an unknown tropical disease in November 1945.
(2) The Van Kirk Memorial: This stone bench and plaque was dedicated in the early 1950s in honor of First Lieutenant John Stewart Van Kirk, who died in combat on 30 November 1942 in Tunisia. He had previously attended Officer Candidate School at Fort Monmouth.
(3) The Kain Memorial: This small bronze plaque affixed to a stone marker honors Wesley L. Kain, who died in action on 16 December 1944.

Originally located in Brooklyn, NY, the deceased's family requested that it be moved to Fort Monmouth in September 1994.
(4) The D-Day Memorial: This stone marker with carved inscription commemorates the 40th Anniversary of D-Day and was originally dedicated on 6 June 1984 (Rick Harrison, personal correspondence 2020).

The Dean Memorial (a bronze plaque on stone) still sits in its original location near the currently abandoned baseball field on the North Side of the Avenue of Memories. The site was christened "Dean Field" on 19 May 1959. The designation honors Sgt William H. Dean, Jr., a member of Headquarters Company 3rd Battalion, 330 Infantry, who died in combat on 7 December 1944 in France.

Not only are the "left-behind" memorials safe, for now, a new one has been added. Dedicated in 2019, it pays homage to the history of Fort Monmouth at large. According to an article by Kevin Soto in *Shore News Network,* the newest marker was "dedicated as part of the official opening of East Gate Park, a professionally designed and landscaped open space sponsored and curated by RPM Development Group on the 1,226-acre former army post" (Soto 2019). The memorial is made of granite and brick, with a cast metal plaque honoring the people who served at Fort Monmouth. It also features cast metal seals representing the major military branches that operated at the post. A 6 November 2019 *Shore News Network* article quoted Michael Hong, Assistant Vice President of Development at RPM, as saying, "This will be a monument the entire community can be proud of and a humble remembrance of all who made Fort Monmouth a special piece of American history. We're honored to officially unveil it" (*Shore News Network* 2019). In correspondence for this piece, retired Lieutenant Colonel John Edward Occhipinti, who served at the Fort as the last Director for Plans, Training, Mobilization, and Security till the Fort closed in 2011, and then as the Fort Monmouth site manager and Army liaison to the FMERA from 2011–2018, expressed his hope that the memorials will resonate with the land's new residents, saying, "It is important . . . that the memory of all the great people who were part of Fort Monmouth are preserved; the military personnel, their families, and our government civilians and contractors" (John E. Occhipinti, personal correspondence 2021).

Conclusion

In his 2009 book, *Monument Wars,* Kirk Savage writes, "People and history get in the way, and they force the commemorative landscape to change and adapt. For that we should be grateful: change keeps monuments alive" (Savage 2009:7). And based on the experience at Fort Monmouth, one would have to agree. Memorialization can be hard work, it can be unappreciated, is often underfunded, it is often political, but it can help us remember who we are, and what we aspire to be (and in some cases, who we do *not* want to be, but that is another story). What our memorials mean to us, and where they stand, and how they are presented, and who they are owned by can and should change over time as circumstances necessitate.

A representative of the Tradition Committee promised the family of Edmund P. Karr in 1949 that, "all . . . memorials will be kept sacred and beautiful . . ." It was a big promise to make, but it seems, to date, the promise has been kept by the Army and by the people, and corporations, and government entities who have, through unseen twists of fate, become the memorials new caretakers.

Acknowledgments

The author would like to thank John E. Occhipinti, Rick Harrison, Floyd Hertweck, Bruce Steadman, Lillian Burry, and John Tobia for their help with this piece, and Richard Veit for encouraging her to write it.

References

Army Base Realignment and Closure (BRAC) Program
    2021   *BRAC 2005.* https://dcsg9.army.mil/brac/sites.html?state=NJ, accessed 15 January 2021.

Bicknell, Jeanette, Jennifer Judkins, and Carolyn Korsmeyer, eds.
    2019   *Philosophical Perspectives on Ruins, Monuments, and Memorials.* New York, NY: Routledge Publishing.

Davison, Andrew
    2011   Thorne Middle School Honors Tie to Battle of Bulge Hero. https://archive.centraljersey.com/2011/06/02/thorne-middle-school-honors-tie-to-battle-of-bulge-hero-2/, accessed 25 December 2020.

Galton, Lawrence, and Harold J. Wheelock
    1946   *A History of Fort Monmouth New Jersey 1917–1946.* Fort Monmouth, NJ: Signal Corps Publications Agency.

Headquarters Department of the Army
    2006   *The Army Memorial Program (AR 1–33).* Washington, DC: Government Printing Office.

InfoAge Science History Learning Center
    2010   *Camp Evans: The Untold Story.* NJ: RFG Publishing.

Phillips, Helen C.
    1967   *United States Army Signal School 1919–1967.* Fort Monmouth, NJ: U.S. Army Signal Center and School.

Reilly, Chrissie
   2011   C4ISR Honors Past, Preps for Future with Memorials. https://www.army.mil/article/65714/c4isr_honors_past_preps_for_future_with_memorials, accessed 15 January 2021.

Rejan, Wendy, Chrissie Reilly, and Melissa Ziobro, eds.
   2008   *A History of Army Communications and Electronics at Fort Monmouth, New Jersey.* Washington, DC: Government Printing Office.

Rejan, Wendy
   2009   *Fort Monmouth.* Mount Pleasant, SC: Arcadia Press.

Savage, Kirk
   2009   *Monument Wars: Washington, D.C., the National Mall, and the Transformation of the Memorial Landscape.* Oakland, CA: University of California Press.

Shore News Network
   2019   Veterans, Developers Dedicate New Monument At Historic Fort Monmouth. https://www.shorenewsnetwork.com/2019/11/06/veterans-developers-dedicate-new-monument-at-historic-fort-monmouth/, accessed 14 December 2020.

Soto, Kevin.
   2019   New Monument Dedicated at Opening of East Gate Park. https://patch.com/new-jersey/littlesilver/new-monument-dedicated-opening-east-gate-park, accessed 15 December 2020.

Spinelli, Nick
   2012   Fort Gordon Receives, Rededicates Monuments. https://www.army.mil/article/75201/fort_gordon_receives_rededicates_monuments, accessed 15 January 2021.

Gobel, David, and Daves Rossell.
   2013   *Commemoration in America: Essays on Monuments, Memorialization, and Memory.* Charlottesville, VA: University of Virginia Press. [e-book version]

United States Army Communications-Electronics Command Archive.
   2009.   *Landmarks, Memorials, Buildings, and Street Names of Fort Monmouth, New Jersey and the U.S. Army CECOM Life Cycle Management Command.* Aberdeen Proving Ground, Maryland. 6585 Surveillance Loop, Building 6002, Aberdeen Proving Ground, Maryland 21005. Electronic document, https://cecom.army.mil/PDF/Historian/Feature%201/Fort%20Momouth%20Landmarks%20and%20Placenames%202020.pdf, accessed 21 December 2020.

U.S. Army CECOM LCMC Historical Office
   n.d.   Memorandum, folder "Establishment of Tradition Committee 1948–1951." *Memorialization and Tradition Committee Records*, Box 1, "1945–1949." Available via the U.S. Army CECOM LCMC Historical Office, APG, MD.
   n.d.   Memorandum, folder "Fort Monmouth Memorialization Committee, Men to be Memorialized." *Memorialization and Tradition Committee Records*, Box 1, "1945–1949." Available via the U.S. Army CECOM LCMC Historical Office, APG, MD.
   n.d.   Memorandum, folder "Letters on Implement." *Memorialization and Tradition*

Committee Records, Box 1, "1945–1949." Available via the U.S. Army CECOM LCMC Historical Office, APG, MD.

n.d.   Memorandum, folder "Tradition Committee 1948." *Memorialization and Tradition Committee Records*, Box 1, "1945–1949." Available via the U.S. Army CECOM LCMC Historical Office, APG, MD.

n.d.   Memorandum, folder "Tradition Committee 1949." *Memorialization and Tradition Committee Records*, Box 1, "1945–1949." Available via the U.S. Army CECOM LCMC Historical Office, APG, MD.

Ziobro, Melissa

2010   "Breslin Memorial Returns to Belmar." *Monmouth Message, The*. 19 February 2010. U.S. Army CECOM LCMC Historical Office, APG, MD.

15

Cannons by the Courthouse

War Memorials, Memory, and Commemoration in Modern Suburbia

Richard Veit, Mark Cianciosi, and Joshua Butchko

The Old Monument Speaks
Here I have stood for many years.
Placed here by patriots mid lusty cheers.

Millions of people have passed me by,
Millions of hearts have heaved a sigh.

I am a memory of living and dead,
who struggled for the Union as Lincoln said.

The struggle was bitter and the toll was great.
Brother killed brother, love turned to hate.

I must give way to the automobile.
That is the way I was made to feel.

Surely some spot can be found.
The ideals I stand for I still can propound.

But alas, here comes the junkman with stout rope.
He has pulled me to the concrete and my back is broke.

Where are the citizens of yesteryear,
who placed me here with lusty cheers?

I think the citizens of Hackettstown
could at least have gently taken me down.

I was a memorial to the
boys of Sixty-Five,
but few of them are now alive.

Who remembers the famous day and year
when the patriots of Hackettstown placed me here?

The boys it seems are not forgotten,
as I lie in the junk pile to rust and rotten.
    Charles Augustus Stewart Gulick, January 14, 1927

Etched on the reverse of the granite shaft that supports the Hackettstown Civil War memorial in Warren County, New Jersey, is a curious poem written by local resident Charles Augustus Stewart Gulick in 1927. Hackettstown's original Civil War memorial, affectionately known as "Billy Yank," was dedicated with great local fanfare on 30 May 1896 (Figure 15.1). Manufactured by the J.W. Fiske Iron Works of New York City, the monument stood 19 ft. tall and included a life-sized, bronze-colored statue of a Union soldier.[1] Nearly three decades later, "Billy Yank" was dismantled and sold for scrap when a court order mandated its removal as part of an effort to widen New Jersey State Highway 46 (Brock n.d.). Gulick's poem, penned in the immediate aftermath of Billy's demise, recounts the life history of a war memorial, from its initial erection by citizens, who placed it with "lusty cheers," to its somewhat callous removal spurred by roadwork expansion; "I must give way to the automobile." The poem ends on a mixed note, stating, "The boys it seems are not forgotten, as I lie in the junk pile to rust and rotten." It would take over 70 years for Billy to reemerge from that junk pile. Today, a new Civil War memorial stands in Hackettstown. The new "Billy Yank" was dedicated on 28 May 2001, almost exactly 105 years after the original. This memorial is well cared for and stands near the center of town. It celebrates both the area's Union heroes as well as the monument that came before it, illustrating the power of community spirit and the importance of local commemoration. Gulick's poem is a fitting reminder that monuments go through many phases; they are dreamed, planned, erected, celebrated, forgotten, removed, replaced and sometimes restored. Memorials and the spaces they occupy evolve corporeally and symbolically, often in tandem with the changing society around them.

This chapter examines the history of New Jersey's war memorials through an archaeological lens, with a focus on understanding how and why some conflicts are commemorated and others are seemingly overlooked. Memo-

---

1 While Fiske Iron Works memorials appeared to be bronze, they were in fact "white bronze" or cast zinc, painted to appear like bronze (Grissom n.d.).

Figure 15.1. "Billy Yank" Hackettstown's Civil War Memorial. It was erected in 1896, only to be scrapped during a road widening project in 1926. A replica monument commemorating the town's Civil War veterans was erected in 2001. Photograph by Craig Walenta, 2022.

rials commemorating the Revolutionary War through the current War on Terror are examined. A wide variety of memorials occupying a myriad of public spaces are discussed, among which are formally designed monuments contrived by gifted artists as well as local memorials inspired by community efforts, static displays of military ordnance, and even modest monuments created by erstwhile gravestone carvers. Particular attention is paid to two factors that drive commemoration: periodicity, for example, celebration of significant anniversaries, 50, 100, and 200 years after the conflict, and monument life course, for example, how monuments change, and memorialization evolves over time. We argue that periodicity and public memory are the major factors driving commemorations, that memorials are less permanent than they seem. Commemoration is selective and driven largely by sociopolitical circumstances of the moment. Indeed, how we interpret monuments depends very much on who we are and the times we live in. Working from that understanding, this article attempts to provide a baseline for better contextualizing the creation of military memorials in a representative northern state.

Monuments have featured in current events for some time now and have provided useful material for study by historians, political pundits, and to some degree, historical archaeologists (Shackel 2003; Venables 2012; Upton 2015; Allison 2018). Much of the discussion has focused on understanding the erection of Confederate memorials and now their removal (Levinson 2018; Domby 2020). This chapter is less about the sociopolitical ramifications of monument removal, even if well warranted, and more about the creation and subsequent evolution of monuments and what that reflects about society. It attempts to bring the archaeological lens to bear on the construction and life course of military memorials (Appadurai 1986). It builds from the material record, the monuments themselves, rather than documents. It also seriates the erection of monuments by conflict. While based on extensive research, it is not all-inclusive; rather, it is intended as a starting point for further study.

The Setting

New Jersey is a small state located in the northeastern United States. One of the original thirteen colonies, New Jersey first saw European settlement in the 1620s and, following the English conquest of 1664, experienced rapid colonization (Lurie 2012:33). Its history has been characterized as a microcosm of American history (Cunningham 1976; Lurie and Veit 2016) and given its location between New York and Philadelphia as well as Boston and Washington, it has played a central and strategic role in American history. Residents of the state have participated in nearly all the nation's major conflicts (Lender 1991; Bilby 2017). Although initially agrarian, widespread industrialization began transforming the landscape by the mid-nineteenth century (Israel 2012:177). Today, New Jersey is largely suburban or urban (Gillette 2012:264). At the same time, it is a small state divided. Due to a complicated political history, it has over 566 municipalities, some smaller than a square mile (Karcher 1988).

In this context, New Jersey provides an excellent test case for examining the material history of military memorials.

Memorials in the state are diverse and range from the very modest—small granite markers with bronze plaques or aluminum interpretive signs, to the gargantuan: monumental buildings—the Trenton War Memorial, and retired naval vessels—the battleship USS *New Jersey*. The primary focus of this study are the statues, obelisks, and static displays of military hardware found in many communities, the seemingly omnipresent cannons by the courthouse.

While some monuments are multifaceted installations purposefully erected following major fundraising campaigns and organized architectural competitions such as the New Jersey World War II Memorial in Trenton (DMAVA NDa), the Korean War Memorial in Atlantic City (DMAVA NDb), and the Vietnam War Memorial in Holmdel (New Jersey Vietnam Veterans Memorial [NJVVM] n.d.), others are simple roll-call monuments, erected by municipalities and veterans' organizations, most notably the American Legion and the Veterans of Foreign Wars. Often, these community memorials evolve in an accretional style as new conflicts arise and those who participated and were lost are remembered. Many of these monuments are the focus of community activities, such as parades and celebrations built around patriotic holidays.

The exact number of memorials in the state remains unknown, and a complete formal census of such monuments has not yet been performed. The project involved extensive fieldwork coupled with a review of online sources including the Historical Monument database (HMDB) (HMDB n.d.), and consultations with the New Jersey National Guard Armory Museum, New Jersey Historical Commission, and State Historic Preservation office. Through these channels, we identified 855 monuments which form the basis of this study. In our calculations, multicomponent memorials are accounted for both as the sum of their parts and the individual elements contained therein.

Research Methods

This case study is, in part, an above-ground archaeology project. Our procedures were straightforward; when possible, we visited, photographed, and examined the individual monuments. We also employed online databases to build out our catalog, and examined resources compiled by the New Jersey National Guard and Militia Museum. The Museum had extensive materials about Revolutionary War and Civil War memorials. Indeed, these two conflicts may be overrepresented because of the National Guard Museum staff's previous recording efforts. Data processing and analysis were organized using Excel spreadsheets in which basic information about the markers was compiled. Among the items noted were location, date, creator, form, distinctive styles or features, and who or what they commemorate.

As previously noted, all major conflicts involving the United States ranging from the American Revolution through the War on Terror are remembered in New Jersey's memorials. It is worth noting that New Jersey has been spared the local presence of most of our major national conflicts—the clear exception is the American Revolution.

That said, New Jerseyans have participated in robust numbers in all of the nation's conflicts (Figure 15.5). The Civil War, World War I, and World War II, saw extensive participation. Here the sampled monuments are discussed beginning with monuments that commemorate all conflicts, then proceeding chronologically from the American Revolution through to the War on Terror.

New Jersey War Memorials, a Chronological View

Out of the 855 monuments examined, 117 commemorate multiple conflicts, others honor "veterans of all wars." Most of these date from the mid-late twentieth century. Often, these began with memorials to World War I or World War II, and then had additional components added for the wars in Korea, Vietnam, and subsequent conflicts. These are generally community monuments situated on public land (for example, city hall, schools, parks, etc.). Many consist of plaques, generally bronze on granite bases, often augmented with flags, and static displays of military hardware, either captured or indigenous. They may list war dead, or individuals from the community who served. Many are visually democratic, in that, the lists of names are alphabetical, and they tend not to highlight individual actions. There are several notable examples of what we call accretional monuments, such as Paterson's Hill of Heroes or the All-Veterans Memorial of Mount Olive (Figure 15.2a and 15.2b).

Veterans Memorial Park at Hayden Heights in Paterson is a grand, albeit complex, example of a multicomponent commemorative site that celebrates the legacy of those who served. Also known as the "Hill of Heroes," this park literally holds its veteran memorials in high regard on a promontory overlooking the surrounding area. Dedicated by the City of Paterson's Park Commission in December 1969, the park centers on an obelisk originally commissioned by the Works Progress Administration (WPA) in 1930 as a memorial to the Great War. The granite obelisk, built by celebrated sculptor Gaetano Federici, also includes a bronze statue of two soldiers at its base. Additional features were added to the obelisk noting several additional conflicts when it was rededicated by the Paterson Veterans Council in 1993. Overall, the park

Figure 15.2. *A*, Hill of Heroes, Paterson, and, *B*, the All-Veterans Memorial, Mount Olive. These are two examples of accretional multi-component monuments. Photographs by Joshua Butchko, 2022.

features over 20 elements. The monuments at the Hill of Heroes celebrate veterans from all American-involved conflicts from World War I through the current War on Terror. Earlier conflicts, such as the Civil War, are commemorated in other spaces across the city.

Tonya Davidson, writing about Canada's National War Memorial, reminds us that monuments are "more than a creation of bronze and granite" (Davidson 2016:56). Conflict memorials provide a unique opportunity to not only learn about these objects and what they represent, but to also learn from them. Social variables in the present can often instigate contests between the already complex meanings of these memorial spaces. The Hill of Heroes exists as an exceptionally hallowed and consecrated gathering space, yet it is not without its share of complications. In addition to being a frequent victim of local vandals, this sacred space was also the subject of some criticism when disabled veterans raised concerns that they had limited access to the park. With the coordination of city officials, Veterans Council, and others, as well as funding from the Passaic County Board of Chosen Freeholders, a handicap-accessible driveway was added to the park in 2019. This situation reminds us that memorials, perhaps intended to be static pillars of solemnity, are inherently forced to adapt due to the evolving nature of the human connection to them. These connections, for good or bad, provide an opportunity that Davidson suggests "allows us to learn from indifference, outrage, love, and loyalty in significant ways" (Davidson 2016:53).

Next most common in our dataset are monuments commemorating the American Revolution. New Jersey's Revolutionary War history is the single best-represented conflict in the state, with 235 individual monuments (just over 1/4 of the state's total monuments). As previously noted, the state, then colony, saw extensive military activity during the Revolution so much so that parts of the state have been characterized by historian Michael Adelberg, as the "Theatre of Spoil and Destruction" (Adelberg 2010:1). Since it was the United States' first conflict, the Revolution has had longer to acquire monuments than other conflicts. Indeed, since the eighteenth century, the state's Revolutionary War sites have drawn many visitors from near and far (Rice 1963; Chambers 2012).

Even before the Revolution ended, grave markers and personal memorials were being erected for its veterans. Several formal memorials were constructed almost immediately after the war ended. The Halyburton Memorial on Sandy Hook may be the earliest example in New Jersey. Erected by Katherine Hamilton, Dowager Countess of Morton, this monument served as both a grave marker and monument to the memory of her son, Lieutenant Douglas-Halyburton, who succumbed to exposure with thirteen companions while attempting to recapture British deserters on Sandy Hook. The impressive marble monument was erected between 1785 and 1788 but was subsequently destroyed by gunfire from a French warship in 1808. In 1939, a new monument was erected at the site of the original by the WPA (Moss 1964:31–32).

Despite early examples like Halyburton, or the circa 1829 memorial at Red Bank Battlefield in National Park, Gloucester County, the number of Revolutionary War memorials remained fairly small until the late nineteenth century (Catts 2021). These numbers increased over several notable peaks particularly in the early twentieth century, 1930s, 1970s, and the 2000s (Figure 15.5). These peaks may correspond with the Centennial, 150th anniversary, and Bicentennial of the Revolution. The early peak conforms with the height of the colonial revival movement, but also might be seen as an effort to make visible aspects of American history at a time when large numbers of new immigrants were coming to America from eastern and southern Europe. The peak in the 1930s may reflect WPA and Civilian Conservation Corps (CCC) monument construction efforts. The peak in the 1970s corresponds well with the Bicentennial and a renewed interest in the American Revolution, and has continued since, perhaps in part due to the creation of the Crossroads of the American Revolution National Heritage Area in 2002 and their efforts since to celebrate the state's Revolutionary War heritage.

Monuments to the Revolution range from the very elaborate, such as Princeton's Battle Monument, sculpted by Frederick MacMonnies in 1922 to the modest, such as the aluminum sign in Piscataway noting a location where General Howe's troops stopped and turned. Static displays of Revolutionary War–era cannon are also found in several locations including Morristown, Elizabeth, and Scotch Plains. Such displays of cannon and other retired ordnance were important focal points for community activities and pride. Many cannons were named, such as "Old Nat," formerly displayed at Morristown National Historical Park and the "Jackson-Gildersleave Cannon" displayed in Bloomfield. One of the most curious is a well-traveled and much celebrated cannon named "Old One Horn" a Revolutionary War 12 pounder.

According to tradition, the cannon was left behind by British troops during a raid on the Pierson family homestead in Westfield in 1780 (Honeyman 1923:510). One of its pins was knocked off, rendering it unusable. Another story has the cannon left on the green near the Baptist church in Scotch Plains following a skirmish. After the war it became a coveted relic, claimed by local militia troops from Westfield, Scotch Plains, Plainfield, Springfield, Rahway, and New Market (Honeyman 1923:510). Employed at public celebrations, it was captured and recaptured in raids by local militia men and fire departments (Figure 15.3). In the late nineteenth century, it came into the posses-

Figure 15.3. Old One Horn, a Revolutionary War cannon that was the focus of commemorative activities throughout the nineteenth century. Much coveted by towns in central New Jersey, volunteer fire companies, such as the Plainfield firefighters seen here, went to great lengths to capture it from their neighbors. It is now in Westfield's Fairview Cemetery. Plainfield Fire Department, Hose Company #2, Corner of Front and Duer Streets, c. 1890s. Photograph by Guillermo Thorn, courtesy of Kean University.

sion of the Winfield Scott Post, Grand Army of the Republic, before finally coming to rest in Evergreen Cemetery in Westfield (Honeyman 1923:510).

The War of 1812 and Mexican War are not well represented in this study, but there are a few noteworthy static displays. Among them are a pair of well-traveled cannons on display in Salem County, one in Salem City named Il Sannito and one at Pole Tavern named Il Lugano. According to the marker with Il Lugano, the cannon was manufactured in Naples in 1763, used against the Austrians captured by Napoleon, given to Joseph Bonaparte, when he was King of Spain, captured by the Duke of Wellington, shipped to Canada, captured in 1814 by United States troops at the Battle of Plattsburg and sold to Salem County as surplus during the Civil War (Swing 1889:61; Martin 1979:32). Since 1913 it has been displayed in the Pole Tavern area. Both cannons have been meticulously restored. Here, what is celebrated and remembered is not so much the War of 1812, but a pair of antique artillery pieces that are focal points of local pride and reflect a long tradition of military service. There appears to be only one monument to the Mexican War in the state, a bronze plaque commemorating General Winfield Scott in Elizabeth, New Jersey. Scott, who served from the War of 1812 through the American Civil War, was a sometime resident of the city (Thayer 1964:254–255).

The Civil War, which saw intense participation by New Jerseyans, is the second most represented conflict among the state monuments. These include numerous statues, some mass-produced, others individualized, and a large number of displays of contemporary ordnance. A graph of Civil War monuments shows a steady drumbeat of commemoration, from the war's end through the 1930s, and then scattered pulses of commemoration in later decades (Figure 15.5). One of the most interesting Civil War monuments features a cannon, nicknamed the "Swamp Angel," a 16,500 lb. rifled Parrott cannon with an 8 in. bore that briefly shelled Charleston in August 1863 (Robertella 2017). After the war, the Swamp Angel was transported to the Phoenix Iron Works in Trenton, New Jersey, where it was to be scrapped. Recognized by veterans, it was saved, and moved to the heart of the Trenton. Later, it was relocated to Cadwalader Park, in north Trenton, where it stands today as part of a Civil War memorial.

The Spanish–American War was a brief imperialist foray, inspired by Yellow journalism and colonialist fervor. Many New Jersey cities erected Spanish–American War memorials, including Morristown and New Brunswick. The latter has a memorial to the USS *Maine* as well as a captured Spanish howitzer dating from the eighteenth century. This study identified 11 Spanish–American War memorials. Others may have been erased by First World War scrap drives. Following the Spanish–American War, the Veterans of Foreign Wars was founded. This patriotic fraternal organization became a major force in commemorative activities.

World War I saw an incredible variety of exceptionally well-designed monuments, representing the artistic canons of the time, including statues and other pieces that evoke mythological Greek and Roman imagery. The most elaborate is Atlantic City's World War I memorial, which comprises a classically styled rotunda graced by a stunning statue by Frederick MacMonnies, titled *Liberty in Distress*. Other noteworthy memorials, all classically inspired, stand in Westfield, Plainfield, and Montclair. There are also numerous *Spirit of the American Doughboy* statues by E. M. Viquesney (Kopel 2010).

In the aftermath of World War I, the American Legion, a new fraternal organization of veterans, also lent their support to the creation of military monuments. Their 1925 handbook notes:

> World War memorial projects are matters of direct interest to The American Legion and inasmuch as they are primarily educational along patriotic lines, the Americanism committee is intimately concerned. Posts have been identified with memorial projects ranging from costly buildings and monuments to the planting of memorial trees and the dedication of bronze tablets. The extent and cost of memorials must be determined by local circumstances; however, the post, and particularly

its Americanism committee, is responsible that example of patriotism and sacrifice shall be fittingly memorialized for the benefit of posterity. (American Legion 1925:22)

Indeed, the American Legion argued for the creation of memorials in all communities as a form of Americanism (American Legion 1934:34). By the 1960s, as part of their Americanism program, the American Legion was offering naval vessels, aircraft, ordnance, jeeps, tanks, and field artillery for donation to American Legion and VFW posts as well as museums for "monumental and decorative purposes" (American Legion 1969:176–177).

Even before these rules were promulgated, captured and decommissioned pieces of ordnance were being employed for monuments. Both homegrown American and captured German cannons were very popular for displays, with examples in Scotch Plains, Millburn, and Wayne. French 75 mm field pieces are especially common. However, both sites are represented. Captured German mountain howitzers are on display in the Laurel Grove Cemetery in Totowa. There is a captured German artillery piece in Red Bank, New Jersey, and the Wayne American Legion Post displays a Krupps 105 mm field gun, with a spectacularly exploded barrel (Figure 15.4a). Arguably, the state's most interesting World War I static display is a M17 light tank at Manville's American Legion (Figure 15.4b). Interestingly, World War II saw the scrapping of some WWI memorials. For instance, Dunellen had received a Krupp's cannon captured on the Western Front, which was displayed at the American Legion (Triolo and Marren-Licht 2012:59), only to be scrapped and replaced by a Stuart light tank after the war.

Memorials for World War II are generally more restrained than those that followed the Great War. Somber, gray plinths resembling gravestones, with bronze plaques, honor rolls of the war dead, are especially common. New Jersey did not erect its official state World War II Memorial until 2008. Situated prominently across the street from the State Capitol in Trenton, New Jersey, it is an elaborate, copper-capped classical temple, with striding liberty and colorized black granite wall plaques recounting major events in the history of the conflict.

The Korean War is less clearly represented by these displays. Many communities simply added a bronze plaque to their existing World War II memorials. However, Westfield has a unique memorial, where a granite tablet is pierced by a void shaped like a map of Korea. The official state Korean War Memorial is in Atlantic City. It features heroic statues, representing the service members who fought in Korea.

a

b

Figure 15.4. *A*, A captured German cannon with an exploded barrel in Wayne, New Jersey, and *B*, a restored M 17 Light Tank from WWI in Manville, New Jersey. Photographs by Richard Veit, 2022.

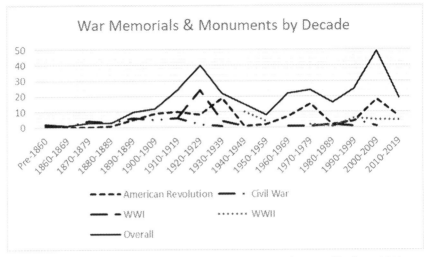

Figure 15.5. Graph showing the number of markers erected per conflict from 1860–2020. Note the cyclical peaks for the Civil War, and the exceptional peaks in memorialization in the early twentieth and early twenty-first centuries. Image by Richard Veit.

Artillery pieces displayed at the Clark and Readington American Legion Posts also appear to be Korean War vintage. More modern weaponry is somewhat challenging to date as some pieces of ordnance were used from WWII through the Vietnam era. Although an unpopular war, the Vietnam War is well represented in the state, especially in central New Jersey. Helicopter gunships, and tanks guard numerous American legions and memorial parks. While there are numerous community memorials to the Vietnam War, the most noteworthy is a pavilion with memorial panels and statuary at the state's Vietnam Era Education Center in Holmdel.

New Jersey has recently seen a remarkable increase in the number of memorials being installed across the state. Our data indicates that between 1990 and 2010, at least 94 war memorials have been erected or revitalized across the state. This striking increase could be explained in part by its correlation with what historian Erika Doss refers to as memorial mania (see Figure 15.5). Memorial mania is a national issue, comparable to a wave of statue mania that swept the country in the late nineteenth and early twentieth century. Doss argues this obsession with memorials "is grounded in a vastly expanded U.S. demographic" and "is contextualized by a highly successful public art industry, burgeoning interests in 'memory studies' and 'living' or experiencing history and shifting understanding of American national identity" (Doss, 2010). Many of New Jersey's most recent war memorials appear reflective of this trend, perhaps none more evocative than the All-Veterans Memorial in Mount Olive Township (AVM).

The AVM is a distinct memorial space featured prominently at Turkey Brook Park and nestled beside the historic Seward House, a state- and nationally registered historic site. This varied assembly of monuments, artwork, architecture, and vigil space was created by a diverse group of volunteers and funded by 100 percent private donors; the official AVM website touts it as "New Jersey's premiere veteran's memorial" (AVM n.d.). Visiting the AVM in person, it is easy to see that they are worthy of consideration for the title. The AVM consists of over a dozen unique and interconnected elements that celebrate veterans of all conflicts, big and small, from yesteryear to today, recognizing heroes from all walks of life, including those who were awarded high honors and even the four-legged friends who served beside them. The park is centered around the original Mount Olive War Memorial, which was dedicated in 1968 at nearby Budd Lake Beach. This monument was relocated and restored at its present location by the AVM team in 2007, and the surrounding scene has grown exponentially since then. Over the course of five significant installation phases between 2008 and 2018, a reverent and evocative ceremonial landscape was created. While the state by and large has reached a denouement in its memorial obsession of late, remarkable places like the AVM in Mount Olive suggest the mania will persist as long as the drive and desire to celebrate the past endures.

Interpretations and Conclusions

Military monuments are reminders of past wars, and serve as places of public commemoration, highlighting shared sacrifice and loss and emphasizing community values. They range from elaborate monuments, the work of sculptors and architects, to simple brass plaques. Others are multifaceted and accretional, while many include static displays of military hardware. Several are situated on the actual sites of former military engagements. Most importantly, they are products of a particular time and particular cultural contexts. As is true of other artifacts, memorials have their own material biographies. Witness, the complicated life histories of Old One Horn in Westfield, Il Lugano at Pole Tavern, and the Swamp Angel in Trenton. Organizations like the American Legion played a major role in shaping monuments through their donations of military hardware and captured ordnance or war trophies. This was purposefully done in order to build interest in and support of military service and veterans' groups.

Military monuments are a pervasive aspect of the American cultural landscape. Our study suggests that monuments to the the American Revolution, Civil War, World War I, World War II, and the Vietnam War dominate the landscape. Meanwhile, Korea and the Spanish–American War get short shrift. In New Jersey, a state that lost 674 citizens in the attack on the World Trade Center, there are numerous new memorials to 9/11 and the subsequent War on Terror, all deserving further study. Realistic portraits of women and African Americans are underrepresented in the state's historic memorials—though most late twentieth-century artistic memorials appear to make a concerted effort to represent diverse individuals.

A cursory evaluation of the dataset suggests intriguing patterns may exist when concentrating on the style of memorial. Allowing for the previously noted limitations of the data and overall variability of memorial type, the memorials (855 objects and groups of objects total) can be broadly sorted into four style categories: standard, sculpture, natural, and mixed media (Figure 15.5).

Standard form comprises common stone markers, plaques, signs, and the like (343 objects or 40% of the total). The sculpture form (175 or 21%) considers memorials embellished with elaborate figural, relief, scenic, or symbolic sculptural and architectural details (eagles, obelisks, soldiers, etc.). The natural form accounts for less embellished organic variants of standard markers, particularly unfinished boulders bearing plaques (70 or 8%). The remainder of the memorials identified as mixed media (267 or 31%) includes all other forms and combinations thereof (gardens, parks, retired ordinance, vehicles, vessels and other structures).

Style patterns emerge predictably from those conflicts that have a wider sample set from which to discern. For example, nearly two-thirds of American Revolution memorials are in the standard form (153 of 234 objects or 65.4% of the conflict total). In contrast, Civil War memorials are exhibited predominantly in the sculpture form (47 of 71 or 66%). Memorials to WWI, WWII, and Vietnam tend to be mostly distributed between standard and mixed media forms; WWI yielding a slight uptick in sculpture form compared to the other two.

Unsurprisingly, memorials dedicated to all wars and veterans, multiple conflicts, and the like (274 of 855 or 32%) present the most variable style forms and mostly consist of mixed media forms (127 or 46% of multiple memorials). These style choices, while no doubt linked to the conflict being remembered, are also likely a product of the time they were produced as well as the agenda and resources driving those who created them.

New Jersey's military monuments and conflict memorials shape and create community pride and memory. They help establish a sense of place and a particular version of history that draws on ancient traditions of military commemoration. They also serve a didactic function and keep memories of past conflicts alive. As part of an evolving cultural landscapes, monuments are erected, added to, removed, forgotten, and reinterpreted. While many monuments were erected shortly after conflicts ended, others reflect the celebration of major anniversaries and may be linked to the aging of veterans. Perhaps most surprisingly, monuments are often impermanent and mobile. In the nineteenth century cannons were maintained with pride by local militia groups and were sometimes stolen by one group from another, thereby moving from town to town. While most monuments are long-lasting, we found several examples of monuments that were removed and recycled, as well as cases of monuments being demolished and then replaced.

Through this preliminary study, we hope to illuminate some of the factors driving material commemoration and argue that the monuments in our midst are worthy of study and debate. It is, however, only a first step. A more comprehensive database and mapping project would allow the themes presented here to be explored in more detail. Moreover, additional study of the individual markers could provide considerable information about the motivations behind their construction and, in some cases erasure, and, in the words of Charles Gulick, "allow the monuments to speak."

Acknowledgments

We wish to thank a number of our colleagues and friends who shared useful information with us about New Jersey's war memorials and military monuments. This article is richer for their assistance. They include Joe Bilby, Melissa Ziobro, Mark Nonestied, Tom D'Amico, Nick Woods, Marvin DeRuyscher, Sadie Dasovich, Steven Santucci, Allison Butchko and Sgt. Andrew Walker. We also benefited from the assistance of the New Jersey National Guard Militia Museum, New Jersey State Historic Preservation Office, and the American Legion's archives.

References

Adelberg, Michael
    2010   *The American Revolution in Monmouth County: The Theatre of Spoil and Destruction.* Charleston, SC: The History Press.

All Veterans Memorial [AVM]
    n.d.   All Veterans Memorial. https://www.allveteransmemorial.org/avm-design.html, accessed 21 February 2021.

Allison, David B.
    2018   *Controversial Monuments and Memorials, A Guide for Community Leaders.* New York: Rowman and Littlefield.

American Legion
    1925   *Post Handbook of the American Legion.* 4th Edition. Indianapolis, IN.
    1934   *Post Handbook of the American Legion.* 9th Edition. Indianapolis, IN.
    1969   *Post Commander's Guide.* Indianapolis, IN.

Appadurai, Arjun
    1986   *The Social Life of Things: Commodities in Cultural Perspective.* Cambridge, UK: Cambridge University Press.

Bilby, Joe
    2017   *New Jersey: A Military History.* Chicago, IL: Westholme Press.

Brock, Donna
    n.d.   The Story of Billy Yank. *Historic Hackettstown* (hackettstownhistory.com), accessed 21 February 2021.

Catts, Wade
    2021   *Memorialization, Reconstruction, Erosion, and Sham Battles: Multiple Ways of Remembering the Battle of Fort Mercer, New Jersey.* Paper presented at the 2021 conference of the Society for Historical Archaeology.

Chambers, Thomas A.
    2012   *Memories of War: Visiting Battlegrounds and Bonefields in the Early American Republic.* Ithaca, NY: Cornell University Press.

Cunningham, John T.
    1976   *New Jersey, America's Main Road.* New York: Doubleday.

Davidson, Tonya
    2016   Mica, Pedagogy and Defacement. *The Public Historian: The Journal of the National Council of Public History* 38(2): Pp. 42-61.

Department of Military and Veterans Affairs [DMAVA]
    2020   World War II Memorial at Veterans Park. https://www.nj.gov/military/community/civic-engagement/war-memorials/wwii-memorial.shtml, accessed 21 February 2021.
    NDb   New Jersey Korean War Memorial. https://www.nj.gov/military/community/civic-engagement/war-memorials/korean-war-memorial.shtml, accessed 21 February 2021.

Domby, Adam H.
    2020   *The False Cause, Fraud, Fabrication, and White Supremacy in Civil War Memory.* Charlottesville, VA: University of Virginia Press.

Doss, Erika
    2010   *Memorial Mania: Public Feeling in America.* Chicago, IL: University of Chicago Press.

Gillette, Howard, Jr.
    2012   Suburbanization and the Decline of Cities, Towards an Uncertain Future. In *New Jersey: A History of the Garden State.* Maxine N. Lurie and Richard Veit, eds. Pp. 264–286. New Brunswick, NJ: Rutgers University Press.

Grissom, Carol
    n.d.   Cemetery Monuments Made of Zinc. https://www.si.edu/mci/english/research/conservation/zinc_cemetery_monuments.html, accessed 21 February 2021.

Historical Markers Database [HMDB]
    n.d.   Historical Markers Database https://www.hmdb.org/

Honeyman, A. Van Doren
    1923   *History of Union County New Jersey, 1664–1923.* New York, NY: Lewis Historical Publishing Company.

Israel, Paul
    2012   The Garden State Becomes an Industrial Power: New. In *New Jersey: A History of the Garden State.* Maxine N. Lurie and Richard Veit, eds. Pp. 175–201. New Brunswick, NJ: Rutgers University Press.

Karcher, Alan
    1988   *New Jersey's Multiple Municipal Madness.* New Brunswick, NJ: Rutgers University Press.

Kopel, Les
    2010   The E. M. Viquesney Doughboy Database. https://doughboysearcher.weebly.com/

Lender, Mark Edward
    1991   *One State in Arms: A Short Military History of New Jersey.* Trenton, NJ: New Jersey Historical Commission.

Levinson, Sanford
    2018   *Written in Stone: Public Monuments in Changing Societies.* Durham, NC: Duke University Press.

Lurie, Maxine N.
    2012   Colonial Period: The Complex and Contradictory Beginnings of a Mid-Atlantic Province. In *New Jersey: A History of the Garden State.* Maxine N. Lurie and Richard Veit, eds. Pp. 33–63. New Brunswick, NJ: Rutgers University Press.

Lurie, N. Maxine, and Richard F. Veit, eds.
    2016   *Envisioning New Jersey: An Illustrated History of the Garden State.* New Brunswick, NJ: Rutgers University Press.

Martin, Mary Coates
    1979   *The House of John Johnson (1731–1802) Salem County, New Jersey.* Baltimore, MD: Gateway Press.

Moss, George H., Jr.
    1964   *Nauvoo to the Hook: The Iconography of a Barrier Beach.* Locust, NJ: Jersey Close Press.

New Jersey Vietnam Veterans Memorial (NJVVM)
    n.d.   New Jersey Vietnam Veterans Memorial https://www.njvvmf.org/, accessed 21 February 2021.

Rice, Howard C., Jr.
    1963   *Travels in North America, in the Years 1780, 1781, and 1782.* Volume I. Chapel Hill, NC: University of North Carolina Press.

Robertella, Louis A.
   2017   *The "Swamp Angel": The Cannon that Fired on Charleston, South Carolina, 1863.* CreateSpace, Independent Publishing Platform.

Shackel, Paul A.
   2003   *Memory in Black and White: Race, Commemoration, and the Post-Bellum Landscape.* Walnut Creek, CA: AltaMira Press.

Swing, Gilbert
   1889   *Biographical Sketches of Eminent Men: Events in the Life and History of the Swing Family.* Camden, NJ: Graw, Garrigue, and Gaw Printers.

Thayer, Theodore
   1964   *As We Were: The Story of Old Elizabethtown.* Elizabeth, NJ: The Grassman Publishing Company.

Triolo, Joh, and Liz Marren-Licht
   2012   *Images of America, Dunellen.* Charleston, SC: Arcadia Publishing.

Upton, Dell
   2015   *What Can and Can't Be Said: Race, Uplift, and Monument Building in the Contemporary South.* New Haven, CT: Yale University Press.

Venables, Brant
   2012   A Battle of Remembrance: Memorialization and Heritage at the Newtown Battlefield, New York. *Northeast Historical Archaeology* 41:144–165.

16

Contested Monuments, Contested Spaces, and Contested Narratives

Lu Ann De Cunzo

Building this volume around, and then beyond, the memorial landscape of the American Civil War is timely in this historic moment of renewed iconoclasm during which we are witnessing the re-enactment of centuries-old divisions along similar geopolitical lines. "Monumental action" and "actions against monuments" have become a potent tool in the battle to intervene in public memory about histories and legacies of slavery and racism (Baugher et al., Introduction in this volume). The Black Lives Matter movement has produced powerful examples of how material culture, monuments, and memorials matter; consider the way that the almost two-century-long tale of the "slave auction block" in Fredericksburg, Virginia, concluded with its removal just weeks after George Floyd's murder (Barile Tambs, chapter 3 in this volume).

The power of objects, buildings, and landscapes and their challenge for those of us who study them lie in their ability to communicate, to evoke emotion, to "mean" in ways that inform our thinking and our action. Every object embodies the application of mind and body to material with purpose and imagination, within contexts of time, place, skill, and resource access that guide makers' choices. Every object relates to other things and to living beings, human, and other. Every object has a history and is a product of history. Every object is, by definition, cultural, social, political, and economic (and you can easily expand this list). Every object evokes and creates *memory*. But not every memory is commemorated in material form or performance. The implications of what is memorialized and how can be far-reaching, as this volume's authors attest.

In this chapter, I first review the questions that guided this volume's authors and others' explorations of material commemoration for the insight they offer into the scope of an archaeology of memorialization. Memory politics forms the critical thread connecting the contributions to the volume, and

I ponder the politicization of heritage next. Then, I turn to the distinctiveness of memorializing war, the materiality of war monuments and memorials, and the volume's lessons for archaeologists. To conclude, I reflect on the future of commemoration as a productive, even necessary, mode of cultural expression.

Monumental Questions, Arguments, and Concerns

> In this volume, we examine monuments, famous and forgotten, great and small, to understand the cultural and historical factors that shaped their creation, maintenance, and removal.
> Baugher, Veit, and Jameson, Introduction in this volume

The questions that guided the editors as they imagined this volume and invited authors to contribute warrant rehearsal as we conclude the volume. The first queries address why people commemorate some events and individuals and forget or erase others, and what factors drive the erection of monuments and other forms of commemoration. Other questions target what, how, when, where, and why of monuments representing historical stories and national myths and of people's interactions with them. And finally, the consequences of monument building raise questions about our long-term responsibilities to the individuals and events memorialized—their preservation, adaptive reuse, removal, replacement, and/ or destruction (Baugher et al., Introduction; Green, chapter 6; Litteral and Wallman, chapter 7; Ziobro, chapter 14).

Other memorials scholars have attended to the relationship between the objects' materiality and their changing meanings. In their introduction to *Philosophical Perspectives on Ruins, Monuments, and Memorials,* for example, editors Jeanette Bicknell, Jennifer Judkins, and Carolyn Korsmeyer (2019:2) query, "How, exactly, is the memorial task of objects accomplished, and how do such objects function to sustain memories, honor historical events, convey meanings, or bind communities together? How are their historical, ethical, and aesthetic values related, and how are they to be assessed over time?" Erika Doss (2010:15), in her influential work, *Memorial Mania,* much cited by this volume's authors, examines "how metaphors of agency, subjectivity, rights, and citizenship work in visual and material [memorial] cultures." Subtitled *Public Feeling in America,* Doss's work also highlights the inevitable emotional nature of people's relationship to memorial objects. "How," she asks, "are feelings of grief, fear, gratitude, shame, and anger mediated in America's memorial cultures?" How do memorials represent, and repress, our nationalist sentiments, and how do they help us negotiate "racism, violence, and terrorism?" Dell Upton (2015:1) steps back and poses a more fundamental query, and I conclude this cascade of questions with the interrogatory framing in his book on Southern civil rights memorials, *What Can and Can't Be Said*: "What is it possible to say using the medium of the monument?" And more fundamentally, what is it "possible to say in public discourse at any moment?" In other words, what can monuments and memorials do and what can they not do? And how does historical context inform the answers to these questions?

Responding to these queries often begins with trying to articulate what memorials and monuments *are* and what they *do*. In a brief act of bricolage, let me summarize our authors' thinking.

In this volume's Introduction, Sherene Baugher, Richard Veit, and John Jameson begin by explicating the "power of place" to which monuments contribute. Monuments often symbolize past conflicts. They archive public affect and comprise material and narrative repositories of feelings and emotions (Doss 2010:14). Because they are "acts of remembrance," S. Matthew Litteral and Diane Wallman (chapter 7) remind us that memorials are intrinsically "imbued with political and historical struggle" as they keep memories of past conflicts present and often unavoidable in the landscape. There, Baugher, Veit, and Jameson explain, they may symbolize reconciliation and be subject to reinterpretation (Veit et al., chapter 15). Monuments constitute "prisms through which we can understand the values and attitudes of the people and communities that erected, visited, and supported them" (Smith, chapter 4). They say less, Upton (2015:20) elaborates, "about the people, times, and places they honor." But they also do the cultural work of "corporally and symbolically" negotiating social change (Veit et al., chapter 15), a temporality that Walter Benjamin characterized as "the past and the present constructing one another in an ongoing dialectic" (Dawdy 2010:769).

For archaeologists, Baugher, Veit, and Jameson propose, the problem that memorials have created is one of inclusion and respect of diversity versus silence, polarization, and conflict. How, to introduce yet one more question, can archaeologists create dialogue and develop a narrative that represents diverse stakeholders? And how do archaeologists negotiate *our* political beliefs in the process? This volume emerged in response to the recent re-eruption of fundamental unresolved inequities at the core of American society. Our authors are committed to effecting change through and beyond our work surrounding memorials. I consider memory politics in greater depth in the next section.

Commemoration and Erasure: Memory Politics

> The issue of control over heritage is political because it is a struggle over power . . . heritage itself is a political resource.
> Smith 2006:281

In her book, *Uses of Heritage,* another inspiration for many of this volume's authors, Smith (2006:44) distinguished between monuments and heritage. "Monuments are not heritage; it's the acts at the monument," the experience that is heritage. Monuments are tools to facilitate remembering, commemorating, passing on knowledge, and expressing values and meanings (Smith 2006:83). Heritage is therefore, by definition, "dissonant and contested" (Smith 2006:3–4). It is what she has labeled the "Authorized Heritage Discourse" (AHD) that suppresses contest through passive instruction (Smith 2006:31; see also Baugher et al., Introduction; Venables, chapter 2). AHD is comparable to John Bodnar's (1992:13–15, 246) "public memory" that presents an idealized, simplified, timeless past of a society, naturalizing and reifying the existing structure of power. Monuments can make the intolerable seem appropriate and even commendable, as Hilary Green demonstrates so powerfully in her essay about the 2005 erection in Pennsylvania of a monument to Confederate Brigadier General Albert Gallatin Jenkins, enslaver of free African Americans—and about its removal 15 years later (chapter 6).

The problem, James Young expounded in *The Texture of Meaning,* is our tendency to "divest ourselves of the obligation to remember" the intolerable and deplorable once memory is manifested in monument (Young 1993:5, quoted by Bakshi 2017:210). As Jay Stottman astutely states in his chapter on the Louisville Confederate Monument, controlling the message of the landscape further empowers the creators of that landscape. The central and constant question and challenge for such public memorialization, Bodnar (1992:253) insists, is how effective the people will be in containing this cultural offensive of the powerful embodied in the landscape (see also Green, chapter 6, regarding the removal of Confederate monuments, and Spencer-Wood, chapter 10, regarding the struggle of women for representation in the memorial landscape).

"The politics of worthiness" (Ramos-Zayas 2007, quoted in Delerme 2011:7) that elevated some conflicts to materialized national narratives and silenced and erased others is especially insidious in the context of "postmemory." Marianne Hirsch (quoted in Bakshi 2017:49) explained that postmemory "is not the memory of direct experience, but of generational distance." It is the experience of people whose lives are dominated by a narrative which they inherited and can challenge only indirectly. But challenged it is, through debates and performances such as those surrounding the monuments narrated in this volume. Memory is persistent and resistant in its dissonance, erupting into action and even violence in times of anxiety and of enlightenment such as that which marks our present (Doss 2010:2; Moody 2020:258).

Memorializing War

> It is fundamentally human to remember and commemorate the fallen, not merely for the sake of our own peace of mind, but to instruct future generations that they might recognize the price of freedom.
> Khosronejad 2011:15

In the United States, at least since the Revolutionary War, we have lauded and commemorated military heroes, for the reasons Khosronejad states, and, as this volume demonstrates, to control the narrative about conflict, sacrifice, and "truth." (Venables, chapter 2; Veit et al., chapter 15). Christianity's veneration of martyrdom shaped the beliefs of many Americans that death on the battlefield was the ultimate sacrifice and the highest act of patriotism. Thus, monuments to the war hero and the war dead were regarded as historical and truthful, rather than interpretive and biased (Upton 2015).

In the decades after the Civil War, sacrifice to the cause of the South was elevated to cultic status (Bodnar 1992:28; see also Baugher et al., Introduction). This volume's authors chart the actions of Southern women to protect and heroize their men (Stottman, chapter 8), creating a mortuary landscape that became a stage on which Southern martyrdom was performed (Ylimaunu and Mullins, chapter 12). The memorializing of Confederate male bravery and sacrifice became an important element of reconciliation, spurred by a need for Southern soldiers to fight international battles (Baugher, chapter 5). But the real story here is how, having lost the war, the South won the battle over the narrative for at least one and a half centuries (Baugher et al., Introduction). The grand "Lost Cause"—a narrative of gallantry and patriotism, a conflict over states' rights and preservation of the Southern way of life—was born of the ideological crisis of abolition and the dramatic changes it wrought in people's lives (Stottman, chapter 8; Bodnar 1992:27). It was through monuments, Kirk Savage concluded in *Monument Wars* (2009), that the South resolved this "momentous struggle over the idea of race and the terms of citizenship in a nation supposedly dedicated to equality" (quoted in Greene 2013:201). By the turn of the twentieth century, anxiety about national unity spawned by modernization and mass immigration added fuel to the monument mania that marked the era (Doss 2010:27). Today, neo-Confederates propounding White Southern nationalism have re-appropriated Confederate monuments as sites to celebrate White privilege, racism, and hate (Ylimauna and Mullins, chapter 12). They challenge both the conception of "freedom"—from what, for whom—and its price (Khosronejad 2011:15).

Chapters about memorializing the Finnish Civil War, World War I, and the Korean War highlight the diversity of ways that people have deployed and politicized war losses in the service of their present. In the generations following their civil war, unlike in the United States, Finns created a memorial landscape that conveys the "inexpressible tragedy of death and a national grief that all Finns can claim as their national heritage" (Ylimauna and Mullins, chapter 12). The deaths of almost one million British soldiers and civilians, and the wounding of another 1.7 million British military personnel, in World War I (Mougel 2011) provoked a transformation of the martial memorial landscape of Great Britain from one of national victory to one honoring those lost. The U.S. experienced one-tenth the losses of Britain (Byerly 2014), and only in 2021 did a national memorial open in Washington, D.C., an initiative spurred by the World War I Centennial. In the years immediately following the war, traditional community monuments were erected, and ultimately dominated by "living memorials"—schools, parks, athletic stadiums—and at the University of Delaware, a library. These "memorials erased the boundary between commemorative space . . . and the ordinary spaces where Americans worked . . ." and met. "The idea was to make war remembrance a part of everyday life" (Trout 2017). Over time, however, function trumped memory and at memorials like the University of Delaware Memorial Hall (library), most students do not know what the building memorializes. The new national memorial, sited in a small park just east of the White House, commemorates those members of the U.S. Armed Forces who served in the conflict. It incorporates the traditional—an existing statue of General Pershing—with contemplative park spaces, and a yet-to-be installed bas-relief sculpture and wall of remembrance, *A Soldier's Journey,* which follows the journey of an Armed Forces member from reluctant soldier to homecoming hero (Gershon 2021).

The "Say Their Names" (2020) mantra of the Black Lives Movement embodies a particular democratizing paradigm for remembering victims of violence that the U.S. Vietnam Memorial (1982) deployed so powerfully. Transcending the controversy over the memorial form (nicknamed, among other labels, the "black gash") were the grief, loss, and guilt evoked by the names of individual dead soldiers inscribed on the wall. Even the national memorial for the Korean War (1995), the "Forgotten War," the war without end, the global war against communism (Fox, chapter 13), is a veterans' memorial. The larger-than-life steel statues of soldiers, sailors, and aviators walking ghost-like through the rice paddies is haunting, inducing in visitors a visceral connection with the warriors, almost a shadow memory of being there among them, that "Freedom Is Not Free." The wall of names encompassing the voids that were the World Trade Center towers in New York City also elide the national and the individual; we know by name those who died on 11 September 2001. They are us, and we are them.

We have long histories of raising monuments to, and of, those who led warriors into battle, for altruistic reasons and for horrifying ones. More recently, we have begun, beyond the cemetery, to publicly inscribe memories of individuals lost in war, and those whose violent deaths should provoke shame and change. Plenty of space remains on the global landscape to honor accomplishment as well as loss, the accomplishments of those who, in large ways and small, engendered peace, and otherwise aided, saved, and raised up their fellow human beings.

Archaeological Lessons

> In memory, time becomes "place."
> Alessandro Portelli 1997:32

Monuments and commemoration events comprise a public memory discourse about who matters, what happened, who served, and often who won, reifying power and privileged memories. Some reflect historical amnesia informed by historical shame, and others inspire change or depict a vision of a different future. As Portelli wrote, all create places that connect past, present, and future, thus emplacing time (1997:32). Together, the authors offered at least three recommendations to guide an archaeology of the monumental and the memorial.

First, understand the past choices and factors informing public memorialization to help us refine our questions and decide how to proceed in the future. This volume provides much of that background and context, especially regarding monuments and memorials of modern wars. Contributors have demonstrated the need to undertake detailed case studies, compare memorials and memorialized events, and attend to local knowledge and oral narratives (Green, chapter 6 and Casello, chapter 9, offer compelling examples of both the process and dissonance troubling the narratives of the African American experience). The "winners" and the "losers" perspectives matter;

the losers, especially, do not forget. The temporality of the event monumentalized also matters, whether it occurred within living memory, or has entered "postmemory," and the periodicity of memorial events.

Second, attend to the power of place and materiality. Place matters; place is authentic. Form, scale, material, and surfaces also matter. Architect Juhani Pallasmaa (2016:177–8) has described it thus: "materials and surfaces have languages of their own." Durable materials are intended to ensure the permanence of a monument, so it can inspire future generations (Loewen 1999/2018:43). Marble, granite, and bronze monuments, for example, were meant to perform specific didactic functions (Doss 2010:37). Stone has been the material of choice for monuments across the ages, and the subject of considerable exegesis. "Stone is a primordial thing" (Higgins 2019:10). Stone speaks of distant geological origins, of permanence, of immutability, of resistant power. It appears in everyone's environment and is a site of human technological, artistic, and documentary action, resulting in everything from small tokens to grand shelters and barriers (Higgins 2019:10–7; Pallasmaa 2016:177–8).

"Bronze evokes the extreme heat of its manufacture, the ancient processes of casting, and the passage of time as measured by its patina. Wood speaks of its two existences and time scales; its first life as a growing tree and the second as a human artifact made by the caring hand of the carpenter" (Pallasmaa 2016:177–8). Water, Levi Fox explains in his analysis of Korean War memorials (chapter 13), represents liminality, zones of transition for those who died far from home. Stone, bronze, wood, and water are materials and surfaces that speak of "layered time," unlike the flat, silent industrially made materials of today (Pallasmaa 2016:178). More ephemeral materials, such as the paint on plywood and projected light that formed the media for many recent memorials to slain African Americans, are no less meaningful, and warrant similar analysis and interpretation.

Memorial form and representation also matter. Although Dell Upton (2013:15) rightly reminds us of the "ambiguities of visual metaphor," the meaning of the numerous cannons and other ordnance comprising war memorials that Veit, Cianciosi, and Butchko (chapter 15) have documented in American communities, is clear. Baugher's exegesis of the obelisks marking Civil War POW (prisoner of war) dead illuminates the process of assigning and appropriating the meaning of dominant forms (chapter 5). Fox (chapter 13), in contrast, reminds us how formal details also communicate in subtle and abstract ways. Korean War Memorials, for example, often incorporate sharp angles, dividing lines, hollow forms, and empty spaces, reminders that the conflict remains unresolved.

Third, in advance of any memorial renewal or removal, create partnerships for cooperative decision-making, including all the stakeholders—agencies, property owners, interested community members, university faculty, and students. It is our responsibility to "pay it forward" in engaging students to value inclusive memory and help negotiate contested memory. Litteral and Wallman's intervention at the Judah P. Benjamin Confederate Memorial exemplifies the approach, which involves "critically explor[ing] power, politics and activism around public monuments and memorials . . . , unit[ing] artists, academics, activists, politicians, organizations, institutions, descendant and local communities to address public memory, heritage and memorialization and promote restorative justice, social equity and legislative action" (chapter 7). Alliances forged in and beyond Pennsylvania brought down the Confederate Brigadier General Jenkins Monument, demonstrating that "both-sideism, whitewashed myths, and top-down solutions no longer had a place in defining how the Civil War should be commemorated" (Green, chapter 6).

Future Remembering

> If every group heroifies its past leaders and actions, we still end up honoring boring, perfect heroes while ignoring and forgetting the common history that divides us.
> James Loewen 1999/2018:42

In *Lies Across America,* Loewen (1999/2018:7, 10) critiques this approach to future commemoration efforts, having declared that previous monumentalizing has crafted an American "landscape of denial." Now any "questioning [of] the myths told on the . . . landscape is inherently subversive." What kinds of paths forward might be blazed to acknowledge and act when the subversive is truth-telling? Let's consider some of the responses that memorial scholars have shared.

Paul Ricoeur has famously stated that the "work of remembering" in the "public space of discussion" can move people beyond the compulsion to repeat the past, and truly reconcile the present with the past (quoted in Bakshi 2017:162). Archaeologist Cristobal Gnecco (2022) describes monuments and memorials as "battlefields" on which different conceptions of the past, of time, and of life are deployed, and difficult struggles for meaning and identity play out. Struggle itself may be fruitful, inspiring public participation and community involvement. Controversies over public memorialization may encourage people to reflect on how and why to remember, as well as the stories themselves. Counter memories of the Confederate Civil War narrative were forged during the Gettysburg invasion in 1863 and the abduction of free Blacks. Sustenance of this counter-memory contributed to the Brigadier General Jenkins's monument falling 15 years after its erection during the national summer of 2020 reckoning (Green, chapter 6).

Other authors entreat us to encourage the material public discourse, rather than removing, silencing, or otherwise making the dispute invisible. Removal, creating absence, promotes forgetting, concealment, and remoteness (Bakshi 2017:66, 69). Rather, we must acknowledge and promote people's ability to confront the past. Digital media offer one platform for confrontation and conversation, for understanding if not acceptance. Commemoration may take digital form in innovative ways with wide-reaching implications. In one case, the prompt is the literal disruption of the seabed by mining and other actions. To date, there is no international recognition of those enslaved Africans who lost their lives at sea and were relegated to the seabed. A group of archaeologists have proposed "Memorializing the Middle Passage on the Atlantic Seabed," a series of virtual ribbons following slave traffic routes across the Atlantic that will appear on all International Seabed Authority maps of the seafloor (Turner et al. 2020). Besides memorialization, the ribbons will raise awareness, a first step in the dialogue to preserve shipwrecks bearing the remains of enslaved individuals that now rest on the international seabed and are threatened by human action.

Counter-monuments constitute another approach to dialogic material memorialization. Peace monuments and memorials are one example, related in intent but widely variant in execution. Edward Lollis (2010:416–421) has chronicled more than 2,000 peace monuments around the world. While some may question the inclusion of some memorials in this category, Lollis argues that all those he enumerated "reject war and violence and help promote a *culture of peace.*" They include the "permanent": the classical Peace Monument in Washington, D.C. (1877–1888), comprising a stone base on which stands a figural personification of peace; the disquieting Hiroshima Peace Memorial with its skeletal Genbaku Dome; Coventry Cathedral in England, with its High Altar Cross crafted from charred beams and nails recovered after bombing during World War II; the innovative Glass Wall for Peace that frames the Eiffel Tower in Paris, inscribed with "peace" in diverse languages and alphabets; and the "ephemeral": The Fallen, dedicated to all who died on D-Day, soldiers' silhouettes stenciled in the beach sand and washed away by the evening tide (*The Urbanist* 2008; *Guardian* 2015).

In Harrisburg, Pennsylvania, counter-monuments have replaced the Brigadier General Jenkins Monument. Inspired by the International Institute for Peace through Tourism (IIPT) Global Peace Park project, Harrisburg became one of the first U.S. state capitals to create a peace park. Forty civic organizations and hundreds of individuals collaborated to commission *A Gathering at the Crossroads* and River Front Park. Like other peace parks, these interventions strive "to nurture the growth of peace and understanding at home and throughout the world and create common ground for the community to come together in celebration of their nation's people, land, and heritage, and the common future of all humankind" (IIPT) (Green, chapter 6; Mealy 2021).

Despite their emotional power, these monuments to peace are not considered counter-monuments by all memorial scholars (Young 1993; Doss 2010). The latter are characterized by brazen and painful challenges to "the very premise of their being." They may involve defacement and assault, but most importantly, their transformative potential lies in their positing of new understandings of commemoration and discourses of representation (Doss 2010:356, 361, 363). They often employ collage, bricolage, and assemblage to unite materiality and non-linear narrative time. Like the projection of George Floyd's face on the base of the Confederate General Robert E. Lee statue in Richmond, counter-monuments work "through the juxtaposition of fragmented images deriving from irreconcilable origins" (Pallasmaa 2016:179; Margry and Frink 2011:8). The *New York Times Style Magazine*'s naming the graffiti-laden statue the most influential work of protest art since World War II recognizes the power of such juxtaposition (La Force et al. 2020).

Not even counter-monuments accomplish the goals of what Loewen (1999/2018:44) calls "authentic history," however. It is about truth-telling on the landscape as a tool to "bring forth justice in the future" (Moody 2020:268). It is about monuments that explain why African Americans have such a long history as victims of violent, state-sanctioned death, rather than just memorializing those who died. Yoon and Alderman (2019:121) propose that memorials should enact a "place-based ethics of care for victimized groups" and a reckoning by states that perpetuated that violence.

For those waiting for models of memory work achieving this state of truthful reckoning and reconciliation, I must disappoint you. Rather, I invite you to ponder a complicated monumental discourse that has evolved over two international wars and recently threatened to prompt another, or rather the re-eruption of one which remains unresolved. War and women stand at the heart of the discourse. Spencer-Wood (chapter 10) critiques the memorial landscape of the U.S. for its glorification of the cultural dominance and ideals of militaristic masculinity. This case reinforces her argument in a global context, engendered in a monument depicting a teenage girl. In January 2022, the *International Policy Digest* reported on another North Korean missile test aimed at provoking renewed aggression against South Korea (Flanakin 2022).

During the year, the number of missile tests aimed toward South Korea and Japan escalated. Any dialogue leading to containment was compromised by South Korea's significantly worsening relationship with Japan over an "intractable grievance." The grievance: Japan has not adequately addressed the exploitation and effective enslavement of Korean "comfort women" to serve the sexual desires of the Japanese Imperial Army during World War II.

Over the past decade, comfort women have become the subject of a global campaign for awareness, truth-telling, apology, and reconciliation for hundreds of thousands of women. The women and their descendants, academics, government officials, activists, news reporters, and artists have employed testimony, protests and rallies, arts and performances, films, videos, documentaries, and books. And memorials (Yoon and Alderman 2019:119–120; Olivo 2014; Constante 2019; Ward and Lay 2018). The first, the *Statue of Peace*, was erected in 2011 in front of the Japanese Embassy in Seoul. The *Statue of Peace* has come to represent the global movement to stop sexual violence against women and has become ensconced in global memory space (Shim 2021).

The memorial consists of a bronze, life-sized, unsmiling teenage girl with a bird on her shoulder seated on a simple chair with an empty chair beside her. The girl's shadow depicts an old woman. The bird symbolizes liberation and links the victims who passed away and those (now few) still alive. The shadow symbolizes the women's enduring hardship, and the empty chair represents the "interplay between presence and absence" (Shim 2021; see also Woo-young 2016; Han and Griffith, 2017; Mackie, 2017).

Japan has formally apologized several times following a government study that demonstrated the validity of the enslavement narrative. In 2015, during the 70th anniversary of World War II, Japan again acknowledged responsibility and agreed to an $8.3 million payout to survivors. By then, comfort women had become *the* main geopolitical dispute disrupting relations between Japan, South Korea, and China (Gluck 2019; Shim 2021). Activist groups subsequently erected replicas and similar statues in Australia, Canada, China, Germany, and the U.S., and this "restive memory" reverberated globally (Shim 2021; Gluck 2019). David Shim has analyzed what the *Statue of Peace* does and what consequences it has for those who engage with it, what he refers to as its "material rhetoric." The empty chair, he argues, is the crucial element. It makes the absent present and invites the viewer to take a seat and remember, mourn, reflect, console, or even protest. The statues have been stroked, hugged, clothed for winter, and brought food and flowers. They have also been slapped, and had money thrown at them, invoking the initial dispute over whether the comfort women were forced or willingly engaged in prostitution (Shim 2021).

The statues have become a contested presence in the global discourse over human rights because the truth-telling is unfinished. Japan has acknowledged and apologized for its exploitation of Korean women. But the Japanese comfort women remain excluded from the South Korean–centric global narrative. Moreover, South Korea's human rights violations during the Vietnam conflict, including torture and mass rape, remain unacknowledged and silenced. So too does the history of South Korean complicity in providing prostitutes to service the U.S. military camps following the Vietnam War. Suppression of these truths stymied U.S. efforts to intervene with both Japan and North Korea in the recent controversy (Flanakin 2022). The U.S. must reconcile its own military's history of violence against women and accept the obligations of that truth. We must embrace the comfort women statues with our own "place-based ethics of care," before we can honor a "universal right" to memory and fulfill our obligation to secure that right (Chow 2015:198; Yoshida 2022a, 2022b). Only the strength of truth-telling can empower the U.S. to speak with an honorable voice of unity that may prevent the brothers and sisters, sons and daughters of George Floyd and Breonna Taylor, Latoya James and Robert Howard from dying on another battlefield.

Concluding Thoughts

> I ♥ Archaeology . . . because we can "enlist and serve diverse allies . . . with interests in justice, intercultural reconciliation, and the mitigation of pernicious effects of late modernity."
> John Welch 2020:29–30

Even the unsmiling bronze teenager seated in a simple chair, who came to represent global acknowledgment and eradication of violence against women, has become weaponized. Women's suffering has been exploited and served up as a distraction for complicit nations. Hate and violence permeate this volume, and this essay, but so do honor and sacrifice. And care. And that is where archaeologists come in. In *Archaeologies of the Heart,* John Welch (2020:23) enumerates all the reasons why *he* loves archaeology, and advocates for an archaeology that guides and helps people to take care of the world and of each another. Heart-centered archaeology promotes an ethical space for thinking through a rigorous, relational archaeology grounded in care for the living and the dead (Lyons and Supernant 2020:5). In their own words and in their own ways, that is the message of this volume's authors.

References

Bakshi, Anita
    2017   *Topographies of Memories. A New Poetics of Commemoration.* New York, NY: Palgrave McMillan.

Bicknell, Jeanette, Jennifer Judkins, and Carolyn Korsmeyer
    2019   Introduction. In *Philosophical Perspectives on Ruins, Monuments, and Memorials.* J. Bicknell, J. Judkins, and C. Korsmeyer, eds. Pp. 1–6. New York, NY: Routledge.

Bodnar, John
    1992   *Remaking America: Public Memory, Commemoration, and Patriotism in the Twentieth Century.* Trenton, NJ: Princeton University Press.

Byerly, Carol R.
    2014   War Losses (USA). *International Encyclopedia of the First World War: 1914–1918 Online.* Updated 8 October. https://encyclopedia.1914-1918-online.net/article/war_losses_usa, accessed 17 January 2022.

Chow, Pok Yin S.
    2015   Memory Denied: A Commentary on the Reports of the UN Special Rapporteur in the Field of Cultural Rights on Historical and Memorial Narratives in Divided Societies. *The International Lawyer* 48(3):191–213.

Constante, Agnes
    2019   Who are the 'Comfort Women,' and Why are U.S.-based Memorials to them Controversial? *NBC News Online,* 7 May. https://www.nbcnews.com/news/asian-america/who-are-comfort-women-why-are-u-s-based-memorials-n997656, accessed 20 January 2022.

Dawdy, Shannon Lee
    2010   Clockpunk Anthropology and the Ruins of Modernity. *Current Anthropology* 51(6):761–93.

Delerme, Simone
    2011   Latinization of Space and the Memorialization of the Borinqueneers. *Anthropology News,* In Focus on Memorials and Memorialization 52(6): 7 September.

Doss, Erika
    2010   *Memorial Mania: Public Feeling in America.* Chicago: University of Chicago Press.

Flanakin, Duggan
    2022   Comfort Women' Issue Continues to Sour Japan-Korea Relations. *International Policy Digest,* 20 January. https://intpolicydigest.org/comfort-women-issue-continues-to-sour-japan-korea-relations/, accessed 24 January 2022.

Gershon, Livia
    2021   How D.C.'s Newly Unveiled WWI Memorial Commemorates the Global Conflict. *Smithsonian Magazine,* 20 April. https://www.smithsonianmag.com/smart-news/world-war-i-memorial-unveiled-180977551/, accessed 17 January 2022.

Gluck, Carol
    2019   Memory in Hypernationalist Times: The Comfort Women as Traveling Trope.

Mnemonic Solidarity. Global-e archive 12(7): May. https://globaljournal.org/global-e/may-2019/memory-hypernationalist-times-comfort-women-traveling-trope, accessed 20 January 2022.

Gnecco, Cristobal
    2022   Engagement and the Politics of Authority. In *Cambridge Handbook of Material Culture Studies*. L. A. De Cunzo and C. D. Roeber, eds. Pp. 128–45. Cambridge, UK: Cambridge University Press.

Greene, Sally
    2013   Judge Thomas Ruffin and the Shadows of Southern History. In *Commemoration in America: Essays on Monuments, Memorialization, and Memory*. D. Gobel and D. Rossell, eds. Pp. 202–22. Charlottesville, VA: University of Virginia Press.

Han, Sol, and James Griffith
    2017   Why This Statue of a Young Girl Caused a Diplomatic Incident. *CNN*, 10 February. https://www.cnn.com/2017/02/05/asia/south-korea-comfort-women-statue/index.html. Accessed 6 June 2024.

Higgins, Kathleen
    2019   Life and Death in Rock: A Meditation on Stone Memorials. In *Philosophical Perspectives on Ruins, Monuments, and Memorials*. J. Bicknell, J. Judkins, and C. Korsmeyer, eds. Pp. 9–20. New York, NY: Routledge.

Khosronejad, Pedram
    2011   Remembering the Sacred Defense: Iran-Iraq War Memorials. *Anthropology News,* In Focus on Memorials and Memorialization. 52(6): 15 September.

La Force, Thessaly, Zoë Lescaze, Nancy Hass, and M. H. Miller
    2020   The 25 Most Influential Works of American Protest Art Since World War II. *New York Times Style Magazine,* https://www.nytimes.com/2020/10/15/t-magazine/most-influential-protest-art.html, accessed on 18 April 2021.

Loewen, James W.
    1999   *Lies Across America: What Our Historic Sites Get Wrong.* 2018 edition. New York, NY: The New Press.

Lollis, Edward W.
    2010   Peace Monuments. In *International Encyclopedia of Peace*, Vol. 3. N. Young, ed. Pp. 416–21. Oxford, UK: Oxford University Press.

Lyons, Natasha, and Kisha Supernant
    2020   Introduction to an Archaeology of the Heart. In *Archaeologies of the Heart*. K. Supernant, J. E. Baxter, N. Lyons, and S. Atalay, eds. Pp. 1–19. New York, NY: Springer.

Margry, Peter Jan, and Liam Frink
    2011   Thou Shalt Memorialize: Memory and Amnesia in the Post-secular. *Anthropology News,* In Focus on Memorials and Memorialization 52(6): 8 September.

Mackie, Vera
    2017   One Thousand Wednesdays: Transnational Activism from Seoul to Glendale. In *Women's Activism and "Second Wave" Feminism: Transnational Histories*. B. Molony, J. Nelson, eds. Pp 249–271. London: Bloomsbury.

Mealy, Todd
    2021   A Gathering at the Crossroads: Memorializing African American Trailblazers and a Lost Neighborhood in Harrisburg. *Pennsylvania Heritage.* Spring. http://paheritage.wpengine.com/article/a-gathering-at-the-crossroads-memorializing-african-american-trailblazers-and-a-lost-neighborhood-in-harrisburg/, accessed 20 January 2022

Moody, Jessica
    2020   *The Persistence of Memory: Remembering Slavery in Liverpool.* Cambridge, UK: Cambridge University Press.

Mougel, Nadège
    2011   World War Casualties. *Reperes.* Julie Gratz, translator. Centre européen Robert Schuman. http://www.centre-robert-schuman.org/userfiles/files/REPERES%20%E2%80%93%20module%201-1-1%20-%20explanatory%20notes%20%E2%80%93%20World%20War%20I%20casualties%20%E2%80%93%20EN.pdf, accessed 17 January 2022.

Olivo, Antonia
    2014   Memorial to WWII Comfort Women dedicated in Fairfax County amid protests. *Washington Post,* 30 May. https://www.washingtonpost.com/local/memorial-to-wwii-comfort-women-dedicated-in-fairfax-county/2014/05/30/730a1248-e684-11e3-a86b-362fd5443d19_story.html, accessed 20 January 2022.

Pallasmaa, Juhani
    2016   Matter, Hapticity, and Time: Material Imagination and the Voice of Matter. *Building Material* 20:171–89.

Portelli, Alessandro
    1997   *The Battle of Valle Giulia: Oral History and the Art of Dialogue.* Madison, WI: University of Wisconsin Press.

Ramos-Zayas, Ana Y.
    2007   Becoming American, Becoming Black? Urban Competency, Racialized Spaces, and the Politics of Citizenship among Brazilian and Puerto Rican Youth in Newark. *Identities* 14(1–2):85–109.

Say Their Names
    n.d.   https://sayevery.name/, accessed 24 January 2022.

The Urbanist
    2008   12 Compelling Monuments Dedicated to Peace Instead of War. *The Urbanist.* 16 May. https://weburbanist.com/2008/05/16/12-compelling-monuments-dedicated-to-peace-reversing-the-typology-of-the-war-memorial/, accessed 19 January 2022.

The Guardian
    2015   The 10 Best Monuments to Peace. *The Guardian.* 30 October 30. https://www.theguardian.com/culture/2015/oct/30/ten-best-peace-monuments/, accessed 19 January 2022.

Peace Tourism
    2018   Harrisburg Peace Promenade a Model for IIPT Global Peace Parks Project.

International Institute for Peace Through Tourism. https://peacetourism.org/harrisburg-pennsylvania-peace-promenade, accessed 20 January 2022.

Savage, Kirk
 2009 *Monument Wars: Washington, D.C., the National Mall, and the Transformation of the Memorial Landscape.* Berkeley, CA: University of California Press.

Shim, David
 2021 Memorials' politics: Exploring the material rhetoric of the *Statue of Peace. Memory Studies.* 22 June. https://doi.org/10.1177%2F17506980211024328, accessed 20 January 2022

Smith, Laurajane
 2006 *Uses of Heritage.* New York: Routledge.

Trout, Steven
 2017 Commemoration and Remembrance (USA). Updated 26 June. *International Encyclopedia of the First World War: 1914–1918 Online.* https://encyclopedia.1914-1918-online.net/article/commemoration_and_remembrance_usa, accessed 17 January 2022.

Turner, Phillip J., Sophie Cannon, Sylvia DeLand, James P. Delgado, David Eltis, Patrick Halpin, Michael I. Kanu, Charlotte S. Susman, Ole Varmer, and Cindy L. Van Dover
 2020 Memorializing the Middle Passage on the Atlantic seabed in Areas Beyond National Jurisdiction. *Marine Policy* 122:104254. https://www.sciencedirect.com/science/article/pii/S0308597x20309003, accessed 20 January 2022.

Upton, Dell
 2015 Introduction. *What Can and Can't Be Said: Race, Uplift, and Monument Building in the Contemporary South.* Pp. 1–24. New Haven, CT: Yale University Press.
 2013 Why Do Contemporary Monuments Talk So Much? In *Commemoration in America: Essays on Monuments, Memorialization, and Memory.* D. Gobel and D. Rossell, eds. Pp. 11–35. Charlottesville, VA: University of Virginia Press.

WebUrbanist
 2008 12 Compelling Monuments Dedicated to Peace Instead of War. *WebUrbanist.* 16 May. https://weburbanist.com/2008/05/16/12-compelling-monuments-dedicated-to-peace-reversing-the-typology-of-the-war-memorial/, accessed on 19 January 2022.

Welch, John R.
 2020 Archaeology: An Experiment in Appreciative Inquiry. In *Archaeologies of the Heart.* K. Supernant, J. E. Baxter, N. Lyons, and S. Atalay, eds. Pp. 23–37. New York, NY: Springer.

Woo-young, Lee
 2016 'Comfort Women' Statues Resonate with Koreans. *Korea Herald,* 3 March. https://www.koreaherald.com/view.php?ud=20160303000844. Accessed 6 June 2024.

Yoon, Jihwan, and Derek H. Alderman
 2019 When Memoryscapes Move: 'Comfort Women' Monuments as Transnational. In *The Routledge Handbook of Memory and Place.* S. De Nardi, H. Orange, S.

High, and E. Koskinen-Koivisto, eds. Pp. 119–28. London, UK: Taylor & Francis Group.

Yoshida, Kenji

 2022a Philadelphia Art Commission Votes to Go Ahead with New Divisive 'Comfort Women' Park. *Japan Forward*, 13 October. https://japan-forward.com/philadelphia-art-commission-votes-to-go-ahead-with-new-divisive-comfort-women-park/, accessed 2 December 2022.

 2022b Statues of Division: Korean Intellectuals Contest 'Comfort Women' Monuments. *Japan Forward*, 22 July. https://japan-forward.com/statues-of-division-korean-intellectuals-contest-comfort-women-monuments/, accessed 2 December 2022.

Young, James E.

 1993 *The Texture of Memory: Holocaust Memorials and Meaning.* New Haven, CT: Yale University Press.

CONTRIBUTORS

Sherene Baugher, Ph.D., is professor emeritus of anthropology and landscape architecture at Cornell University, focusing on the historical archaeology of the Northeastern U.S. From 1980 to 1990, she was the first official archaeologist for New York City. She is the author and editor of five books and numerous articles.

Joshua Butchko is an archaeologist with a BA in anthropology and classics from Drew University and an MA in public history from Rutgers University—Camden. Over a twenty-year career, he has worked on hundreds of culture resource projects in the Mid-Atlantic region, primarily with Hunter Research, Inc.

Mark Cassello is chair of the Department of Humanities at Calumet College of St. Joseph in Whiting, Indiana. His interests include the practices of public memory and American literature (1880–1945). He is founder and president of the Pullman National Monument Preservation Society.

Mark Cianciosi completed his graduate studies in anthropology at Monmouth University in 2021. He is historic preservation specialist with Pinellas County, Florida, as well as an engineer officer in US Army Reserves. In his free time, Mark is an active member of the Great War Association in Newville, Pennsylvania.

Lu Ann De Cunzo is professor of anthropology at the University of Delaware specializing in the Middle Atlantic region of the U.S. Research interests include comparative colonialism, borderlands, decolonizing archaeology, and post-disciplinary material culture.

Levi Fox studied Korean War public memory while obtaining his Ph.D. in history from Temple University. Fox now advises social studies education majors as assistant professor of history in the Civic Engagement Department at Immaculata University and operates a walking tour company called Jersey Shore Tours.

Hilary Green is the James B. Duke Professor of Africana Studies at Davidson College. She is the author of *Educational Reconstruction: African American Schools in the Urban South*, 1865–1890 (Fordham University Press, 2016).

John H. Jameson is retired from the U.S. National Park Service, where he was a leader in the public interpretation of archaeological and cultural heritage sites. He was a founding member of the ICOMOS cultural heritage interpretation Scientific Committee. The author/editor of numerous articles and books, he serves on a UNESCO working group and several editorial boards including the *European Journal of Archaeology.*

S. Matthew Litteral, MA RPA, is archaeologist consultant with Atkins Global. He specializes in historical archaeology and has worked on projects nationally (New England, Kentucky, and Florida) as well as internationally (United Kingdom, Mexico, and the Caribbean). He has presented at conferences and written publications regarding the standardization of field worker wages and archaeology as activism.

Paul R. Mullins was professor of anthropology at Indiana University-Purdue University Indianapolis, Indiana. His studies focused on racism, consumption, and difficult heritage. He was a docent in the University of Oulu, Finland. He passed away in spring 2023.

Harold Mytum is professor of archaeology at the University of Liverpool, UK. He has been recording and researching historic mortuary monuments for many years and has published many articles and books on the subject.

Jeffrey Smith is professor emeritus of history living in St. Louis. He is author of *The Rural Cemetery Movement: Places of Paradox in Nineteenth Century America* and has written related chapters in *Till Death Do Us Part: Ethnic Cemeteries as Borders Uncrossed.* He has written for Ohio Valley History, Markers, and the Washington Post.

Suzanne Spencer-Wood, professor, Oakland University (2001–present) and associate, Peabody Museum, Harvard University (1992–2019) pioneered feminist historical archaeology by organizing the first two conference symposia on gender research (1989); most recently, guest co-edited a 2022 special issue of *Archaeologies* on intersectionality theory and research; and co-edited a book on the archaeology of childhood and parenting.

M. Jay Stottman is assistant director of the Kentucky Archaeological Survey at Western Kentucky University. His research focuses on public and activist archaeology, heritage landscapes, and urban environments. He is the editor of the book *Archaeologists as Activists: Can Archaeology Change the World?* (2010).

Kerri Barile Tambs is president of Dovetail Cultural Resource Group in Fredericksburg, Virginia. Dually trained as an archaeologist and architectural historian, her research interests include urban archaeology, architectural construction methods, and giving voice to the historically marginalized.

Richard Veit is professor of anthropology and provost of Monmouth University. His research focuses on the archaeology of the colonial Middle Atlantic region. He is the author of eight books and has been the recipient of Monmouth University's distinguished teacher award.

Brant Venables is a principal investigator at ASC Group, Inc., in Columbus, Ohio. His dissertation analyzed the heritage narratives of several Revolutionary War sites and Loyalist monuments. His community outreach work has involved designing museum exhibits and brochures on local archaeology for the Friends of Robert H. Treman State Park.

Diane Wallman is associate professor of anthropology at the University of South Florida. She is a Fulbright Scholar, as well as a National Geographic Explorer and National Science Foundation grant recipient for her current work on the Caribbean island of Dominica. Dr. Wallman has diverse publications and awards for her archaeology and community-based research.

Timo Ylimaunu works as a university lecturer and he is a post-medieval archaeology docent in the University of Oulu, Finland. His studies are focused on historical archaeology in general, difficult heritage, and memory studies.

Melissa Ziobro served as a command historian for the U.S. Army Communications-Electronics Command at Fort Monmouth, NJ, from 2004 to 2011. She is currently the specialist professor of public history at Monmouth University in West Long Branch, NJ.

INDEX

Page numbers in *italics* refer to illustrations.

Aberdeen Proving Ground (APG), 246, 247
Abolitionists, 5, 11–12, 83, 173, 176
"About Ten Days After the Battle of Gettysburg" (Winters), 96
Absolution, 35
Activism, 8
Adelman, William, 151
African American: history and culture, 154, 284, 285; monuments, 5–6, *7,* 16, 87–88, *87,* 98, 100–103, *100,* 166, 172–73, *174,* 175–76; resistance, 83, 94; soldiers, 92, 97–98, 100–101; women, 5, 163, 176, 178, *179. See also* Slave auction; Slavery, African American
A Gathering at the Crossroads (Ault), 100–103, *101,* 176, 285
Ahauton, Sarah, 177–78
Alabama, 233
All-Veterans Memorial (AVM), 269
American Civil War, 6, 16, 63; causes of, 4–5, 77–78, 87, 89, 212; dead, 12–13, 56, 59–60, 63–64, 66, 74, 75–76, 80–81, 204; immigrants in the, 32, 35; narrative alterations of the, 74, 79, 82. *See also* Lost Cause of the Confederacy
American Legion, 265–66, 269
American playground movement, 178, 180
American Railway Union (ARU), 146
American Revolution, 8–10, 21, 23–24, 32, 34, 238
American South: identity, 56, 58–59, 122, 131, 137, 138–39; school history textbooks of the, 5, 63, 77; way of life, 4–5, 63, 71, 76, 108, 279–80. *See also* Lost Cause of the Confederacy
Ancient Order of Hibernians, 34
Andersonville POW Camp, 71, 75, 82
Antiquities Act of 1906, 155
Archaeology, 1; archival research in, 47–49, 259–60; conflict, 1, 12; excavation projects, 46–48, *47,* 113–14, 122, *123;* public, 42–43, 49, 113, 114–15, 283; study of monuments in, 6, 133, 140, 281–82; and the study of subjugated groups, 42, 109, 118, 122, 284, 287
Arlington National Cemetery, 79
Armed Occupation Act, 110
Arthur, Clara, 178, 180
Artifacts: contested, 40, 45–46, 50–51; definition of, 1; monumental, 7, 21, 269
Association of Critical Heritage Studies (ACHS), 6
Ault, Becky, *A Gathering at the Crossroads,* 100–103, *101,* 176, 285
Authorized Heritage Discourse (AHD), 6, 23, 28, 34, 278

Barnes, Amos, 97
Battlefields, 2, 5, 23, 32
Battle of Bennington, 24
Battle of Saratoga, 25, 33
Benjamin, Judah P., 107, 111, 112
"Billy Yank," 256, 256n1, *257*
Black Lives Matter, 11–12, 15, 164, 168–69, 173, 275, 280
Boston marriage, 175

Brady, T. M., "Lion of the Confederacy," 69–71
Brantford, Ontario, 21, *28*
Brant, Joseph, 21, 26–27, *28*, 28–30, 36
British Army, 23–27
Brotherhood of Sleeping Car Porters, 153–54
Burgoyne, John, 23–26
Butler, John, 26–27

Cabrini, Mother, 173
Camp Alfred Vail, 237–38
Camp Little Silver, 237
Cannon, Martha Hughes, 172
Cannons, 29, 68, 263–64, *264*, 265, 266, *267*, 271, 282
Carriage step, 40, 47
Carty, Chandra, 115
Carwardine, William H., 151–52
Cemeteries, 57–58, 226; Confederate, 5, 12, 56, 58, 60–61, *62*, 67–69, 210–12; Finnish, 205, 207, 213; national Union, 75–76, 78; POW, 13, 75–76, 78–82; as reflections of social values, 58–59, 63–64, 81; as sacred spaces, 63, 64–66, 70–71
Charleston Massacre, 6, 98
Civilian Conservation Corp (CCC), 263
Civil rights, 97–98; of women, 166–67, 170–72, *171*, *172*, 178, 286–87
Civil Rights Movement, 5, 93, 132
Cold War, 33, 247
Colonialism: as depicted in statues, 169–70; and racist patriarchy, 177–78; reverence for, 41
Columbus, Christopher: monuments of, 3, 6
Combahee River Raid, 6
Comfort women, 286–87
Commemoration: memorialization events as, 149–50, 186, 259, 263–64, *264*, 281; motivations for, 1–3, 4–5, 14–15, 56, 111–12, 126–7, 167, 215, 239–40, 258, 276; rolls of honor as, 187, 259, 266, 280; using digital media for, 284
Communications-Electronics Command (CECOM), 246–47
Communism, 222, 225, 233, 234
Confederate: burials, 13, 65–66, 76, 79–81, 82–83; cemeteries, 5, 12, 56, 59–61, *62*, 63–64, 67–69, 210–12; narratives, 4–5, 13, 63, 67, 71, 76, 79, 98, 112–13, 122, 131, 203, 213; veterans; 69, 77, 81–82, 127, 128, 132, 138–39, 210. *See also* Monuments: Confederate
Connecticut, 225
Continental Army, 24–27
Corby, Father, 35
Cormany, Rachel, 95–96
Cornerstone deposit, 13, 66; Louisville Confederate Monument, 126, 133–41, *134*, *135*, *136*
Cowan, Arthur S., Col., 247
Culture: official, 145, 155; vernacular, 149–50
Cushman, Charlotte, 175

Damnatio memoriae, 6–7
Davis, Jefferson, 66, 76, 128, 137; monuments of, 56, 202, 210, *211*
Descendant communities, 94, 97–98, 103, 113, 114–15, 170, 283
Debs, Eugene V., 146
Demographic changes, 147, 148, 268
De Oñate y Salazar, Juan, 3–4, 169
De Vargas, Diego, 4
Discourse, 21–22, 281, 285, 287
Domestic work, 167
Douglass, Frederick, 11, 16, 77
Dunwoody, Henry, H. C., Brig. Gen., 248

Eleanor Cross, 187, *189*, 190–91, *190*, 197–98
Elmira POW Camp cemetery, 13, 75, 82–88
Elmwood Cemetery, 66, 69
Ethics, 287
Explorers, European, 3–4

Fairview Cemetery, 68, 69
Feminist intersectionality theory, 163–64
Finland, 14, 202–3, 204–5, 207, 214
Finnish memorial landscape, 202, 203, 204, 205–7, *206*, 213–14, 215, 280
Finn's Point Cemetery, *80*, 81
First Nation forces, 26–27, 28–31
Florida, 13, 107, 109–11, 112–16, 227
Floyd, George, 6, 51, 88, 94, 285
Forgotten Victory, 229, 234
Forgotten War, 219, 220–21, 222, 225, 229, 232, 233, 280
Fort Delaware POW Camp, *80*, 81
Fort Gordon, 238, 247, 248

Fort Monmouth, 14–15, 237–38, 245–46; memorials, 239–41, *242,* 243–45, *245,* 246–51
Fraser, Simon, 25, 33–34
Fredericksburg, Virginia, 12, 40, 43–44, 49–51, 76
Freedom is Not Free, 226, 227, 229, 233, 234, 281

Gamble Plantation Historic State Park, 13, 107–9, *108,* 110–16, *117,* 122–23; landscape biography of, 117–18, *119,* 120–22
Gamble, Robert, 107, 110, 112, 118, 120
Garibaldi, Guiseppe, 10–11, *11*
Gates, Horatio, 24
Gender, 14, 137, 140–41; ideology, 164, 166–67. *See also* Women
George III (king), 8, 9–10
Georgia, 8, 16–17, 69–70, 74, 233
Germans, 24, 25, 28, 195, *196,* 197, 198
Gettysburg, 5, 13, 35, 76, 92–94
Grand Army of the Republic, 131–32, 133
Gravestones, 13, 58, 61, 64, 76, 78–81, 82, 83–84, *85*
Great man theories, 41–42, 136, 137, 163, 166
Green Howards, 187, 188, 198

Harrisburg Peace Promenade Monument Project, 101
Haudenosaunee, 21, 26, 27, 31, 36
Heg, Hans Christian, 11–12
Hepburn, Susan Preston, 128, 136, 138
Heritage: dual, 52; tourism, 23, 40, 50, 107–8, 148, 149–50, *150,* 220, 221–22, 235
Heritage narratives: alternative, 42, 48–49, 52, 101–3, 115–16, 156; basis for, 40–41, 44–45, 79, 145, 152; challenging, 12, 15, 17, 22–23, 34, 42, 94, 109, 114, 122, 283–84; control of, 1–3, 5, 14, 31, 74, 76, 87, 112, 131, 278–79; multiple perspectives of, 4, 16, 19–50, 52, 144, 149, 277; mythic, 219, 283
Heroism, military, 81, 87, 138, 208, 215, 262, 269, 279, 283
Heterosexualism. *See* Sexuality
Historic Pullman Foundation (HPF), 151, 152
History: authentic, 285, 287; mediated, 58–59, 76–77, 87, 94, 107–8; reconstructed, 144. *See also* Silenced history

Hollywood Cemetery, 65–66, *65*
Hostelries, 43–44
House museums, 41

Identity politics, 3, 23, 42, 50, 51–52, 58–59, 63–64, 157, 263, 266, 268
Indigenous people, 177–78; dispossession of, 78, 110; monuments of, 8, 28–30, *28, 29,* 166, 169–70; protest of statues by, 3, 4, 164, 169, 170; sacred sites of, 2; silenced history of, 3–4, 26, 31
Illinois, 13–14, 81–82, 147, 175, 220, 226
Illinois Labor History Society (ILHS), 151–52
Immigrants, 12, 31–36, 78, 173, 178
Indiana, 222, 232
Indian Wars, 31
Interpretation, 41, 42–43, 50, 51, 52, 112
Iowa, 221
Irish, 21, 33–35
Irish Brigade monument, 35

Japan, 286–87
Jenkins, Albert Gallatin, 13, 94–95, 100; monument, 92–94, *93,* 98–100, *99*
Jim Crow, 5, 78; laws, 88, 108, 127
Johnson, Adelaide, *The Women's Movement,* 170, *171*
Johnson Island POW camp, 78–79
Jones, John, 75, 82–83, 87–88, *87*
Judah P. Benjamin Confederate Memorial, 107, 109, 111–13, 116, 283

Kalevankangas memorial, *206,* 207, 208
Kansas, 225, 233
Kentucky, 13, 68–69, *69,* 126–41, 171–72
Kentucky Women's Confederate Monument Association, 128–29, 132, 135–36, 138
Kitula monument, 208, *209,* 210, 213
Know-Nothing Party, 32, 34
Korean War, 14, 219–223, 225, 227, 232–33, 235, 280, 282, 285–86
Korean War Veterans' Memorial Committee, 230, 232

Labor history, 14, 151–54, 156
Ladies Memorial Associations, 12, 56, 60, 65–67, 68, 69–70, 76, 112, 128, 210–11

300 · Index

Lanahan, Francis, Maj. General, 239–40, 241
Landscape, 117, 131, 132–33, 141; altered, 148; designed, 144, 145–46, 152
Lazarus, Emma, "The New Colossus," 35
Lee, Robert E., 79, 137, 210; statues of, 56, 68, 169, 285
Lewis, Alexander, 96–97
LGBTQIA. *See* Sexuality
"Liberty in Distress" (MacMonnies), 265
Liberty poles, 8–9
LiDAR, 113, *114,* 118
Life course, 15, 256, 258, 262, 269, 271
Liminality, 213, 235, 282
Lion of Lucerne (Thorvaldsen), 70
"Lion of the Confederacy" (Brady), 69–71
Local history, 42, 213–14, 225, 228–29, 232, 248, 259
Lost Cause of the Confederacy, 4–5, 12, 13, 56–57, 59, 63–64, 66–67, 70–71, 76, 210; buy-in to the, 202, 203; challenging commemorative landscape of, 94, 98, 126; rhetoric at planation sites, 108, 111–12, 122; symbolic expressions of the, 135–39
Louisville, Kentucky, 13, 126–27, 225; Confederate Monument, 128–31, *130,* 132–41
Lowenthal, David, 3
Loyalists, 26–27, 28

MacMonnies, Frederick, "Liberty in Distress," 265
Magnoni, Carlo, 192
Maine, 226
Mannerheim, Field Marshall, 208
Maryland, 221, *223*
Massachusetts, 5, 58, 59, 70, 173, *174,* 175, 177, 225, 229
Materiality, 22, 270, 275, 282
McGavock Confederate Cemetery, 60–61, *62*
McNeill, Archibald, 110–11
Memorial Day/Decoration Day, 65, 66, 68, 69, 98
Memorial landscapes, 32, 41, 56–59, 63, 71, 88–89, 103, 116–117, 126, 190, 234–35, 269, 280; battling for, 131–32, 278; challenging, 132, 141, 214–15, 285, hidden, 205, 284; preserving, 246, 247, 250–52. *See also* Judah P. Benjamin Confederate Memorial

Memorial mania, 268–69
Memorial motifs, 29, 173, 191, 220, 225, 229–30, 235, 245, 282; of domination, 167–68, 169–70, 286; cemetery, 58, 84, 207–8, *209*
Memorials, 1, 8, 109; life-course of, 256, 258, 262; peace, 101–2, 284–85, 286; place-based, 213–14; in public spaces, 22, 71, 77, 94, 101, 122, 126–29, 131–32, 169, 204, 212–13, 219, 226, 248–49, 260; by water, 220, 221, 222, 233, 234, 235, 248
Memorials, war, 16, 167, 222, 247, 260, 264, *268,* 279; American Civil War, 5, 56, 63–64, 71, 79, 128–131, *130,* 255–56, 264–65; Boer War, 190; Finnish Civil War, 205–8, *206, 209,* 210, 213–14; Korean War, 219–22, *223, 224,* 225–30, *228, 231;* 232–35, 266, 280–81, 282; Revolutionary War, 9–10, *10,* 28–30, *28, 29,* 175, 262–63; Spanish-American War, 248, *249,* 265; Vietnam War, 249, 268, 280; World War I, 186, 189–91, 192–95, *196,* 197–98, 199, 260, *261,* 265–66, 280; World War II, 199, 214, 241, *242,* 243–45, *245,* 248–49, 250, 266 *See also* Monuments; Statues
Memory: boom, 41, 220, 235; collective 41, 49, 52, 57–58, 59, 63–64, 67, 88, 94, 97–98, 144, 271; condemning of, 6–7; exclusionary, 3, 41–42, 88–89, 109, 112–13, 166–67; places of, 2, 144, 154–55, 205, 281–82; politics of, 41, 56–57, 77–78, 203, 277–79, 283–84; popular, 144–45; post-, 278–79, 282; public, 145, 155, 234, 278, 281
Michigan, 178, *179,* 222, *224,* 225
Military base closure and realignment, 238, 245–47
Military heritage site, 21, *22,* 23, 27–28, 32, 33–35, 88; Fort Monmouth, 239–45. *See also* Memorials, war
Minnesota, 227
Minorities, 5–6, 15, 163, 165, 166, 168, 169, 176–77, 180
Missionaries, Franciscan, 4
Mississippi, 228, 232
Monmouth County, 250
Monuments, 1–2, 89, 277; building of, 8, 10–11, 16, 36, 126–29; Confederate, 4–5, 12, 13, 56–58, *57,* 60, 64, *65,* 67–70, *69,* 77, 79–82, 84–87, *85, 86,* 92, 126, 128–41, *130,* 202,

210–12, *211;* counter- , 284–85; debates surrounding, 6, 22, 52, 56, 71, 98, 129–30, 157, 208, 286–87; destruction of, 6–7, 9–10, *10,* 11–12, 40–41, 207; national, 8–9, 144–45, 147–48, 153–56; relocation of, 15, 141, 226, 246–50, 265, 269; removal of, 3, 6, 13, 15, 51, 93, *93,* 94, 98–100, 103, 126, 141, 168–69, 215; Union, 70, 131–32, 256. *See also* Cemeteries; Memorials; Memorials, war; Military heritage site; Statues
Morgan, Daniel, 25, 33–34
Mortuary practices and beliefs, 58, 75–76, 80–81, 213
Mosler, Henry, "The Lost Cause," 68–69, *69*
Mount Auburn Cemetery, 58, 59, 70
Mount Olivet Cemetery, *57,* 64, 69
Muldoon, Michael, 129
Murphy, Timothy, 21, 25, *32,* 33–34, 36

Naming: cannon, 263–64; street, 2, 16–17, 239
National A. Philip Randolph Pullman Porter Museum, 13–14, *153,* 153–54
National Historic Landmark District, 147, 153, 155
National mythologies, 1, 28, 31, 41, 219, 283
National Prisoner of War Museum, 74
Native Americans. *See* Indigenous people
Nativist movements, 32, 34
New Jersey, 14–15, 237–38, 258; Civil War memorials, *80,* 264–65; non-war memorials, 6, 10; war memorials, 229–30, *231,* 232, 238–41, *242,* 243–52, *245, 249, 257,* 259–60, *261,* 262–63, 266, 268–71, *268;* war cannon memorials, 263–64, *264,* 265, 266, *267*
New Mexico, 3–4
Newtown Battlefield, 26–27, 31
New York, 6, *7,* 8, 9, 10–11, 23, 32, 75–7, 221, *223, 224,* 227, 232; map of, *22;* statues of women in, 165, 173, 175

Oakdale Cemetery, 66, 67–68
Oakland Cemetery, 69–70
Oakwood Cemetery, 82
Obama, Barack H., 145, 154, 155–56
Obelisks, 9, 56, 60, 69–71, 92, 260–61; meanings conveyed by, 81, 282

Ohio, 78–79, 81, 220, 226, 232
Oppression, 28, 41, 42, 163, 168
Oral history, 40–41, 42–43, 44–45
Ordnance, military, 257, 263, 265, 266, *267,* 268, 269, 282

Parks, Rosa, 175
Patriarchy, 14, 16, 137–38, 170; racist, 163, 164, 166, 169, 177–78
Peace parks, 101, 284–85
Pennsylvania, 13, 35, 92–103, 176, 227–29, *228, 231,* 232–33, 284–85
Permanence, 15, 88, 238, 244, 245, 258, 271, 282
Place, power of, 2, 63, 131, 277, 281, 282
Plantations, 107–8, 110–11, 116–17, 120
Pocahontas, 169, 175
Polish, 21, 32–33, 175, 178
Polish American Congress, 33
Power: agendas and influence, 3, 16, 56, 59, 63, 128, 131, 132, 157; expressed by statues, 163, 166–68, 169, 170, 172–73, 180; of objects, 275; relations, 1, 2, 5, 6, 58, 109
Prejudice, 88, 173
Preservation: artifact, 1–2, 8; historic, 147, 151, 155, 157–58; obligation for, 23, 244, 247, 249–50, 252
Prisoners of war (POW), 74; camps, 74–75, *80,* 81; cemeteries, 13, 75–76, 78–88
Proclamation 9233, 155
Public memory, 144–45, 157–58
Pueblo, 3–4
Pulaski, Casimir, 175
Pullman Civic Organization (PCO), 147, 149, 151, 152
Pullman, George M., 13–14, 145–47, 148, 152, 154, 156
Pullman National Monument, 144, 147, 148, 153, 154–57, *158*
Pullman Palace Car Company, 145–46, 148, 153
Pullman porters, 14, 145, 148, 152–55, 156

Race relations, 5, 50, 51–52, 63, 127, 147, 203
Racism, 4–5, 6, 14, 15, 31, 34, 78–79, 88, 127, 176, 203; patriarchal, 163, 164, 166, 169, 177–78; symbols of, 40–41, 51, 93, 132, 280
Randolph, A. Philip, 148, 153–55, *153*
Ray, Sarah Elizabeth, 178

Reconciliation, 74, 77, 79, 81, 95, 101–3, 145, 149, 156, 202, 283; failure of, 89, 92–94, 100
Reconstruction, 71, 76, 203
Recontextualization, 5, 29, 98–99, 130
Reds, 14, 202, 203, 204–8, *206,* 210, 213–14
Remembering and forgetting, 77–78, 88–89, 97–98, 155, 280, 283–84. *See also* Memory
Restorative justice, 116, 285
Reunification, Finnish, 204–5, 206, 210, 214
Rhetoric of mourning, 12, 56–57, 63–64
Rhode Island, 226
Right foot, 4
Rural Cemetery Movement, 57–58

Sacagawea, 166, 169, 170
Sacred sites, 2, 63, 64–65, 70–71, 213
Sanctification, ideological, 56–57, 64, 71, 150, 156, 166, 167–69, 172, 177, 180
Sanford, Joseph, 43
Saratoga National Military Park, 23, 32
Serra, Junipero, 169
Sex discrimination, 163–64, 165–66, 170
Sexuality, 173, 175
Shaw, Robert Gould, 5
Sherman, William Tecumseh, 31
Signal Corps, 238, 239–40, 241, 246–47
Signal Corps Tradition Committee, 239–41, 243–44, 246–47
Silenced history, 3–4, 5–6, 13, 112–13, 120, 270; rectifying, 101–3, 109, 153–55, 156, 284, 287
Six Nations people, 28–30, *29,* 31, 35–36
Slave auction, 44, *44,* 48; block, 12, 40, 42–43, 44–51, *45, 47*
Slave labor, 4, 107–8, 110, 117, 118, *119,* 120, 122
Slavery, African American, 6, 12, 63, 71, 76, 109–11, *117;* cruelty of, 4–5, 107–8, 122; and enslavement of free Blacks, 13, 92–97, 100; revealing the history of, 112–18, *117. See also* Slave auction; Slave labor; Slave villages
Slavery, Indigenous, 3, 4
Slave villages, 113, *114,* 118, 123
Sledmere Memorials, 14, 188, 189–90; book of commemoration, 187; Eleanor Cross, 187, *189,* 190–91, *190,* 197–98; Wagoners', 187, 187n1, *189,* 192–95, *196*
Smith, Laurajane, 6

Social order, 63–64, 71, 127, 137–38, 199
Social values, 177, 178, 180, 277
South Carolina, 61, 169, 220, 222, 229
South Korea, 285–87
Spanish-American War, 79, 248, *249,* 265
"Spirit of the American Doughboy" (Viquesney), 265
Stamp Act of 1765, 8
Static displays, 262, 269, 282; of cannon, 29, 68, 263–64, *264,* 265, 266, *267;* of military vehicles, 266, *267,* 268
Statues, 1, 163, 268; contested, 3, 4–5, 6; 164, 169, 170, 173, 208; individualized, 102, 165–66, 190–91; of LGBTQIA persons, 175; of minorities, 166, 169, 172–73; power of, 163, 166–68, 169, 170, 172–73, 180; of women, 164–66, 169–73, *171, 172, 174,* 175–78, 286–87. *See also* Memorials; Monuments
Stevenson, Jim, 112–13
Stone, 210, 245, 282
Subordination, 88–89, 163, 164, 166, 168–70, 173, 177–78
Suffragists, 170–72, *171, 172,* 178
Sugar mills, 120, *121,* 122
Sullivan, John, 26, 27, 31
Swamp Angel, 265
Sykes-Picot agreement, 189
Sykes, Sir Mark, 14, 187, 188–93, 195, 197–99
Symbolic capital, 64, 66–67, 71

Taylor, Susie King, 17
Tennessee, 64, 66, 69, 171, 212, 222
"The Lost Cause" (Mosler), 68–69, *69*
"The New Colossus" (Lazarus), 35
The Women's Movement (Johnson), 170, *171*
Thorvaldsen, Bertel: Lion of Lucerne, 70
Tomochichi, 8, *9*
Town of Pullman, 13–14, 144, 145–46, *146,* 152; annual House Tour, 149–50, *150,* 155; redevelopment of, 147, 148, 157–58. *See also* Pullman National Monument
Trouillot, Michel-Rolph, 3
Truth, Sojourner, 16, 165, 172–73, 175
Tubman, Harriet, 5–6, *7,* 165, 166, 175

Underground Railroad, 5, 83, 96, 101, 176
Union: cemeteries, 75–76, 78; memorials, 131–132; veterans, 77

Union prisoner of war camp cemeteries, 13, 74, 78–83
United Daughters of the Confederacy (UDC), 5, 12, 13, 56, 61, 77, 78–79, 85, 87, 122; and the Gamble Plantation, 107, 109, 111–13, 116
United States Colored Troops (USCT), 92, 97–98, 100–101
United States Hotel, 43–44
Unite the Right 2017 rally, 99, 169
Utah, 172

Valentine, Edward Virginius, 210
Valiants Memorial, 36
Veterans of Foreign Wars (VFW), 265
Veterans Memorial Park at Hayden Heights, 260, *261*, 262
Vietnam War, 287
Viquesney, E. M., "Spirit of the American Doughboy," 265
Violence: against Black people, 5, 6, 78, 88, 98–99, 168, 285; against Indigenous people, 3–4; sexual, 5, 286–87
Virginia, 6, 67, 170, 176, 202, 212

Wagoners, 192
Wagoners' memorial, 187, 187n1, *189*, 192–95, *196*
Washington, George, 26
Water, 235, 282, 284

Whites, 14, 202, 203, 204–5, 207, 214
White supremacy, 5, 13, 63–64, 67, 76, 78, 168–69, 203, 280
Winters, Joseph R., "About Ten Days After the Battle of Gettysburg," 96
Winter War, 205–6, 214
Wireless communication, 238
Wisconsin, 11–12, 220, 226, *228*
Wolds Wagoners Reserve, 192, 193–95, *196*, 197
Women: American, 14, 164, 177; Black, 163, 172–73, 178, *179*; Confederate, 5, 12, 13, 56, 59–61, 65–66, 67, 128–29, 137–38; comfort, 286–87; deserving of statues, 176–78; enslaved, 4, 5; monuments of, 14, 16, 164, 169–73, *171, 172, 174,* 175–76, 286–87; suffragists, 170–73
Works Progress Administration (WPA), 260, 263
World War I, 186, 188–89, 192, 194–95, *196,* 197, 199; training bases of, 237–38
World War II, 33, 203, 240, 286–87
Wyoming, 170–71

Xenophobia, 14, 173, 199

Yandell, Enid. 128–29, 138
Yorkshire, England, 14, 187, 190, 198–99

Zakrzewska, Maire, E., Dr., 178, *179*

Cultural Heritage Studies

Edited by Katherine Hayes, University of Minnesota

Heritage of Value, Archaeology of Renown: Reshaping Archaeological Assessment and Significance, edited by Clay Mathers, Timothy Darvill, and Barbara J. Little (2005)

Archaeology, Cultural Heritage, and the Antiquities Trade, edited by Neil Brodie, Morag M. Kersel, Christina Luke, and Kathryn Walker Tubb (2006)

Archaeological Site Museums in Latin America, edited by Helaine Silverman (2006)

Crossroads and Cosmologies: Diasporas and Ethnogenesis in the New World, by Christopher C. Fennell (2007)

Ethnographies and Archaeologies: Iterations of the Past, edited by Lena Mortensen and Julie Hollowell (2009)

Cultural Heritage Management: A Global Perspective, edited by Phyllis Mauch Messenger and George S. Smith (2010; first paperback edition, 2014)

God's Fields: Landscape, Religion, and Race in Moravian Wachovia, by Leland Ferguson (2011; first paperback edition, 2013)

Ancestors of Worthy Life: Plantation Slavery and Black Heritage at Mount Clare, by Teresa S. Moyer (2015; first paperback edition, 2023)

Slavery behind the Wall: An Archaeology of a Cuban Coffee Plantation, by Theresa A. Singleton (2015; first paperback edition, 2016)

Excavating Memory: Sites of Remembering and Forgetting, edited by Maria Theresia Starzmann and John R. Roby (2016)

Mythic Frontiers: Remembering, Forgetting, and Profiting with Cultural Heritage Tourism, by Daniel R. Maher (2016; first paperback edition, 2019)

Critical Theory and the Anthropology of Heritage Landscapes, by Melissa F. Baird (2017; first paperback edition, 2022)

Heritage at the Interface: Interpretation and Identity, edited by Glenn Hooper (2018)

Cuban Cultural Heritage: A Rebel Past for a Revolutionary Nation, by Pablo Alonso González (2018; first paperback edition, 2023)

The Rosewood Massacre: An Archaeology and History of Intersectional Violence, by Edward González-Tennant (2018; first paperback edition, 2019)

Race, Place, and Memory: Deep Currents in Wilmington, North Carolina, by Margaret M. Mulrooney (2018; first paperback edition, 2022)

An Archaeology of Structural Violence: Life in a Twentieth-Century Coal Town, by Michael P. Roller (2018)

Colonialism, Community, and Heritage in Native New England, by Siobhan M. Hart (2019)

Pedagogy and Practice in Heritage Studies, edited by Susan J. Bender and Phyllis Mauch Messenger (2019)

History and Approaches to Heritage Studies, edited by Phyllis Mauch Messenger and Susan J. Bender (2019)

A Struggle for Heritage: Archaeology and Civil Rights in a Long Island Community, by Christopher N. Matthews (2020; first paperback edition, 2022)

Earth Politics and Intangible Heritage: Three Case Studies in the Americas, by Jessica Joyce Christie (2021)

Negotiating Heritage through Education and Archaeology: Colonialism, National Identity, and Resistance in Belize, by Alicia Ebbitt McGill (2021)

Baseball and Cultural Heritage, edited by Gregory Ramshaw and Sean Gammon (2022)

Conflict Archaeology, Historical Memory, and the Experience of War: Beyond the Battlefield, edited by Mark Axel Tveskov and Ashley Ann Bissonnette (2022)

Heritage and Democracy: Crisis, Critique, and Collaboration, edited by Kathryn Lafrenz Samuels and Jon D. Daehnke (2023)

Memory and Power at L'Hermitage Plantation: Heritage of a Nervous Landscape, by Megan M. Bailey (2024)

Monuments and Memory: Archaeological Perspectives on Commemoration, edited by John H. Jameson, Sherene Baugher, and Richard Veit (2025)

Printed in the United States
by Baker & Taylor Publisher Services